THE EARLY
CHURCHILLS

An English Family

By A. L. ROWSE

DORSET PRESS
New York

This edition published by Dorset Press,
a division of Marboro Books Corporation,
by arrangement with
Curtis Brown Ltd.
1990 Dorset Press

ISBN 0-88029-587-2

Printed in the United States of America
M 9 8 7 6 5 4 3 2 1

Contents

PROLOGUE, 1

I. DORSET BEGINNINGS, 5

II. CAVALIER COLONEL, 15

III. THE RESTORATION: IN ENGLAND AND IRELAND, 31

IV. SIR WINSTON CHURCHILL: WHITEHALL AND DUBLIN, 45

V. HOUSE OF COMMONS: COURT MEMBER, 64

VI. PARLIAMENT AND POPISH PLOT, 79

VII. ARABELLA, 97

VIII. JOHN AND SARAH, 114

IX. COURT LIFE AND HOME LIFE, 132

X. THE REVOLUTION, 148

XI. WILLIAM III AND MARLBOROUGH, 170

XII. THE DUKE, 192

XIII. SUMMIT AND FALL, 213

XIV. SARAH AND THE QUEEN, 241

XV. EXILE AND RETURN, 263

XVI. BLENHEIM PALACE, 282

XVII. THE THREE BROTHERS, 305

XVIII. SARAH IN OLD AGE, 330

EPILOGUE, 355

NOTES, 359

INDEX, 371

Preface

FOR QUITE a number of years now, in the intervals of researches into the Elizabethan Age, I have had this book in mind. The Churchills are by origin a West Country family, from that part of England which is closest—not only geographically—to America and which, along with East Anglia, made the most marked contribution to the historic foundations of the American people. (By one of those grand reversals which give rhythm and richness to the study of history it was the West Country that was occupied by the American invasion forces in the heroic months of 1944 and from which they set out on their momentous task of the liberation of Europe. The old West Country became in those unforgetable days, happily and naturally, an American colony.)

I hope, therefore, that it is not inappropriate for a West Countryman to write the story of this family whose origins lie across my road from Cornwall to Oxford, country fought over by the earlier Sir Winston, the Cavalier Colonel in the Civil War of the seventeenth century, a landscape familiar to many earlier generations of Churchills. It seems that the stock may be traced to a family of freehold farmers going right back to the twelfth century in Devon. It is a long way from Churchill in the parish of Broad Clyst to Blenheim, from the slow immemorial routine on the land to the sudden ascent of John Churchill, first Duke of Marlborough, to European eminence.

The stock has extended its range more widely across the Atlantic: one branch has been of long continuance in Virginia; another offshoot achieved distinction with the novelist, Winston Churchill. While, with the latest of the name, English and American blood shares an unparalleled achievement with equal pride.

My chief obligation in writing this book is to Sir Winston Churchill himself, for his interest and warm encouragement and help; some of my earlier pages have had the honor, and the benefit, of his corrections. His own researches and those of Archdeacon Coxe before him, in the

PREFACE

Blenheim archives, are basic for the story of John Churchill and his wife Sarah, and I am deeply in their debt, as all writers on this subject must be. But I have been able to bring to light a good deal of new material on other members of the family: on old Sir Winston, the Cavalier Colonel, Arabella, Admiral George, General Charles and their families. I am most grateful to the Duke of Marlborough for permission to work in his archives.

I have received much help from many quarters, for which I should like to record my thanks: to the Countess Zamoyska for her hospitality and help in Dorset; to Lord and Lady Digby for their kindness in showing me their Churchill treasures at Minterne; to the Honorable Mrs. Cubitt for putting me on the track of some Churchill portraits; to Mr. Howard Colvin and Mr. W. C. Costin, Senior Tutor of St. John's College, Oxford, for information about Winston Churchill's residence there; to Miss Grace M. Briggs for information as to Sir Winston's reading at the Bodleian; to Professor H. G. Hanbury for clearing up an antiquarian legal point; and to Professor Robert W. Rogers, of the University of Illinois, for some new light on Pope and the Marlboroughs.

My obligations to libraries and manuscript collections on both sides of the Atlantic are considerable, particularly to the Bodleian and Codrington at Oxford, the Public Record Office in London, the National Library of Wales, the Huntington Library in California. At the last Mr. Tyrus Harmsen drew my attention to some unpublished letters of Sarah, upon which I have drawn, by no means exhaustively. I am much indebted to Miss N. McN. O'Farrell for constant help with original documents at the Public Record Office, British Museum and Somerset House.

A prime obligation is to Professor Jack Simmons of Leicester University, who has greatly improved the shape of the book by pruning the earlier chapters of much that was not the more interesting for being new. Mr. K. B. McFarlane of Magdalen has conducted a masterly massacre of my commas; but I am grateful to him, too, for some very neat corrections both of fact and of style. I should like to express my warm appreciation to Mr. Cass Canfield for his constant interest in the progress of this book and for his valuable suggestions for improving its literary form.

A. L. ROWSE

All Souls College
Oxford

THE CHURCHILL FAMILY

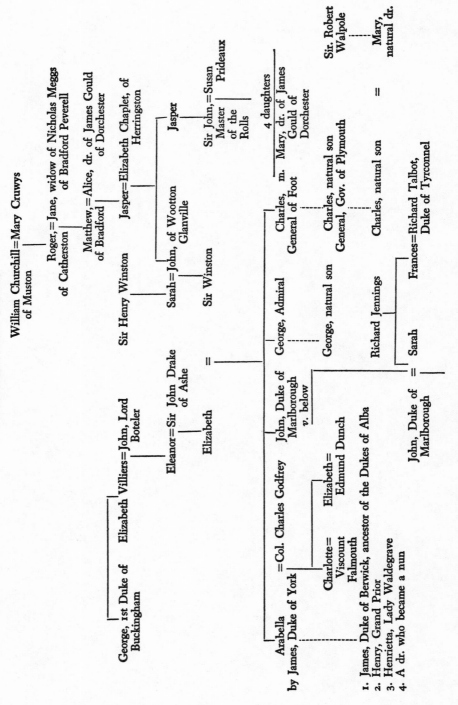

William Churchill=Mary Cruwys
of Muston

Roger,=Jane, widow of Nicholas Meggs
of Catherston   of Bradford Peverell

Matthew,=Alice, dr. of James Gould
of Bradford   of Dorchester

Jasper=Elizabeth Chaplet, of
Herringston

Jasper

Sir John,=Susan
Master   Prideaux
of the
Rolls

4 daughters

Sir Robert Walpole

Mary,
natural dr.

Sir Henry Winston

Sarah=John, of Wootton
Glanville

Sir Winston

Charles,   m. Mary, dr. of James
General of Foot   Gould of Dorchester

Charles, natural son
General, Gov. of Plymouth

Charles, natural son

Frances=Richard Talbot,
Duke of Tyrconnel

George, 1st Duke of
Buckingham

Elizabeth Villiers=John, Lord
Boteler

Eleanor=Sir John Drake
of Ashe

Elizabeth

=

George, Admiral

George, natural son

Richard Jennings

Sarah

Arabella   =Col. Charles Godfrey
by James, Duke of York

John, Duke of
Marlborough
v. below

Elizabeth=
Edmund Dunch

Charlotte=
Viscount
Falmouth

=

John, Duke of
Marlborough

1. James, Duke of Berwick, ancestor of the Dukes of Alba
2. Henry, Grand Prior
3. Henrietta, Lady Waldegrave
4. A dr. who became a nun

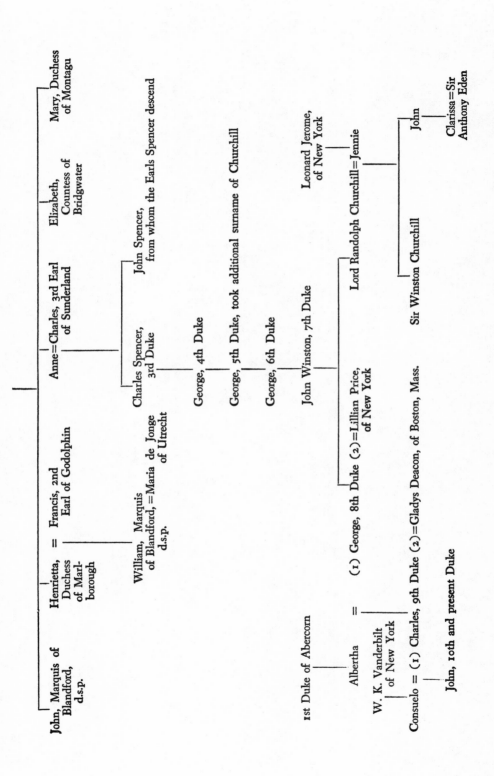

Prologue

CIVIL WARS are much to be deplored for the damage they do to property and things of beauty, for the destruction they work upon men's lives and the intangible, the not always calculable, harm they inflict upon standards of conduct. On the other hand, they provide opportunities for the heroic in man's spirit, for deeds of valor, for the common man's loyalty, courage and endurance as for the moral grandeur of a great man, a Lincoln or Lee, or an Oliver Cromwell. This is as true of the English Civil War of the seventeenth century, which provided so much of the tinder and steel for the American Revolution, as it is of the heroic and terrible struggle of the years 1861 to 1865.

The Civil War of the seventeenth century appeared to its participants to have come down upon them like a thunderstorm out of a blue sky—as we may see from a famous passage in Clarendon's autobiography. "It was about the year 1639, when he was little more than thirty years of age, and when England enjoyed the greatest measure of felicity that it had ever known . . ." he begins. He proceeds to specify the troubles desolating Europe—civil wars in France and Spain, mutual incursions and invasions, the Thirty Years' War in Germany. "Of all the princes of Europe, the King of England alone seemed to be seated upon that pleasant promontory that might safely view the tragic sufferings of all his neighbours about him without any other concernment than what arose from his own princely heart and Christian compassion. His three kingdoms flourishing in entire peace and universal plenty; and his dominions every day enlarged by sending out colonies upon large and fruitful plantations. . . . In this blessed conjuncture, a small, scarce discernible cloud arose in the north, which was shortly after attended with such a storm that never gave over raging till it had shaken and even rooted up the greatest and tallest cedars of the three nations, blasted all its beauty and fruitfulness, brought its strength to decay and its glory to reproach and almost to desolation."

1

King Charles I, a moment before the deluge overwhelmed him, thought himself fortunate. He told his nephew, Prince Rupert of the Rhine—who was to fight beside him in battle later and prove the King's most dashing cavalry leader—that he believed himself to be the happiest king in Christendom.

It only shows that one can never dare to be complacent in the realm of politics: eternal vigilance is the price of safety, or of any security there may be. For shortly the serpent of dissension entered into this paradise, and all came to pass as it is summed up in Marvell's lines:

> O thou, that dear and happy isle,
> The garden of the world erewhile,
> Thou Paradise of the Four Seas
> Which Heaven planted us to please,
> But—to exclude the world—did guard
> With wat'ry, if not flaming, sword:
> What luckless apple did we taste
> To make us mortal and thee waste?

Such was the background to the story of the Churchills, a family of good yeoman-farmer stock, living there in the West Country through the centuries close to the land, coming up via the law to make their appearance among the gentry in this quiet prosperous time before the Civil War. Then they were caught in the war on the losing side, that of the King, and were set back into impoverishment and neglect so long as the Puritans and Oliver Cromwell ruled at Whitehall. As our Sir Winston shows in the life of his ancestor, the Duke of Marlborough, the circumstances of that time are deeply reflected in the character and career of the family, the personalities of its members.

Cromwell's rule proved only an interlude; for all his greatness, he could not give it permanence. Again and again he tried to provide a constitutional foundation, but all to no avail: it was founded on the sword and it perished with him. Even before his death the country had begun to react strongly against Puritanism, the rule of the embattled good:

> Such as do build their faith upon
> The holy text of pike and gun;
> Decide all controversies by
> Infallible artillery;
> And prove their doctrine orthodox
> By apostolic blows and knocks:

Who

> Compound for sins they are inclined to
> By damning those they have no mind to.

On Cromwell's death, the country felt its way back to the ancient ways of government—King, Lords and Commons. The two sections of the governing class that had fought each other in the Civil War came together to bring back Charles II on a compromise footing. He proceeded to compromise himself and his country in the ambivalent years of his rule. More than half French, he sympathized with the autocratic ideas of his cousin, Louis XIV. He would not pursue the foreign policy that the country's interests more and more demanded; he would not carry out the demands to resist Louis's career of aggression against other European powers. Indeed, for a consideration—to gain a measure of independence from Parliament—he accepted his cousin's subsidies. Thus Louis XIV was enabled to build up that position of domination in Europe from which it took a quarter of a century of war and diplomacy to dislodge him, and to reduce France to a more equal place with other European powers.

It was by a strange turn of fate, an exciting, unpredictable chance, that the son of that house impoverished by the Civil War should turn out to be the effective instrument in the reduction of Louis XIV and France's ascendancy. This Marlborough proved himself to be, not only as a soldier—as such the greatest, perhaps, of English stock—but as the diplomatic agent, the linchpin of the Grand Alliance. It was a prophetic foreshadowing of the career in our time of his descendant, a second Sir Winston.

The history of a people—and the history of our stocks, in the island and overseas, is now a long and immeasurably rich one—carries these reverberations, these memories, back and forth across intervening seas and times: backward to Marlborough's war fought on the battlefields of Europe against one form of aggression, and forward to our own time when the struggle is against worse forms, more evil assaults upon the liberty of the human spirit.

The story of how our common ancestors faced earlier dangers and surmounted them can never be without interest for us, and possibly may provide encouragement and inspiration, give us heart, in the somber tests of our own time.

CHAPTER I

Dorset Beginnings

———————

THE CHURCHILLS are good West Country stock, of considerable antiquity. When they first appeared on the public scene in the good days of the Restoration, with the original Sir Winston Churchill and his famous progeny, the old Cavalier insisted that they had come over with the Conqueror. "Otho de Leon, Castellan of Gisors, (whom we may call our common ancestor) . . . had two sons, Richard lord of Montauban and Wandril lord of Courcelle . . . Wandril had issue by his wife Beatrice de Tria, Raoul and Roger, who took the name of Courcelle: Roger, the youngest brother, came into England with William the Conqueror," and so on—a regular baroque genealogical rigmarole.[1]*

In the grand days of the return of the King and the aristocracy to power, after the Civil War and the rule of saints and heroes, it was *de rigueur* to have come over at the Conquest. Sir Winston was not an antiquary for nothing, and he read Blue Mantle at the College of Arms a lesson, *à propos* of his arms, that is a nightmare of bogus genealogy and problematic heraldry. This kind of thing did not impress the positive, Whiggish spirit of Duchess Sarah later on, who was no historian but commented on a fulsome life of the great Duke, her husband: "this history takes a great deal of pains to make the Duke of Marlborough's extraction very ancient. That may be true for aught I know; but it is no matter, whether it be true or not, in my opinion. For I value nobody for another's merit."[2]

In fact, the Churchills were pretty thick upon the ground, and very close to the soil, in Dorset, Somerset and East Devon. We find them scattered over that Dorset countryside with the delightful, evocative

———————

* Numbers refer to notes which will be found, arranged by chapters, beginning on page 359.

names—Melbury Osmond, Melbury Sampford, Melbury Bubb; Bishop's Caundle, Purse Caundle and Caundle Marsh; Piddlehinton and Piddletrenthide; Winterborne Herringston and Winterborne Came. It seems that the stock can be traced to a family holding a freehold farm at Churchill in the parish of Broad Clyst in Devon as far back as the twelfth century.

But we are interested in the country on either side of the main road from Dorchester to Sherborne, at first upheaved and hilly as the way goes through the narrow valley to Cerne Abbas and Minterne Magna, then broadening out toward Sherborne into what was once the Forest of Blackmore, with its heaths and copses and its medieval legend. The story is that King Henry III, when hunting there once, spared a beautiful white hart, which was afterward killed by some local gentry. The King was so annoyed that he imposed a special tax on their lands—White Hart Silver.[3] It continued to be paid, in the English way, for centuries; the Churchills paid it in their time.

For this is the soil upon which the family we are pursuing emerged. And like all good things—or rather, like all that is most characteristic in the modern story of our people—they seem to have emerged in the Elizabethan Age. An enemy of theirs in the eighteenth century asserted, in the pretty way that enemies have, that "John Churchill's great grandfather was a blacksmith, who worked in the family of the Meggs."[4] If so, they have nothing but good reason to be proud of it; for in the course of time they threw up a titan of a Wayland Smith, who forged upon the anvil of his people's courage an instrument for overthrowing a tyranny far worse than that encountered by his ancestor in Louis XIV.

Certainly the Duke's great-great-great-grandfather, Roger Churchill, married the widow of Nicholas Meggs of Bradford Peverell, as even Sir Winston the old Cavalier admits; and with this we at last reach firm ground. The Sir Winston of our day comments that this circumstance "seems very suspicious and even disquieting." But who wouldn't prefer a real live blacksmith to a companion of the Conqueror, a figment of Restoration snobbery and hypothetical heraldry?

This Roger had a son Matthew, who had a son called Jasper, who married a girl from Herringston. They had two sons, John the elder, Jasper the younger. John took to the law and made a marked step up in the world; he became a gentleman. He was followed by his nephew, Jasper's son, another John, who became an eminent figure at the bar and ended up as Attorney General to the Duke of York and Master of the Rolls: Sir John Churchill.

His uncle John did not attain such eminence, nor did he have such luck as the younger generation: his generation came to an end with the Civil War. Before this catastrophe he had had time to do well enough out of the law. A member of Middle Temple, he rose to be a Deputy Registrar of Chancery. He was enabled to buy the pleasant little estate of Newton Montacute in the parish of Wootton Glanville, not half a dozen miles from Sherborne, in the open heathy country of the Forest of Blackmore. There was a common of some five or six hundred acres belonging to the manor, and, since he was a man of some initiative, he sought to improve his grounds by taking in a few acres—the beginnings of a park. At once he found himself up against opposition, the obstinacy of a tough old individual, so characteristic of our countryside.

In November, 1639, the Deputy Registrar brought a case in Chancery.[5] The previous autumn, wishing to enclose some of the common, he had obtained the consent of his tenants and set workmen to hedge, ditch and plant the enclosure. When he had already spent some money on it, some of the tenants went back on their agreement. At the next court-day, his steward debated the matter with them and their renewed assent was entered in the court book. In September a bridge was made over a rivulet between the house and the common—the stripling Caundle—and two fishponds were made for the use of the house. Then an old lady protested that the boundary was too far to the east, so that it inconvenienced her going on horseback to church, when she was so disposed. She intimidated her son, who had agreed in the matter, threatening that his assent should be £200 loss to him. (I have seen just such a tough old Dorset harridan up before the magistrates at Dorchester for the fourth or fifth time, for some repeated farming offence.) Not content with this, she drove her sons on to dig up the earth and level the banks as fast as the workmen made them, so that the workmen were defeated and forced to give over.

It does not appear that the Deputy Registrar got his way. In the next generation, with the victory of the gentry, Sir Winston was able to go further and undertake measures for enclosing and parceling out the whole common—and a good thing too.

In addition, John Churchill leased Minterne from Winchester College: a pretty little estate deep in the valley toward Dorchester, the house conveniently near the road next the church, woods all round and a sounding trout stream below. He had, besides, house property in and near Dorchester, and one or two farms in the neighborhood. In short, the typical estate of a small West Country gentleman, the status to which he had risen. At the time of his troubles, later, it was worth some £168 a year; perhaps we should multiply by fifteen for a contemporary valuation.

Just like such a man going up in the world, he married into the class above him: Sarah, daughter of a Gloucestershire knight, Sir Henry Winston of Standish, an heiress in a small way. More important than her inconsiderable possessions, she bequeathed the Gloucestershire name of Winston to the Churchills. It was to have a resounding reverberation.

She presented her husband with two sons: John, the elder, who died shortly after birth, and Winston, who survived. He was born about the year 1620. At some time before the Civil War, the mother died, for John Churchill made a second marriage in 1644. Some years before, in 1639, he resigned his official post as Deputy Registrar of Chancery to his promising young nephew and namesake, and settled down at Wootton Glanville to live the life of a country gentleman.[6]

But the lives of all country gentlemen at this time were broken into, disturbed, distracted, and not seldom ruined, by the odious, the superfluous Civil War that lasted from 1642 to 1646. At least it is possible that the Civil War might have been avoided if the King, Charles I, had had any grain of political sense. But like those other casualties of revolutions they brought down on their own heads—Louis XVI and Nicholas II—he had none. He had that fatal characteristic of most Stuarts—most marked in his grandmother, Mary Queen of Scots, and in his son James II—hopeless bad judgment. Of two possible courses of action, one plainly right, the other plainly wrong, these two instinctively and infallibly chose the wrong one. Charles wavered, but usually managed to take the wrong turning.

People are apt to forget how alien the Stuarts really were in England. On his father's side Charles was a Franco-Scot, on his mother's a Germano-Dane. So perhaps it is the less surprising that he never had any instinctive feeling *with* his people, or much real knowledge of them.*

---

* "But though he moved from palace to palace with a restlessness on which foreign ambassadors remarked, he did not know his people well and was a stranger to the greater part of his own dominions." C. V. Wedgwood, *The King's Peace*, 70-71.

This made all the more ludicrous, and in the end disastrous, his obstinate determination to govern the country against its wishes. Henry VIII and Elizabeth I were both just as authoritarian as Charles; but they had the sense to govern their people along with their wishes and interests. They were English and they had the *feel* of their people; their progresses about the country, their extrovert contacts with life, kept them in touch. Charles lived his essential life withdrawn, in the inner dream of an aesthete, a man of refined and distinguished sensibilities, a man with no common touch: a man who had received a profound wound with the beloved Buckingham's assassination—and never forgave the English people for it. At heart, he was alienated from them.

This, of course, played into the hands of the Puritan extremists. Though, in a sense, the Parliamentary leader, John Pym, was no revolutionary—or, at any rate, a very conservative one. A man of immense political ability, very grave and competent at multifarious business, capable of carrying it all in that taciturn secret brain, he was the true successor to the Elizabethans. He was forced into a revolutionary line, to capture power for Parliament, because he knew that the King could never be trusted to govern along with Parliament. Nor could he, ever—to the end.

To swing the balance of power and to give his cause a rallying cry and a religion, Pym—no fanatic himself—had to give Puritanism its head, base himself on the embattled forces of Presbyterianism, call in the Scotch. That gave the King, by reaction, a party: effectively the King's party was the Church party; it might be said that the Church of England was the Cavalier party at prayer—except that it was not always, or indeed often, at prayer. Sense and reason, as always, were on the side of the moderates: either the moderate Royalists like Hyde and Falkland or the moderate Parliamentarians like Bedford and John Hampden. Some of the most intelligent men, like Falkland or Edmund Waller or Anthony Ashley Cooper, found it difficult to make up their minds. If such people could have had their way, there would have been no Civil War: the change in the balance between King and Parliament would have taken place within our political institutions, without bursting their integuments and disrupting the life of the nation.

But perhaps it is too much to hope that people should ever be sensible politically: the extremists and the fanatics had their way, and the issues were fought out—though, of course, not settled—in overt civil war.

Without the Civil War, English history would be the poorer for the want of a romantic story, some heroic and appealing episodes, a tumultuous and colored canvas crowded with events and characters—something like a contemporary Rubens. But one can have romance in history at too great cost—in suffering, loss of gallant lives, ruin and devastation. And people never realize how much of the last there was in the English Civil War; it was all so long ago and fought in such gentlemanly fashion —there lies an afterglow upon it. In fact, it was not all so gentlemanly; there was a trail of houses and towns partly burned, countrysides despoiled and impoverished, people starving, their menfolk slain; trade, commerce, industry held up, the wealth of the land going into munitions of war. No wonder that toward the end of it the peasantry in the western counties—Dorset, Somerset and Wiltshire—suffering from the depredations of three or four armies crossing and recrossing their land, rose in great bands of Clubmen with the cry "A plague on both your houses." And then, there were the usual losses of things of beauty, the wreck of churches and cathedrals, the deliberate destruction of stained glass, monuments, woodwork, paintings, the leveling or blasting of innumerable treasure houses like Basing House, Raglan or Wardour Castles: the loathsome ferocity of barbarians against the innocent objects whose very beauty and distinction affront their inflamed sense of inferiority at what they cannot comprehend.

We are apt to forget all this and how much England lost by it: it is a wonder that so much remains in the fortunate island, till lately inviolate. Here is the background to our story; it is the very texture of the earlier Churchills' lives. This is the experience they went through, and, though they left no record of what they felt about it all, it not only left a mark upon their lives and fortunes, but explains a good deal in their character and behavior: candor and partisanship in one generation as against disingenuousness and ambivalence in the next; the simple party fervor of the old Cavalier against the cool detachment, always betwixt and between, of the son; the gnawing insecurity and frustration compensating themselves in piling up security in the form of cash: all the family with a keen eye to the main chance, the keenest of all making, in addition to everything else —undying fame, incomparable glory—an immense fortune.

When the Civil War opened and party alignments sharpened, the western counties were dominantly with Church and King. Particularly with the conservative society of a county like Dorset. There, the sympathies of almost all the gentry were Royalist. Of the leading families only the Trenchards, the Sydenhams, the Erles and Denzil Holles were Parliamentarians. The coastal and clothing towns were apt to be Parliamentarian: both Poole and Lyme undeviatingly so—the resistance of the latter, in a prolonged siege, gave heart to the Parliamentarians and seriously impeded Royalist progress in the West. Dorchester, too, was with Parliament in its sympathy: the Churchills of that place took the protective coloring of the environment. The celebrated minister of Holy Trinity, John White, an eminent Puritan and a leading figure in the founding of Massachusetts, "one of the subtlest and wisest of that sort of men," was much to the fore in managing the affairs of the town and keeping the burgesses to the path of virtue.[7] Two Royalist strongholds were very important—Sherborne Castle in the north of the county, Corfe Castle in the south—for each was very strong and they held the keys of communications with the West.

The nationwide unpopularity of the King's long, incompetent and irresponsible personal rule gave Parliament an advantage at the start; and for the first half of 1643 Parliament controlled Dorset. The Parliamentary forces signalized their supremacy by spoiling the town of Sherborne, capturing all Lord Bristol's plate that had been hidden there and destroying much of the glass of Wells Cathedral.[8] Deliverance for the Royalists came from the West, from Cornwall, where the Cornish were organizing a little army of their own under their local leaders, Sir Bevil Grenville, Nicholas Slanning, Charles Trevanion, Killigrew and Sidney Godolphin—all of whom, with their bravery, their varied talents and gifts, were killed. Their little army, bravely led by Hopton and Grenville, worked wonders. In a succession of surprising victories against superior forces, from Braddock Down in January, Stratton in May, to Lansdown, Roundway Down and the surrender of Bristol in July, it rolled back the Parliamentary forces, defeated that excellent soldier, Sir William Waller, and won the West for the King.

It was natural that John Churchill and his son Winston should share the sympathies of the rest of the Dorset gentry: the father in a quiet enough way, as befitted an elderly man in retirement, the son furiously in action, fighting in the field, a gallant captain of horse. At Wootton Glanville they were within the aura of, and naturally looked to, Sherborne Castle. In these years of Royalist ascendancy in the West, John

Churchill acted as one of the King's commissioners while his son was away fighting in the King's army.

When the fighting was over and the King had lost, the Churchills had to pay pretty heavily for their delinquency. The victorious Parliament, much more competent at administration than the King had ever been, rapidly brought into play its instruments for reorganizing a disrupted society and making its opponents pay: the Committee for Compounding, which sat at Goldsmiths' Hall, with its commissioners in every county. It is impressive how effectively it got to work. How it must have piled up rancor and undying resentment in the defeated—who got their long-delayed revenge with the return of the King in 1660.

John Churchill's case came before the Dorset Committee in March, 1646, which reported to Goldsmiths' Hall, mildly enough, that he had issued warrants for raising money for the King, but that since last November twelvemonth, i.e., November, 1644, "we find not that he hath acted anything to the prejudice of the state." Also he had advanced £300 for supplying the Parliament's garrison at Weymouth "in full of his fifth and twentieth part"—the levy laid upon Royalists for their delinquency.[9] He had already paid £100 for his personal estate, and taken the National Covenant and the negative oath of submission to Parliament. He desired of their honors that he might proceed to his final composition. We may take this as a neighborly, and in no way vindictive, statement of the case.

In his petition to Goldsmiths' Hall next month, the elderly lawyer put the best color he could upon his proceedings.[10] He submitted that his "house and estate being within four miles of the garrison of Sherborne, he was amongst others nominated a commissioner for the King and required to do some acts in pursuance thereof or to suffer the violence of the King's party, under whose power his person and estate then was." He recited his certificate of good conduct since November, 1644, from the local Committee, his payments of £300 and £100, and petitioned that "in regard he is aged about sixty years and at this time of infirm body, unable to travel," he might make his composition by deputy.

A return of Churchill's estate was made, which we may be sure did not err on the side of exaggerating its value,[11] and in August his fine was fixed at £446.[12] But his case dragged on, in the way these things did.[13] In May, 1647, he was assessed to pay £300. On September 26, 1648, he was summoned before the county commissioners at Dorchester

—his triumphant Parliamentarian neighbors, Sir Thomas Trenchard, Sir Walter Erle, Denzil Holles, Sydenham, with the mayors of Dorchester and Poole—and had fourteen days' warning given him according to the order of Goldsmiths' Hall.[14] In November, 1648, he was summoned before the Committee to pay his assessment. It was not until June, 1650, that the matter was finally settled by a certificate from the local committee to that effect.

How vexatious and worrying it all was! This kind of thing, and far worse—eviction, liquidation, wholesale transfers of property, the end of families—was going on all over England.

There remained the son to deal with, and his affairs were more complicated: the consequences of the Civil War bore much more hardly upon him.

Meanwhile, life went on in the fields and in the country manors in England, glumly, resentfully, bitterly, as the sequence of events unfolded itself: the attempt of the King to renew civil war, the terrible, the unforgivable scene of his execution—however much he had brought it upon himself—the return of the young king to Scotland, his escape after Worcester through the Western counties, his concealment in Dorset (not a breath from Wootton Glanville), his flight to France; the subjugation of Scotland and Ireland by the triumphant army, the emergence of a military dictatorship whose splendid achievements abroad gave no pleasure in the surly, disaffected manor houses at home, awaiting another day.

At some time during the Civil War—probably about the year 1644 —John Churchill had married again. From a case that came into Chancery after the father's death, we can see that there was no love lost between Winston and his stepmother and can descry something of the state of affairs at Wootton.[15] The stepmother claimed that John Churchill's estate was worth £600 a year, and that on marriage he had contracted for her to have her dower out of his estate and promised to leave her £500 at his death. He made his will on July 23, 1657, leaving her an annuity of £80 for life and appointing her sole executrix. On her threatening proceedings against the son, Winston Churchill, for withholding her dower and not fulfilling his father's will, which he had got into his possession—according to her—he came to her along with the rector of Wootton, Thomas Mewe, and "proposed that although there had been difference between them, he was willing to make friends," the rector "not only persuading but almost enforcing her to agree." It seems that the point at issue was whether she was to receive the lump sum she claimed for dower or the annuity of £80 that John Churchill had left her.

Winston Churchill's contention seems perfectly clear. As his father's only son and heir, he had entered the manor; he had given his stepmother no dower because "she did make her election to have the said annuity, which she had since received and accepted." She had had a whole day's perusal of his father's will to acquaint herself with its terms. To avoid further differences between them, it was agreed that she should have the annuity, and that for the next seven years "she should enjoy the mansion house and outhouses of Glanville's Wootton to her own proper use"; but that on extraordinary occasions he with his family should "make use of so much of the said house as should be meet and convenient," and that he should be allowed to brew there. His step-mother had assigned to her "furze, fuel and wood fitting for her chamber and dressing meat, diet and other uses necessary for housekeeping." He had let a proportion of the farm land and the grove to his stepmother at a rent of £50, and pleaded that her mother return his father's bonds for his debt to her, which had been claimed to be £700.

One sees something of the picture: Winston Churchill kept out of his own home by the exigencies of these hard times. For does it not look as if John Churchill may have had to raise this large sum from his new wife's mother in order to compound for his delinquency? How Winston Churchill was affected by it all we shall shortly see.

His descendant and namesake turned with relief from "these scraps and oddities" to contemplate the vast panorama of the Europe of Charles II. But it is from such scraps and oddities that history, in the intimate sense, is made and the lives of men and women long dead stand frag-mentarily revealed.

CHAPTER II

Cavalier Colonel

I

WINSTON CHURCHILL is the first member of the family whom we can depict at something near full length, in whom we can descry the lineaments of his personality, grasp the gist of his character, give a framework to his life and career.

We have seen that he was born about the year 1620, for in 1636 he matriculated at Oxford as a member of St. John's College, on April 8, at the age of sixteen.[1] It was still the practice for undergraduates to come up to the university at the same youthful age as they had done in Tudor times: the tone of their college had all the more influence in forming their outlook. The young Winston may have been under sixteen when he came up to St. John's, it would seem about the middle of February. The college was at the full tide of Laudian favor and Laudian principles.* Its former President was now Archbishop of Canterbury and only a short time before had endowed his college with the most beautiful of Caroline buildings—the Canterbury building, where Winston Churchill shared a room for his first year. He left in the term ending Michaelmas, 1638, when the caution money he had paid, £5, was returned, as usual upon good behavior. The two and a half years he spent at Oxford as a member of St. John's College may now, for the first time, be seen to have their proper importance.[2] For it was there that he imbibed the Laudian principles—in politics devotion to the Crown, in religion High Church, himself remaining undeviatingly Protestant—to which he adhered all his life.

Meanwhile, he had been entered as a student at Lincoln's Inn, and

---

* William Laud, President of St. John's, subsequently Bishop of London and Archbishop of Canterbury, was in high favor with Charles I and became a dominant influence in Church and State. His campaign to restore discipline in the Church and extend High Church principles led to a bitter conflict with the Puritans. His persecution of them at home had considerable influence in driving numbers of them across the Atlantic to New England.

15

admitted on January 30, 1637.[3] The Inns of Court were an alternative university, where it was the regular thing for the sons of country gentlemen to study, to complete their training with the more practical and worldly accomplishments of the law. Such a course was doubly indicated in his case, the son of one who had made his way by the law: here he was entered, the "son and heir of John Churchill of Glanville Wootton, gentleman."

Life at the Inns of Court was very much the same for the students as at the university, with the same framework and following the same routine, except that there was rather more liberty and there were the opportunities and excitements of the capital. Within the Inn, the students were summoned to dinner and supper in hall by the blowing of a horn. Their proper wear in hall was cap and gown, as at the university; but fashion challenged this sobriety and the young men ruffled it booted and spurred, in cloak and lace collar, and wearing their hair long. Hall and chapel were the scene of an intensive, crowded life. In the former took place the readings, moots and bolts—the public exercises that tested the knowledge acquired by the students from their seniors, sharpening their wits against each other. The same bell that rang them to the chapel, then newly built, still clangs upon the scene. The young men shared chambers in those crowded buildings, some of which still stand—having survived fire and bombs—looking out on Chancery Lane.

Within, their life proceeded: readings every week, services and sermons in chapel (Donne's sermons had not long ceased to echo within those walls), meals in common in the hall, feasts at All Saints, Candlemas and Ascensiontide; at Christmas, Revels and the young men dancing before the assembled Benchers.

Of Winston Churchill's progress in the law we have no knowledge —it must have been that of any other young lawyer. But here, in these years at the end of the 1630's, he laid the foundations of the stock of knowledge, acquired the rudiments of legal training, which stood him in sufficient stead for a career after the long interruption of the Civil War. The only notice we have of him concerns a characteristic fracas in the Three Cranes tavern, a convenient resort nearby in Chancery Lane. It was the usual affair of silly young men throwing wine at and over each other and the glasses after: two West Countrymen, Glanville and Churchill, against Skelton and Hosier, a painter in the service of the Earl of Northumberland. Skelton tried several times to hit Churchill over the head with a tankard, for which the young lawyers pumped Hosier—who reported the proceedings.[4]

What brought them to the notice of the authorities was that Glanville had drunk to the confusion and destruction of the Archbishop of Canterbury. It might have been serious for the young gentlemen, who were called before the Council, had not the Earl of Dorset stood their friend and suggested that it was all a mistake, that they had really drunk to the Archbishop of Canterbury's *foes*. Honor was preserved: Glanville, Churchill and their friends were dismissed with a caution.

Laud was at the apex of his unpopularity. It was not the first time that a benefactor had been reviled by a lot of young cubs, who were to learn better. Political conflict was approaching a crisis: things were moving ineluctably toward "this fiery declination of the world" wrote a country gentleman as the Long Parliament gathered and Pym rode into Westminster attended by an escort of three hundred gentlemen.[5]

Churchill was in his twenty-second year when the Civil War broke out and desultory fighting first crackled in the West. The situation changed with the march of the Cornish army into Somerset: the war became professional, and we know that he fought in the Royalist horse at the battles of Lansdown and Roundway Down.[6]

The Parliamentarian army, in this high hot summer of 1643, was posted under Sir William Waller—a professional soldier, personal friend of Hopton—at Bath. The Royalist strategy was to drive him out of the way, link up with the King's forces at Oxford, the Cavalier capital, for a joint march on London.

Waller had taken up an almost impregnable position on the summit of Lansdown ridge, which one sees with its steep escarpments running north from Bath. This he made stronger with breastworks and earthworks. The Royalist army hesitated to attack such a position. When Waller saw them withdrawing, he "sent his whole body of horse and dragoons down the hill to charge the rear and flank of the King's forces; which they did thoroughly, the regiment of cuirassiers so mating [i.e., terrifying] the horse they charged that they totally routed them."[7]

The Cornish foot stood firm, however, and saved the situation by beating back Waller's reserve of dragoons. The Cavaliers were enabled to rally their horse, and "winging them with the Cornish musketeers, charged the enemy's horse again . . . and routed and chased them to the hill; where they stood in a place almost inaccessible. On the brow of the hill there were breastworks, on which were pretty bodies of small shot and some cannon . . . Yet the Cornish foot were so far from being appalled at this disadvantage that they desired to fall on, and cried out that 'they might have leave to fetch off those cannon.' "

In the end, they had their way: order was given for the assault. Musketeers were sent into the flanking woods; horse and foot made their way slowly up the winding steep road, taking advantage of what shelter they could from wall and hedge, but all the time exposed to a galling fire. Again and again they were charged; the ghastly ascent went on. "Sir Bevil Grenville advanced, with a party of horse on his right hand . . . and his musketeers on the left, himself leading up his pikes in the middle, and in the face of their cannon and small shot from their breast-works, gained the brow of the hill, having sustained two full charges of the enemy's horse. But in their third charge, his horse failing and giving ground, he received, after other wounds, a blow on the head with a pole-axe, with which he fell, and many of his officers about him." The Cornish had gained the edge of the ridge. Here they clung—good cliff climbers as Cornishmen should be—until the whole army gained possession of the ridge. Waller's army was too exhausted to dispute it any further, and in the night he decamped, leaving the Royalists in possession of the field.

It was a barren victory, however; for the Royalist losses were at least equal to Waller's. Some losses were irreparable; as Clarendon says, the death of Sir Bevil Grenville "would have clouded any victory."

Waller's army, being in friendly country—for the manufacturing and freeholding district of North Somerset was Parliamentarian in sympathy—was able to refresh itself and recruit its strength. The Royalists had received further loss in the blowing up of an ammunition wagon, which killed a number of officers and temporarily blinded Hopton. They moved east into Wiltshire, where, within three miles of Devizes, Waller's horse fell upon their rear. Here, at a ford, the Royalist horse were able to hold up the pursuit and cover the retreat of the army into Devizes.

Devizes was an open town, quite unfortified; and from his vantage point high up on Roundway Down, Waller's batteries could dominate it. The position of the Royalists was critical; supplies were running low, ammunition was short. Urgent messages for reinforcements were sent to Oxford, and for once they arrived in time—a large contingent of 1,500 horse under Wilmot.

Waller still had the advantage of his excellent position on Roundway Hill. But again he lost it, as at Lansdown, by ordering a charge of all his horse downhill into the valley and up the opposite slope where Wilmot's cavalry was posted. The charge failed to shake them, and, instead, Waller's horse were caught between the two wings of the Cavalier army. Their check turned into a rout and they were flung headlong down the steep precipices of the hill, plunging to destruction. Waller's foot held firm, until they saw the Cornish foot approaching, when they turned and fled.

Waller managed to fly, with a few contingents, to Bristol; for the rest, it meant the destruction of the Parliamentarian army in the West— many killed, the rest prisoners. Prince Rupert now joined the victorious army with further reinforcements from Oxford. A total force of 14,000 foot and 600 horse beleaguered Bristol, behind its very strong defenses of wall and ditch, streams and forts. The city was sealed off, and in the early hours of the morning of July 26 the assault was launched. Resistance was fierce, especially on the south side, where the Cornish had to cross a ditch that was too wide for their scaling ladders. Their bravery again led to disproportionate losses, especially among their officers.

Meanwhile, on Prince Rupert's side, Colonel Washington found a weak place in the curtain wall and managed to enter. Prince Rupert called up 1,000 of the Cornish foot to the support, and though only 500 could be sent, the city shortly after surrendered.

The surrender of the second city in the kingdom and the destruction of Waller's army were great triumphs, and brought to an end this phase of the war in the West. The Western counties were now solidly under Royalist control. Only the seaports, Plymouth, Poole and Lyme Regis, were holding out for Parliament, and their resistance was to have serious consequences for the future of the Royalist campaign.

We know that among the Cavalier horse, a young and obscure trooper, Winston Churchill, fought at Lansdown and Roundway Down. It seems, too, that he was present with the victorious army that entered Bristol.

In the midst of these excitements, the young captain of horse married, probably in Maytime of 1643, just before he went off on the campaign that carried the Royalists to victory.[8]

War has never been averse to love; but no doubt other calculations entered into this marriage that was to be so important to the Churchills. John Churchill, like a sensible man, had married above him in marrying a Winston. He must have had a hand in making a further step upward in his son's marriage to Elizabeth Drake, a daughter of Sir John Drake of Ashe. For the Drakes of Ashe were one of the leading families of Devon, a medieval family that had been going for generations, intermarried with the oldest Norman gentry of Devon, Grenvilles, Fortescues and such. Sir Bernard Drake, Sir John's grandfather, had been a foremost figure in the county in the reign of Queen Elizabeth. He had had an angry pass with Sir Francis Drake, on the latter's assuming the Drake coat of arms on his return from the Voyage Round the World, the most celebrated Englishman of his day. This was not good enough for Sir Bernard, who thought him an upstart and is *said* to have boxed the upstart's ears.[9] This is the kind of thing that is important to human beings: birth of more consideration than being the first circumnavigator of the globe. But indeed any relationship between Sir Francis and the Drakes of Ashe never has been established, though he may well have belonged to a poor, forgotten offshoot of the tribe.

Sir John Drake had married Eleanor, daughter of Lord Boteler, who had married the sister of George Villiers, first Duke of Buckingham. Since that handsome young man had been promoted to the favors of the susceptible James I by the respectable party at Court, headed by the Archbishop of Canterbury, against the unrespectable Howards, three generations of Villiers exerted an irresistible fascination, in various members—men and women alike—upon three generations of Stuarts. It is an extraordinary story. Something in that errant, vivacious, brilliant blood, with its wonderful looks, passed an electric current into the stocks with which it mingled. Nothing in the Churchills so far, earthy and commonplace, could have foretold their astonishing future—nothing until that marriage.

Sir John Drake died young, in 1636; but his wife was not a Villiers for nothing: she was a personality, and she took charge.

We learn from complicated proceedings they were subsequently involved in, through the troubles brought down on them all by the times, that Elizabeth had been left by her father 1,000 marks toward her marriage portion.[10] She was then only a girl. Now she was twenty-one. Lady Drake agreed with John Churchill to give her a dowry of £1,500, in return for which he was to settle upon her lands worth £160 a year. The marriage went forward.

Their famous descendant comments, "it is remarkable that such contracts should have been effected between persons so sharply divided by the actual fighting of the Civil Wars"[11]—for Lady Drake and her son were Parliamentarians. In truth, there was nothing remarkable in this: the life of society must go on, families were divided, enemies married, sometimes a besieger married a fair besieged.[12] We have such instances as the Puritan Milton marrying the daughter of the Cavalier squire of Forest Hill—and very good reinsurance it was for them: the Powells took full advantage of it to quarter themselves upon the poet in the days of their adversity. And so it came about with Winston Churchill.

However, with the Royalist ascendancy in the West, Lady Drake was the first to taste adversity.

Her fine house of Ashe—a large Elizabethan E-shaped mansion—lay right on the main road, on the right-hand side going south, from Axminster to the sea. There a fragment of it, one wing with its detached chapel, still remains, looking out over the fat pastures of that shallow valley on one side, across to Colyton and up to the dark woods of Shute lining the horizon to the west. To the east, there is the little village of Musbury, with its Devon church tower and, within, the monuments of generations of Drakes. It is a pleasant place, though only a fragment, within its formal gardens, the remains of the old fishponds, the emplacements of the earlier great house: surrounded now by its orchards, a white foam of appleblossom in spring, the red and russet and gold of autumn.

Ashe lay exposed to the road, and to whoever was passing up and down. It stood on the direct route between Axminster in Cavalier hands and Lyme that was obstinately, irreducibly, Parliamentarian. It was hardly possible that the mansion of a flagrantly Parliamentarian lady should escape attention.

At Christmas, 1643, a friendly neighbor heard talk at the Royalist headquarters at Axminster, where Lord Paulett was commander in chief, that there would have to be a garrison placed at Ashe or else it would have to be burned.[13] This neighbor, a Devon yeoman, at once sent word by his sister to Lady Drake, warning her to ask Lord Paulett to place some musketeers in the house to save it from destruction. But she had already got the Parliamentarian garrison of Lyme to put in a few soldiers. So that it was hardly surprising that, a week later, Lord Paulett let loose his Irish soldiery on the place, who burned it down.

Lady Drake had already left for Lyme, though in her petition to

Parliament she makes the most of her sufferings, giving the impression that she had been stripped "almost naked and without shoe to her foot but what she afterwards begged" and so "fled to Lyme for safety."[14] Here for many months she endured the privations and hardships of the siege, and for a livelihood was "reduced to the spinning and knitting of stockings, in which miserable condition she continued until the siege of Lyme was raised." With the arrival of the Parliamentarian army under the Earl of Essex in the summer, on its way through to disaster and surrender to the King at Lostwithiel, Lady Drake was able to escape and make her way to Parliament and the shelter of London.

Here her necessities were relieved in September by the grant of £100, a pension of £5 per week for her support, and the house in the Strand of a Royalist gentleman, Sir Thomas Reynell, to live in rent free.[15] Here she remained encamped, one might say "embattled," till July, 1647; for not all Sir Thomas's petitions could get her out of it, even when fighting had ceased and he had made his submission. He claimed that she had "broken down great part of the walls, digged up the ground and pulled up the flowers to find treasure."[16] But this was common form.

Lady Drake's residence in London is no part of our story; but it seems that she had her daughters with her, while her son was held prisoner by Prince Maurice in 1644. For on Lady Drake's getting her sister, the Royalist Countess of Marlborough, to petition the Prince for John Drake's freedom, he replied that he could not do it, for then Lord Paulett's house would be fired—John Drake having given out that he would burn it in revenge for his own.[17] Such was the spirit that was building up on either side in this deplorable war.

When the war ended with the victory of the Parliament, Lady Drake was awarded £1,500 compensation out of Lord Paulett's estate; while he had to settle £200 a year on faithful Lyme—a permanent knock to the finances of that noble house.[18] It took the active and clamorous lady some years, however, before she got her money.

Her story has led us some way ahead of affairs in the West. To return to the summer of 1644: Lyme—with Lady Drake within it—was regularly besieged by Prince Maurice's army, from April to the end of June.[19] The defense, directed by Blake—the Somerset soldier who became the grand Admiral of the Commonwealth—was very spirited. When Essex's army marched into the West in June, the Royalists had to draw off and Lyme was saved. Behind the shelter of Essex, Parliament regained temporary ascendancy in Dorset.

We do not know where Winston Churchill was in this year 1644; but it is reasonable to suppose that he was fighting in the field, either with the forces in his own native county under Prince Maurice, or with the King's forces that pursued Essex into Cornwall, cooped him up in the peninsula and forced him to surrender.

The war, however, was not decided in the West; but by the superior resources of the eastern counties and London, Parliament's control of the navy and sea power, and, ultimately, by the fruition of Pym's long-term strategy in bringing Scotland in to make the balance against the King certain and secure. The result was to be seen in the great defeat of Marston Moor in 1644, by which the King lost the North, and in the disaster of Naseby, 1645, by which he lost the Midlands and his cause received a fatal blow.

In the last phase of the fighting in the West Winston Churchill was present; for we know that he was wounded in the arm by the forces under his fellow Dorsetman, Colonel Starr, that he was at the siege of Taunton and engaged in the defence of Bristol, and that he was still in arms against Parliament as late as December, 1645.[20]

There is no point in tracing further the breakup of the Royalist cause: the retreat into the far West, the escape of the Prince of Wales—hope of the future—from the Scilly Islands to France, the surrender of the Royalist remnant to Fairfax at Truro.

2

The Civil War was over. It remained to gather up the threads of life, resume the broken diurnal routine, accustom oneself to the new and unprecedented situation in which England found itself; for the country to find, if possible, a basis of settlement; for the individual, to make the best of things.

In the year 1647, in the summer of which Lady Drake left London, the Cavalier captain was at length free to come together with his wife; for on February 23 next year their first child, Arabella, was born at Ashe and baptized in the chapel there on March 16.[21] Thereafter Mrs. Churchill presented her husband with fruitful increase, with monotonous annual regularity, till the complement of a dozen was reached. As usual in those days, most of them died in infancy. Winston, the first-born son, born in 1649, did not live. Their next son, the famous John, who became the Duke of Marlborough, was born at Ashe in 1650 and baptized there on May 26. Of their remaining children, those who survived were George, born at Ashe in 1653, who became an admiral; Charles, born in 1656, who was a general under his brother, the Duke; Theobald, born in Dublin in 1663, who took orders but died in his twenties.[22]

We see that the family life centered upon Ashe. His father was still alive at Wootton Glanville, with a second wife. There was Minterne: why did not Winston occupy that? We have evidence that he was not on good terms with his stepmother and, perhaps, his father. Then, too, they were all impoverished. Lady Drake's son, John, was living at Trill, a farm not far from Ashe. There remained what there was undamaged of the great house and to put that in a state of repair. Lady Drake estimated her losses at £6,000, toward which she was awarded £1,500 out of Lord Paulett's estate in March, 1648.[23]

No doubt this helped to repair some part of the house—every penny was needed—and enabled her to shelter her daughter and son-in-law and their young family.

But what about the Colonel's delinquency?

For some time it seems that it escaped attention or that Churchill was sheltered by Lady Drake's connections. But in June, 1649, he was informed against by two Parliamentarian captains, Dymock and Chapman.[24] They informed the Committee for Compounding that Sir Henry Rosewell of Ford owed Churchill £150 and Colonel William Fry of Yardley—who was Sir John Drake's executor—owed him £1,200. Here was a sum of £1,350, evidently Mrs. Churchill's jointure, liable to be made available for delinquency fines. The Churchills naturally turned and twisted every way to escape it.

The simple explanation of the protracted proceedings that ensued appears to be that Mrs. Churchill's marriage portion had not been paid over to her, owing to her separation from her husband by the wars, and now they were trying to take advantage of that fact not to compound for it, while suing Fry and Rosewell for its payment to them.

In April the facts of the marriage contract agreed upon by John Churchill and Lady Drake were brought out: Winston Churchill did not deny his interest therein and desired to compound for it. At the end of the month Winston Churchill compounded for an annuity of £100 on Wootton Glanville and other lands of his father—which may have represented his father's contribution to his living. His fine was fixed at £480. On November 11 the fine was paid and Churchill's estate discharged.

These proceedings, though I have given them in a very abbreviated form, reveal so much—the disruption of the times, the disturbance to people's lives, the insecurity and strain, the actual impoverishment. But think of the resentments, the rancors and hatreds it piled up in the countryside, the inability of the defeated to forgive or forget! It was all the more insupportable in that it was the gentry, the natural ruling class, who were harried and humiliated by Cromwellian captains from the lower middle class.[25] They never forgot that experience: it was the rift within their own ranks between Crown and Parliament that had enabled the natural order of things to be reversed and Cromwell's lower-class sectaries to rule England. It was only the ascendancy of the army, and the genius of Cromwell, that enabled this unnatural order to continue: it would not long survive Cromwell's own life. When the rule of the army foundered upon the indefeasibly civilian spirit of the English people, the two wings of the governing class—Royalist and Parliamentarian—came together again to restore the King and the country's ancient institutions, the accustomed ways. They would never let in the lower classes again, however bitterly they might be divided by party spirit.

The experience of civil war and revolution explains the intense bitterness of party spirit in the years to come. It also explains much in the outlook and characteristics of the Churchills. Defeat and frustration gave an edge to long-smothered ambition, sharpened the determination to make the most of opportunity when it came. Wants denied and financial stringency all through their youth must have determined them that they would not be poor when they grew up: they would make money and hold on to it—as every one of them did. Those dark years must have had a subtler impact: it made each of those children reserved, capable of keeping his or her own counsel, bent on inner independence.

Their descendant sees with imagination the effect it must have had within the household at Ashe. "It would be strange indeed if the children were not conscious of the chasm between their elders; if they never saw resentment on the one side, or felt patronage from the other; if they were never reminded that it was to their grandmother's wisdom and faithful championship of the cause of Parliament they owed the bread they ate."[26] And the effect on the boy among them in whom there one day

matured a military genius second to none in our history? "The two prevailing impressions which such experiences might arouse in the mind
of a child would be, first, a hatred of poverty and dependence and,
secondly, the need of hiding thoughts and feelings from those to whom
their expression would be repugnant. To have one set of opinions for one
part of the family, and to use a different language to the other, may have
been inculcated from John's earliest years. To win freedom from material
subservience by the sure agency of money must have been planted in
his heart's desire. To these was added a third: the importance of having
friends and connections on both sides of a public quarrel . . . Certainly the
whole life of John Churchill bore the imprint of his youth. That
impenetrable reserve under graceful and courteous manners; those un-
ceasing contacts and correspondences with opponents; that iron parsimony
and personal frugality, never relaxed in the blaze of fortune and
abundance; that hatred of waste and improvidence in all their forms—
all these could find their roots in the bleak years at Ashe."

In these years Winston Churchill made one appearance that we
know of in London, June 23, 1652, when he was called to the bar; but
this seems to have been a purely formal, much-belated measure: he made
no use of it and did not keep term.[27]

Down in the country, in remote east Devon, sunk in glum resentment, he had at any rate the consolation that intelligent people have who
are defeated and out of favor: reading and writing. He was reading hard,
for he was going to write a book. Now that the sword had been struck
from his hand, he would take up the quill in defence of his cause. His
spirit was not defeated: it burns with unquenched ardor in what he wrote.
He had plenty of time for reading and writing in those long winter nights
when the south westerlies blew up the valley from the sea and the candles
guttered in the drafty damaged house; or when snow lay upon the pastures
and up the slopes to Musbury church, where a Puritan intruder held
forth in place of the pulpit's rightful occupant. The Colonel was not
likely to patronize his ministrations or to entrust the education of his
children to him. It is said that he used the services of a neighboring
sequestered clergyman, whose sympathies he shared.

The book helped to fill the black years when Oliver ruled at
Whitehall and the faithful waited, almost without hope, for the King
to come back to his own. It was not published till long after the Restora-

tion, in 1675, when it was dedicated to "His most Sacred Majesty, Charles II," and the old Cavalier offered it "as the only instance of duty I could give at that which was indeed the worst of times; being begun when everybody thought that monarchy had ended and would have been buried in the same grave with your martyred father . . . When none of us that served that blessed Prince had any other weapons left us but our pens to show the justice of our zeal by that of his title; when, for want of ink black enough to record the impieties that followed, we designed to write them in blood: writing and fighting being alike dangerous, and necessary."

Macaulay, with his frequent superciliousness, refers to the work as that of "a poor Cavalier knight, who haunted Whitehall, and made himself ridiculous by publishing a dull and affected folio, long forgotten, in praise of monarchy and monarchs."* The omnivorous Macaulay cannot have read it. The author's descendant is more just, and more percipient, when he says, "to quote from this book is to meet its author across the centuries." The truth is that the book is neither dull nor affected: it is learned in an old-fashioned way, it may be naïve, but it is full of the writer's personality, which means that it is alive, when many more famous authors are dead.

The book is a history of the country, only a monarchical history. That the government of this isle has always been monarchical is its theme; its title: *Divi Britannici*. Disagreeable old Anthony Wood tells us that it did sell—among the novices, because of the arms of all the kings of England, rather than for the matter therein. At Oxford it was held, in the kind way that academics have, that the book could not possibly be Churchill's, but must have been written by Clarendon.[28] A don at Christ Church wrote to his crony, "we call Churchill's book here the Chancellor's. I know not whence we had the information, but if it be worth the reading, as you write me, sure it cannot be Churchill's, although it bear his name."[29] From which we see the silliness of academic opinion: Sir Winston had written a better book than they thought him capable of, so it must be the Chancellor's. But, indeed, the book and its author are remembered, when they are forgotten.

---

* Macaulay, *History of England*, ed. C. H. Firth, I, 452. Note the injustice of Macaulay's phrase "haunted Whitehall." Sir Winston was a permanent official of the Board of Green Cloth, besides being a Member of Parliament; it would have been a dereliction of duty if he were not in regular attendance at Whitehall.

It is pleasant to observe that the wheel has come full circle with Sir Winston's namesake, who also has written his history of England, though, with the wider scope of our age, his has broadened out into the history of the English-speaking peoples.

We soon discern that the dominant influence upon Churchill in writing his book was that of his fellow West Countryman Ralegh's *History of the World*, even before we come to a marked tribute, which may record something of family tradition in Devon as to Ralegh's fate. "Herein those that were his particular friends and relations were not more surprised than all the world beside. For as they expected to have been indebted to his sword for bringing home more gold than would have paid the price of his forfeited head, so everybody else hoped to have been no less indebted to his pen for finishing that most excellent piece of his, the History of the Old World, which ended as untimely as himself, by attempting a discovery of the new one."[30]

The book, like Ralegh's, displays an astonishing amount of diverse and divagatory learning, not only from classical authorities, but from medieval chroniclers and lawyers, and coming up to publications of the day. In this respect, Churchill's manner and approach were old-fashioned; but he was an old-fashioned person: not for him the streamlined prose, the elegant spareness, of the new Royal Society. He has a natural eloquence not unworthy of his descendant, and phrases that are not unlike; he has the gift of style. Of the function of the historian: "if the reading of history in general be not only a recreation, but a restorative, and such as by which some princes have recovered the health of their bodies, others the distempers of their minds, many have learnt to settle, and most to preserve the weal of their estates," then possibly his book may be not less pleasant than useful. This was addressed to Charles II, who certainly would have done better to pay more attention to history and less to women. Of historians themselves: "there have not been wanting in all times some faithful ministers of fame, who, rescuing out of the jaws of time the memory of such renowned persons, whose names have been less mortal than their bodies (their honour continuing like the perfume in their ashes, uncorrupted in the midst of corruption) . . ."[31] One sees that the old Cavalier's temperament gave his prose an excellent natural rhythm.

The whole approach is that of a naïve patriotism—in that very like the Elizabethans. The succession of the kings in this island is the most ancient; our monarchs were the first to be anointed. The efficacy of the sacrament continues: is it not notoriously known "how a maid at Deptford, born blind by reason of that distemper [the king's evil], was cured by no other visible means but the touch of a cloth dipped in the blood of the late King Charles the Martyr"?[32] No doubt. As to the providential advantage of our insularity, he quotes Waller:

> Tis not so hard for greedy foes to spoil
> Another nation, as to touch our soil.[33]

It might have been quoted in 1940. Another phrase recalls his descendant: the bounds of Britain appear now to be boundless, "extending to those far distant regions (now become a part of us and growing apace to be the bigger part) in the sun-burnt America."[34]

The book begins, like Leland, Camden and the chroniclers, with the kings of Britain, the origin and etymology of the name: a great deal of genuine learning is displayed, a nightmare of authorities cited in the Elizabethan fashion. Thence it passes in succession to the Roman rulers, the old English, then the Normans. These end, surprisingly, with Queen Elizabeth, to whom a just tribute is paid. "And happy it was for her that she was so unhappy; for, by being a subject she had learned to rule and, from the sense of her own sufferings, was much inclined to compassionate others. All that were swordmen admired her courage, as having a spirit too great for any woman but such as was born to rule over men. All that were gown-men as much magnified her understanding, as having by her wisdom made her way through all the snares made by her sister's ministers to entangle her."[35] The case of Mary Queen of Scots was awkward for a devotee of the Stuarts; like Camden (after James's accession), he takes the received Stuart line. Mary's misfortunes are put down to envy and an unkind fate.

A comment in passing, when writing of Drake's career, may express something of the family feeling about their namesake, their dislike of the upstart—may represent their private tradition. Of Drake's return from the 1585 expedition, when he "stormed through the Indies like a conqueror," Churchill writes: "he returned even surfeited with victory, his head being giddy with new contrivances, as his men's were with the calenture."[36] The tone is not friendly; the treatment of Drake not generous.

As he comes near to the events of his own times, the Cavalier gives vent to his feelings: he has a fine line in Churchillian invective. Of the origin of the Scots he gives this account. "The Scots would be thought a branch of the Scythian stock . . . and they have this colour among many others, that as their ancestors are entitled to as ancient barbarity as those of any other nation whatever, so like those rude Scyths, they have always been given to prey upon their neighbours . . . some thinking them a by-slip of the Germans, others of the Scandians; some affirming them to be outcasts of some mongrel Spaniards that were not permitted to live in Ireland; and others yet fetching their descent from the Vandals . . . And some there are that with no small probability take them to be a miscellany of all these nations."[37]

At the end of the book there is a magnificent outburst of Cavalier feeling about the rule of the regicides. "Here seemed to be the *Consummatum est* of all the happiness of this kingdom, as well as of the life of this King. For upon his death the veil of the Temple rent, and the Church was overthrown. An universal darkness overspread the state, which lasted not for twelve hours only, but twelve years. The two great luminaries of law and gospel were put out: such as could not write supplied the place of judges, such as could not read of bishops. Peace was maintained by war, licentiousness by fasting and prayer. The commonalty lost their property, the gentry their liberty, the nobility their honour, the clergy their authority and reverence. The stream of government ran down in new-cut channels, whose waters were always shallow and troubled."[38]

This is an eloquent summing up of the state of Royalist feeling. As for the constitution of the Commonwealth, "whether the plot of this imaginary structure came first from Hell or Holland matters not much; but so it was that (like the new buildings there) it cost more to make good the ground it stood on, than the superstructure was worth; which made the people in a very little time so weary both of the projection and the projectors, that it was not long ere it fell into visible decay.[39]

And so to the Restoration.

CHAPTER III

The Restoration: in England and Ireland

THE EARLY months of 1660 witnessed a landslide in favor of the King in exile. Neither Parliament nor the army, Republican politicians nor generals, Presbyterians nor Independents, had been able to give the country a permanent settlement or provide a firm constitutional structure. Only the genius, the prestige, the power of Cromwell had been able to hold things together; even after his death, that mighty shadow had prevailed for more than a year. Now cracks appeared on every side; innumerable schemes were put forward by clever doctrinaires—all to no avail; a gulf opened beneath men's feet. The whole country was demanding a free Parliament; everyone knew that that meant the restoration of the King.[1]

Slowly General Monk marched south from Scotland with his army, watching the currents of opinion, keeping his thoughts to himself. At last arrived in London, he formed the conclusion that nothing but the restoration of King, Lords and Commons—the country's ancient constitution—would do. A West Country royalist himself by origin, Monk's friends and relations brought about the decisive contact between him and the King in Holland. Sir Peter Killigrew, "Peter the Post," passed to and fro with frequent messages. In Bevil Grenville's son John—who, as a boy, had been lifted into his father's saddle at Lansdown when he was mortally wounded—Monk and the King found an intermediary whom both could trust. The restored Long Parliament voted him £500 to buy a jewel for his services. For the impecunious King they voted £50,000 for immediate expenses. When the money arrived at Breda, he took his brothers and his sister in to see the portmanteau in which it lay: never had they seen so much money.*

---

* There is a parallel to this in their grandfather Henri IV's reaction when he saw the money Elizabeth I sent over to subsidize him. See my *Expansion of Elizabethan England*, 397.

In glad Maytime, Admiral Montague was sent over with the fleet to fetch home the King, with his brothers, the Dukes of York and Gloucester. Pepys was with the Admiral on board the *Naseby*, so that we know all about the homecoming. At Dover, painters were sent out to pull down the state's arms and put up the royal arms. When the King came aboard, the royal standard was hoisted; cheers resounded through the fleet, and the sailors threw their caps and even their doublets into the sea. The ships were renamed: the *Naseby*—name of ill omen—became the *Royal Charles*. On board, the King surprised Mr. Pepys by his activity and affability. "All the afternoon the King walked here and there, up and down (quite contrary to what I thought him to have been) very active and stirring."[2] The King's mind was full of the last days he had spent in England, and Mr. Pepys was touched to tears by his Majesty's stories of his escape and the hardships he had undergone on his flight, after Worcester, to the coast.

At Dover, crowds lined the shore. There was General Monk kneeling, whom the King embraced and raised up, hailing him as "Father." The mayor approached with a large Bible, which Charles accepted with the memorable words that "it was the thing that he loved above all things in the world." The English have always been more susceptible than most peoples to humbug, and some humbug is no doubt necessary to government. This was designed to appeal to the Protestantism of the nation; it will be seen later how far the remark was true.

Charles II's first proclamation, against drinking, swearing and debauchery, was read to the ships' companies in the fleet, where it seems to have given particular satisfaction. In London the enthusiasm was immense; similar scenes were enacted. At St. Paul's door the ministers presented Charles with another Bible for his collection, to whom he replied that "he would make that book the rule of his life and government.[3] But he left it behind him. John Evelyn watched the King's entry into London on his birthday, "with a triumph of above 20,000 horse and foot, brandishing their swords and shouting with inexpressible joy; the ways strewed with flowers, the bells ringing, the streets hung with tapisserie, fountains running with wine, the Mayor, Aldermen and all the companies in their liveries, chains of gold and banners; lords and nobles clad in cloth of silver, gold and velvet; the windows and balconies well set with ladies; trumpets, music and myriads of people flocking even so far as from Rochester, so as they were seven hours in passing the city, even from two in the afternoon till nine at night. I stood in the Strand and beheld it and blessed God!"[4]

The thaw had come; it was happy springtime; the King was home to enjoy his own again. With his pleasant cynical turn of humor, he "said, smilingly to some about him that he doubted it had been his own fault that he had been absent so long, for he saw no-one that did not protest he had ever wished for his return."[5]

I

On his father's death, Winston Churchill—or the Colonel, as we henceforth find him popularly called—went to live at Minterne. He made that his seat in the country. At the Restoration he was a man of forty: if ever he was to make a mark in the world, now was the moment —even so, it was rather late.

The Convention Parliament of 1660 having called home the King and passed an Act of Indemnity and Oblivion—which the Cavaliers described as "Indemnity for the King's enemies and Oblivion for his friends"—dissolved itself. The full tide of Royalist reaction was evident in the Parliament that was elected next year, the Cavalier Parliament. It contained a large number of the younger generation that had grown up since the Civil War. On someone commenting on these beardless young men, Charles said that he would keep them until they had beards.

And so he did: this Parliament was kept in existence for eighteen years, from 1661 to 1679. So overwhelming a majority for one side, so strong a reaction, was neither representative of the nation nor good for it. It represented the victory of the Anglican country gentry, the alliance between squire and parson henceforth in every parish, not to be broken until the social revolution of our own time; it expressed their accumulated resentments at their sufferings, the insults and humiliations they had received at the hands of their inferiors. Never again! was their watch-word. They were far more reactionary than Charles, or even Clarendon, his Chancellor. The Cavalier Parliament forced upon them both the "Clarendon Code," enforcing uniformity in the Church, driving out the moderate Puritans, proscribing their dissenting services, riveting serious disabilities upon them in regard to civic office and education, depriving them of any share in government and trying to extrude them from public life.

fines upon them for their delinquency, the proscription of their Church. It was contrary to the spirit of the Restoration, which rested upon a compromise between moderate Parliamentarians and Royalists. It went beyond what Clarendon wished, for, a stanch Anglican, he was a man of his word and saw the unwisdom of it; it went far beyond anything the King wished, for that "expert hedonist took less pleasure than the virtuous in punishing other people for their opinions."[6] Moreover, a crypto-Catholic, anxious to tolerate and advance Catholics, he had the political sense to see that that could not be effectively done without the alliance and support of the Dissenters. The reaction was the triumph of a class, rather than of the monarchy; the Cavalier Parliament was not generous to the King with its money grants: it wished to keep him in leash and dependent on it. This, in time, drove the King to look abroad for financial support and to free himself from dependence on Parliament—to look to his cousin, Louis XIV, who successfully developed an absolute monarchy that was the model and the despair of his fellow monarchs all over Europe.

These fractures and conflicts of interest and opinion are the clue to the bitter political struggles under the later Stuarts, to the rise of the Tory and Whig parties; nor did they die down and cease to convulse the nation until the Hanoverian succession in 1714.

Such was the background—or rather the foreground—to all the political activity of the Churchills during this period.

In March, 1661, Winston Churchill was returned as a member for Weymouth, and so he remained till the end of the Cavalier Parliament in 1679.[7]

At once we find him one of the most energetic and active members of the House, serving on most of its important committees. His legal training was useful; his long service in the field gave him an advantage over younger men. In May he was placed on the most important committee, that on elections and the privileges of the House.[8] Three days later he was on that for preserving His Majesty against treasonable and seditious attempts: there were several attempts against his life about this time. At the end of the month Churchill was on a large committee to consider the bill for repairing and enlarging the common highways, and on another to enable churchwardens to assess and levy money for the repair of churches and other purposes—we observe a return to the old order in the parishes.

In June he served on committees considering bills to suppress tumults and for providing necessary carriages for His Majesty in his progresses.[9] In July he was helping to draw up bills establishing articles and orders for regulating the navy, and reporting on that for discharging the loyal party of all interest exceeding 3 per cent. The Commons resolved to lay an imposition on sealed paper and parchment toward the advance of the revenue. This was referred to the Solicitor General, Winston Churchill, Sir Henry Bennet and two or three others.

In November this busy committee work was resumed: inspecting the accounts of commissioners for disbanding and paying off the army and navy; preventing unnecessary charges to sheriffs in passing their accounts; restoring the Marquis of Hertford—his old commander in the West—to the dukedom of Somerset, and the Earl of Arundel to the dukedom of Norfolk.[10] The oligarchy was strengthening itself and taking up position: no more major generals or Puritan captains with their inconvenient convictions, or dotty sectaries holding forth in public places. At the end of the month he was on an important committee to consider ways for the further supply and reparation of His Majesty's loyal and suffering subjects, who had faithfully served His Majesty or his father.

This opens up an acute source of dissatisfaction among the Cavaliers. The landed gentry wanted compensation for their losses; they wanted the return of the lands they had had to sell to pay their fines. It was impossible for the government to give them this. On this fundamental issue, Clarendon had effected a compromise at the Restoration: the lands of the Crown and of the Church, the estates of Cavalier magnates which had been confiscated outright, were restored. This was as much as could be done for the Cavaliers. The lands that they had themselves sold to pay their fines had to be left to the purchasers. Any attempt to go back on that would have disrupted the countryside once more. It was politically impossible. But it remained a festering resentment at the back of Tory minds; for, in many places, on the proceeds new men had risen, ex-Roundheads, with a footing in the squirearchy, to become local leaders of the Whig party of the future.

All this committee work is dull stuff—but Parliament is like that. I have given it in some detail to show how strenuous the work of Parliament was in these early years of the Restoration. There were three kingdoms to get in order, a new deal to be worked out and as securely grounded as the shifting circumstances of the Restoration permitted.

The Colonel was one of the foremost committeemen in the House, and a faithful follower of the King. His service was at length taken notice of by the Court.

Churchill owed his introduction at Court to the patronage of Sir Henry Bennet, later Earl of Arlington. We do not know exactly when this took place, but Churchill definitely became Arlington's protégé.* We have seen them serving on a House of Commons committee together. They had more in common. Arlington came from a similar family of Berkshire small gentry who had risen through the law. He, too, was an Oxford man—one sees his grand portrait over the door of Christ Church hall, very dignified in his deportment and his sweeping robes, with the black patch he always wore on the bridge of his nose to remind people of his service to the Crown. For, like Churchill, he too had received a wound: a saber-cut in a skirmish at Andover. It did not amount to much, but he made the most of it. Anthony Hamilton said that "the plaster-patch so well suited his mysterious looks, that it seemed an addition to his gravity and self-sufficiency."[11]

He was a favorite with the King, for he was an amusing man, with "the best turns of wit in particular conversation that I have known," said Sir William Temple; he had the art, wrote Bishop Burnet, "of observing the King's temper and managing it beyond all the men of that time."[12] Even Clarendon admitted, generously—for Arlington in the end supplanted him—"he may well be reckoned in the number of the finest gentlemen of the time . . . The King received him with great kindness, as a man whose company he always liked."[13] He shared more with the King: Charles and he had been seen in a Catholic church together in Madrid; they had the same skeptical turn of mind, combined with secret Catholic sympathies; both were witty, cynical men, disingenuous and uncandid—perhaps understandably when idiot fanaticisms were rampant in the world around them. Arlington, like Harley later, was also a subterranean wirepuller—such men are indispensable in politics. The King had made Clarendon find him a seat in Parliament; though, as the old constitutional lawyer, the Chancellor, protested, "he knew no more of the constitution and laws of England than he did of China."[14]

One thing Arlington understood better than the Chancellor was

---

* For the sake of simplicity I call him Arlington, the name by which he became notorious, though he did not acquire it until his peerage in 1663.

foreign affairs; and another was the art of intrigue. He was engaged now in bringing together a group of the new generation in the Commons, whom the Chancellor neglected: country gentlemen on whose votes the King could rely and who, when the time came, could be turned against the antiquated, honest, monopolizing Chancellor.

Such was the Colonel's political patron, and, in time to come, he was to suffer—or at any rate, be traduced—for his associations.

It may be thought that the royal recognition was exiguous enough. Charles had little to give, except to personal favorites and intimates who took advantage of his good nature to pester him: anything rather than be bored! It was typical of the circumstances of the Restoration that the Parliamentarian John Drake was knighted within a fortnight of the King's return.[15] The faithful Colonel had to work and wait four years for his. All that he got now was an augmentation of honor to his coat of arms. On December 11, 1661, the King ordered Garter King-at-Arms to grant an augmentation of a St. George's cross gules on a canton argent to the arms of Winston Churchill of Minterne, for service to the late King and for his present loyalty as a member of the House of Commons.[16] A cheap enough way of recognizing service; but we may take it as an earnest of better to come. As for the Colonel, he blazoned above his new coat of arms an uprooted oak with the motto *Fiel pero desdichado* ("Faithful but unfortunate")—again with the personal touch of the sense of his own misfortunes. Such is the motto his descendants continue to bear. "Faithful" certainly, but never was the cant of heraldry more belied than in the second epithet, "unfortunate."

Even the Colonel's fortunes were turning.

After Christmas he returned to work on bills for the relief and employment of the poor and the punishment of vagrants, and for preventing abuses in the Customs.[17] This brought him into association with another West Countryman who became prominent: Clifford, later Lord Treasurer, another friend with incriminating associations for Churchill in subsequent years, for Clifford resigned office after the Test Act, a declared Catholic.

All through the session of 1662, the Colonel continued to be employed on numerous committees: bills for providing transports by land and water for army and navy, for preventing seditious abuses in unlicensed books and pamphlets, for regulating the excise, for the better observance of the Lord's day.[18] This was a very hardy annual. The com-

mittee met in the Speaker's chamber very early on a beautiful May
morning: a gathering of country gentlemen, many of them from the West
Country, Mr. Clifford, Sir John Strode, Sir John Rouse, Mr. Boscawen
and the Colonel—these last two to be connected by a family tie after
some unexpected and exalted divagations.

Churchill's assiduity in the House at length brought him to the
notice of the King, by Arlington's means. We have Clarendon's sub-
acid account of it in his autobiography; self-satisfied, as always, he did
not see the necessity of bringing in the younger men.[19] "When those two
persons, Sir Harry Bennet and Mr. Coventry, (between whom there had
been as great a league of friendship as can be between two very proud
men equally ill-natured) came now to sit together in the House of Commons . . . they made friendships with some young men, who spake con-
fidently and often and upon some occasions seemed to have credit in the
House. And upon a little conversation with those men, who, being
country gentlemen of ordinary condition and mean fortunes [Clarendon
himself had been no more: they were all from the same class, small
gentry], were desirous to have interest in such a person as Sir Harry
Bennet, who was believed to have great credit with the King."

"He recommended those men to the King 'as persons of sublime
parts, worthy of his Majesty's caressing; that he would undertake to fix
them to his service, and when they were his own, he might carry what
he would in the House of Commons.' These men had parts, indeed, and
good affections, and often had resorted to the Chancellor, received advice
from him and thought themselves beholden to him . . . But now these
gentlemen had got a better patron; the new courtier had raised their
value and talked in another dialect to them, of recompenses and rewards,
than they had heard formerly. He carried them to the King and told his
Majesty in their own hearing 'what men of parts they were, what
services they had done for him and how much greater they could do'; and
his Majesty received and conferred with them very graciously and dismissed them with promises which made them rich already."

Charles naturally asked Clarendon's opinion of these men, "and
particularly named Mr. Clifford and Mr. Churchill and some other men
of better quality and much more interest, who he said, 'took it ill that
they were not particularly informed what the King desired and which
way they might best serve him'; and bade him that 'at the next meeting
of the rest, these men might likewise have notice to be present.'" This

was the nightly meeting that took place at Court, during the session, to discuss government business. Clarendon could not but give a good character of Clifford and Churchill, "who were honest gentlemen, and received the advice they were to follow from Sir Hugh Pollard, who had in truth a very particular influence upon all the Cornish and Devonshire men."

Upon this the King said that "he would have Sir Harry Bennet, Mr. Clifford and Mr. Churchill called to the next meeting; and because they were to be introduced into company they had not used to converse with, that it should be at the Chancellor's chamber, who should let the rest know the good opinion his Majesty had of those who were added to the number."

We observe the Chancellor's art, in the days of his power, of making enemies, of alienating those who should have been his supporters. Sir Hugh Pollard was a good friend of his; now two of Pollard's most forward recruits were added to the number of Arlington's friends.

It was to him that Churchill owed his introduction at Court, and shortly the connection brought him the reward of an employment under the Crown, a job at last.

2

The Restoration was presented with a far more intractable, and a more complex, situation in Ireland. The rebellion of Celtic and Catholic Ireland in 1641 had been a prelude to the Civil War in England; it was accompanied by massacres and barbarities, which made an undying impression on the English and forfeited all claims of the Irish to sympathy now. After years of warfare, civil war, calling in papal nuncios to do what they could not do for themselves, i.e., govern, the Cromwellian conquest made a clean sweep—swept the native Irish landowners west of the Shannon and settled the rest with Puritan soldiers and adventurers. Whereas the majority of Irish landowners up to 1641 had been Catholic, they were now Protestant.[20] In 1660 the Cromwellian colonists had accepted the Restoration; the King's declaration gave them guarantees. Through all the subsequent tangle of negotiations, bargaining, resettlement, this remained the fundamental factor: the Cromwellian conquest of Ireland remained essentially unchanged.

Great unrest and a universal sense of insecurity prevailed until the new settlement was confirmed and put into operation. For there was a welter of claims, old and new, to land. The native Irish were encouraged by a Royalist reaction and the King's known sympathies to entertain exaggerated hopes; but the King could do little for them. As in England there was not enough money to go round, so in Ireland there was not enough land.[21] The government had been assured that there was enough to meet everybody's claims—innocent Protestants, innocent Papists, Royalists who had fought for the King, whether Catholic Irish or old English settlers, Cromwellians who had conquered Irish rebels. The claims and counterclaims were inextricable; many of them were false, or put forward for ulterior motives. Those who had some legitimate claim, but were at present occupying lands to which others had a better, were to be given "reprisals," i.e., compensation, elsewhere. The confiscated lands of regicides, lands forfeited in the course of rebellion, constituted a kind of fund from which reprisals were to be made.

Such was the purpose of the Act of Settlement of 1662. There was nothing like enough land to provide for reprisals, let alone for the legion of conflicting claims that arose. As Ormonde wrote, whom the King made Lord Lieutenant: "if the Adventurers and soldiers [i.e., Cromwellians] must be satisfied to the extent of what they suppose intended unto them by the Declaration; and if all that accepted and constantly adhered to the peace in 1648 must be restored, as the same Declaration seems also to intend . . . there must be new discoveries made of a new Ireland, for the old will not serve to satisfy these engagements."[22] A gallon was expected out of a pint pot.

The situation within Ireland was sufficiently intractable: the bulk of the claims were incompatible and abstract justice could not be achieved. To this was added the rapacity of English courtiers. The Civil War, like all such wars, had resulted in a decline of public virtue and private morals: gone was the old idealism that had led men to die for their principles: there had been too much of that, and too much suffering in consequence of it. The new generation, led by Charles himself—who had grown up in the penurious squalor, the seedy circumstances of hanging round foreign courts and capitals, often not knowing where their next meal was coming from—were all on the make. The Chancellor, an antiquated survival from a nobler generation, stood out; but he was completely out of touch with the younger generation, who detested him and whom he for his part despised.

The first commissioners, a large body of thirty-six, who had been appointed to look into Irish claims, had been defeated by their task—after months, they succeeded in relieving one widow. In 1662 the government made the best choice it could of seven commissioners to carry out the Act of Settlement. Clarendon says that it would have been impossible to find fitter men.[23] There was Henry Coventry, who had served on committees of the Commons with Churchill; but the King found he could not dispense with him at home and his place was taken by Sir Allen Brodrick. There were Sir Edward Dering of Kent; three judges, Rainsford, Beverley, Smith; Colonel Cooke; and Winston Churchill, whose legal training gave him a qualification. Clarendon describes them as "gentlemen of very good extractions, excellent understandings and above all suspicion for their integrity, and generally reputed to be superior to any base temptation."[24]

In the late summer, after the Parliamentary session was over, the commissioners went across to Dublin and by October they were well into their work. The job was not a lucrative one, but it offered opportunities to advance the interests of his patron, from whom Churchill might expect some reward. The work, which was expected to take some weeks, in fact took years. The Colonel transported his family to Dublin, where they spent most of the year 1663, and in subsequent years they were in Dublin part of the time. The youngest son, Theobald, was born there and was baptized in St. Bride's Church, January 11, 1663.[25] The eldest son, John, for some time attended the Dublin Free Grammar School. The commissioners met at the King's Inns—where the Four Courts now stand, on the bank of the Liffey on the way to Phoenix Park, which was just now being emparked: one thing that Dublin owes to the Restoration.

The first thing the commissioners discovered was that there was an immense amount of land being withheld from the King which should be at his disposal.[26] Arlington had been made Secretary of State in October, 1662, and all Irish affairs now passed through his hands. Like everybody else—or perhaps more than most, for he was very extravagant—he was avid to make up for the years that the locusts had eaten. Not far from Dublin, in the pleasant country of the upper Barrow, in King's and Queen's Counties, lay the very large estate of Lord Clanmalier, head of the O'Dempseys. Lord Clanmalier had been a rebel, though not one of the worst. He was held to have forfeited his estate and the King now granted it to Arlington, for services which he had for long been unable to recompense. Ormonde was against the grant. There was no love lost between him—so great a magnate that he had no need to be any other than honest—and Arlington.[27] As the greatest of Irish landowners, Ormonde's sympathies were with his class: he would have restored Clanmalier and many others; moreover, the lands were occupied by a large number of Cromwellian soldiers and adventurers. The King had granted it to Arlington, but the problem was how to secure it for him. It became a vexed issue, tied up with Irish politics and perplexing legal difficulties.

It was not improper for the Colonel to advise his patron on the matter and to look after his interests. There is a long series of letters from him to Arlington about it—all of his correspondence, unfortunately, that remains. From this one-sided correspondence, we derive glimpses of the commissioners and their work. The Colonel went on pressing Arlington's claims in spite of innumerable difficulties.

At length Arlington's bill was drafted: no need to go into its complexities here; the legal stumbling block was that the adventurers and soldiers refused to quit their hold until they were assured of their reprisals.[28] In January Churchill received a summons from the King, but "the Duke will not let me go yet and says he will excuse me to the King. You will hear the state of affairs from my brother Coventry. The work is tedious, more troublesome than killing of men at 4s a week."[29] Ormonde wrote to Clarendon that the few decrees of the commissioners so far had raised them many enemies.[30] At the same time, he paid them a tribute with the King: "I cannot doubt but that their decisions have been very just and impartial and agreeable to the Act." Clarendon consoled his friend over his increasing difficulties, with sentiments on a different plane from the scum around him: "Alas, what do we speak of 'Reason'? It hath a very small jurisdiction in the world. Passion and appetite have a large province; and we do not with more reluctancy do anything than what we ought to do with most cheerfulness."[31]

Ormonde had instructed Churchill to remain at his work unless the King again commanded him to England. He could report no progress to Arlington: "I am sorry your bill is so difficult to pass. It has been disappointed often when we thought all was going well and appears like the enchanted isle of O'Brasil, nearest when furthest off."[32]

The commissioners had been much impeded in their work by being divided three to three, so that at present almost every case was dismissed, "and the parties, thought never so innocent, without any visible remedy." The Irish House of Commons had passed a vote of censure on them; but in it the English interest was dominant. The common saying in Dublin was that the commissioners were loyal and honest, at least Rainsford, Beverley, Brodrick and Churchill were; but that they were divided, three for the King—Rainsford, Beverley and Churchill; three for the English interest—Smith, Deering and Cooke; and one for himself—Brodrick.[33]

Clarendon wrote of Arlington in his majestic way, which as usual did not conceal the edge of his disapprobation: "he was in his nature so very civil that no man was more easily lived with, except his interest was concerned . . . He practised such a kind of civility and had such a mean in making professions that they were oftentimes mistaken for friendship, which he never meant or was guilty of to any man." This was true enough: Arlington had no friends. But the Colonel's devoted efforts on his behalf—characteristic of his naïve loyalty of nature—deserved some reward, and Arlington made him some professions and promises which were fulfilled. The Colonel hoped that through him he might enjoy that elusive happiness, the King's favor.[34]

The unsatisfactoriness of the Act of Settlement had set people upon the idea of a new Act—which would postpone Arlington's bill still further. Churchill began to wonder whether it would not be better for him to go half shares with Clanmalier, and obtain the rest of his grant out of some other forfeited estate.[35] The proposal to rest the Irish settlement upon two Acts seemed to him "like Sir William Petty's invention here with two bottoms, which may hold in fair weather but never in a storm."

The new Bill of Settlement was now sent over to England for the King's and Arlington's opinion. The King was considering summoning Churchill over to hear his views on the bill. For his part, the Colonel found that it was not enough to send his wife over to look after his private affairs: he needed to go himself.[36] The King left the matter to the Lord Lieutenant, and Churchill got his leave. His last words to Arlington before coming were the advice "not to pen the Act so as to suffer any parties to be judged." This, at any rate, was virtuous counsel. He went on to add, "for, as I have ever told you in the business of Ireland, you will find yourself strangely deceived if the King be not absolutely despotical. I shall say no more till we meet."

The Colonel's mind was of a disconcerting simplicity. He never concealed what he thought, and such thoughts gained him much opprobrium later.

On his return, he received a somewhat belated recognition of his services: on January 22, 1664, he was knighted by the King at Whitehall.[37] No one can say that he had not had to work hard for it. Arlington, who had been raised to the peerage in the previous year, received rewards of a more substantial kind. In that same month, January, 1664, he was given £10,000 out of the gift made to the King by the Adventurers in Ireland.[38] No doubt this had its effect on the shaping of the new Act of Settlement, the Act of Explanation, which leaned heavily on the side of the English interest, the Cromwellian settlers and adventurers. In February he was given the custody of Lord Clanmalier's estate.[39] In 1666 he made a politic marriage: a leading figure in the English government now, he was able to marry a daughter of Louis of Nassau, natural son of Prince Maurice, William the Silent's famous son. The lady brought with her a dower of 100,000 guilders—and was, moreover, a sister of the wife of the Duke of Ormonde's eldest son, Lord Ossory. The small squire had gone a long way. He could now expect £4,000 a year from his estates alone, apart from his offices, which, he had feared, would not give him "wherewithal to dine the next day after his loss of them." He cleared large sums from the Post Office and in fees and bribes. In 1667 he at length gained outright possession of Lord Clanmalier's estate: the portion in King's County to be made the manor of Charleston, that in Queen's County the manor of Portarlington.[40] This year he had his revenge upon Clarendon: Arlington's long cabals with the King's mistress, Lady Castlemaine, at length bore fruit in the old statesman's dismissal. Now the younger generation could do what they liked. On leaving Whitehall for the last time, Clarendon saw Arlington looking down on him "with great gaiety and triumph" from the window of Lady Castlemaine's lodging.[41] Such is the heartlessness of high politics.

His triumph enabled him to build his magnificent pile at Euston, not far from Saxham where he was born. The King gave him a license to impark 2,000 acres in the neighboring parishes—fifteen miles from Newmarket, the King's favourite resort. In London he lived in opulent ostentation at Goring House, which occupied the site of Arlington Street. In 1672, for his part in the nefarious Secret Treaty of Dover, he was made an earl and a Knight of the Garter; and in the same year, his only daughter and heiress was married to Charles II's son by Lady Castlemaine, the Duke of Grafton. After all, the young Duke's father had made the patrimony for the son: the Graftons have been there ever since.

Truly, Sir Winston Churchill's rewards were exiguous in comparison.

CHAPTER IV

Sir Winston Churchill: Whitehall and Dublin

I

SIR WINSTON was able to spend the years 1664 and 1665 happily in England. The new Act of Settlement for Ireland had as yet taken no satisfactory form; it was for long under discussion, bandied about between the English Council and Ormonde's government in Ireland. Through Arlington, Churchill could represent his views.

His presence was much needed in the House of Commons, for one of the chief weaknesses of the Restoration government was that it was quite inadequately represented there.[1] Clarendon did not sufficiently recognize the importance of this; he was a man of the generation of 1640, and though he wished for co-operation with Parliament he also thought that it should not interfere with every concern of government. Arlington saw the point, though he had been no good in the House himself: he had never once opened his mouth there—popular assemblies were not the place for his secret and insinuating arts. He had done what he could in bringing together a group of King's friends, who could be relied on in all weathers, in the fluctuating conditions of Charles II's reign. Of these the most reliable and unquestioning was the Colonel—he did not cease to be known as such for having been knighted. And it was an index to the estimation in which he was held: though no fool, an educated and even a bookish man, he was too much of a piece, cut after too obvious a pattern, to weigh much with that assembly, where the strings were pulled by more sophisticated, more disingenuous men. As a regular dependable Court member, soon to become an official of the royal household, he remained a prominent House of Commons man throughout the Cavalier Parliament, serving on committees and frequently speaking on behalf of royal policy. As that policy became increasingly unpopular and distrusted, the Colonel became a target for attack. With the Whig triumph in 1679 he was made a victim; fortunately for him he was a secondary figure, he was not important enough for anything more than extrusion.

All that was in the horrid future: for the present he could enjoy himself, and no year was more propitious to him than the year 1664.

The brief session of Parliament which began March 16, 1664, was yet an important one.[2] The Anglican reaction was still at full flood. The Act of Uniformity and the Corporations Act, which had re-established the Church of England as the national church and proposed to extrude Nonconformists from municipal corporations, where they were strong, were now followed by the Conventicle Act. This forbade the meeting of more than five persons, outside the family, for religious services, and was aimed at Dissenters' meetings. In fact, it was never really applied. The English were not any good at religious persecution. The best thing about the Restoration was its clemency: it stood out as an anomaly in that cruel age. Never was there a counterrevolution that shed so little blood. This was due both to Charles and Clarendon in particular, and to the good sense of the nation in general. More important than any nonsense about conventicles was the approach of a commercial war with Holland. This was not wished by Clarendon or his party; it was urged on by the new men, and Clarendon found himself in the unfortunate position of conducting a war of which he disapproved.

Attendance at the House was not very regular in those days, and even for important divisions not much more than a couple of hundred members registered their votes. The Colonel was back and busy on committees. In addition his own private affairs needed attending to. Let us hope that he was able to spend the summer at agreeable Minterne. All the more so since at the end of the summer he forfeited his freedom to become a permanent official of the royal household. On September 13, 1664, he was appointed Junior Clerk Comptroller to the Board of Green Cloth:[3] the first fruits of the King's favor, which he had besought through Arlington, and the limit of the King's generosity. It was no very grand post, but through it came that intimate contact with the Court from which flowed, in the next generation, all the fortune of the Churchills.

The Board's business was to take the accounts of the daily expenditures of the royal household, make the necessary provisions for it, undertake the contracts and the payments, control the discipline and pay the wages of the household servants belowstairs.[4] It fell into the Lord Chamberlain's province to pay the wages of the servants abovestairs, where the royal apartments were. The head of the Board was the Lord Steward of the household, who throughout the reign was Ormonde; so perhaps Sir Winston owed his promotion to the Duke, who thought well of him, as much as to Arlington, who was a man of professions rather than performance: a cold heart, where the Duke was warm. Once the Colonel had served Arlington's purposes over the Clanmalier estate, we do not find them in association again.

Under the Duke, who can hardly have attended the Board much, for he was absent for long periods in Ireland, there were eight officers: the Treasurer and the Comptroller, both usually peers, the Cofferer, who actually paid out the moneys, and the Master of the household.[5] In addition, there were a Senior and a Junior Clerk of the Green Cloth, a Senior and a Junior Clerk Comptroller: all four knights. Promotion was by seniority and its members were well preserved. Sir Winston entered at the bottom as Junior Clerk Comptroller; and in twenty-two years he moved up only two places to become the Junior Clerk of the Green Cloth. The four Clerks received their full board and wages of £88.13.4 a year; when the Court was absent they got board wages at the rate of £365 a year. On James II's accession, they were moved up to £500 a year. This post gave them lodgings at Court, wherever it was, at Whitehall, Windsor or Hampton Court. As with all Court posts, there were fees and tips, perquisites and considerations, more rewarding than the salary. Sir Winston's private affairs, so long under a cloud, the outlook discouraging, began to take a rather more cheerful hue. By 1667 he was able to lend the King £2,000 in his necessity.*

The Board must have been an agreeable little body; but it was no sinecure providing for Whitehall with its scores of servants, liveried and otherwise. Altogether there must have been hundreds of them, though the Board had to provide for only its own section, of which the core was the kitchen—always a fruitful source of profit.[6] Whitehall was a small town in itself, the residence not only of the royal family and the

---

* *Cal. Treasury Books*, 1667-68, 63. Sir Winston Churchill, called before the Treasury officials, said he was willing to lend £2,000 to the King, if he could get it out of the hands of Sir Robert Viner—the great capitalist with whom it was evidently invested. We must remember that Sir Winston was a gentleman of property, who had now succeeded to his estate.

Court, but the seat of government. It covered the whole area from the present Great Scotland Yard on the north to Richmond Terrace on the south, from St. James's Park on the west to the riverbank.[7] There was a wide thoroughfare down the middle, more or less following the present one, terminating in a fine Tudor gateway, with a lesser gate at the southern exit. Inigo Jones's much-admired Banqueting Hall was the latest addition to the congeries of buildings. The royal apartments were on the side of the river. There were the stairs leading up to the apartments *en suite*: the Great Chamber, with the Yeomen of the Guard in attendance; the Presence Chamber, where public audiences took place; the Privy Chamber, where only nobles and privy councilors had the right of entry; the Privy Gallery, which was near the Council Chamber and led down the stairs on the other side into the Park.[8] Behind these was the King's Bedchamber, which, for all that few had the entry to it, was often occupied by a crowd of Charles's cronies laughing with the King over his broad and frequently repeated stories. Unlike his father, he was very friendly, familiar and all too accessible. Sir William Temple, after some experience of his ways, wrote: "the first thing that a king should learn is to say No, so resolutely as never to be asked twice, nor once importunately."[9] This Charles could hardly ever bring himself to do, and never to women. He had an agreeable nature.

In addition, there were chapels and closets, the Queen's apartments and the Duke of York's and, no less important, Lady Castlemaine's at the Cockpit—for that was her abode: on the site of the garden of 10 Downing Street. Altogether it was a rabbit warren of perhaps a couple of thousand rooms: a jumble with its little privy gardens, its naughty alleys and its open spaces; not magnificent like the Louvre, but far more convenient and comfortable in the English manner, for it housed everybody of importance attached to the Court. There was virtually free access to it, as we may read in Pepys' and Evelyn's diaries, with hundreds of people bustling about, hurrying in and out on business, or lounging about the galleries, waiting for the great to appear, tattling, gossiping, quarreling, eying each other or ogling the ladies, who "in good King Charles's golden days" were not at all averse, and few were those who were all that they should be.

At the Restoration, the Court was reorganized on former lines, though only Clarendon remained to continue the gravity and decorum of the old ways and to become the butt of the ridicule of the brilliant but graceless Buckingham, Tom Killigrew, Charles's favorite wag, Lady Castlemaine and their set. Nevertheless, the ancient routine, the elaborate ritual, the external splendor and formality remained. When the King dined in public, he was served by peers on bended knee. When he went to chapel—and there was daily chapel—the "ladies of the Bedchamber to our Dearest Consort the Queen" sat in the first seat "on the left hand of Our Closet."[10] That was where Lady Castlemaine sat, one of the ladies of the Queen's Bedchamber—until she chose to announce her conversion to Catholicism. Amid the ritual and the frolics moved the familiar figure of the King, with natural dignity, but free and easy; tall and slender, with his swarthy Bourbon complexion, his long stride followed by his spaniels in the Park, sauntering with the ladies or paying his nocturnal visits to the Cockpit, recognized by the sentries on his return.

Such was the scene upon which Sir Winston Churchill was a well known figure for the rest of his life; taking a regular official part, which, though a secondary one, was not negligible.

One of the characteristic creations of the Restoration was the Royal Society. After the ravages of fanaticism, all too certain about the universe, the spirit of inquiry got its chance—from which the astonishing developments of modern sciences proceeded. Along with the scientific experiments and investigations of serious people like Wilkins, Wren, Hooke, Boyle, Sir William Petty, there were not wanting curiosities like the promise of the Duke of Buckingham to bring to the Society a piece of a unicorn's horn—like most of his promises, unfulfilled.[11] Sir Kenelm Digby reported that the calcinated powder of toads reverberated, being applied in bags upon the stomach of a pestiferate body, cured it by several applications. The sky was said to have rained seeds and ivy berries in Warwickshire, Shropshire and other counties. The spirit of wonder was abroad in the world. Captain Silas Taylor related that Virginians, when they would kill rattlesnakes, tied some of the plant called dittany of Virginia in a cleft stick and held it to the snake to smell, "who presently coils herself up, turning her head away from the plant as long as she can; then she opens herself on a sudden and, being stretched out in length, is found quite dead."[12] Dr. Charlton was to provide two male vipers against the next meeting. Dr. Hooke had observed with a microscope how leaping cheese maggots put their tail into their mouth and, when they leap, spring it out with great force to leap a great way like fleas.[13]

Meetings of the Royal Society must have been amusing in those days. Along with the diversions, there went the serious intellectual aim of the Society: to analyze things as they are, not to picture them as they are supposed to be. Science became fashionable. The King himself was amused by scientific experiments and was willing to become the Society's patron and founder. It attracted an aristocratic membership. Viscount Brouncker became its president; the Duke of Buckingham, the Earl of Devonshire, Lord Shaftesbury, Lord Cavendish and other peers sparkled among the scientists and physicians, the general gentlemanly membership.

At the end of this year, December 21, 1664, Sir Winston Churchill's name was proposed by Sir William Petty: evidently they had become friends in Dublin.[14] At the next meeting, December 28, Sir Winston was elected, along with Sir William Portman, another Dorset squire. On January 4, they were admitted Fellows.[15] They heard three accounts of the new comet, which had caused such perturbation in December. Mr. Pepys was with child to see it; the King and Queen sat up all night to glimpse it, and did, it seems.[16] Of course, it portended dreadful horrors: the horrors were not slow in coming. Mr. Hooke showed a way of applying a thermometer to a weather clock. Francis Willoughby, home from his travels, was desired to communicate his philosophical observations made abroad. Mr. Boyle reported on his experiments on the congelation of animals and vegetable substances. What a future this line of investigation was to have, to be sure!

Whether it was that this menu was too much for Sir Winston Churchill or no, true it is that he never appeared *there* again. Some years later, when that excellent administrator, Samuel Pepys, was president, a list of members who were in arrears, contrary to the statute, was drawn up and it was ordered that their names should be left out of the next list.[17] Among them was the Duke of Buckingham, which was not surprising, considering that he was far advanced in bankruptcy. With him —some fifty all told—were Sir William Portman and Sir Winston Churchill.

His lack of interest in science offers a contrast with his descendant, who has kept remarkably *au fait* with the portentous developments of which his ancestor saw the beginnings without curiosity.

An equally striking contrast across the centuries is provided by their respective contributions, in the Commons, to the Poor Law: the original Sir Winston playing his part in constructing the code that kept the poor and the unemployed in their place all through the classic period of the rule of the squirearchy, his descendant contributing constructively to the social revolution of our time with his labor exchanges, trade boards and introduction of unemployment insurance. Nothing bespeaks more the class-character of the Restoration, the return of the gentry to power, the gentlemanly counterrevolution, than its treatment of the poor and the unemployed. They had got out of hand; they were now put into a straitjacket. They were not to wander from their native places; they were not to move from one parish to another.[18] If they became a charge on the rates, it was to be in the places where they belonged. The eyes of squire and parson, churchwardens and overseers, were upon them. Their workhouses and bridewells were "prisons under another name." At the same time, sparsely, harshly, if they were "deserving," they were given relief.

That summer, in the middle of the fiercely fought sea war with Holland, befell one of the horrors portended by the comet: the great plague that ravaged London. It began in April; by June the death rate was 600 a month, in August it reached the appalling total of 26,000. All well-to-do people left the City; business was suspended. The Court fled from Whitehall; many thought the plague a judgment for its licentiousness. They were certain when, in 1666, a second visitation hit the City. Yet, oddly enough, the Great Fire spared Whitehall.

The autumn session of Parliament met in October at Oxford, away from the plague. This gave Sir Winston an opportunity to renew acquaintance with his old college of St. John's; for when Parliament met at Oxford, it was usual for members to stay in the colleges where they had been students. The House of Commons sat in the Convocation House; the Commons' committees conveniently nearby in the Schools— it is pleasant to think of that long-dead heart of the University humming with Parliament men coming to and fro. It is agreeable, too, to find Sir Winston, at the beginning of the month, on arrival at Oxford, being admitted as a reader to the Bodleian Library.[19] No doubt, with his bookish interests, he found it enjoyable, as well as useful, to vary attendance at the committees of the House, meeting in the Schools below, to mount the stairs to Duke Humphrey's library in all the panoply of bookcases and painted ceiling furnished by Sir Thomas Bodley.

Sir Winston was, as usual, on the Committee for Elections and

Privileges.[20] The committee to consider a bill to prevent the spread of infection of the plague met in the Physic School. The Anglican reaction reached its high-water mark in this Laudian center: the Oxford Parliament passed the Five Mile Act, by which Nonconformist ministers and schoolmasters were forbidden to reside in cities and corporate towns. It remained entirely inoperative; the best comment on the Act was that in Oxford itself a supposedly excluded Dissenter presently became mayor.[21] Sir Winston sat on the committee in the Divinity School, from which this pious bill emerged. He was on another to amend the bill for regulating the press.

Actually, in the English environment, it was impossible to operate these Acts. They were understandable enough, after the long and intolerant rule of the sectaries. But the Anglican reaction had passed its peak and was already receding. Clarendon and his friends were exceedingly, and undeservedly, unpopular; Buckingham, Arlington, Shaftesbury* were rising to power. The membership of the House of Commons was changing; new men were entering all the time, altering its inflection; new currents of opinion were flowing, with which these men were in touch.

Far more important in its effects than any Five Mile Act was the exclusion of Irish cattle. An Act of 1663 had excluded Ireland from the colonial trade and forbidden the importation of Irish cattle every year from July 1 to the end of the year.[22] The jealous interests of English landowners, particularly of the West Country and the North, were in the ascendant. Cromwell's policy had been more enlightened: union with Ireland, Irish members sitting at Westminster, free trade between the two countries, Ireland sharing in the benefits of the Navigation Act. Clarendon and Ormonde were anxious for the repeal of the restrictions on Irish cattle, in the interests of Ireland, and if the English settlers there were ever to make a success of the country. They were true statesmen.

Pepys tells us that the Prohibition Bill was the work of the Western members, "wholly against the sense of most of the rest of the House, who think, if you do this, you give the Irish again cause to rebel."[23] The Eastern counties, whose interest was feeding, not breeding, cattle, were in favor of allowing Irish cattle in. But the Eastern counties, responsible

---

* For simplicity again, I use the name of Shaftesbury, by which Anthony Ashley Cooper is best known to history, though at this time he was Lord Ashley.

for Cromwell's victory and rule, were now under a cloud: the Restoration was the heyday of the West Country.

The King entirely shared Ormonde's views on the matter, who represented to him "the cruelty of such a treatment of a colony, which all wise states, especially the Roman, thought it their interest to encourage."[24] Now, in 1665, there was an agricultural depression. The brilliant, the unscrupulous Shaftesbury was intelligent enough to know that the depression had nothing to do with the importation of Irish cattle; but to gain popularity with the Western members against Clarendon, he inflamed their passions and led them on with that compelling voice of his with its irresistible cadences. So far from the majority being in favor of repeal, they pushed for total prohibition. In committee, the strongest opposition to the majority was put up by Sir Winston Churchill and Sir Allen Brodrick, much to their credit. In the Lords the Duke of York and the Chancellor were outspoken against it, and the King several times declared that he could not give the royal assent to it with a safe conscience. Nevertheless, the second reading was carried by 103 votes to 52, and so the matter stood when Parliament was prorogued—to meet at Oxford in the autumn.

There, toward the end of October, the struggle was resumed. Sir Winston continued to fight as stoutly as ever for justice for Ireland, and the cause even made some progress. But the situation was rendered hopeless by a complete change in the attitude of the King. With the cost of the Dutch war, the losses by the Plague and the Fire, he was desperate for money to carry on the government. If he had remained firm, he could have carried the peers with him. Charles II, however, always took the line of least resistance: he was now as anxious to carry the bill, and placate the majority, as he had previously been to oppose it. Sir Winston and Sir John Talbot fought on in vain: at the end they were tellers for the Noes, who mustered 68, as against 81 Yeas. It had been a gallant fight; but "so it was resolved in the affirmative."

This was the main business of the Oxford session for Churchill, though he played an active part on a number of other committees. On the last day of October the House voted its thanks to the University for its eminent loyalty to his late Majesty and for refusing to be visited by the usurped powers or to subscribe to the Solemn League and Covenant. So many members of both houses had subscribed—including the disingenuous Shaftesbury. After all, there is nothing easier to eat than words.

2

During these two years when Sir Winston Churchill was in England, a great deal of time and attention was given to the Act of Explanation, which was to define and make clear the Act of Settlement.[25] Ormonde had had to come over from Ireland, the Solicitor General drew up the bill with the aid of a committee consisting of the Duke, all the Irish privy councillors then in London and the Commissioners of Claims, so that Sir Winston had his part in drawing up the measure he went back to Ireland to execute.[26]

In Ireland the English interest had consented to surrender one sixth of what the Act of Settlement gave them. In London the Irish agents thought that too little, and in the end the English interest agreed to raise the one sixth to one third. On that basis the Act was drawn up. Having made this considerable concession, the Protestants—Royalists, Cromwellians, adventurers, soldiers—expected theirs to be the first claim upon the Act; and they were now confirmed in possession of two thirds of their former holdings. The rest, along with the mass of forfeitures to the Crown, of rebels and regicides, constituted a reservoir from which to allot reprisals and make grants to those qualified under the Act.

This Act was considerably more generous to the Irish and represented a larger measure of justice, considering the historic tangle of rebellion, reconquest and new settlement. All would depend on how it was implemented. Full powers were given to five of the former commissioners to execute it: Chief Justice Smith, Dering, Colonel Cooke, Brodrick and Churchill.[27] As early as August, 1665, Lord Orrery wrote that the English interest was very much startled at Sir Allen Brodrick's and Sir Winston Churchill's being commissioners, "but for the last of them I have, I hope, given satisfaction."[28] These two were both sympathetic to Irish claims.

Once more Sir Winston transferred himself and his family to Dublin, to the tedious treadmill of the Court of Claims. We have indications that his lady, who inherited something of her mother's temperament, did not relish this Irish sojourn and longed for England. Moreover, the children were growing up, of an age to be placed and provided for; in Ireland they were out of sight and out of mind.

The Irish Treasury paid out £20 a week for the commissioners' common table—presumably in the King's Inns, where they sat—and

£1.5 each a week for their lodgings.[29] Here they settled down to the weary work, though with better prospects now of getting it finished.

First, there was the difficulty of getting the bill through the Irish Parliament, where there was much opposition from English interests that had been sacrificed. We have a vivid and characteristic letter of Sir Winston, describing the scene in the House that December as stormy as the weather outside.[30] "On Saturday last was sevenight, the humour was most virulent, the members confronting each other with swords half drawn and with words sharper than they: some being heard to say that the lands they had gotten with the hazard of their lives should not now be lost with Ayes and Noes. In this distraction 'twas yet more dismal to see how little my Lord of Orrery could prevail, much less my Lord of Anglesey, both at the same time tormented in their feet [i.e., with gout], but more in their heads; who, keeping their chambers as I did my cabin in the late great storm, dreaded the effects of every wave, I mean of every vote. Some whereof were so violent that, in despite of all our pilots, they made the bill leak (as your lordship will find by the exceptions). Neither was it in the power of any man's single reputation, but the Duke's only, to have kept it from sinking: who by an eloquence peculiar to himself, seemingly unconcerned, but certainly extemporary, so charmed their fears and jealousies that they that were most displeased with the bill were yet so pleased with the overtures he had made them, that when it came to pass it had only one negative. On Saturday last it had the royal assent, which hath put an end to all our fears and made us merrily begin our Epinicia [i.e., songs of victory] with that noted cantilene *Per varios casus, per tot discrimina rerum**—being confident of such a peace to be established hereupon that we shall need to fear no war but what we have with Heaven, and that I hope will cease. If it please God to stop the plague, I doubt not but his Majesty will by Easter find the people of this kingdom in so good a temper and so settled a posture that they may be very considerable in his service."

This is one of Sir Winston's best letters. I have given it practically in full, for it gives us a fair picture of his personality: the old Cavalier who had been brought up on the classics before the Civil War and can quote his tag from Vergil; the enthusiasm of temperament, the sanguineness, with a strain of excitability, the essential simplicity and candor of mind. Such a man was not likely to rise above the second rank among

---

* "Through manifold chances, and so many vicissitudes."

the sophisticated wits of the Restoration. At the same time we recognize a literary expressiveness, a certain flair for writing, that not many of *them* possessed.

In January, 1666, Sir Winston wrote to thank Arlington for recommending his younger son to Lord Sandwich, "for though (as times go now) it is no great preferment to be a page, I am not ignorant of the benefit of disposing of him (in such a juncture of time as this) into that country where all the boys seem men and all the men seem wise."[31] He was glad that the boy would have Lord Sandwich's example before him. (Lord Sandwich was the Cromwellian Admiral Montague who had brought over the King in 1660.) The boy being so provided for must be the second son, George, who went to sea and had a prominent naval career, ending up as an admiral and administrative head of the Admiralty in the day of his brother the Duke's power.

In April Churchill sent by his son a letter of congratulation to Arlington on his marriage.[32] We do not know whether this refers to the same son George or to the elder John. Whichever it was, "I hope he may appear first at Court (as I did) under your patronage." In return, he was able to report that Arlington's business about the Clanmalier estate was at length settled. "The Commissioners were not to blame, but the Act, for the delay as to your proviso." So Arlington at length came into full possession of this large estate. The manor of Portarlington was erected with exceptional privileges and the right of sending two members to Parliament. Arlington set forward the work of improving the estate, cultivating, planting, building a glassworks: in the heyday of the English patricians it became a chief part of the patrimony of the Graftons. Where the old inhabitants were ousted, they were apt to take to a life of robbery and violence, making what depredations they could upon the intruders. Such people came to be known by the Irish name of Tories (i.e., robbers). "It is not surprising to find that Tories were numerous near the new borough, and that some of them bore the name of Dempsey."[33]

In June Sir Winston wrote to Arlington, "I must present my most humble duty to my lady, though I have not yet the honour to be her known servant."[34] Next month his brother commissioners begged him to use his favor with Arlington to get a warrant for their diet and lodging: the Irish Treasurer had not enough money in hand to answer urgent state occasions—a not unusual state of affairs in that country.[35] They hoped that the importance of their services was appreciated: they were so acquitting themselves "as to settle the minds no less than the estates of all the people here, who give that ready obedience to our injunctions that I may boast that our precepts have made their way where the county troops could not; several of those outlaws they commonly call Tories declaring they would submit, if they might have leave to come fairly before the Commissioners for Justice." Churchill was hopeful that their work would make a firm foundation for a settled Ireland, able to resist any attempt from a foreign enemy, "whereunto I stand in my own particular resolutions as ready to serve his Majesty with my sword then, as with my pen now."

The work of the commissioners went forward steadily and regularly; from it resulted the land settlement that endured throughout the eighteenth century—on the whole the quietest and least disagreeable stretch of Irish history—until the work was undone by the land legislation of the later nineteenth century.

The commissioners sat all through that winter and spring, by which time they had dealt with the bulk of the claims that were fairly clear. In the spring Sir Winston was anxious to get back to England, or his presence was desired at Whitehall, where he had other duties to perform. There were still so many questions to settle that Ormonde thought it "better to send Sir Allen Brodrick back to his business here, to avoid equality in voices, than to let any of them go till their work is over."

At the end of May, the Court adjourned till October: "today [May 25] Sir Winston Churchill and Colonel Cooke have gone to sea."[36] He was in England that exciting, distracted, contentious summer of 1667. During the peace negotiations, when the government decided to send no fleet to sea in order to economize, the Dutch took the opportunity in June to break the boom at Chatham, burn four ships of the line and coolly tow the *Royal Charles* off home undamaged. It was a national humiliation, and let loose a fury of contempt and anger against Charles's government. While he was largely occupied with Lady Castlemaine, the only man to show any capacity for war or resolution was the old Cromwellian Monk.

To divert popular clamor and share responsibility, Charles called a session of Parliament in July. Sir Winston was thus able to be in his place. The King gained nothing by his move. Parliament passed a unanimous resolution demanding the disbandment of the 12,000 men he had

raised under the guise of resisting the Dutch. The Commons were beginning to suspect him, and rightly, for he was already negotiating secretly
with France for support: a course contrary to the interests of the nation,
which culminated later in the disgraceful, the treacherous, Secret Treaty
of Dover. The King hastily prorogued Parliament till October, when the
Commons were able to employ their time in impeaching Clarendon, and
the King his in sacrificing him. That summer before his fall the old man
was able to prove himself much abler in diplomacy than in conducting
a war he had never sought and tried to avert. He managed to make
peace with Holland on a very favorable basis, one which brought an
acquisition of the utmost importance for the future. The Dutch ceded
New Netherland, so closing the gap in the English possessions along
the American coastline, and giving us the command of the trade route
from the Great Lakes to what was to become the greatest city in the
world.[37] New Amsterdam became New York.

Clarendon had indeed deserved well of his country; he was rewarded
by impeachment, banishment, exile for the rest of his life.

By now Sir Winston was back in Dublin. He and Sir Edward
Dering arrived together, two days within their appointed time, so that
apprehensions that the Commission would lapse were allayed. They had
had a stormy October passage. At Beaumaris the pleasure boat was
waiting for them, "but it was too wild to go to sea, and after waiting
eight days we went on to Holyhead, resolved to take the first opportunity
of landing anywhere in Ireland."[38] They had to wait nine days more,
"and thus when we had despaired of reaching Ireland on the appointed
day, it pleased God to send a northerly wind, and we at once embarked
on a packet-boat." They landed at Rathdown, fourteen miles away
from Dublin, and so were able to meet, a quorum of three, on the
appointed day.

Work, and such diversions as Ireland could afford, went on till
June. In that month a most important issue, which could have had
very awkward consequences for Sir Winston—considering the stand he
took up—came to a head. This was the question of the Duke of York's
claim. He had been granted practically all the lands of the regicides,
Cromwell's, Ireton's, Ludlow's and others—something between 100,000
and 150,000 acres. And this without any protection for the old proprie-
tors. The Duke left his claims to be prosecuted by a rapacious set of

agents, of whom the most shameless was a Captain Thornhill. These delayed the settlement of the Duke's claim as long as they could, in order that they might enjoy the gifts upon lettings from year to year. This held up a large number of other claimants and suitors, whose affairs could not be settled until the Duke's were.

Sir Winston, who, as we have seen, was never wanting in courage, took the lead against the Duke's agents, and gave Captain Thornhill a dressing down in open court.[39] In a passion Sir Winston attacked the Duke's agents, calling them all a pack of knaves and cheats engaged in betraying their master. Thornhill then tried to provoke the Colonel into saying something that might be reported as treasonable. Captain Thornhill visited him in his chamber that afternoon and asked who he meant by "the Duke's agents." Sir Winston replied hotly, "What are you come to challenge and hector me? I meant you." Thornhill returned that the words were "the Duke's agents" and it could not be that Churchill meant only him. "No," said Sir Winston, "I meant you and Dr. Gorges and the whole pack of you." Thornhill: "Sir, will you give it under your hand that I am a knave?" Sir Winston: "Alas, how long is it since you became so squeasy-stomached that you could not brook being called a knave? You shall have it under my hand." Thereupon he called his man to fetch pen and ink. The Captain, drawing Sir Winston into committing himself—never a difficult operation—pointed out that the influential Sir Jerome Alexander was the Duke's chief agent: he presumed that Sir Winston would not dare call him a knave. " 'Yes,' in passion replied the Knight, 'He's the chief knave and so I can prove you all'—and with that directed the Captain to the stairs, who seeing the necessity of either running down the stairs or being thrown down, as the least of two evils elected the former."

Churchill's colleague, Colonel Cooke, reported that this passage at arms did nothing but good. "We expected hereupon that a public complaint would have followed, but on the contrary we find a far different and composed, out-of-countenance temper in the man of war. For, though yesterday and today many provocations were offered on Sir Winston's part in open court, contrary to the late custom, all have been borne with great patience." And, in fact, this courageous stand of Sir Winston's fortified his brother commissioners in docking the Duke of York's lists of 30,000 acres, which were to be distributed in reprisals, while a similar acreage was to follow.[40] Cooke was able to report to Ormonde that he "can neither say, nor hope, that the Duke's agents went away satisfied, for the horse-leech will sooner cry 'Enough'; but certainly they both went away perfectly silenced."[41]

Good for Sir Winston, we may say. For he was perfectly aware of the risk he was running. Already in March he had written, "I am quite tired out with the continual duty I am upon here, having obtained no other rewards from the Duchess but to be represented to the Duke as the very greatest enemy he hath of all the Commissioners."[42] This immensely long letter lets us behind the scenes of the commissioners' work—the difficulties, personal and political, the tedious, but hardly avoidable, legal quibbling. As for the Duke of York's claims, "the lands of the Archbishop, the Lord Treasurer, etcetera, are particularly mentioned to be left out of his highness's certificate, because given to them . . . Certainly the King, if it was reported to him that we had given judgment for his highness, would compel us to give him the fruits of his judgment; and if the merest adventurer of holders might demand that justice of us, much more his highness . . . The King will not suffer us to come away as yet, in respect of watching the petition of the Adventurers, which is not yet come in, but is framed with great malice and backed with a very considerable party." Sir Winston's hatred of the Cromwellians made him sympathetic to Irish claims as against the adventurers. He complains again of tiredness with all the press of suitors and attendance upon him. "'Tis impossible for you to [imagine] the disorder and destruction that is here amongst us, entertaining no motives willingly but with favours of distinction." But he was unwilling to leave it and "come away, as you desire, before we see the effects of this great design."

What makes Sir Winston's courage in standing up against the Duke's claims all the more admirable is that his daughter had been given a place at Court as maid of honor to the Duchess of York, and had already been for some time the Duke's mistress. In later years, enemies would say that the old Cavalier had promoted his daughter to the Duke's favors. We see how unjust an aspersion that was: he had not even wanted his daughter to go to Court.

It is indeed far more probable that Lady Churchill managed to get her daughter a Court post. We have seen that she detested being in Ireland, and we have had some indication that she inherited her mother

Lady Drake's temper: Sir Winston may not have had too comfortable a life with her.

The week following the fracas with Thornhill, the Chief Justice and Sir Winston were at dinner at the King's Inns when they heard that Dering and Cooke had obtained license to return. "The license gave my brethren a furious alarm," wrote Cooke.[43] Sir Winston's lady saluted him with such a tempestuous epistle, "as if the only reason he sought not the same liberty was because he was more delighted with his divertisements than obliged by his business to continue here." Their asking for leave was so much resented by the Chief Justice and Sir Winston that they petitioned the Lord Deputy—Ormonde's son-in-law, Lord Ossory, in the Duke's absence in England—to stop it. "Whereupon yesterday after dinner, Sir Edward Dering and I [Cooke] directed our visit to his lordship, enthroned at the upper end of his table between the two Knights. His lordship vented himself very passionately at our unfriendly behaviour in seeking leave, without having first obtained his leave. Our silence encouraged Sir Winston Churchill to second him. After storm came calm, so we all went brotherly together to attend Council concerning petitions put in for prolonging our time."

It seems that Sir Winston, contrary to his lady's wishes, was prepared to put duty first. However, they got leave later, when their work was in a satisfactory shape, and were able to spend the summer in England.

That summer a great change threatened the direction of Irish affairs. After the fall of Clarendon, there remained only the magnificent figure of Ormonde between the young men and the attainment of full power. The weakness of the Clarendonian regime had always been finance. That gifted jackanapes and spoiled crony of the King's, the second Buckingham, made himself—of all people—the spokesman of financial reform. A hopeless squanderer, he was already well on the way to bankruptcy. This did not impair his popularity with the Commons. He deserved everything that Dryden said of him:

> A man so various that he seemed to be
> Not one, but all mankind's epitome.
> Stiff in opinions, always in the wrong;
> Was everything by starts, and nothing long:
> But in the course of one revolving moon

Was chemist, fiddler, statesman and buffoon . . .
In squandering wealth was his peculiar art:
Nothing went unrewarded but desert.
Beggared by fools, whom still he found too late:
He had his jest and they had his estate.

This man, in the cause of financial virtue and out of resentment that Ormonde had not been more lavish with him over the marriage of his niece, made himself the Duke's leading opponent.[44]

Ormonde thought that he had reached an understanding with the subtle Arlington, who had married his son's sister-in-law. Arlington feared above all things that Ormonde would lead a party to bring Clarendon back. He assured the Duke that he would prevent an attack on him from Buckingham. Ormonde, secure in these assurances, went down to Moor Park "to enjoy the company of friends and the coolness of the place."[45] No sooner was his back turned than commissioners were appointed to examine into the malversation of the government and revenue of Ireland. This was but a foreshadowing of what was to come.

In October the Commissioners of Claims returned to Dublin to wind up their work. We learn that "Sir Edward Dering and Sir Winston Churchill arrived late last night [16 October], and today had a formal sitting of their Court and adjourned till Tuesday."[46] Lord and Lady Aungier had arrived and Lord Dungannon was on his way, "so that now our city begins to feel itself again, having been very empty these three months past."

It took the Commissioners another three months to complete their work. On January 21, 1669, Churchill, Dering, Brodrick and Cooke arrived at Holyhead in the King's pleasure boat *Mary*.[47] Irish matters followed Churchill over to Whitehall; for we find him writing thence, February 20, to a fellow commissioner sending an order in council to be communicated to the rest, "grounded upon a petition of Thornhill and some of that gang."[48] Ormonde had advised Churchill to solicit the King about the commissioners' diet money—so it was still in arrear: Churchill's regular attendance gave him the opportunity. But he was about to "begin my journey . . . towards my new home" and would not be back till April. This must mean that Sir Winston was now building at Minterne.

When we consider its long endurance, we may regard the Restoration settlement of Ireland, as human affairs go, as a not unsatisfactory achievement. As for the great man who had presided over it, in spite of Buckingham's calumnious campaign, the King repeatedly affirmed his confidence in Ormonde. Then suddenly, in February, 1669, he was dismissed. Pepys regarded it as "a great stroke to show the power of Buckingham and the poor spirit of the King, and little hold that any man can have of him."[49]

Little Mr. Pepys was not wrong: the best days of the Restoration were over.

CHAPTER V

House of Commons: Court Member

WHEN Sir Winston Churchill came back from his Irish exile, he found that the world had moved on without him, leaving him rather behind. The disappearance of Charles's tiresome mentor, the great man, Clarendon, left the King free to conduct a policy of his own—and a very disingenuous affair it turned out to be. Politics were, in any case, in a state of confusion, for the bounds of the royal power and that of Parliament, the boundaries of jurisdiction between Lords and Commons, were by no means clearly defined; they were in course of definition in the political struggles of the time. This is what makes these years so interesting constitutionally. Finance was a fundamental trouble of the period. The Commons here had undoubted power, but could they trust the King, with adequate supplies, to conduct a policy of which they and the nation approved?

Here was the issue that dominated politics up to its resolution in 1688; for, of course, the Stuarts could not be trusted. Charles II was a clever, indolent man, willing to make concessions, to compromise in order to keep his throne and not have to go on his travels again. But, underneath, he was not much more willing to conduct the nation's business in accordance with its will than his father had been. So far as he could, he followed his own personal policy of a French alliance, subsidies from Louis XIV in order to rule independently of Parliament, favor for Catholics and—since this was a necessary coating for the pill—for Dissenters. (Not that he liked Dissenters: he thought theirs was "no religion for a gentleman.") This line was in accordance with neither the interests nor the wishes of the nation. When his brother succeeded, who had no conception of compromise ("Nobody will kill me, Jamie, to make you king"), it took James a mere three years to lose the throne.

This condition of affairs made the situation of loyal supporters of the monarchy, who were at the same time Protestants, increasingly uncomfortable. It created acute difficulties under James II, difficulties that dominated, as their solution decided, the careers of the Churchills. They were all monarchists, but they were all Protestants. They would not succumb to the inducements of the King to become Papists.

It has been usual to write the history of the Restoration in terms of the Court and its personalities: never have they been more amusing and scandalous, more variegated or fantastic: they pullulated around the easygoing Charles II. And certainly we have had far too much adulation of the "merry monarch." The truth about him was no secret to the penetrating eye of the philosophical Halifax. "This principle of making the love of ease exercise an entire sovereignty in his thoughts would have been less censured in a private man than might be in a prince . . . Ease is seldom got without some pains, but it is yet seldomer kept without them. He thought that giving would make men more easy to him, whereas he might have known it would certainly make them more troublesome . . . The love of ease is an opiate, it is pleasing for the time, quieteth the spirits; but it hath its effects that seldom fail to be most fatal."[1]

The truth is that the backbone of the nation was the House of Commons. In spite of everything. In spite of bribery and corruption, the extremes of partisanship, the asininities of which all collective assemblies are capable, the disloyalties, the mutual antagonisms, the contradictions, the panic that seized them over the Popish Plot. The Commons represented the nation, assembled and embattled. Everybody who was anybody in his county was there: the gentry who not only ruled, but ran, English society. This institution, and its power, distinguished this country from all others. It was not, as supercilious monarchs like Louis XIV thought, a mark of inferiority; it was a mark of the greater political maturity of the English people and their governing class. This peculiar institution, which grew to express the political instinct of the nation, was to have an astonishing career wherever English-speaking people settled in the world, and to have its influence wherever other peoples were capable of self-government.

In spite of crises and distractions, Parliament followed, in the event, a moderate course that attained its objective in 1688. Beneath the excitements and alarms of the time, and in spite of the opposition of the monarchy fighting a rear-guard action to preserve power for itself, the work of building a constitutional state went forward. Parliament wanted a monarchy, but a Protestant one. It wanted a foreign policy in the interests of the nation, i.e., an alliance with other European powers, particularly Holland, to check the growing ascendancy of France. It wanted responsible Parliamentary government, not the irresponsible absolutism of a Louis XIV. It was now ready for a measure of toleration for Protestant Dissenters, but not for Catholics with their exclusive claims.

In circumstances of great complexity and confusion, Parliament's achievement in these years was remarkable. An American scholar has summed it up: "it settled the relations of church and state, of Anglican and Noncomformist, which have endured in part almost to our own day, in part still remain. It made good in principle and practice the control of finance by the Commons. It determined the status of Catholics for a century and a half. It enunciated those protests against illegal taxation and against government by a standing army—with its consequent abuses, the quartering of soldiers and martial law—which have found place in every Anglo-Saxon constitution since. It reformed the judicial system," and secured the liberty of the individual, by the enactment of habeas corpus, which remains today a fundamental difference between democratic freedom and the absence of any personal security where there are no representative institutions. The Restoration Parliament "made good the doctrine of ministerial responsibility to Parliament, in so far as the constitutional arrangements then permitted, and began that series of changes which led to the present system. It overthrew royal powers in matters ecclesiastical and substituted for them those of the Commons. It made an inroad on the royal prerogative in foreign affairs, the last great line of defence short of the succession; and it not only suggested the Exclusion Bill, but began that connexion with William III which culminated in his accession to the throne . . . The House of Commons indeed supplies the real connexion between the Civil War and the Revolution of 1688; and it is the Commons, rather than the leaders, which give us the correct measure of public opinion."[2]

In all this activity of the Commons, Sir Winston Churchill took a regular, a fairly prominent, but not a central, part. He was now, first and foremost, an official of the royal household; that not only circumscribed his freedom, but turned him into a Court member—someone whose line on any important matter of policy in dispute could be foretold.

He was there to defend the King's policy, and his wishes. As Charles's government became more unpopular and lost command of any majority in the Commons, so Sir Winston was considered simply a placeman of the Crown. One watches the decline of his personal position, the sacrifice he made; for, with the victory of the Whigs, he became a target of abuse, was eventually driven from his post at the Board of Green Cloth and lost his seat in Parliament.

He sacrificed his independence; but then, as we have seen, any independence of the Crown was contrary to his high monarchical principles: he may be described as a Passive Obedience Tory. He was a man set in his ways, simple and rigid, in that snake pit of a Court with its twisting, turning, reptilian creatures, glittering, deceitful and insincere. He had become fixed somewhat early, and had now reached the limit of his development. There was something obstinate, even *borné*, about him: something of a West Country bull.

In the House, besides being a Court member, he had a secondary classification as a lawyer: one of the "gentlemen of the long robe," more frequently put on committees than others, apt to be called on for an opinion on legal points. Even so, he was a lawyer of the second rank. His interventions in debate were not weighty: he usually delivered himself of one simple point, and that an emotional one. All the same, he always spoke *to* the point; and his speeches had the importance that they invariably expressed the official point of view. As a leading spokesman of the Court in the House—throughout the whole period—he incurred unpopularity when opinion turned more and more against the Court. And in the public prints he was traduced for the undignified situation he was placed in by his daughter's relation to the heir to the throne. It was a strange turn of fortune for a respectable West Country squire. But there was nothing to be done: his fate was fixed by his position at Court. It may have been a source of unhappiness and disquiet to him; one will never know. There is a look of anxiety and sadness in his eyes, all the more striking in the big, heavy, masculine features, tricked out in all the Court finery of slashed sleeves and satin. At the same time, what made him a target for abuse and subsequent depreciation in history opened up the astonishing possibilities that made his children's fortune.

In the session that began on October 19, 1669, Sir Winston was back in his place to play a full part. We find him serving, as usual, on committees to consider the poor laws and seditious conventicles.[3] The destruction of churches in London by the fire had given the Dissenters an advantage: they had raised a number of tabernacles in the City. The Conventicle Act of 1664 was due to lapse; the committee was to report on its continuance. It reported that there were several conventicles in Westminster itself, near Parliament: an affront to the government and its laws. In the debate, Sir Winston observed seditious people whispering with many of the House, "to give themselves reputation."[4] He meant apparently some old Republicans, his ancient enemies—Henry Neville, Major Salloway and such.

In November Churchill was concerned with the bill to enable Sancroft, Dean of St. Paul's, to build a new deanery. It is pleasant to think that we owe that beautiful Wren house, which has survived, in part to him. Later that month came up an address of the House against Lord Orrery for malversation in Ireland. Churchill tried to defend this member of the government, a friend: he argued that he knew no way of proceeding against a privy councilor.[5] In vain. The House held that that gave him no privilege and that treasonable matter was contained in the charge. This was voted by 182 to 144, from which we may judge the state of parties. It was resolved that Lord Orrery should be sent for in custody of the Serjeant of Arms. Party spirit was running high; the majority of the House was already against the government. It does not seem that Lord Orrery was guilty of anything much.

In this session and the next, Sir Winston was busy with the question of the import duties on brandy, wines and other liquors.[6] He was on a small and interesting committee to prepare a bill for regulating and making brandy: the Solicitor General, Serjeant Maynard, Sir Robert Howard, poet and dramatist, Colonel Birch, Sir John Duncombe and others. From this emerged a proposal to prohibit the import of foreign brandy—though Sir John cannot have agreed, for we find him in the debate observing that, in the Guinea trade, all the English strong waters perished. "Brandy must be redistilled to make it fit for the East Indies: how then can our *aqua vitae* carry?"[7] What a world of Caroline trade and early expanding prosperity this conjures up! The poet was to take care of the bill, in the interest of home producers of spirits.

In March, Churchill was called upon to defend both the government and the King's prerogative in ecclesiastical matters. In the wartime conditions prevailing in the Channel, a score of privateers were held up at Dover, their prizes uncleared. The question was whether their accounts should come before the Commons. Churchill found a legalistic argument to defend the Crown's point of view in the matter. The commissioners who had taken the accounts of the prizes were but substitutes; "but if the Lords Commissioners of Prizes have approved of what they have done, the question is, then, whether the Lords have done their duty and are accountable to you?"[8]

Into the bill amending the Conventicle Act, the Lords inserted a proviso reserving the King's ancient prerogative in ecclesiastical matters or any power at any time enjoyed by any of his ancestors. Andrew Marvell reported to his Whiggish constituents, the mayor and corporation of Hull, "there never was so compendious a piece of absolute universal tyranny": he thought it would leave it in the King's power to dispense with the execution of the whole bill.[9] Sir Winston, of course, defended the Lords' proviso. He thought it "necessary to recognise the King's Supremacy now. It is not whether his ecclesiastical right be infringed, but whether the King thinks so or no. The Lords, the two estates, have thought this requisite; the Lords think the Supremacy in question, and they advise it. He cannot give his negative till he hears the Lords' reasons."[10] One detects the note of cant on both sides—but perhaps some cant is necessary in politics. As Lord Halifax observed, "the comfortable opinion men have of themselves keepeth up human society, which would be more than half destroyed without it." In spite of Sir Winston, the House negatived the proviso by 122 to 88.

At the end of March there was a committee of the whole House on the bill for Lord Roos's divorce, a case which made a tremendous scandal; but the political importance of it was greater, for the Whigs intended it as a precedent for a divorce for the King and the provision of a Protestant succession. Such a subject provided matter for an immensely long dispute, in which all the leading members spoke with much ardor and learning in the canon and civil law. Churchill contributed a legal point, which bore against the divorce.[11] However, the bill passed.

We observe that Sir Winston is constantly in the minority. So far as the King was concerned, all were fooled. As a secret Catholic, he had no intention of marrying again—and no intention of giving up his pleasures. Halifax, who was "near him," observes: "men that were earnest Protestants were under the sharpness of his displeasure, expressed by raillery, as well as by other ways. Men near him have made discoveries from sudden breakings out in discourse etcetera, which showed there was a root. It was not the least skilful part of his concealing himself, to make the world think he leaned towards an indifference in religion."[12]

This was a very busy session, for Churchill as for others. Marvell wrote his excuses to Hull, that "the crowd of business now toward our rising obliging us to sit both forenoon and afternoon, usually till nine o'clock, which indeed is the occasion that I have the less vigour left at night, and cannot write so frequently to you."[13] He added, "that which is extraordinary is that his Majesty hath for this whole week come every day in person to the House of Lords and sat there during their debates and resolutions. And yesterday the Lords went in a body to give him thanks for the honour he did them therein." What Marvell may not have known was His Majesty's reason for going: he thought it "better than a play."

This was the last session that gave Charles any satisfaction; for he was now engaged in the underground negotiations with Louis XIV that led to the Secret Treaty of Dover. After that, when news of its purport leaked out and suspicions were confirmed, there was never any more confidence in Charles on the part of the majority in the House. That treaty was his greatest mistake. Not so much the secret clauses by which he promised to declare himself a Catholic and to bring the country over to Catholicism—as if that were possible! The rumor of this design did immeasurable damage; but he was left free to declare himself when he liked, and he had the political sense never to do so. What was unforgivable was that the collusion of the King of England with Louis XIV, in a treacherous attack on Holland and in the general course of French policy, immensely aided Louis to achieve that domination of Europe which, in consequence, it took twenty years of European war later to reduce. The Treaty of Dover was personally a clever instrument: Charles got the cash and was free to keep his promises or no as he liked. One half of the Cabal government was duped as to what the other half had agreed; everybody was fooled, not only one half of the government and the English Parliament, but to some extent Louis and the Catholics too. It is better, in the end, to be direct and sincere where the fates of nations are concerned.

The collective capacities of the Cabal were very considerable; the trouble was that they could not be collected. Two of them were crypto-Catholics, the other three crypto-Protestants. Only one of them had any genuine belief, and he the least intelligent: Churchill's old West Country associate, Clifford. Clifford's ability was purely financial and administrative. One notices in this session how frequently and to the point he speaks on all such matters. He had quite outdistanced Churchill, was now Treasurer of the Household and on his way to become, at the momentary full deployment of Charles's Catholic policy, Lord High Treasurer. The response of the Commons to all this was the Test Act, driving all Catholics from public life. Clifford died shortly after—it was said, by his own hand. Perhaps it was as well: if he had survived to the time of the Popish Plot, he would probably have been hanged.

In the autumn session of 1670, there were a couple of old-Cavalier outbursts from Sir Winston. The first was à propos of one Hayes, who had attempted to seduce the Lord Mayor of London from executing the Conventicle Act. Sir Winston: "If we recriminate any, let us recriminate all. It is hard we cannot have an Act of Indemnity for those that served the King, seeing we had one for them that were against him."[14] That session the King was putting pressure upon Parliament for large supplies to pay his debts—at the same time as selling himself to Louis for a big subsidy. The Commons took up the question of the payment of his debts in good faith—they were some £1,300,000 at interest, "the debts not at interest making it above £2 millions."[15] The discussions led to reflections not only upon the royal administration but upon the royal habits, Charles's extravagance, especially where his women were concerned. Sir John Coventry was particularly free with his criticisms.

That Christmas recess, Charles's eldest bastard, the Duke of Monmouth, planned a beating up for Coventry. On the night of the adjournment of the House, twenty-five of Monmouth's troop lay in wait for Coventry outside his house in Suffolk Street, threw him down and slit his nose. The House was angered by this incident, nor did it help the King to get his bill of supply without assurances as to his policy. Sir Winston burst out, "those persons who sit quiet in their sovereign's blood wonder this thing should be so pressed. It seems to him a cutting the King over the face."[16] The report says that "the words gave offence." Sir Winston had to explain himself. He went on to say that "not only our own affairs, but of Christendom, are upon their crisis." He urged that the King be put into a capacity to defend the kingdom, and that the bill of supply should take precedence of Sir John Coventry's nose.

Sir Winston Churchill, however, was not aware of the King's real plans; nor was anyone else. The strangest thing about this affable, talkative monarch was his silence and secrecy. No one knew what his real convictions were: he could never utter them. No one knew his plans, not even his mistresses; he had the advantage that his relations with them were not those of any love. Among them all he moved, a solitary, lonely man, very *désabusé*: underneath the gaiety and easy nature, really rather a sad man, as one perceives between the lines of Halifax's discerning *Character*.

From April, 1671, to February, 1673, Charles kept Parliament in recess: nearly two years in which to unfold his own policy and try out, as his father had done, his personal rule. He had got large supplies out of Parliament by a trick, further subsidies from Louis by his promises. With these, Louis had sent over Louise de Quérouaille, a former waiting woman of Charles's favourite sister, Henriette, to keep him quiet and, if possible, attached. The Breton beauty became a figure in English politics: to Charles a cosier one than the exacting, the clamorous, the tempestuous Castlemaine; all the same, she needed to be subsidized largely too. Supported on both fronts, Charles felt in a position to launch his religious policy at home and to attack the Dutch, alongside of Louis, abroad. In March, 1672, he issued his Declaration of Indulgence, suspending by his own absolute authority all the country's repressive laws against Roman Catholics and Protestant Dissenters. On this, the King said he would never withdraw. Two days later, he declared war against Holland.

The importance of the war for us was that it produced a complete revulsion of opinion with regard to Holland, and revealed in a flash the overriding danger from France. The tough little republic had to sustain the onslaught of the immense forces the greatest power in Europe could bring to bear on her land frontier and, at sea, the weight of attack of the one sea power that rivaled her own, *plus* Louis's growing navy. It was a moment fraught with danger for Europe. In Holland, the dikes were broken, the sea let in: the irresistible might of the French army was held up at the water's edge; a revolution threw out the appeasers of France and brought the young William of Orange to power, to save the state and launch him on his lifelong task of reducing Louis. From the grave, through the brain and arm of Winston Churchill's son, he accomplished it in the end.

At sea, the Dutch saved themselves by the drawn battle of Sole

Bay. It was a tremendously hard-fought contest between English and Dutch, in which the French, obviously under instructions, held off and left the contestants at it hammer and tongs. When this happened again at the battle of the Texel next year, it became too obvious that the French game at sea was to watch the English and Dutch immolate each other for France's benefit. Public opinion in England, which had devoted to these sea battles the intense feeling usually reserved for sport, veered sharply from the treacherous ally to the gallant opponent. What was the purpose of the war? What could possibly be gained by it? It could only result in ensuring the domination of Louis XIV over Europe. Holland had saved herself by her exertions and was now to save Europe by her example. William set to work to bring together the Grand Alliance which alone could keep France within bounds—an alliance of which this country should have been the keystone, if its King had not virtually been a traitor to the interests of the nation. That is, briefly, the reason for the Revolution of 1688, and why William became King in England.

During those two years, Charles had, as the historian of the reign observes, "committed acts which had a profound reaction on the fate of his dynasty and the history of his country."[17] When he was forced, in February, 1673, to summon Parliament for supplies for a war which now had no purpose, he was faced with a House of Commons inflamed with rage and frustration. The real purport of the Secret Treaty of Dover had leaked out. There were going to be no supplies until the Catholic advisers of the King were removed and a Protestant succession assured. The nation was determined not to allow Catholics in power—at a time of European crisis, when Louis was driving his Protestant subjects into exile, and the House was constantly engaged upon bills for naturalizing them. His policy pointed straight to the revocation of the Edict of Nantes, the expulsion of scores of thousands of his best and most industrious subjects, the forced conversion of others, the *dragonnades* and fire and slaughter in the Protestant Cévennes. (The atmosphere of the time was very much of the Nazi 1930's, the issues for English policy not dissimilar.) It is from this time that the bitterest party spirit dates, when Marvell, who had been able earlier to report well of the King to his Whig constituents, now writes in "An Historical Poem":

> This isle was well reformed and gained renown,
> Whilst the brave Tudors wore the imperial crown:

But since the royal race of Stuarts came,
It has recoiled to Popery and shame;
Misguided monarchs, rarely wise or just,
Tainted with pride and with impetuous lust.
The poor Priapus King, led by the nose,
Looks as a thing set up to scare the crows . . .
The royal evil so malignant grows,
Nothing the dire contagion can oppose.
In our weal-public scarce one thing succeeds,
For one man's weakness a whole nation bleeds.
Let Cromwell's ghost smile with contempt, to see
Old England struggling under slavery.

The Commons were not going to have it, and in a continuous campaign drove the King from position to position, marked out the course the nation would have him follow. Otherwise: no supplies. Within a month Charles "took a step which no other male Stuart would have taken": he withdrew the Declaration of Indulgence.[18] Such toleration as there was going to be was not by royal grace and favor, but by Parliamentary authority, and for Protestants only. This was followed up by the Test Act, which forced the heir to the throne to resign his public offices and go into exile, and drove the Lord Treasurer into retirement. The Cabal was split in pieces. Shaftesbury, furious at having been outsmarted over the Treaty of Dover, when he thought nobody smarter than himself, went over to the Opposition. Buckingham and Arlington were made to give an account of themselves to Parliament.

The temper of the Cavalier Parliament was changing with its composition: by now, one third of its members were new men, who knew not David or the blithe promise of May, 1660. Churchill remained a prominent member, not to be ignored. At the beginning of the session he was placed, as usual, on the most important committee of the House, that dealing with Elections and Privileges, which controlled the Commons' internal affairs.[19] Sir Winston's membership of the House was clearly no sinecure: it earned his keep at the Board of Green Cloth.

The character of the House was changing too. Gone were the more idealistic days of Clarendon: with the organization of parties, the struggle for influence and votes, the House was becoming much more open to bribery. After the disaster to the Cabal, Charles turned to a House of Commons man, Danby, who bribed members right and left to secure a party for the King. In January, the House took note that a member had been reported to say that he hoped to make this session worth £5,000 to him.[20] The House was very delicate about this matter: no lady is so conscious of virtue as a lady of easy virtue. Sir Winston was on the committee to look into the matter, and on another to consider the more interesting question of the water pumps invented by Sir Samuel Morland, a fascinating figure in an age full of them. (Restoration England was bursting with vitality, the country poised—once it had got on the right constitutional basis and was free to follow the right foreign policy —for its classic period of expansion and power.) Morland was the inventor of a calculating machine and a speaking trumpet; he endeavored to harness steam pressure to use and suggested it for the propulsion of vessels. A bill that he might enjoy the benefit of his invention was introduced, and Sir Samuel's plunger pump shortly raised water to the top of Windsor Castle—where it might have done a great deal of good.

A trivial episode at Windsor was taken notice of by the House in its anger against members of the Cabal. It was informed that when Buckingham was Master of the Horse, one day when the King would not stay so long at a drinking bout as the Duke wished him, Buckingham took the King's horse by the bridle and would have forced him—to the danger of the King's person. In the circumstances of the time, the House was obliged to proceed in these canting terms; but what nullified many of its personal proceedings in relation to the King was his subtle sabotage: he had no intention of allowing them to rid him of his boon companions.

Sir Winston came to the Duke's defense: he knew the business at Windsor; he wished the particulars might be as easily proved as charged. The House would do better to read the letter with its information of more consequence. "The Duke is not far from you, and if the letter be not of importance, the Duke has forfeited his understanding, as the charge makes him forfeit his reputation. Men of quality will not inform you of trifles."[21] This lets us into another side of Sir Winston's personality: the snobbishness of the man who had risen into an exalted society from below. We are allowed condescendingly to see the company he keeps at Windsor. Actually, the Duke of Buckingham's reputation was not worth a farthing; but on this occasion Sir Winston was in the right and the information was withdrawn. He had the courage to say a word on behalf even of Lauderdale, though an indirect one. On the motion of an address to the King to remove him from his counsels, Churchill observed that "though we are satisfied, yet the King knows none of our reasons": they should be specified.[22] In the attack on Arlington, Churchill did not come to his defence. Nobody loved that unlovable character. He was well able to look after himself. Kicked out of the Secretaryship of State, he sneaked upstairs to become Lord Chamberlain, from which post of vantage he intrigued to supplant those who had supplanted him.

On the decisive matter of the independence of the judiciary, Sir Winston took, as usual, the Crown's line. The issue was the historic one that had come up under Charles I, whether the Judges' patents were to be made out according to the form *Durante bene placito* (during pleasure) or *Quamdiu se bene gesserint* (during good behavior): according to the first, they held office at the pleasure of the Crown; by the second, Parliament could be the only court to determine their record of behavior. The future independence of the judiciary, throughout the English-speaking world, depended on this decision.

The old poet, Edmund Waller, had become a kind of Father of the House and its most admired speaker. His speeches stand out by their style and by their allusions, even in the crabbed reporting of those days. On the transformed status of the Member of Parliament, he said: "Times are much changed now. Formerly the neighbourhood desired him to serve; there was a dinner, and so an end. But now it is a kind of an empire. Some hundred years ago, some boroughs sent not: they could get none to serve. But now it is in fashion and a fine thing, they are revived."[23] On this issue Waller, who had become the memory of the House, said: "Fifty years ago this came in question; the House of Commons ever favoured *Quam diu se bene gesserint* . . . Lord St. John said, it was no great matter their fining Justices; the only arbitrary power was fining one hundred pounds, it may be, for a wry look, and no remedy."[24] The poet, who was very famous in his old age, put his finger on the crucial issue here—as it remains today with those countries that have no justice independent of political power.

This session a dispute concerning the Board of Green Cloth came before the House: it adds a little to our information about that esoteric body. The King's Purveyor of Fish had had his servants beaten by the orders of one Sir Thomas Byde, who was in the habit of extorting unreasonable sums for fishing within his manor of Ware. In order to escape jury duty in Middlesex, Byde had had himself made one of the Privy Chamber; and thus, like any other of the King's servants, came under the jurisdiction of the Green Cloth. The Board was a court, with the right of trial, with an appeal to Westminster Hall. Byde had, therefore, been quite properly brought before it, and was dismissed, with payment of £5 fees. Sir Thomas Byde was a member of Parliament, and so able to state his own case there. Sir Winston put the Board's case moderately and persuasively, going out of his way to say that Green Cloth men were no more to be exempted from the law than in the common condition of other men. The matter was satisfactorily referred, without more fuss, to a committee.[25]

When Parliament met again on April 13, 1675, after fourteen months' prorogation, the Commons at once pressed forward with anti-Popery measures. Bills were introduced applying tests of such specific Catholic doctrines that every loophole against Papists in power might be stopped. Every loophole, that is to say, except the largest: the throne itself; for the heir to the throne was a Catholic, and nothing would induce James to compromise his faith. In November, the Commons introduced a measure that "the children of the royal family should be educated in the Protestant religion and no Popish priest to come near them."[26] Popish priests were too much in evidence at Whitehall and Somerset House, Marvell reports dryly to his Protestant constituents at this moment: "the Pope hath given a Cardinal's hat to Father Howard, the Queen's almoner."[27] Why could not the Stuarts take warning from the temper and will of the nation? Charles did, and at the opening of this session he asseverated "that for his part he should always maintain the religion and the Church of England as now established, and be all his life constant in that profession."[28] Nor did he ever dare to withdraw publicly from that position.

From the constitutional point of view, the historian of the reign tells us that "the central theme in the attempt to establish a clearly defined relationship within the trinity which consisted of Crown and both Houses."[29] The formative years of his life Charles had passed in exile; his ideal of government, as of conduct, was that of his cousin, Louis XIV, the grandest monarch in Europe. He associated "absolute kingship with order, and political experiment with anarchy. Of English patriotism, or respect for English tradition, there was no trace in his career." Subsequent history has underlined the relative values, the respective worth, of French and English models of government. Neither Charles nor James was English, however: they were five eighths French, the rest a mixture of Scot, Dane, German. Of course, Charles, like Louis, was a fine gentleman—though Halifax thought that "his fine gentlemanship did him no good." The House appreciated that he was a gentleman, but was increasingly of the opinion that he could not be trusted. In the circumstances of gathering tension between them, the unfailing courtesy that was preserved was a triumph, "a distinctively English achievement."[30]

The Commons became more and more sensitive as to its rights and privileges, and this led to conflicts not only with the King, but with the Lords. Sir Winston Churchill took a prominent part in the dispute over Shirley v. Fagg, which had the importance of settling the appellate jurisdiction of the House of Lords. Over this, Sir Winston was, for once, and not the last time, on the winning side. It also fell to him to defend his cousin, Sir John Churchill, Jasper's son, who followed him as a student at Lincoln's Inn. He was a more distinguished lawyer than Sir Winston, and no less of a royalist; Attorney General to the Duke of York, on James's accession he was made Master of the Rolls.

CHAPTER VI

Parliament and Popish Plot

PARLIAMENT met again in October, 1675. Sir Winston was as prominent as ever on the Commons' committees.[1] A new bill to prevent the growth of Popery was brought in. With the tension in Europe and the advances being made by Louis XIV, the Commons were determined to maintain the Protestant foundation of the state. Even James might have survived as King, if he had had the sense to respect this determination.

Not content with the largest army in Europe, Louis XIV was now engaged in building a navy to rival England's. It was like the determination of pre-1914 Germany, and had the same result: it brought on a clash between the two countries. Why should they expect to be dominant on both land and sea? No English government could survive such a threat to the nation. Even Charles's government took defensive measures and proposed a program of naval building—which would cost money. Some members were in favor of going slow and saving the burden of taxes. Not so Sir Winston. "Saving money is no argument, when saving the nation is the case. We are now upon the shallows, upon the fewest ships; but we consider not the great man on t'other side of the water, the King of France." Sir Winston wanted the larger number of ships put to the question first. If you put five before nine, if we vote not five, how shall we vote nine? If nine be put first, then five may come naturally.[2]

How strange a foreshadowing it seems of his descendant's introduction of the naval building program of 1912 and the popular cry:

> We want eight,
> And we won't wait!

There followed a typical wrangle over procedure—nothing more boring—whether the greater or lesser sum necessary should be put to the

79

question. The debate is enlivened for us by a nostalgic phrase of Colonel Birch. "The more diffusive the work, the better it is for the nation. He has had occasion to ride through the Forest of Dean; for half a mile together he saw not one tree in fifty decayed, and of great height—the bravest echo of woods he ever heard."[3] It is a phrase in which the beauty of Restoration England stands revealed.

The House resolved one first-rate, five second-rates and fourteen third-rates be built and that the money, £300,000, should be raised by land tax. This was voted by 176 to 150, which gives us the rough division of parties, the Whigs being mainly in favor of raising money from the land, rather than from trade and excise. This division of interest between parties becomes the classic one for the next half century. The imposition of the whole cost upon the land did not, of course, disturb Marvell's commercial constituents at Hull. A rider was attached to the vote: "and that no other charge be laid upon the subject this session of Parliament." Here too the Opposition won, by 145 to 103, Sir Winston being a teller for the Noes.[4]

The next step was to see that this sum was appropriated to the proper object. In such efforts we see the forms of our constitution gradually taking shape—against the wishes of a Tory like Sir Winston. A committee of the whole House resolved that the moneys for the ships be kept separate and distinct in the Exchequer: they did not trust Charles's government. Churchill was named as being against appropriation. He explained, with moderation, that he was against it only until there was proof given that such a branch of the revenue was misapplied, as had been said. "Till that be, we ought not to appropriate."[5] Distrust of Charles was responsible for this—actually it seems that money voted for the navy was not misappropriated and that Churchill was in the right. It must have been a thankless task defending the government in these mistrustful years—the fruits of Charles's personal policy; and the temper of public opinion was rising the whole time. A motion for the adjournment was lost and candles were called for, i.e., that the debate might continue, Mr. Boscawen commenting from long experience, "one candle may always be on the table, when it grows dark, without a question; and at a division, that you may see who goes out and who in."[6]

We may still see these vanished gentlemen, as by the mellow light thrown by candles, upon their canvases in the corridors of English country houses: in their wigs, full faced or half turned away, with their long,

coarse country faces, their hawk noses and their curled wigs, their lace
cravats, their wine-colored velvets and silver buttons. One still sees
these names that occur so frequently in the Commons' proceedings—
Sir Courtenay Pole, Sir Coplestone Bamfilde, Sir Jonathan Trelawny, Sir
Joseph Tredenham, Mr. Boscawen—upon the walls of West Country
houses, their former occupants gone to join the shadows that fell from
those candles.

For the present, the King had had enough of them. Besides, his
simultaneous negotiations for a subsidy from Louis enabled him to
dispense with their services. Since 1671 Charles had got £600,000 out of
his cousin.[7] Louis now paid him £100,000 to prorogue Parliament for a
year—which would enable him to go forward unhampered on the Continent—and offered the same amount to keep Parliament in recess during
1677, with an addition if this disagreeable institution might be prevented
from meeting till 1678.[8]

Charles could not see his way so far; but he kept Parliament prorogued for fifteen months, while Louis went ahead.

I

During the interval, public anxiety grew with the French advances
on the Continent. Cambrai and Valenciennes fell to Louis XIV and the
Netherlands were again in danger. Louis offered Charles two million
livres to delay the meeting of Parliament.[9] Charles attempted to stave off
Parliament's anger by forwarding the Protestant marriage of James's
daughter, Mary—heiress-presumptive to the throne—to William of
Orange: a marriage that had revolutionary consequences. Charles even
entered into an alliance with the Dutch; but he reneged, and maintained
his secret understanding with Louis. Besides, the Duchess of Mazarin
had now come over, to vary her more masculine attractions with the
feminine appeal of the Duchess of Portsmouth.

Party feeling in the Commons was becoming more and more
inflamed. The Whig party, under the impulse of the organizing and
demagogic talents of Shaftesbury, was gaining strength. The Court was
losing ground rapidly in the Commons.

Up to this time, Churchill had been a respected figure in the
House; he was a House of Commons man in spite of his holding a place
at Court. But it is clear what a struggle he increasingly had to put the
government point of view to the House. In the hectic atmosphere of the
last sessions of the Cavalier Parliament, he was sometimes cried down

or laughed out of court. (It was a reversal of fortune, of which his descendant has not been without experience too.)

Even before the prorogation, Sir Winston had felt the derision of the House. The King had pricked Sir Edmund Jennings as sheriff of Yorkshire. Jennings was a member of the Opposition; and they were afraid of this proving a weapon in the hands of the King: after all, his father had made opponents in the House sheriffs, to get rid of them from Westminster. The thankless job fell to Sir Winston, to stonewall on behalf of the Court.[10] He agreed that the appointment was inconvenient to the House, but not that it was a breach of privilege. Before they decided that, he wanted to be satisfied whether the King was taking something that was not his right—to prick a sheriff. Not a Yorkshire gentleman had yet offered anything against it. It was too light a thing, on half an hour's debate, to jump into a breach of privilege: the Lords would cast it back at them.

The situation was rendered more critical by the posture of foreign affairs, the constantly growing power of France. Charles was using this to demand large supplies from the Commons; but they had no guarantees as to his foreign policy. It was much like the situation in the 1930's, when the Opposition could hardly be expected to vote supplies for a policy they rightly distrusted. At both junctures, the correct policy was that of a Grand Alliance against the aggressor. The Opposition in 1677 had no more confidence in Charles II than that in our own day had in Neville Chamberlain. One was engaged in appeasing Louis XIV, as the other in appeasing Hitler. In either case it increased the danger the country would have ultimately to meet. Waller summed up the situation in a sentence: "No man can love England that seeks not after the balance of our neighbours."[11]

Parliament was recalled in January, 1678, in circumstances of mounting tension. The European war was still going on; the Commons were determined to force the King into the Grand Alliance against Louis. Charles was playing an even subtler game than usual. He was preparing to yield to their demand, in order to increase the pressure on Louis for subsidies. A general alliance was, in fact, signed at Westminster in March, but never ratified by Charles.[12] He meant to have an easier life, and was engaged in bidding up both sides. Louis's reply to that was to direct a barrage of bribery against the Commons, and use them against Charles. The French now had two powerful emissaries in London: Barillon, to look after the Court, its master and its ladies; Ruvigny, now dispatched with large sums to operate with the Commons. To assert some control of the nation's affairs against France, Danby organized a countercampaign of bribery against Ruvigny. The effect was, at this juncture, that England was completely neutralized in European affairs. And so she remained until this intolerable situation was resolved by the Revolution of 1688. To such a state had the Stuarts reduced their—but one hardly say "their"—country!

One result was that Charles had now, on the expectation of his entering the war, got his standing army. Another was that the very threat of our joining the allies and making an effective Grand Alliance had some effect in inducing Louis to make peace on moderate terms—the Peace of Nijmegen. It showed what could be done, if England would only play her part and not leave it too late. (As in the 1930's—the whole burden of speech after speech in the Commons by Sir Winston's descendant, while the locusts ate up the years.)

The agitated state of opinion was reflected in a crowded opening of Parliament. On the return of the Commons to their own House, Sir Winston complained, in his impulsive manner, that "we cannot follow the Speaker to the Lords' House without hazard of our lives, the disorder is so great, by reason of crowding. You, Mr. Speaker, tell us many great things, declared from my Lord Chancellor in his Speech. I desire he would give you a copy of what he spoke to us."[13] This was a move in the hope, no doubt, of mitigating the ill effect of the speech, and worse reports of it, by a copy of the text.

For the first time Sir Winston was omitted from the Committee of Elections and Privileges. No doubt the dominant majority left him out as merely the spokesman of the Court—as he was. He was placed on one or two other committees of not much importance: on a bill to erect a register of pawnbrokers; on another, to prevent the export of wool, in the interest of our own manufacture.[14] The *Prosperous*—suitable name for a Restoration trader—had arrived at Portsmouth, laden with French commodities. There was a doubt as to the meaning of the word "imported" as attached to these. Churchill's legal ability was recruited to the committee to report on defects in the law and to provide remedies. A more important committee was that to inquire whether Quakers or any dissenting Protestants had been convicted as Popish Recusants, and whether the penalties on the latter had not been levied. The committee was to frame a distinction between Popish Recusants and other Dissenters. The day after their meeting, the House would consider the danger the Church of England was in by the growth of Popery.[15]

The truth is that the Catholics in England were an inconsiderable minority and, as such, no danger. What injected fever into feeling on the matter was the influence of Catholics at Court, the constant proselytizing that went on in the proximity of the royal family—though it is true, as the Archbishop said on Lady Castlemaine's conversion, that if the Church of Rome gained no more than the Church of England lost by her, it was no great matter. There was, above all, the certainty of a Catholic on the throne—and James was known to be resentful, vindictive, implacable.

The House set itself to take what steps it could to safeguard the future—the extreme section of the Whigs, led by Shaftesbury, wanted to exclude James altogether from the succession. The Commons passed a bill disabling all Papists from sitting in either House of Parliament, with a proviso exempting the Duke of York from taking the oaths. The Lords accepted the principle of the bill, but sent it back with amendments, which the Commons would not agree to. This disagreement was referred to a committee, upon which Churchill had to be placed.

In the debate, he spoke up for the proviso and the Duke: it took some courage, in the awkward relationship in which he stood to the Duke.[16] "Upon this disadvantage, when I hear so loud a cry, 'To the Question,' I should not speak, but to discharge my conscience. Though I think not to prevail, when I heard so loud a cry against what I am moving. The Lords are so near the government, that they see more than we . . . I think that the monarchy of England is concerned in this. Consider the consequence, if you reject this Proviso. How far will you force so great a prince to declare? . . . Suppose the Duke takes not the oaths, etcetera. All that do not take them, will you make them Papists? There were some at your bar that were Quakers, who would not take them; will you drive all that herd of swine into the sea of Rome at once? If those that sit in Parliament must take them, those out of Parliament must too." The report records, "And so he sat down abruptly."

Emotions ran very high in the debate, particularly among the loyalist West Countrymen.[17] Sir Jonathan Trelawny, who was a pensioner of the Crown, burst out—What would happen on the King's death?

"For God's sake, accept the Proviso." It is noted that "those against the Proviso sat silent." Sir William Killigrew, who was a placeman, cried, "I dread taking the Duke from the King," and broke down in a flood of tears. We see, in all this, how impossible a position was that in which the Stuarts were placing their most loyal Protestant subjects. These last had to bear the accusation of advancing the Papist projects of their masters—unfairly in the case of Sir Winston. Actually the proviso passed by only two votes, 158 to 156.[18] It is an indication how near the Cavalier Parliament was to exclusion, and how determined it was on a Protestant succession.

Already the political situation was boiling over, the first manifestations of the monstrous experience of the Popish Plot. Titus Oates, who had seen something of Catholic society and been at the Jesuit College of St. Omer, had already made his depositions before the King and Council, as to a plot to bring England under Catholic sway. The Council took his depositions seriously; the people were hardly likely to reject what those hardened sinners, the privy councilors, had swallowed—whatever their motives. This was the spark that ignited a raging prairie fire: there was the combustible material of all the distrust that had been mounting up for years, the frustration of the efforts to deal with Catholicism in the highest quarters, the indignation and humiliation at our rôle, when Europe was burning. The nation was convulsed by panic and hysteria. A concatenation of circumstances made people crazy with fear and suspicion—we must remember the crudity and brutality, the credulity and volatile emotionalism, of the age. It was a time of informers, spies, perjurers; of confessions extorted, made, recanted and again sworn to; of clubs with their oaths and secret rites; of meetings in dark alleys, hired assassins, duels and beatings up. Mysterious documents were found in unexpected places, in garden or thatch—though no one appears to have thought of a pumpkin in a field.

Indeed, we in our time can well visualize the horror of the experience the nation went through: it was not very dissimilar to that which the United States experienced a short while ago. The point about each indefensible episode is that there *was* a certain amount of justification for it; then fear, fanned and made use of by designing politicians, made the thing pass all bounds. Again, the seventeenth-century experience in England has this in common with the American version in the twentieth century, that in each case it was absorbed and overcome by the normal functioning of the political system, without resorting to any extra-constitutional measures: tribute to the fundamenal health and soundness of the respective polities, the English and American conception of constitutional, representative government.

What wrought public feeling to such a pitch was that, beneath the wicked lies of Titus Oates—who had the psychological intuition of the pathological, the half insane, for he was an informer of genius—there really *was* a Popish Plot. It was not a very important matter, but it came from an exalted quarter. There had been a secret Jesuit conference that spring, not—as Oates thought—at the White Horse tavern, but at St. James's Palace itself. The papers of Father Coleman, who was the Duke of York's secretary and then the Duchess's, were impounded and revealed, to a maddened public, negotiations for substituting James for Charles in the French king's favor and for advancing Catholicism in England. Coleman was a megalomaniac exhibitionist; of all the people who went to the gallows or the scaffold in that time of horror, he was the only one who, in some sense, partly deserved it. The murder—or was it suicide?—of Sir Edmund Berry Godfrey finally clinched the terror; for he was mysteriously associated with Coleman, had shown alarm and apprehension at having, as a magistrate, to take Oates's depositions and, shortly after, had been found transfixed with a sword through the back on some waste ground on Primrose Hill.

On November 28, Titus Oates was called to the bar of an already convinced House to give his evidence.[19] He claimed that at Whitehall he had been placed under restraint and denied the use of pen, ink and paper. Sir Winston dared to contradict the liar, and said that he had seen him busy writing something as if for print only a week ago at Whitehall. The House knew better; the report says that "he was laughed at." The cataract was in full career; nothing could now stop it. Five Catholic peers —harmless, retired backwoodsmen—were impeached and sent to the Tower. All through next year, "Charles was forced to acquiesce in the judicial murders which were removing men whom he knew to be innocent." Such were the fruits of the distrust he had sown. Men thought it was 1641 come again; and the parallel appeared very close when the King's chief minister, Danby, was sent to the Tower.

In December, the House purged itself. The names were called of all members who had defaulted in their attendance, and not taken the oaths of allegiance and supremacy or subscribed to the declaration against transubstantiation according to the Test Act.[20] The case of Sir Richard Graham was put to the question. It was lost, and it was then ordered that the list of members be sent for in custody of the Serjeant-at-Arms. Sir Winston Churchill bravely acted as a teller for the minority, and this is the last time that he saw the inside of Parliament in the reign of Charles II.

For the next two years, the King was not in control of events: the reaction against his rule swept him off his feet and almost swept the traditional constitutional boundaries away. He was driven at last to dissolve Parliament and to call a new one. This represented the high-water mark of the reaction against the Stuarts and the height of the power attained by the Whig extremists, who drove events forward furiously.

There was no place for a Winston Churchill in this over-whelmingly Whig Parliament, or in any of the three elected in these years, 1679, 1680, 1681. A dead set was made against all who were attached to the Court, and apparently Sir Winston dared not stand for the seat at Weymouth he had held so long. He was certainly not returned. It seems that he even lost his place at the Board of Green Cloth for a time. At least, unkind Anthony Wood reports this as appearing in a newsletter at the end of the year 1678.[21] And he does not fail to record the attack on Churchill in an anonymous pamphlet of 1677, *A Seasonable Argument to persuade all the Grand Juries to petition for a new Parliament*.[22] This accused him of being a pensioner in Parliament, of being a principal laborer in the great design of bringing in Popery and arbitrary government, of getting £10,000 in boons and of preferring his own daughter to the Duke of York. The same charges were repeated in the vituperative *Flagellum Parliamentarium*. Not one of these charges was true; but such were the amenities of Restoration politics.

In the way that often happens in fatuous human affairs, the grand opportunity having come to the Whigs, they behaved disgracefully—far more cruelly than ever Charles had behaved, for they sent innocent people to their deaths. Under the leadership of that vindictive spirit, Shaftesbury, the former Cromwellian, the Whigs tried not merely to exclude James from the throne, but to make Charles's eldest bastard, Monmouth, King. Instead of attempting to unite the nation on a moderate course, in which they could easily have reached agreement with Charles for limitations on his successor, whose stupidity and folly none knew better than he, they drove furiously on, affronting the moderate sentiments of the nation, which did not want a Venetian oligarchy, but an ordered, constitutional monarchy. In 1679 Charles had a stroke and James, who had been sent into exile at Brussels, returned to be with him in case of his death. When Charles recovered, there was no keeping James by him. He was packed off to Holyrood, with his favorite, Winston Churchill's son John, with him.

In time, the Whigs wore out their welcome; the popular enthusiasm for extreme courses diminished rapidly, in the English fashion. The King recovered his popularity and, skilful politician that he was, took advantage of the reaction against the Whigs to defeat and disperse them. He called no more Parliaments. A verbal treaty with Louis in 1681 obviated the disagreeable necessity: Charles was to receive 2 million *écus* for the first year and half a million in each succeeding year.[23] Louis felt secure in the knowledge that Charles, *"étant dans une alliance secrète avec moi, ne fera rien contre mon intérêt."* Nor did he: he gracefully—or, rather, disgracefully—accepted a supplement of a million livres to raise no opposition to Louis's acquiring Luxembourg.[24] Retrenchment in the navy indicated appeasement. With that, and these subsidies, Charles was able to jog along without Parliament. With Nell Gwyn as the stanchest supporter of Protestantism in the most intimate sector of the royal circle, in comfortable domesticity with her and the Duchess of Portsmouth, Charles had peace for the last four years of his life.

2

James succeeded quietly to the inheritance which Charles had so skillfully—and, on the whole, successfully—maneuvered to hand on to him unimpaired. During the Tory reaction in those last four years, the borough corporations, which had been the strongholds of the Whigs, were remodeled in the Tory interest. So that it is not surprising that a Tory majority was returned to James's one and only Parliament. Never had the Court so exerted itself to secure the return of well-affected members.

The reconstructed corporation of Lyme Regis returned its old opponent Sir Winston Churchill—perhaps the shade of Lady Drake lent propriety to the transaction.[25] In any case, he had for a number of years been on the Commission of the Peace, one of the deputy lieutenants for Dorset, a name in the county, though he himself was usually away at Court.[26]

At once Sir Winston resumed his activity as spokesman for the Court. If he had temporarily lost his post at the Board of Green Cloth in the Whig blizzard, he soon recovered it. On James's accession, the remuneration of the four clerks was fixed at £500 a year.[27] Next year, on Sir William Boreman's death, Sir Winston moved up to the second place.[28]

In the House, he was more active than ever—though in very different circumstances; he could now speak with authority: he had the majority behind him. We find him serving on a large number of committees, lesser and greater.[29] In June, there was a committee to inspect the accounts of the commissioners for disbanding the forces which had been raised to deal with Monmouth's rebellion. Another committee was to inspect the journals of the House and report what was fit to be expunged —which strikes an ominous note. There were many minor matters dealt with: a bill to provide carriages for His Majesty in his progress and removals. (James was moving about the country with the idea of collecting popularity for his religious policy. Rather like the tour Edward VIII made of South Wales before his abdication, with a similar result.) There were bills to create a new parish in Westminster, to be called after the King's patron saint, St. James: of which the church, which we know as St. James's, Piccadilly, was to be built by the Tory architect, Wren. Later in that month of June, we find Sir Winston serving agreeably with Sir Christopher on the committee for the bill for St. Paul's Cathedral.

James was treated far more generously by this Tory Parliament than ever Charles had been by his. Even so, the Commons did not hesitate to address him to enforce the laws against *all* dissenters from the Church of England.[30] James proceeded to use his dispensing power and instruct the Treasury not to collect the statutory fines on Recusants. Parliament held firm to both habeas corpus and the Test Acts, which James was initiating a campaign to undermine and overthrow. And both Houses were uncompromising about James's employment of Catholic officers. In spite of Parliament's generosity to him, James regarded their attitude as merely vexatious and went on appointing Papists to posts in his standing army. It was all very ominous—and he could take no warning.

When Parliament met again in November he read them a lesson about his Catholic officers and his intention to be obeyed—a Speech from the Throne at once provoking and undignified. Charles had never made such mistakes of tact. Poor gouty old Lord Belasyse, who—though a backwoods Catholic peer—was not without *nous,* said to the faithful

Ailesbury, taking him by the hand, "My dear Lord, who could be the framer of this speech? I date my ruin and that of all my persuasion from this day."[31]

But James had got a standing army; and, though this was not yet clear, he intended to use it to enforce his Catholic policy—after all the experience of Charles's reign! The Opposition was set against a standing army, and wished to rely on a militia under Parliamentary control. As Sir Richard Temple said, "it is for Kings to come to this House, from time to time, on extraordinary occasions; and if this army be provided for by law, they will never more come to this House."[32] It fell to Sir Winston, as the spokesman of the Court, to move supply for the army: "some other than the militia is necessary to be found."[33] Sir Richard Temple countered by asking leave for a bill to strengthen the militia. Sir Winston: "the Beef-eaters at this rate may be called an army." To this Sir Thomas Hussey retorted, "the Colonel may say what he will of the Beef-eaters, as he nick-names them; but they are established by act of Parliament."[34] (We need not assume that Sir Winston Churchill was responsible for this famous nickname, but it is interesting that he should have been first to use it in Parliament.)

Supply was voted. Next came the question how it was to be apportioned. The government wanted £1,200,000. There was a motion to grant £200,000 for the present; more to come later. The Colonel: "£200,000 is much too little: soldiers move not without pay. *No Penny, No Paternoster*."[35] No, indeed. It was an unfortunate proverb to quote just then; for it spoke the unspoken thought in everybody's mind—if they lost control over the revenue, the King could enforce his religious policy and arbitrary rule. A motion for £700,000 was introduced; but rather than endure any criticism of his measures James prorogued Parliament. He did not call them together again. They had been dangerously generous to him, in the beginning, in voting him customs and excise for life. It was enough for him to get on without them—and give him rope enough to hang himself.

3

Sir Winston Churchill was getting an elderly man now; and it is not surprising to find him concerning himself more with Minterne in these last years. His father had been buried there, not at Wootton Glanville. When one enters the dark, narrow-chested little church by the roadside up from Cerne Abbas, a stone's throw away from the big house looking out upon that exquisite valley and up the wooded slope beyond, one stumbles upon John Churchill beneath his stone in the central aisle: "Here lies the body of John Churchill esq., who died the 6th of April, 1652. This stone was erected and laid here at the cost of Mrs. Mary Churchill, widow, out of her affection, and in commemoration of her beloved husband, John Churchill, esq." Do we not detect a slight note of reproach that it was left to the widow to place the gravestone at her own cost?

In this age of the improving landlord, Sir Winston was taking steps in 1669 to enclose the common at Wootton Glanville, which his father had been unable to accomplish. At last the tenants agreed to permit its enclosure, each tenant to have his rightful proportion and Sir Winston, as lord of the manor, to have the lion's share. Only one tenant held out, Henry Mullett. Sir Winston and the other chief tenants in the parish claimed that Mullett "could not prove he was a customary tenant, for that in the late rebellious times wherein your orator, according to his duty and allegiance, constantly adhered to his Majesty . . . the records of the manorial courts were totally embezzled and lost."[36] Henry Mullett claimed that the manor lay in the ancient precincts of the Forest of Blackmore, where all the tenants had common of pasture for their beasts. If there should be an enclosure, his cattle would be confined to a narrow close "and the year may so happen that there may be no grass" there, where now they have feeding for so many miles on the commons. Where now he kept twenty head of cattle, he would not be able to keep above five or six. Sir Winston would have "a very considerable allotment as his share," so that the tenants' proportion would be inconsiderable. No doubt; that way lay the path of agricultural progress.

A few years later, Sir Winston made a purchase: the manor of Duntish, near Buckland Abbas, worth £150 a year.[37] It had belonged to a Royalist family, and been sequestered. In the same year, 1674, Sir Winston bought, for £750 a farm at Cattistock, which had common of pasture for 110 sheep, four horses and seven other beasts. Here, too, there was trouble, as to the rents and services due, for "as the defendants knew" that Sir Winston had no court rolls of the manor, "they combined to defraud him of the same."[38]

It is evident that Sir Winston was not at all prosperous. He got little enough for his long service to the Stuarts. He died in debt, and the

large amount he had lent the impecunious Charles II in 1667—£2,000—
was still unpaid at his death. He did not possess the cool, clear, calculating
head of his famous son. Sir Winston had the hot impulsive head of the
Cavalier Colonel, only a little disciplined by his legal training. There is a
letter from the Earl of Arran to Ormonde in January, 1668, complaining
that "Churchill has left his accounts in such confusion that a great many
of your friends are afraid they shall suffer, and amongst them my Lord
Suffolk, who desires you would not pay the money you owed Churchill,
until you see that the administrators desire to do justly with his
creditors."[39]

It appears that this must relate to Sir Winston; but to what accounts?
Irish or, more likely, at the Board of Green Cloth? And can it have
anything to do with his abject petition to the King for pardon, for some
offence as to which we are in complete ignorance? Here it is in full, for
a specimen.[40]

To the King's Most Excellent Majesty. The Humble Petition of Sir Winston
Churchill, one of the Clerks Comptrollers of your Majesty's Household.
Humbly Showeth—That your petitioner being deeply sensible of your
Majesty's high displeasure, by a message received from Mr. Treasurer of the
Household, intimating a command from your Majesty that he should forbear
to wait in his ordinary course of service, according to the duty of his place;

And having nothing to offer in justification of any offence given by him to
your Majesty, but to cast himself with all humility and submission at your
most sacred feet;

Doth therefore humbly pray that it may please your most excellent
Majesty to grant unto him your gracious pardon and to make him once more
happy in your Majesty's good opinion of his integrity and humble affections to
your service, which he shall ever continue to make good with the utmost
hazard of his life and fortune:

And your petitioner shall ever pray etc.

It bears the authentic note of Sir Winston; but in what way can he
have offended so seriously? The petition is undated, so that one has no
clue. To the word "integrity" we are apt to attach the adjective "financial."
But is it likely that the easygoing Charles would attach such personal
importance to financial integrity, even in his own household? From the
state of Sir Winston's private fortune, it is unlikely that he helped
himself to much—at a time when others were helping themselves on a
large scale. No: it would seem rather that it must relate to some more

intimate offense, something that concerned the King more personally. The Colonel may have spoken his mind, hotly and impulsively, to the King, in the course of his waiting. About what? About his private affairs? That seems most likely, for he was linked with the King in a doubly awkward way. There was his daughter Arabella, mistress to the King's brother, mother of his children. There was his son John, carrying on an affair with his cousin, the King's mistress, Lady Castlemaine. It was a very tricksy four-in-hand for a straightforward old Cavalier, against whose own private life there was never a breath of suspicion. Sir Winston may have burst out with something in his children's defense: they were past protecting.

The offense is hardly likely to have been political, though there is a faint possibility still open. In the crisis of 1672, when Charles joined Louis in the attack on Holland, and the Dutch were isolated diplomatically, they had three deputies in England negotiating with the King. A secret report to a Minister at Hampton Court—we do not know who—states: "Sir Winston Churchill (who told me he had your Honour's approbation) dined with them that day and had much discourse with them, whereof I suppose he will give you an account; but to my opinion it did differ from a conference (as I have been informed by one of these) which the three Deputies had the day before privately together: where, it is said, Monsieur Borel did propose to make an absolute submission to the King and his government of their present state, but that the two others did oppose it."[41] And so on. If Churchill were in any way going beyond his brief, or, without any brief, interfering in matters of high policy—which, as we have seen, the King regarded as his own private sphere—that could be enough to earn him a severe reproof.

Whatever it was, it seems to have done no harm to his personal position or favor. On the other hand, he never received any further promotion: nothing, not even a peerage.

It only remains to us to gather up the few fragments that remain to us of his arduous, hard-working, varyingly satisfactory life. We know of one person to whom he sent a copy of his *Divi Britannici*; Arthur Capel, Earl of Essex, the old Cavalier turned Whig, who was sent as Lord Lieutenant to Ireland in 1672. In 1676 he writes to Harbord, "Sir Winston Churchill hath by Colonel Jefferies sent me one of his books; I would have you go to him and give him thanks from me for it."[42]

There must have been others to whom he sent the book: he was not ashamed of it; he must rather have been proud of his work.

It was from Minterne, in June, 1686, that the aging Cavalier wrote his stuffy, snobbish letter to Blue Mantle about his coat of arms and his (largely fictitious) ancestors.[43] "I do not suspect in the least my title to the ancient arms (as you call it) should be forgotten or questioned, since the monuments of my ancestors will clear that dispute, and what arms was born by the father I think no man will deny to belong to the son; besides, the very grant itself by which I am licensed to bear the lion without the bend, evinces that till the time of that grant, it was borne with the bend. And as to the canton, I take it not to be given me as an essential part of my coat (for so I refused to accept it), but (as 'tis expressed in the grant) as an augmentation of honour; and if my son think it not so, I know not but that he is at liberty to omit it, and bear the lion without it." Apparently his son did; and the Dukes of Marlborough carry the lion without that bend. Embedded in this long genealogical letter is a piece of information that brings us back to Somerset earth. Curiously enough, the manor of Churchill came to the Jennings family and was sold only by the father of Sarah, whom Sir Winston's son married, to Sir John Churchill, Master of the Rolls: "it had come to my son in right of his wife, had it not been so unfortunately alienated by her said father . . . The manor is now to be sold, but my son, being disappointed of having it given to him, as Sir John Churchill always did promise him, refuses to buy it." There was a recent disappointment that rankled; Sir John Churchill had died the previous year.

So, too, had Sir Winston's promising youngest son, Theobald. He went up to Queen's College, Oxford, at the age of fourteen in 1677; took his B.A. degree in 1680, his M.A. in 1683, when he was in holy orders.[44] On the visit of the Duke and Duchess of York, with the Princess Anne, to Oxford in that year, they were received by the Provost, Fellows and whole college in the quadrangle at Queen's, where a Latin speech and a copy of English verses were spoken to them by young Theobald.[45] Next year, on a vacancy to a fellowship at Eton, Theobald Churchill had the King's mandate for it, but the Provost and Fellows had already elected someone from King's College, Cambridge, before it came—to the King's displeasure. The year after, the promising young man died—evidently at his father's lodgings in Whitehall, for he was buried at St. Martin's-in-the-Fields.[46] A pity, for with his background he was inevitably bound for a bishopric.

Sir Winston had already, in 1684, made his will.[47] He wished to be buried in his father's grave at Minterne—after all, his father had been his only effectual ancestor, maker of the place he had attained in the world. He left to his wife the farm and demesne of Minterne, as her jointure, on condition of paying the dues to Winchester College. She was to have all the plate, hangings and household stuff, for life, from London, Windsor and Minterne; with the "profits of my fair at Hermitage, Dorset, and of King's Drift in Blackmore, and 90 acres in the new enclosure at Wootton." The manor of Newland was to be sold for the payment of his debts; and any moneys due from the King devoted similarly. He had appointed certain lands to be offered to John Churchill, his eldest son, "if he would give as much for them as anyone else."

This is a pretty cold reference to his famous son, already a well-known figure in the world, and a peer. (There is no reference at all to Arabella.) In their mother's will, made in 1698, the year she died, we read: "Whereas it was my dear husband's mind and intention, oftentimes by him declared, that our son Charles Churchill should, after my said husband's death and mine, have all the house, farm and lands in Minterne, granted . . . for several years still to come, by the Warden of St. Mary's College, Winchester; and as the said Charles Churchill had already paid some of his father's debts charged as mortgage on the said farm," she left all her interest in Minterne and the fair at Hermitage to Charles. He was to pay his father's remaining debts, except £500 "due unto my son George Churchill from my said husband." She left all her plate and household stuff to help pay Sir Winston's debts. All her stock and cattle at Wootton were to go to "Charles, the reputed son of my said son Charles Churchill." From the lands at Wootton, £500 was to be raised for George Churchill, the residue to be divided between George and Charles and the testator's grandson, Francis Godfrey. If Francis should die before he was seventeen, his share was to be divided between his three sisters, Charlotte, Elizabeth and Diana. Their mother was Arabella: she is not mentioned. Lastly, the £2,000 owing to the testatrix's husband by Charles II was to be divided between the same three legatees.[48]

Such were the rewards of long years of service to the Stuarts: nothing very grand. Sir Winston was to be justified in his children.

It seems that he was not buried with his father after all. Anthony Wood tells us that he died March 26, 1688, and was buried three days after in St. Martin's-in-the-Fields with his son.[49] Minterne became the seat of his soldier son, Charles, who resided there during the latter part of his life and completed the building of the house. He was buried under a large monument, which doubtless stood formerly in the chancel of that little church, with a long inscription reciting his career. "Near this place lies interred the body of the honourable Charles Churchill esq., fourth son of Sir Winston Churchill, of the county of Dorset, knight. He was at thirteen made page of honour to Christian, King of Denmark, and at sixteen gentleman of the bedchamber to his brother, the renowned Prince George. His martial genius led him to the wars, and his distinguished courage and conduct made him soon taken notice of by his prince. He was made Major General of Foot and Governor of Kinsale in Ireland, by King William; and, after many battles fought with great bravery and conduct, was esteemed one of the best commanders of foot in Europe. By his royal and gracious mistress Queen Anne, he was made Governor of the Tower of London, General of the Army, and General-in-chief of Foot, and had a great and honourable share in the memorable battle of Blenheim. After which, for his many and great services, he was made Governor of Brussels and Colonel of the Coldstream Regiment of Foot Guards, and Governor of her Majesty's island of Guernsey.

"In the year 1702, he married Mary, daughter and sole heiress of James Gould of Dorchester esq., who in honour of his beloved memory, caused this monument to be erected. His known bravery, generous spirit and friendly temper made him esteemed and beloved by all that knew him, and his unalterable affection for the Church, his fidelity to the Crown and love of his country have justly recommended him to posterity. He died, much lamented, 29 December 1714, in the fifty sixth year of his age."[50]

And that was the end of the family in the county that gave them birth.

CHAPTER VII

Arabella

IT WAS Sir Winston's children, Arabella and John, who made the
fortunes of the Churchills, though their father's post at Court put them
in the way of it.

Never in English history, before or since, has there been a Court
so given up to pleasure, particularly the pleasures of sex, as that of
Charles II. Anthony Hamilton, who lived at the heart of it—or rather,
at the center, for it had no heart—describes it as "entirely devoted to love
and gallantry . . . The Court was an entire scene of gallantry and amuse-
ments, with all the politeness and magnificence which the inclinations of
a prince naturally addicted to tenderness and pleasure could suggest. The
beauties were desirous of charming and the men endeavoured to please.
All studied to set themselves off to the best advantage: some distinguished
themselves by dancing; others by show and magnificence; some by their
wit, many by their amours, but few by their constancy."[1]

After the morose respectability of the Puritans, the seriousness
and sobriety, the Restoration was a time of extravagance and opulent
ostentation, of voluptuousness in decoration and clothes—as one sees
from the half-naked women, who always appear to be in negligee, in spite
of all the flowing silks and velvets, looking down from the canvases of
Lely—of French luxuries and *objets d'art*. "Perfumed gloves, pocket
looking-glasses, elegant boxes, apricot paste, essences and other small wares
of love arrived every week from Paris. But, with regard to solid presents,
such as ear-rings, diamonds, brilliants, bright guineas, all this was to
be met with of the best sort in London, and the ladies were as well
pleased with them as if they had been brought from abroad."[2] French
taste, French standards, prevailed; the plays of Corneille and Racine, the
verse of Boileau were the models; the airs of Lully were the favorites—

the King listening peaceably after dinner, politics suspended for an hour, himself beating time with his hand. The Court was essentially, devotedly, French; though following the fashions of Louis XIV, it was, in its gaiety, its lightness and lack of restraint, in spirit more like that of Louis XV.

The dance was led by Charles—"that known enemy to virginity and chastity, the monarch of Great Britain," as a crony agreeably called him.[3] The second place was occupied by the Duke of York. There was little that the brothers resembled each other in. Where Charles was affable and familiar, James was cold and arrogant; Charles was apt to be generous and was certainly extravagant, James mean and parsimonious. Above all, Charles was good-tempered and humorous; James had no sense of humor whatever: not a joke is recorded of him. Only one thing the brothers shared: that "terrible Bourbon temperament" which Madame de Maintenon complained of in her royal husband in his seventies.

Here, too, the brothers differed. Where Charles was selective and discriminating, and rather considerate, James was omnivorous. He was described as "very amorous, and more out of a natural temper than for the genteel part of making love, which he was much a stranger to." Charles himself, who is usually thought of as the chief offender, said to a French ambassador, "I do not believe there are two men who love women more than you and I do; but my brother, devout as he is, loves them still more."[4]

James's affairs are less well known, partly because they were not politically important, unlike the King's. But they were, if anything, more numerous. There was Miss Price, then there was Lady Southesk, then Lady Denham. He was so clumsily obvious that he was apt to be caught in undignified postures. Hamilton says of one of his affairs, "as he was the most unguarded ogler of his time, the whole Court was informed of the intrigue before it was well begun."[5] Then he took to ogling the beautiful Lady Robartes, in the zenith of her glory and youth, married to a straitlaced Presbyterian, "an old, snarling, troublesome, peevish fellow, in love with her to distraction and, to complete her misery, a perpetual attendant on her person."[6] He was offered "the management of the Duke of York's revenues in Ireland, of which he should have the entire disposal, provided he immediately set out to take possession of his charge . . . He perfectly well understood the meaning of these proposals, and was fully apprized of the advantages he might reap from them: in vain did ambition and avarice hold out their allurements; he was deaf to all their temptations, nor could ever the old fellow be persuaded to be made a cuckold . . . Under the pretence of a pilgrimage to St. Winifred, the virgin and martyr, who was said to cure women of barrenness, he did not rest until the highest mountains in Wales were between his wife and the person who had designed to perform this miracle in London, after his departure."

Defeated, the Duke turned his attentions to Lady Chesterfield. James, who played the guitar tolerably, desired to try out a fashionable new piece upon Lady Chesterfield's instrument, which was the finest in England. When he arrived at her apartments, he found her husband was present; and a very awkward trio they made of it. The Duke paid the lady a complimentary visit at her house, while her husband was engaged at Court, who on his return was surprised and annoyed to find the Duke's coach blocking his way. Lord Chesterfield thought best to whisk his wife off to the country, where she endured what everyone thought the hardship of spending her Christmas at a country house, a hundred and fifty miles from London.

James was laughed at by all the clever ones; but, in truth, he was no laughing matter.

He was married to an excellent woman, Anne Hyde, Clarendon's daughter. He had compromised her—or rather, since he was a royal person, himself with her—in the seedy, impoverished days of exile. She was good enough for him then—indeed, a great deal too good—and, secretly, he contracted himself to marry her. The marriage, as Hamilton says, "was deficient in none of those circumstances which render contracts of this nature valid in the eye of heaven: the mutual inclination, the formal ceremony, witnesses, and every essential point of matrimony had been observed."[7] But when the Restoration Court began to burgeon in all its glory, to bloom with beauties, and "he considered he was the only prince who, from such superior elevation, had descended so low, he began to reflect upon it."

These reflections were aided by some superior wits, though very inferior characters. The Court, which made such a point of fine gentlemanship, abounded in cads. Nothing could be more caddish than the proposal put to James by a group of fine young men who detested Clarendon—a proposal to which James was mean enough to lend himself. James opened his heart to Lord Falmouth, the King's favorite, who engaged himself to fix it for the Duke: the marriage was invalid without the King's consent; it was "a mere jest even to think of the daughter of an insignificant lawyer, whom the favour of his sovereign had lately made a peer of the realm, without any noble blood, and chancellor, without any capacity." We see what lightweights such aristocratic young bloods can be. However, they got together: Falmouth, the Earl of Arran, Harry Jermyn's unappealing nephew, Dick Talbot and smutty Tom Killigrew: "all men of honour, but who infinitely preferred the Duke of York's interest to Miss Hyde's reputation, and who, besides, were greatly dissatisfied, as well as the whole Court, at the insolent authority of the prime minister."

At a prearranged meeting with the Duke, "each began to relate the particulars of what he knew, and of perhaps more than he knew, of poor Miss Hyde; nor did they omit any circumstance necessary to strengthen the evidence." Scurrilous Tom Killigrew, for example, "boldly declared that he had had the honour of being upon the most intimate terms with her. He affirmed that he had found the critical minute in a certain closet built over the water, for a purpose very different from that of giving ease to the pains of love; that three or four swans had been witnesses to his happiness, and might perhaps have been witnesses to the happiness of many others, as the lady frequently repaired to that place, and was particularly delighted with it."

Even James protested against the indignity of that; on the basis of their information, he went in to the King.

In the secrecy of the royal cabinet there was a prolonged wrangle; Charles was a gentleman, if James was not. "The Duke of York appeared to be in such agitation when he came out, that they no longer doubted that the result had been unfavourable for poor Miss Hyde." They all met an hour later in her chamber: "a few tears trickled down her cheeks, which she endeavoured to restrain. The Chancellor, leaning against the wall, appeared to be puffed up with something, which they did not doubt was rage and despair." The Duke of York announced: "As you are the two men of the court whom I most esteem [i.e., Falmouth and Ossory], I am desirous you should first have the honour of paying your compliments to the Duchess of York: there she is." Surprised and astonished, the two young peers yet knew their duty: "they immediately fell on their knees to kiss her hand, which she gave to them with as much majesty as if she had been used to it all her life."

Anne Hyde showed what a sensible woman she was, and of what good nature, by the way she behaved to these scoundrels afterward. "Instead of showing the least resentment, she studied to distinguish, by all manner of kindness and good offices, those who had attacked her in so sensible a part. Nor did she ever mention it to them, but in order to praise their zeal, and to tell them that 'nothing was a greater proof of the attachment of a man of honour, than his being more solicitous for the interest of his friend, or master, than for his own reputation': a remarkable example of prudence and moderation, not only for the fair sex, but even for those who value themselves most upon their philosophy among the men."

Hamilton, who had a very sharp pair of eyes and no illusions about people, pays the new Duchess a marked tribute. He says that the moment her marriage was made public, "the whole Court was eager to pay her that respect, from a sense of duty, which in the end became very sincere." After her elevation, she "conducted herself with such prudence and circumspection as could not be sufficiently admired: such were her manners and such the general estimation in which she was held that she appeared to have found out the secret of pleasing everyone—a secret yet more rare than the grandeur to which she had been raised." She was a kind woman, though, like her father, apt to stand rather more on her dignity than was altogether necessary; and she was an intelligent one. She became the patron of Lely, and brought him into fashion and favor: in that, leaving some legacy of herself to us and posterity, besides her children, Mary and Anne, each of whom became Queen.[8] It was a pity she did not live to become Queen herself: such influence as she could exert upon James would have been in the direction of sense and moderation.

As for him, "the Duke of York, having quieted his conscience by the declaration of his marriage, thought that he was entitled by this generous effort, to give way a little to his inconstancy. He therefore immediately seized upon whatever he could first lay his hands upon: this was Lady Carnegie, who had been in several other hands." And so on.

Such was the Court to which Sir Winston Churchill had not been anxious to promote his daughter. But a Court in which her cousin, Lady Castlemaine, reigned could not be without prospects for the daughter of an impecunious knight; and he could hardly have resisted the offer of a place for her as maid of honor to the Duchess of York.

All the maids of honor were fair game to James, who paid his addresses to them one after another. Arabella was a mere slip of a girl, sixteen or seventeen: tall and thin, with a very pale complexion, as yet undeveloped. James became infatuated with her: no one could understand why. "The Court was not able to comprehend how, after having been in love with Lady Chesterfield, Miss Hamilton and Miss Jennings, he could have any inclination for such a creature."⁹ On this occasion, the Duchess's jealousy was really aroused: "the Duchess beheld with indignation a choice which seemed to debase her own merit in a much greater degree than any of the former." There may have been another motive: the Duchess may well have been indignant at the Duke engaging in a serious pursuit of a girl so young. It is clear that for some time his attentions were resisted, and his ardour began to cool.

In the summer of the plague year, 1665, the Duke and Duchess made a progress to York. There were various motives: to separate the royal family, so that the brothers might not both be struck down by the plague; to make the most of the popularity James had temporarily gained by his conduct at the battle of Lowestoft; to give the North a sight of restored royalty. Hamilton tells us that "the votaries of love" made the most of the expedition and of the opportunities it afforded. "There were continual balls and entertainments upon the road; hunting, and all other diversions, wherever the Court halted in its progress. The tender lovers flattered themselves with the thought of being able to crown their happiness as they proceeded in their journey; and the beauties who governed their destiny did not forbid them to hope."¹⁰

James had two passions, hunting and women, which he was apt to combine. On their way north, he amused himself teaching Arabella to ride. She was gawky, gauche and timid; now a girl of seventeen, he a man of thirty-one. It was his idea of fun to scold her for sitting so ill on horseback. (We know what his conversation was like from his attempts to entertain Miss Hamilton: "telling her miracles of the cunning of foxes and the mettle of horses; giving her accounts of broken legs and arms, dislocated shoulders, and other curious and entertaining adventures; after which, his eyes told her the rest, till such time as sleep interrupted their conversation."¹¹

The maids of honor were usually the worst mounted of the whole

Court, but in order to distinguish Arabella, "on account of the favour she enjoyed, they had given her a very pretty, though rather a high-spirited horse: a distinction she would very willingly have excused them."[12] One day, the horse ran away with her, and she had a bad fall. "A fall in so quick a pace must have been violent; and yet it proved favourable to her in every respect; for, without receiving any hurt, she gave the lie to all the unfavourable suppositions that had been formed of her person, in judging from her face. The Duke alighted, in order to help her. She was so greatly stunned, that her thoughts were otherwise employed than about decency on the present occasion; and those who first crowded around her found her rather in a negligent posture. They could hardly believe that limbs of such beauty could belong to Miss Churchill's face." In short, beneath her clothes, Arabella had the Villiers figure, famous for its perfection in women and men alike.

"After this accident, it was remarked that the Duke's tenderness and affection for her increased every day; and, towards the end of the winter, it appeared that she had not tyrannized over his passion, nor made him languish with impatience."

James's liaison with Arabella was not one of his numerous casual affairs; it was on a completely different footing. It was the chief affair of his life, lasting for ten or twelve years; it gave him some domesticity—for Arabella was an entirely domestic sort of woman—and left him with a family to provide for. There were four children who survived. The first was Henrietta, who married a Waldegrave and was the mother and grandmother of the Waldegraves who made their mark in the eighteenth century. Another daughter, who became a nun, had an immensely long life and lived (in France) to see the accession of George III to her father's throne. Of the two sons, the younger, Henry, was given the Jacobite title of Duke of Albemarle in France after 1688, but was better known as the Grand Prior: the elder, James, Duke of Berwick, became perhaps the finest soldier in Europe after his uncle, the Duke of Marlborough.

There must have been something remarkable in the stock: we need not suppose that it was the Stuart blood that made it so. There was nothing remarkable about James's progeny by anybody else, Anne Hyde, Catherine Sedley or Mary of Modena. Our Sir Winston comments on his ancestor that he "has been accounted one of the most notable and potent of sires. Had he lived . . . he would have witnessed within the space of twelve months his son gaining the battle of Ramillies and his daughter's son that of Almanza; and would have found himself acknowledged as the progenitor of the two greatest captains of the age at the head of the opposing armies of Britain and of France and Spain. Moreover, his third surviving son, Charles, became a soldier of well-tried distinction, and his naval son virtually managed the Admiralty during the years of war. The military strain flowed strong and clear from the captain of the Civil Wars, student of heraldry and history, and champion of the Divine Right. It was his blood, not his pen, that carried his message."[13] Berwick's life and career have always been treated in their Stuart setting, but it is clear that his military genius came from the Churchills.

Little is known of Arabella's life and personality; she was not one of the blatant, exhibitionist beauties always in the public eye, at Court or at the playhouse, making trouble or causing scenes and scandals, like Castlemaine, Portsmouth, La Belle Stuart, Nell Gwyn and the rest of them. She led a quiet, hidden life; after all, she was very young and her time was much taken up with childbearing: it was no sinecure being mistress to the Duke. Pepys mentions her only once. In the cold weather of January 1669—bright moonshine at night and hard frost by day, in which the King and Duke walked abroad, attended sometimes by the little man—one day he ran into his crony, Mr. Pierce, the Duke's doctor. "I asked him whither he was going; [he] told me as a great secret that he was going to his master's mistress, Mrs. Churchill, with some physic; meaning for the pox, I suppose, or else that she is got with child."[14]

The latter supposition was the correct one; though—the Restoration being what it was—everyone talked of the former. Marvell writes:

> His meagre Highness, now he's got astride,
> Does on Britannia, as on Churchill ride.

And on James's marriage to young Mary of Modena:

> Then draw the Princess with her golden locks,
> Hastening to be envenomed with the pox,
> And in her youthful veins receive a wound,
> Which sent Nan Hyde before her underground;
> The wound of which the tainted Churchill fades,
> Preserved in store for the next set of maids.

This was quite unforgivable; but it may be held that the Stuarts had asked for it. Unforgivable, and also untrue: Anne Hyde died of cancer of the breast; Arabella lived to a hale and hearty old age, dying at eighty-two. It is generally held that James had taken some such infection and that this accounts for some of his mental characteristics: the abnormal fixity, the wooden rigidity, the complete crack-up and loss of nerve at the defection of the nation in 1688, the fainting fits and nosebleedings. But I do not think we need go so far to account for a humorless fool.

When children began to arrive, James moved Arabella out of White-hall, and set her up in a house in St. James's Square. This was the new salubrious neighborhood being opened up by Henry Jermyn, who got the grant of the land from the Crown: what with the unearned (or doubtfully earned) increment and the profits of the gaming table (he did not lose), he became very well off. His name is suitably recalled to us by the lower associations of Jermyn Street. Here, in the new square, Arabella set up house: the Marquis de Blanquefort, afterward Earl of Feversham, to whom James as King confided the command of his army, the Countess of Warwick and the Earl of Oxford in the southeast corner; Clarendon's two sons, the second Earl and his brother Laurence Hyde, later Earl of Rochester, on the north side; on the west, Lord Hali-fax, Lord Purbeck, Sir Allen Apsley, Madame Churchill and, as her next-door neighbor, Madame Davis. Madame Davis, appropriately called Moll, was the dancer who danced her way from "a bed on the cold ground to a bed royal." Pepys thought her dancing infinitely beyond Nell Gwyn's; but her hold on Charles's affections was much shorter. Moll Davis's was the first, and Arabella's the second, house on the left-hand side as you enter the Square from the southwest.[15]

Here Arabella lived, discreetly and noiselessly, leaving no traces, except her children, and an occasional entry in the Treasury Books. James was not generous by nature; but a pension of £1,000 a year (multiply by, perhaps, ten)—though a very different matter from the hundreds of thousands squandered on Castlemaine and Portsmouth—enabled Arabella to live comfortably for the rest of her life.[16] She traveled to France, for we learn from the memoirs of her son, Berwick, that he was born at Moulins in the Bourbonnais, "whither Mrs. Churchill had retired to conceal her pregnancy."[17]

Three years later, December 28, 1674, there is a warrant from the Lord Treasurer to the Customs to deliver at Madame Churchill's house—no doubt, duty free, whatever the Commons might say about imported luxuries from France—a box with brass andirons, a box with two mantua gowns, some muffs, two or three garnitures of buttons and loops, stuffs for a petticoat directed to Mr. Pounds for the Duke of York, and a trunk and portmanteau for Sir Henry FitzJames with his wearing clothes in it, which are imported in the *Anne* yacht.[18] It is rather a touching trace of that hidden life to come across in those pedestrian Treasury Books. Two years later, there is a warrant to deliver, on payment of customs, some looking glasses, tables, stands and hanging candlesticks sent from France for Madame Churchill.[19] These things were all the rage just then: one sees them still in Caroline houses. A year later, in October, 1677, an escritoire brought from Italy for the new Duchess of York, Mary of Modena, was delivered duty free; certain trunks brought from France by Madame Churchill in the *Cleveland* yacht (Lady Castlemaine had been made Duchess of Cleveland, to propitiate her after a tiff and a scene she had made) were to be free of customs only if they were wearing apparel.[20] The long liaison was wearing thin; but the Customs official who seized the three parcels of Mrs. Churchill's goods was spoken to: they were to be sent to her house and opened there.

The death of Anne Hyde freed James for what he could regard as a respectable, i.e., a royal, marriage. All Europe was scoured for suitable candidates. James made it clear that he would marry no one who was not a Catholic. The country was very much aroused. The King insisted on the news that poor Anne had died a Catholic being kept secret. He told the French ambassador, Croissy, that he recognized two weaknesses in his brother—religion and marriage; that the first had already produced effects enough and that he had reason to fear worse consequences in the future.[21] The phrase *"la sottise de mon frère"* was frequently on his lips in these conversations. In the end, James took his wife at the hands of their grand patron, Louis XIV, and, for all his haughtiness, wrote him an obsequious letter assuring him of his lasting devotion.

The great man's choice had fallen on Maria Beatrice, sister of the young Duke of Modena: she was only fifteen, lively and healthy, capable of bearing Catholic children for the throne of England. The Commons were certain to protest; the marriage by proxy was hurried on before they could get to work. The news of its having taken place was brought to the Duke in the drawing room at Whitehall by the French ambassador: James turned round and said, "Then I am a married man." He went down to meet his wife at Dover, where Nathaniel Crewe, the sycophantic Bishop of Oxford, pronounced what both the recipients must have regarded as a bogus benediction. The donor must, however, have considered it worth the fat see of Durham which he got for it. He was among the first to go over to William in 1688. He lived to enjoy Durham a long time and salved what he regarded as his conscience by his benefactions to Oxford.

Such a marriage was no interruption to James's liaison with Arabella; within a month he was said to have resumed domestic relations with her.[22] In any case, it was some time before the girl-Duchess took to her husband, and she was slow in producing children. The girl was good-natured and not unintelligent, in spite of her ridiculous *dévote* upbringing. Her worst influence on James was to increase his religious bigotry and cut him off still further from commonsense and the English people. Danby, who did his best to save the Stuarts, complained that whereas the Archbishop of Rheims, when in England, came to our churches and knelt during the services, James would not so much as come to the door.[23] A King of England who drew the line at the Church of England was an intolerable contradiction.

What did interfere with his liaison with Arabella, and bring it to an end, was not his marriage, but a new liaison with another maid of honor. This was Catherine Sedley, in every way a contrast with Arabella. She was the only child of Sir Charles Sedley, the dramatist and wit, rake and poet. Catherine inherited her father's wit, and was to inherit his fortune. It was this that made Sir Winston and Lady Churchill so anxious to have her as a catch for their son John. That cool young man was much attracted by her fortune; he could not have been by her looks, for she had none. Next year, in 1678, when she was twenty, she became a maid of honor to the new Duchess, and that was fatal.

Catherine was not at all attracted by James and had no illusions about her looks. She herself could not understand his infatuation and, with engaging candor, said so: "It cannot be my beauty, because I haven't any; and it cannot be my wit, because he hasn't enough to know that I have any." The fact was that Catherine fascinated James as no one else ever had—as only a clever woman can a really stupid man, whatever her looks. Catherine caused the Duchess much more grief than Arabella had, for James was unable to emancipate himself from the spell of her personality. When he became King, he created her Countess of Dorchester, to the Queen's annoyance and distress.[24] When he ceased to be King, Sir Charles Sedley was one of the Commons who voted his daughter Mary to the throne: "her father made my daughter a Countess; I have been helping to make his daughter a Queen." And Catherine said of Queen Mary: "if I broke one of the Commandments *with* her father, she broke another *against* him."

Arabella got no countess-ship; but her children were recognized and brought to Court—to Mary of Modena's disapprobation and jealousy: she still had none of her own when, in September, 1685, young James and Henry, future Dukes of Berwick and Albemarle, were introduced.[25] Their sister, Henrietta, was married to Sir Henry Waldegrave; in January, 1686, he was made a peer.[26] With the beginning of James's liaison with Catherine Sedley, about 1678-79, his relations with Arabella Churchill ceased: she was free to live her own life. On April 7, 1679, she got a pass to go abroad with two of her children and, a younger brother, Mountjoy Churchill, as her escort.[27] About this time, or later, she sold her fine house in St. James's Square for a large sum, £8,000.[28] With this, with a pension of £1,000 a year secured on Irish lands, still only thirty, she was a desirable *parti*.

As the children grew older, James took them away from their mother to provide for their upbringing and education. They were sent to France to be brought up—irresistible magnet for the Stuarts, the model for royal manners and the proper conduct of subjects. Some letters of James to his daughter Henrietta throw light into this dark corner.[29] From Windsor in 1682 he writes, with a characteristic combination of lofty condescension and stiff kindness, that he is glad to hear from his cousin, Princess Louise, that "you behave yourself so well and that she gives you so good a character. I hope you will do nothing to give her reason to alter her opinion of you, and that you will do nothing to make me less kind to you than I am, and you shall upon all occasions find me as kind as you can desire." Next year, he sends Sir Henry Tichborne, a reliable Catholic, over to fetch her back to England, and at Tichborne she is to stay.

The year after he found her a suitable marriage: the heir to the old Catholic family of Waldegrave. We see, in everything he did, what a consistent *dévot* James was. In June, 1684, the head of the family having died, "now that Sir Henry is come to the estate I must recommend you both to be good managers, and to be sure to live within what you have and be sure to have a care not to run out at first." We also see what a careful man he was about money.

Next we hear news of the two boys. "I was very sorry to hear this morning of the accident which happened to your brother Harry, and send this footman on purpose to you, to have an account from you how he does. They tell me his face will not be marked with it . . . Remember me to your brother James, and tell him I am sorry his journey should be stopped for some days, especially by such an accident; and tell Harry I hope he will be carefuller for the time to come, and now that he do what the chirurgeons will have him . . ."

The two boys had been sent early to school in France, under the care of an Oratorian, Father Gough, at the Oratory school at Juilly, and afterward at Plessis. In 1684 they were brought to England to be presented to their uncle, Charles II, and were then sent back, on the advice of the egregious Father Petre, to the Jesuit College of La Flèche. At seventeen, the elder boy had his first experience of war, fighting in the plains of Hungary against the Turks. At the great victory of Mohács, it was rumored that Berwick had been killed. James, now King, wrote September 1, 1687: "Two days ago I was very much alarmed by the letters which came from France about your brother Berwick; but now, God be thanked, I am at ease concerning him, for . . . I find he was very well recovered though still a little weak; and I believe the Earl of Kinnoull, who died at Mohács, was the occasion of that report."

It seems that James was fond of his daughter by Arabella. In this same year, 1687, he made her husband Comptroller of the Household; next year, a month before his flight from the realm, James sent Waldegrave to France with a large sum of money for future use. It was needed. A year later, Waldegrave died at the exiled court at St. Germain. Henrietta was free to follow her inclinations. These led her to fall in love with Lord Galmoye, a Catholic member of the Butler clan. In 1695, Dangeau says, she found herself in a state in which no widowed lady should be: she was sent into a convent.[30] On her emergence it was rumored, though not certain, that she married Galmoye: they had loved each other for a long time and had, says Dangeau, given each other proofs of it.[31] But James and his wife would not receive them. Shortly after, his daughter, sick of exile and silliness, made terms with William III and returned alone to England, where she lived the rest of her days.[32] She may be said to have opted for the Churchills against the Stuarts, for her mother's side against her father's. For she lived in amity with her mother, and was remembered in her will. She died in the same year as Arabella, and was buried at Navestock in Essex, where a monument in the chancel recalls her memory.

It has usually been assumed that after James threw Arabella over, life had nothing more for her; that, impoverished and faded, she passed from the scene. The truth, however, provides no such morosely moral a conclusion.

Charles Godfrey was a fellow officer of her brother, Jack Churchill. Lady Drake had a sister, Mrs. Godfrey; she may have been Charles Godfrey's mother or grandmother, in which case he and Arabella would be cousins. We come upon his tracks in the documents of the time. He was with Churchill and a dozen young Life Guards serving under Vauban at the siege of Maastricht in 1673.[33] These Englishmen, led by Monmouth, were responsible for a gallant exploit: the storming of the half-moon in front of the Brussels gate. Captain Godfrey was given the honor of conveying the news of the fall of Maastricht to Charles II; but he did not get the expected knighthood.[34] At some point, he succeeded in storming Arabella's unoccupied heart, and they made a happy marriage of it.

We do not know when they were married; but in July, 1681, we find Arabella appearing in the family circle as godmother to John's eldest daughter, Henrietta, afterward Duchess of Marlborough in her own right.[35] Arabella and her husband followed her brother's career, and supported his interests, faithfully. They received their reward, which was not inconsiderable.

In the heyday of the Churchills, with the accession of Queen Anne, Godfrey became one of the Clerks of the Green Cloth—it is pleasant to think of him following in Sir Winston's steps—and Master of the Jewel Office. He was a very good sort of fellow, approved of by Swift, though a Whig. Swift tells Stella, September 20, 1711: "Today I was invited to the Green Cloth by Colonel Godfrey, who married the Duke of Marlborough's sister, mother to the Duke of Berwick by King James: I must tell you those things that happened before you were born." (Or perhaps he was thinking, rather, of posterity?) Next day: "Colonel Godfrey sent to me again today; so I dined at the Green Cloth, and we had but eleven at dinner, which is a small number there, the Court being always thin of company till Saturday night."[36] On October 5, "I dined with honest Colonel Godfrey, took a good walk of an hour on the terrace, and then came up to study; but it grows bloody cold, and I have no waistcoat here."[37]

Honest Colonel Godfrey died in the same year as the Queen: 1714.

He left all his lands, furniture, jewels, plate, etc., "unto my dear and
loving wife, Arabella Godfrey," whom he appointed his executrix.[38]
There is evidence of entire affection, complete confidence. To each of
his daughters and sons-in-law Godfrey left £100: token payments of
affection, for they were all well provided for. He left an annuity of £100
a year to his sister, wife of John Waldegrave: a brother-in-law of Arabella's daughter by James—Henrietta. What a small circle this was—
for all its European connections through the Stuarts and Marlborough
himself!

Nor did the Duke forget his sister. In his immense will, made in
1722—the year of his death—with its elaborate dispositions of the vast
wealth he had accumulated, there was included "an annuity of £400 in
trust for his sister Godfrey for life."[39]

When Arabella came to die, she was full of money. She left £4,000
in trust for her daughter, Lady Falmouth, and £1,000 to her grandson,
James, Lord Waldegrave. To Lady Falmouth Arabella left "One pair
of my diamond ear-rings, of four great diamonds each," which she usually
wore (had they been a gift from James?). She left £500 to Lady
Waldegrave, and "my best pearl necklace." All the rest of her property,
which must have been considerable—"stocks in the Bank and South
Sea Company," ready money, plate, jewels, etcetera—she left to "my
dear daughter," Elizabeth Dunch, evidently her favorite, whom she
appointed her executrix.[40]

She left £5 to each of her children to buy a mourning ring. No
mention of the most famous of them, the Duke of Berwick, long since a
naturalized Frenchman and now a Marshal of France. During the long
wars that filled his early life, in which he and his uncle commanded
armies on opposite sides, there is only one inquiry recorded from him of
his mother. When only a boy, on campaign in Hungary, he writes home
an account of his first battle to his brother Henry, "I have taken two lusty
tall fellows and one sabre," and asks him to write his sister that Mr.
Thorp was killed.[41] At the battle of Landen in 1694, Berwick was captured by his uncle, Charles Churchill, and exchanged for the Duke
of Ormonde.[42] With his uncle Marlborough, in the War of the Spanish
Succession, he maintained more important relations.

What kind of a woman was she, whose fate was so curiously interwoven in our history?

An ordinary enough woman, whose inclinations were wholly domestic—if they had not been early wrested out of their course by her royal lover. Hamilton tells us that she was an indolent creature; and that may well have been true: though she inherited the Villiers' figure, she inherited none of their vivacity. She was a kindly, prudent, reserved woman, whose horizons were entirely bounded by the family. Nothing unpleasant or unkind is recorded of her; like all those children born in the ambivalent circumstances of Ashe, she knew well how to hold her tongue. Only a rumor of resentment at her treatment by James reached posterity, and that through Dangeau some years later.[43] He evidently got wind of the view held at St. Germain that Arabella regarded James with detestation after his departure—and this was thought unreasonable of her since he had recognized her children in spite of the Queen's strong opposition. But such a reaction is not unknown in such circumstances: no one ever said that she loved James; he merely took advantage of her.

When Hamilton describes her, she was only a girl, thin and pale. Time remedied that and filled out her lines, though she retained her pale complexion, her milk-white skin. From Lely's portraits of her she seems to have had her father's long nose, a more sensual face; there are the voluptuous lips, the amorous eyes, the hand invitingly defending the too-explicit breasts. Lely gave all his beauties this look—it was the mood, the fashion, the foible of the time: the smoldering eyes, the languor of the expression, the seductive disarray of dress, the suggestiveness of pose.

For the rest, when Arabella died in 1730,* a very old woman of eighty-two, she could look back over it all, in the flickering intervals of her memory, with some satisfaction. Though no countess, and open—like everybody else—to the tart remarks of her sister-in-law, Sarah, it had been a strange, richly fulfilled fate after all, taking an unexpected course from those unpromising, unprosperous beginnings.

Horace Walpole, who had the true historian's unappeasable nostalgia for the life of the past and treasured its evidences in scraps and oddities, carried the memory of Arabella—it is extraordinary to think—up to the end of the eighteenth, the threshold of the nineteenth, century. One day in the hot summer of 1759, we find him visiting Navestock, with its *allées* of limes and green canal; within were the French glasses, the commodes, screens and portraits, "a deal of noblesse *à la St. Ger-*

---

* She died May 4, and was buried May 10, in Westminster Abbey, in the grave of her brother George, the Admiral, near the choir door. J. L. Chester, *Registers of Westminster Abbey,* 328.

main."[44] There were James II, Charles II, the Duke of Berwick and the rest, "above all, *la Godfrey,* and not at all ugly, though she does not show her thighs." Two years later: "I have picked up at Mrs. Dunch's auction the sweetest Petitot in the world*—the very picture of James II, that he gave Mrs. Godfrey—and I paid but six guineas and a half for it—I will not tell you how vast a commission I had given."[45]

One day in 1764, the Berwicks—the third generation of them—came to visit Horace. "They have the grace to call themselves Lirias here, yet they do not go to Court, and say that they are only come to see their relations . . . He had never heard that his great-grandmother married Mr. Godfrey; he told me today that she called herself Churchill, but that her family name was Marlborough."[46] Horace forgot nothing of the past: he was fond of recalling that he had known six generations of the Waldegraves. When very old, in 1785, he recalled his memory of Arabella: "I was a schoolfellow of the two last Earls of Waldegrave, and used to play with them in the holidays when I was about twelve years old. They lived with their grandmother, natural daughter of James II. One evening while I was there, came in her mother, Mrs. Godfrey, that King's mistress—ancient, in truth, and so superannuated that she scarce seemed to know where she was. I saw her another time in her chair in St. James's Park, and have a perfect idea of her face, which was pale, round and sleek."[47]

This was a whole century after the events and days we have been recording. We must return.

---

* Evidently a miniature painted on enamel.

CHAPTER VIII

John and Sarah

I

MEANWHILE, Arabella's brother John was growing up into handsome young manhood.

He had been at school in Dublin and, for a time, it seems, at St. Paul's. But he was never much of a scholar, unlike his father. His genius was for action: action—and diplomacy. He took more after the Villiers side of the family; he certainly had their ravishing looks. To these he added the courtesy and manners that had so distinguished the first Duke of Buckingham. Courts are much more responsive to beauty, whether in women or men; and the youth's striking looks did not go unnoticed. James made him his page and used to take him with him to Hyde Park when drilling the Guards—a favorite amusement with that dullhead. He noticed his young attendant's keenness and, one day, asking him what career he wished for, John fell on his knees dutifully and asked for "a pair of colours" in one of the Guards regiments. On September 14, 1667, his commission was made out as ensign to the King's own company in Colonel Russell's regiment of Foot Guards.[1] John was just turned seventeen: so began the long connection of the greatest of English soldiers with the Grenadiers.

Next year he was sent to Tangier and spent the greater part of three years in that Mediterranean outpost, which had been added to our dominions by Charles's self-sacrificing marriage to Catherine of Braganza. This was the most tangible asset that came to us from the Portuguese marriage, and we should have done well to hold on to it. The King and his advisers realized the strategic value of the place—key to the Western Mediterranean; but it was expensive to garrison and it became a bugbear to the House of Commons, to whose ignorance it was sacrificed in the end. Not till we won Gibraltar in 1704 did we have an equivalent.

114

These three years, though we know nothing of them, were of great importance in the formation of that masterly military mind. Field Marshal Wolseley says, "we know little of Churchill's doings at Tangier, beyond the fact that he was constantly engaged with the enemy, who closely invested the place. He took part in frequent sallies made by the garrison, and showed remarkable daring in numerous skirmishes with the Moors, whose enterprise often took the form of cutting off, by means of cleverly laid ambushes, those who ventured to straggle beyond the British lines. Churchill was thus able whilst a boy to test his nerve, and to accustom himself to danger and to the curious sensation of being shot at."[2] Coolness of nerve was, indeed, one of Churchill's many gifts; he often exposed himself on the field of battle in later years as Commander in Chief, but he was never known to be rattled.

More important, it was these apprentice years that implanted the appreciation of the strategic value of the Mediterranean that Marlborough never lost sight of in all the vast complexities and burdens, military, political and diplomatic, that rested upon him as Generalissimo of the Grand Alliance. To this we must add an equal appreciation of the importance of sea power in the conduct of over-all military operations.

We now know that the young subaltern, eager for experience, in his third year in the Mediterranean exchanged land service for sea, and took part in the expedition against Algiers. He may have returned home on leave before it, for he would need equipment and, of course, there was no money. We have an order from the King to the Vice-Treasurer of Ireland, March 21, 1670, commanding him to pay Sir Winston his arrears of £140 for diet and lodging during service in Ireland, since it had been represented that Sir Winston had bestowed that sum on John "for and towards his equipage and other expenses in the employment he is now forthwith by our command to undertake aboard our fleet in the Mediterranean seas. We, being graciously willing to give all due encouragement to the forwardness and early affections of the said John Churchill to our service, and also in just satisfaction to the father," ordered this sum to be paid "in particular bounty to the said John Churchill."[3]

In the winter of 1670-71, Churchill returned from the Mediterranean, bronzed and fit, eager not only for military experience, to his place at Court, where other arms awaited him. His cousin Barbara, now made Duchess of Cleveland, was still the reigning beauty, though she and the King—like the restless, promiscuous spirits they were—had tired of each other.

In any case, no one could have supported Barbara long, in either sense of the word "support"; for she was both wildly extravagant and of an intolerable temper. Only Charles would have put up with her: he was easygoing and, being King, had the nation's purse to dip into. Gone were the rapturous early days of the Restoration, when Dryden could address the favorite with a perhaps pardonable exaggeration—Dryden was always a gentleman, and always a sycophant:

> You sit above, and see vain Men below
> Contend, for what you only can bestow;
> But those great actions others do by chance,
> Are, like your beauty, your Inheritance:
> So great a soul, such sweetness joined in one,
> Could only spring from noble Grandison:
> You, like the stars, not by reflection bright,
> Are born to your own Heaven and your own light;
> Like them are good, but from a nobler cause,
> From your own knowledge, not from Nature's laws.
> Your Power you never use but from Defence,
> To guard your own, or others' Innocence . . .*

We have seen what she was capable of in her cabal against Clarendon. She was certainly not without resource. When Charles's feelings for Moll Davis grew too high, Barbara had entertained the dancer to supper on her way to the King and administered her a jalap in the sweet, which had the effect of very much disappointing the King in his intentions with her.

Since Dryden wrote his lines, Barbara had presented the King with a whole family of children—though there was doubt about the paternity of one or two. After some protest and mutual recriminations, Charles accepted (and provided for) them all. But she never put herself out to make the King easy; indeed, after she found out that ease was what he valued most, she made him purchase it at a constantly heightened price: scenes, propitiation, gifts, demands; scenes, forgiveness, grants and titles followed in the regular order of the dance she led him. What a fool he was!—she should have been beaten. One day, when the King ventured to put her intolerable cousin and his crony, Buckingham, under

---

* "To the Lady Castlemaine, upon Her encouraging his first Play."

confinement, she called the King a fool openly to his face. When, on the grounds of her intimacy with Harry Jermyn's nephew, Charles refused to own the child she was expecting, she threatened she would bring it to Whitehall and dash its brains out against the walls. The King had to go down on his knees and beg forgiveness. What was more to the point, she got 5,600 ounces of plate from the Jewel House.[4]

She was a relentless gold digger. To console her for the libels circulated about her and the insults she received, Charles was made to present her with Berkshire House at St. James's. Two years later she sold the whole site with its gardens for building plots, making large sums on the transaction: her memory is preserved in this quarter, Cleveland Court and Square, Cleveland Row, St. James's. Next year she got what became an annual grant of £4,700 from the Post Office, and later she got grants for a term of years from excise and customs, in addition to the income she obtained from the sale of offices, the rents she exacted from placeholders. From Charles she extorted large sums—on one occasion £30,000—and grants of plate from the Jewel House. But her extravagance was such that she was still always out of funds. And no wonder—when she could appear at the theater one afternoon wearing jewels worth £40,000 (multiply!) or at night lose half as much at cards. She reached her apogee in 1670 when Charles created her Duchess of Cleveland—with remainder to her first and third sons, omitting the second for obvious reasons—and gave her outright Elizabeth I's favourite palace and park of Nonsuch. This the miscreant proceeded to dismantle and to sell all the contents: for which anyone who cares for the nation's heritage would have had her hanged by the common hangman.*

---

* Rochester seems to have had Barbara in mind in his lines on "Women":

> Her temper so extravagant we find
> She hates, or is impertinently kind;
> Would she be grave, she then looks like a devil,
> And like a fool, or whore, when she'd be civil;
> Can smile or weep, be foolish or seem wise,
> Or anything, so she may tyrannize:
> What she will now, anon she will not do,
> Had rather cross herself than not cross you.
> She has a prattling, vain and double tongue,
> Inconstant, roving and loves nothing long,
> Imperious, bloody, so made up of passion
> She is the very fire-brand of the nation.

One of her more unsuitable affairs with a footman is described in Marvell's "Last Instructions to a Painter."

By this time her amorous activities were as variegated as her financial depredations: she made the King share her favors with Jacob Hall, the ropedancer, whom she had picked up at Bartholomew Fair and whom she paid for his services. He must have been more satisfying than the King. Hamilton tells us that "his strength and agility charmed the public, even to a wish to know what he was in private; for he appeared, in his tumbling dress, to be quite of a different make from the fortunate Jermyn. The tumbler did not deceive Lady Castlemaine's expectations, if report may be believed, and as was intimated in many a song, much more to the honour of the rope-dancer than of the countess. But she despised all these rumours, and only appeared still more handsome."[5]

At this point, her cousin John, "grown a man, bronzed by African sunshine, close-knit by active service and tempered by discipline and danger," says our Sir Winston, "arrived home from the Mediterranean. He seems to have been welcomed . . . and by none more than Barbara, now become Duchess of Cleveland. She was twenty-nine and he twenty . . . Affections, affinities and attractions were combined. Desire walked with opportunity and neither was denied. John almost immediately became her lover, and for more than three years this wanton and joyous couple shared pleasures and hazards."[6] This is a gallant way of putting it: it was rather that Barbara, grown insatiable, setting eyes on the young Guards officer back from Africa, her cousin, felt that she must have him. Certainly, "the cynical, promiscuous, sagacious-indulgent sovereign was outwitted or outfaced."

The situation was not without its comedy, or its escapades. Two stories, which may have something in them, are well known. One is that John was in Barbara's bedroom when they heard the King approaching, and John, to save the Duchess's "honor"—that flexible, expendible commodity—leaped from the high window into the court below. For this, he was said to have been rewarded with a large sum. The other story is that Charles once surprised the couple in bed; but the easygoing monarch, well appreciating such situations, let his young officer off with "You are a rascal, but I forgive you, for you do it to get your bread."

There was a sting to this insult. For after a year or two of this, John was able to invest, in 1674, the considerable sum of £4,500 in purchasing an annuity of £500. It was the foundation of his financial security—no doubt always in view, from the impoverished days at Ashe—and of his immense fortune. It was only from Barbara that he could have got such a sum—and she was as generous with (other people's) money as she was with her own charms. What shocked contemporaries was not that the money had been thus earned, but that the young officer, instead of spending it in the expected fashion, should have proceeded prudently to invest it.

Barbara's last child, a daughter, Barbara, born July 16, 1672, was another fruit of this affair. It was generally held that this was John's child, and the Duchess had to provide for her herself. When she left the English Court in high dudgeon in 1677, she gave the nuns of the Immaculate Conception—a pretty touch—of the Rue Charenton in Paris £1,000, to bring the child up. The little girl grew up and made her profession as a nun, by the name of Sister Benedicta. But convent walls did not prevent the Earl of Arran from coming to her, by whom she became the mother of Charles Hamilton; nor did this prevent her ending happily as prioress of the convent of St. Nicholas at Pontoise.

Altogether, we may consider that, for a young Guards officer, to have known the Duchess must have been a very liberal education.

For the rest, during these years Churchill was living the life of a young soldier of the time who happened to be favored by his family's intimate position at Court. It was a small society in which points of "honor"—or dishonor—were quickly taken up and duels ensued, in which men were idiots enough to kill and get killed for a mere nothing. John, at twenty-one, was not above such nonsense. On January 6, 1671, we hear: "Yesterday was a duel between Mr. Fenwick and Mr. Churchill, who had for their seconds Mr. Harpe and Mr. Newport, son to my Lord Newport; it ended with some wounds for Mr. Churchill, but no danger of life."[7] The quarrel had begun, apparently, at a masquerade.[8] These two were to meet, on the more dangerous ground of politics, years later, when it proved fatal to Fenwick. In August there was a "rencounter" between Captain Herbert and "young Churchill. I know not the quarrel; but Herbert ran Churchill twice through the arm, and Churchill him into the thigh, and after, Herbert disarmed him. But what is the worse, I hear that Churchill has so spoke of it that the King and Duke are angry with Herbert."[9] We see that Churchill is something of a favorite already; in time to come, this same correspondent describes him as "the only favourite of his master."[10]

Meanwhile, the remedy for this sort of thing was action.

Next year, with the joint war of France and England against the Dutch, it came. At the murderous battle of Sole Bay, the 1st Company of the Guards served immediately under James, upon the deck of the flagship, the *Prince*—main target of the attack. There was a ghastly slaughter of officers, and, after the battle, Churchill received a double promotion: from Guards ensign to Marine captaincy. Next year, the Admiralty regiment in which he now held a company was serving on land under the French king. The exploit of the English company under Monmouth, under whom Churchill and Godfrey served, when the half-moon work in front of the gate at Maastricht was carried, took place under Louis's eye. Afterward, Churchill, who had been wounded at Monmouth's side, was publicly congratulated on parade by the great man himself. Another young subaltern had joined in the gallant assault, against orders: Villars. Monmouth wrote home to his father commending Churchill: "here is the brave man who saved my life."[11] What ironic vistas war opens up: Marlborough defeating Monmouth at Sedgemoor, Villars at Malplaquet!

When England withdrew from this indefensible war—product of the Secret Treaty of Dover—a number of troops were left on the Continent in French pay. They were rapidly reduced in number and units were combined. Churchill received the reward of his gallantry at Maastricht by being promoted Colonel of a regiment in the service of France. One sees how ambivalent his career was made by the circumstances of the time, from his earliest days: it was not without its effect on his personality. Before taking command of his regiment, he had to be presented at Versailles and Louis greeted once more the "young Adonis in scarlet and gold" who as an elderly man proved the old King's greatest opponent.

Before his return, he took part under the famous Turenne in the grim battle of Enzheim. On this October day, 1674, Turenne made a surprise attack on the Imperialists' army with only half their numbers. The brunt of the fighting fell upon the English and Irish regiments, especially upon Churchill's, which had half its officers killed or wounded

in the bitter struggle for a wood that lay between the two armies.
Feversham reported: "One and all accomplished marvels . . . No-one in
the world could possibly have done better than Mr. Churchill has done
and M. de Turenne is very well pleased with all our nation."[12] Churchill
had been allotted the post of honor by Turenne, who clearly had confidence in him. What is more arresting is the cool assessment of the
battle made by the young Colonel, with its laconic, implied criticism
of the great Turenne. Churchill wrote to Monmouth: "Half of our foot
was so posted that they did not fight at all."[13] There is a quiet, but
damaging, criticism of the master's dispositions; there speaks, at twenty-
four, an instinct for economy in war, which was a leading characteristic
in Turenne's most brilliant pupil.

More than a quarter of a century elapsed before Churchill had the
opportunity to display his military genius. "From 1671 to 1675 he ex-
hibited all those qualities which were regarded as the forerunners in a
regimental officer of the highest distinction. He won his way up from
grade to grade by undoubted merit and daring . . . At twenty four he
was a colonel. He was fifty-two before he commanded a large army . . .
By the time he arrived at the highest command he was passing the prime
of life, and older than many of the leading generals of the day."[14]

It offers a parallel with his famous descendant, who did not arrive
at supreme power until he was sixty-five, at that moment of supreme
danger in 1940: *annus mirabilis.*

2

The young Colonel came home in 1675* to engage in operations
which proved the most difficult he ever had to conduct, against a formidable opponent. This was Sarah Jennings, then at the mature age of
fifteen. He was ten years older, and—in spite of his experience with his
cousin—by no means a match for her.

Sarah was the younger sister of Frances, "la belle Jennings," whose
dazzling looks made such an impression at the Court of Charles II. But
it was no use: both of them as masterful as they were beautiful, they

---

* He must have returned in the autumn. It is pleasant to note the items in
the two trunks of silver plate, belonging to his equipage, for delivery of which there
is a warrant from the Custom House, October 8, 1675: one basin, two great dishes,
three dozen plates, four candlesticks, two ewers, two massarines (pie dishes),
chafing dishes, one teapot, one chocolate pot, salts, cups, spoons, etc. *Cal. Treasury
Books,* 1672-75, 380.

were impregnable. They took part in all the public activities of the Court—the masquerades and balls, the dancing and routs—but they were proof against more dangerous allurements. Marriage was the only way to their favors, as Churchill had to learn. "La belle Jennings" married first Anthony Hamilton's brother, and, later, tall Dick Talbot, whom we have come across with Sir Winston in Ireland. James II made him Lord Lieutenant of Ireland; so that Frances Jennings ended up as Jacobite Duchess of Tyrconnel, though she managed, in an ambivalent world, to maintain good relations with the Marlboroughs.

Sarah was not quite so startlingly lovely as her sister; but she was quite beautiful enough, with cherry lips, inclined to be petulant, her flashing blue eyes and regular nose, with its indication of willfulness and determination, the gold hair that was washed in honey, people said, and showed never a gray hair even when she was a grandmother. Though younger, she was a more powerful personality than her sister. She early showed her mettle by pushing her mother out of Court: though under age, she was well capable of looking after herself.

The Jennings family were more established than the Churchills and better off; they, too, had been West Country by origin. We have seen that they had owned the manor of Churchill in Somerset, and sold it to Sir John Churchill. They were Royalists, and now the father was dead; so the sisters were heiresses—though not in a large way, enough to add to their spirit of independence. They owned the estate of Holywell, near St. Alban's, which remained always a favorite residence with Sarah, who later bought her sister's share of the inheritance.

The sisters had their place in the household of the new Duchess of York; but Sarah's hold was due to the place she had in the affections of Anne Hyde's younger daughter, the Princess Anne—a favorite with her father, James. Years afterward, Sarah wrote: "the beginning of the Princess's kindness for me had a much earlier date than my entrance into her service . . . We had used to play together when she was a child, and she even then expressed a particular fondness for me. This inclina-- tion increased with our years. I was often at Court, and the Princess always distinguished me by the pleasure she took to honour me, preferably to others, with her conversation and confidence. In all her parties for amusement, I was sure, by her choice, to be one."[15] There is no reason to doubt the essential veracity of this. Poor Anne, to be sure, would not be much good at amusing herself.

A bundle of letters remains to testify to the difficulties John encountered in these years of his courtship.[16] When they open, he is already in love—and, it would seem, for the first time. "My Soul, I love you so truly well that I hope you will be so kind as to let me see you somewhere today, since you will not be at Whitehall. I will not name any time, for all hours are alike to me when you will bless me with your sight." That sounds like the genuine eloquence of love, and he already swears, "You are, and ever shall be, the dear object of my life, for by heavens I will never love anybody but yourself."

To that Sarah could reply, and no doubt did: "What about Barbara? Did you not love her?" The answer was, apparently not.

John sends note after note, urging a meeting. "I fancy by this time that you are awake, which makes me now send to know how you do, and if your foot will permit you to give me the joy of seeing you in the Drawing Room this night." It seems he was not vouchsafed that joy: "My Soul, it is a cruel thing to be forced in a place when I have no hopes of seeing you, for on my word last night seemed very tedious to me; wherefore I beg you will be so kind to me as to come as often as you can this week, since I am forced to wait" (i.e., on the Duke).

Not at all: the girl's heart is not touched; she does not come, sends word she is not well. She keeps him waiting: she well knows the art, young as she is. And indeed the experienced young officer, who knows the ways of women, always did have more heart than Sarah and was at a corresponding disadvantage in dealing with her. Now he is sick, and we hear several times of the headaches that tortured him in the field in later life—perhaps psychological manifestations of the strain he was under and the price he paid for the marvelous self-control he showed, in everything except his love for Sarah. He was now completely under her spell: "I was last night at the ball, in hopes to have seen what I love above my own soul, but I was not so happy, for I could see you nowhere, so that I did not stay above an hour."

Another time: "I stayed last night in the Drawing Room expecting your coming back, for I could have wished that we had not parted until you had given me hopes of seeing you, for, my soul, there is no pain so great to me, as that when I fear you do not love me." There is the authentic note, not merely of passion, but of love itself. But there are shadows in the path: "do not be so ill-natured as to believe any lies that may be told you of me, for on my faith I do not only now love you, but do desire to do it as long as I live."

What were these shadows, the lies told about him? They can only refer to continuing relations with Barbara, or to gossip—in that small circle, where everybody knew everybody else's most intimate affairs— about him and other women. Now he is going away, perhaps being sent by James on a confidential mission to France. "My Soul, I go with the heaviest heart that ever man did, for by all that is good I love you with my heart and soul, and I am sure that as long as I live you shall have no just reason to believe the contrary. If you are unkind, I love so well that I cannot live, for you are my life, my soul, my all that I hold dear in this world."

For an untutored soldier, he was not expressing himself badly— "Love bade me write." "By all that is good" is the favourite phrase by which he swears when thinking of her: evidently he did not think of his relations with Barbara as coming into that category. That was the clue: her youth and innocence, her virtue and chastity. What was it that he wanted? If it were just that and no more, he could wait forever. There had been no word of marriage from his eloquent pen. If she yielded what so many other ladies at Court made no such fuss about, that would be the end of any thought of marriage, his passion satisfied. Fortunately, she was not tempted: she had not been aroused physically: she could wait.

She made a quarrel with him: she turned her back on him in the Duchess's Drawing Room. At once he is at her feet. "To show how un-reasonable you are in accusing me, I dare swear you yourself will own that your going from me in the Duchess's Drawing Room did show as much contempt as possible. I may grieve at it, but I will no more complain when you do it, for I suppose it is what pleases your humour. I cannot imagine what you meant by your saying I laughed at you at the Duke's side, for I was so far from that, that had it not been for shame I could have cried. And, for being in haste to go to the Park, after you went, I stood near a quarter of an hour, I believe, without knowing what I did."

John was plainly in love; the tricks of this girl, now sixteen, were what anyone of his age and experience should have seen through. Per-haps he did see through them, but could not help himself: he could not say the word "marriage"; he had not the means to make her an offer,

certainly not to support a family. It was for her to bring him to the point
—and, with superior tactical sense, she goes straight to it. She takes up
the pen: "If it were true that you have that passion for me which you
say you have, you would find out some way to make yourself happy—it
is in your power. Therefore press me no more to see you, since it is what
I cannot in honour approve of, and if I have done too much, be so just
as to consider who was the cause of it."

John can only fall back on his defenses, like many another man in
a similar predicament. He begins to despair: "as for the power you say
you have over yourself, I do no ways at all doubt of it, for I swear to you
I do not think you love me . . . You must give me leave to beg that you
will not condemn me for a vain fool that I did believe you did love me,
since both you and your actions did oblige me to that belief, in which
heaven knows I took so much joy that from henceforward my life must
be a torment to me for it. You say I pretend a passion to you when I
have other things in my head. I cannot imagine what you mean by it,
for I vow to God you do so entirely possess my thoughts that I think of
nothing else in this world but your dear self." There speaks the usual
man's hope of establishing the innocence of his intentions by asseverating
ignorance.

This did not take Sarah in: "As for seeing you I am resolved I never
will in private nor in public if I could help it. As for the last I fear it
will be some time before I can order so as to be out of your way of seeing
me. But surely you must confess that you have been the falsest creature
upon earth to me. I must own that I believe that I shall suffer a great
deal of trouble, but I will bear it, and give God thanks, though too late
I see my error."

From this exchange of letters we perceive several things. The girl
at last is touched, even agitated; we can see as much in the hurry of the
letter, almost without punctuation, even apart from what she says. From
what both she and John say, a real obstacle raises its head. This can be
nothing else but the pressure of John's parents to marry him to Catherine
Sedley. This was a good idea, an obvious one. John had no money and
little of an inheritance to look forward to; she would one day be rich,
inheriting a fortune from her father; she was intelligent and a good sort.
It was one of those projects that had everything in common sense to
recommend it, and John's parents pressed it hard. Duty and inclination
pulled him in different directions; for he had a strong sense of duty, and

no man was more ambitious. Considering all this, it is a strong tribute to his heart that it prevailed—almost the only time it ever did—against his head. For Sir Winston was certainly in negotiation with Sir Charles Sedley—and this was what was alarming Sarah, perhaps unconsciously acting as a precipitant upon her as yet unfixed affections.

John held firm. By the spring of 1677, the Sedley marriage was off. His crony, Harry Savile, Vice-Chamberlain of the Household and completely in the know, writes: "Mrs. Sedley's marriage with Jack Churchill neither is nor ever will be any more talked of, both the Knight and the Colonel [i.e., Sir Charles and Sir Winston] being willing to break off fairly—which important matter is referred to me by both parties, and for both their goods I think it is best it should cease."[17] A more exalted fate for Catherine was in view: the Duke had become infatuated with her. Instead of marrying John, she was on her way to ousting John's sister from the place of *maîtresse en titre* to the Duke; in time to come, she was to inhabit Arabella's house in St. James's Square, bought for her, with four times the establishment Arabella had ever been given.

In 1677, another obstacle from the path of true love was removed by Barbara packing all her traps and departing in disgust with everybody and everything to France, taking her child with her. This must have been as much of a relief to John as it was to the King, who sank back into the more consoling, if hardly less scrounging, arms of the Duchess of Portsmouth and Nell Gwyn.

The correspondence between John and Sarah could be resumed, the deadlock broken. He returned to the assault on her emotions, now that they had been touched. "It is not reasonable that you should have a doubt but that I love you above all expression, which by heaven I do . . . But Oh, my soul, if we might be both happy, what inexpressible joy would that be! . . . I will not dare to expect more favour than you shall think fit to give, but could you ever love me, I think the happiness would be so great that it would make me immortal."

We see that John is the romantic, the rhapsodist, the one with the ranging imagination; Sarah the rationalist, the woman of practical common sense. This contrast in their characters appears later in other relations, other aspects of their lives. She replies: "I am as little satisfied with this letter as I have been with many others, for I find all you will say is only to amuse me and make me think you have a passion for me, when in reality there is no such thing. You have reason to think it strange that I write to you after my last, where I protested that I would never write nor speak to you more; but as you know how much kindness I had for you, you can't wonder or blame me, if I try once more to hear what you can say for your justification . . . Therefore pray consider if, with honour to me and satisfaction to yourself, I can see you; for if it be only to repeat those things which you said so oft, I shall think you the worst of men, and the most ungrateful; and 'tis to no purpose to imagine that I will be made ridiculous in the world, when it is in your power to make me otherwise."

It is evident from this that tokens of affection had passed between them, and that Sarah, now seventeen, is willing to be married. But he need not imagine that she is going to be made a fool of by him, however fond she may be of him. The fear of being "made ridiculous in the world" always remained with her, a constant motive: it led her to actions later in life which had precisely that effect and made her a raging eccentric; but by then she was too rich, too independent, too careless of what anybody thought—and perhaps too odd—to mind.

John writes, "I have been so extreme ill with the headache all this morning that I have not had courage to write to know how you do; but your being well is what I prefer much above my own health . . . If the Duchess sees company, I hope you will be there; but if she does not, I beg you will then let me see you in your chamber, if it be but for one hour. If you are not in the Drawing-Room, you must then send me word at what hour I shall come." Dangerous? Apparently their understanding is now so clear that there is no danger.

The hussy replies: "At four o'clock I would see you, but that would hinder you from seeing the play, which I fear would be a great affliction to you, and increase the pain in your head, which would be out of anybody's power to ease until the next new play. Therefore, pray consider, and without any compliment to me, send me word if you can come to me without any prejudice to your health."

At that, John blew up. It was rather obtuse of him, in the masculine way, not to see that a woman's teasing is a mode of affection. With hurt feelings, he wrote a letter of resentful protest to Sarah's waiting woman. He got what he deserved from her mistress: "I have done nothing to deserve such a kind of letter as you have writ to me, and therefore I don't know what answer to give; but I find you have a very ill opinion of me, and therefore I can't help being angry with myself for having had too good a one of you; for if I had as little love as yourself, I have been told enough of you to make me hate you, and then I believe I should have been more happy than I am like to be now." The cat shows her claws in that: the unhappy reminder of Barbara and Catherine, the stories, the rumors, true and false, that circulated about him and them, making him "ridiculous in the world." There was no point in arguing with Sarah: John was not clever enough to keep his own end up; nothing to do but capitulate: "I am resolved to take nothing ill but to be your slave as long as I live, and so to think all things well that you do."

And that, in the event, was what came about.

These, in truth, were lovers' quarrels: the crisis in their relations was safely past; it was taken for granted that they were for each other: it was a question of finding ways and means. John still had reason to complain: "it was unkind of you to go away last night since you knew that I came for no other purpose but to have the joy of seeing you; but I will not believe it was for want of love, for you are all goodness, the thought of which makes me love you above my own soul."

Perhaps Sarah's tantrums were going too far—as they certainly were to do in the future. She reproaches John with loving her less than he did. It is necessary to bring him finally, irrevocably, to the point. She announces her intention of going to France with her sister. It was a superbly executed maneuver. John was forced to bring his talks with the Duchess, who is their one hope and looks on it all with a friendly eye, an open purse, to a conclusion.

John: "My heart is ready to break. I wish 'twere over, for since you are grown so indifferent, death is the only thing that can ease me. If that the Duchess could not have effected this, I was resolved to have made another proposal to her, which I am confident she might have effected, but it would not have brought so much money as this. But now I must think no more on it, since you say we cannot be happy." Stupid, that was precisely what Sarah was leading him on to think more on. Back comes the answer: "If your intentions are honourable [Really, at this late stage!] and what I have reason to expect, you need not fear my sister's coming can make any change in me, or that it is in the power of anybody to alter me but yourself, and I am at this time satisfied that you will never do anything out of reason, which you must do if you ever are untrue to me." She had got him exactly where she wanted him: at her feet, bound in marriage by a bond which, however errant he had been before, he would never break. The letters, regarded as a whole, expose a unique example of the art of landing a superb and difficult fish out of recalcitrant circumstances.

The catch was on the hook, the landing about to be made; now Sarah turns to offer a piece of practical woman's advice as to how best to manage the Duchess in the matter: "I have made many reflections upon what you said to me last night, and I am of the opinion that could the Duchess obtain what you ask her, you might be more unhappy than if it cannot be had. Therefore, as I have always shown more kindness for you than perhaps I ought, I am resolved to give you one mark more —and that is to desire you to say nothing of it to the Duchess on my account; and your own interest, when I am not concerned in it, will probably compass what will make you much happier than this can ever do." It did. It was a shrewd piece of advice that Sarah offered, and it clinched the matter. The marriage was made possible for them. Not all the advice that the Duke of Marlborough received from his Duchess, in the distant future, was as sound or as happy.

What the Duchess of York did for the couple we do not know— evidently some arrangements were made with regard to John's post, for he was now gentleman of the bedchamber to the Duke. The sad thing was that Sir Winston could do nothing for his son: he was in debt and John, upon whom the estates were entailed, had to sacrifice some part of his inheritance to raise cash for his father and himself at this juncture. With whatever he could manage to raise, the salary of his post and the annuity he had so gallantly earned, and with Sarah's perhaps equivalent income—she had expectations of more when her mother died—the couple came together. It was not much to live on in such a very grand society, still less to provide for a family; they would have to be very careful: fortunately, by disposition they both were.

When, years after, Sarah came to sum it all up, looking back upon it from an immense distance of age and fame, she said: "I don't know whether it is proper or necessary to add what I am going to write, though I think it a merit, that Sir Winston Churchill had about £1,000 a year from his father,* who liked his grandson better than his own son,

---

* I think that this must be an overestimate on Sarah's part, or that her memory betrayed her after so many years. Perhaps she had never known exactly what Sir Winston's estate was worth. The likely explanation is that the income from his estate and his salary from the Board of Green Cloth together equaled £1,000 per annum.

settled it upon him, that his father could only enjoy it for his life. But the Duke of Marlborough, when he was but eight and twenty [i.e., at the time of his marriage] joined with his father, who was in debt, and let him sell his estate. From the very beginning of his life, he never spent a shilling beyond what his income was. He began with the first commission of an ensign in the army, and went on regularly through every step in that profession; and in King Charles II's time served in France under Marshal Turenne, from whom he learnt a great deal." Then Sarah's radicalism of nature took charge of her pen: "And I think it more honour to rise from the lowest step to the greatest than, as the fashion is now, to be Admirals without ever having seen water but in a basin, or to make Generals that never saw any action of war and only felt from the generosity of their temper that they were not to pursue a flying enemy."[18] One can hear the very accents of her voice, positive, cutting, contemptuous, always in the right.

No one knows when or where precisely the marriage took place—probably in the privacy of the Duchess's apartments, and for several months it was kept secret.

It was, unlike most of the marriages in that age and society,* a love

---

* It is, amusingly enough, Sir Charles Sedley who describes the frequent situation in his poem, "The Happy Pair," in which the man

> values not the woman, but her store:
> Extends his treacherous pledge to golden charms,
> And joins his hands to none but spangled arms.
> He weds her jewels and her amber chains,
> But her rich self (that merits all) disdains:
> Her face he praises, but he courts her ears,
> Catching the glittering pendants that she wears:
> Each eye no longer he esteems a star
> Than flaming rubies hung upon her hair:
> And judging love, without her gold, a curse,
> He scorns her virtue, and adores her purse.

> The woman too no less debased than he
> Gives not herself, but her gratuity;
> Soothes like a merchant with inveigling art,
> Demands her jointure and keeps back her heart.
> On terms and articles with pride proceeds,
> And seals her cold affections to her deeds:
> Stands off and treats like an imperious state,
> And baulks her happiness to be made great:
> Proclaims her fortune of a goodly size,
> And he that offers most obtains the prize . . .

match; and the most courageous and imprudent action that that prudent couple ever committed. They never had cause to repent it. From this time to their dying day, they were in love with each other. Neither of them ever looked at anyone else. Sarah's strength of will, extraordinary for a mere girl, conditioned John in the course of that protracted and argumentative courtship. He had promised to become her slave, and all his life he remained so: in fact, he spoiled her, letting her have her way in all things.

Their passion for each other lasted always. The famous Duke, departing for the wars many years later, wrote: "It is impossible to express with what a heavy heart I parted with you when I was at the waterside. I could have given my life to have come back, though I knew my own weakness so much I durst not, for I should have exposed myself to the company. I did for a great while have a perspective glass looking upon the cliffs in hopes I might have had one sight of you."[19] We know by verbal tradition that on his homecomings the Duke "pleasured" his wife before ever taking off his boots.

On her part: "Wherever you are, whilst I have life, my soul shall follow you, my ever dear Lord Marlborough, and wherever I am I should only kill the time wishing for night that I may sleep and hope the next day to hear from you."

When he was dead, she became his slave, devoting herself to his memory. Hence one of the greatest sayings of any woman in history, when her hand was sought by the proud Duke of Somerset: "If I were young and handsome as I was, instead of old and faded as I am, and you could lay the empire of the world at my feet, you should never share the heart and hand that once belonged to John, Duke of Marlborough."

In the long empty years without him, she often turned over the letters she had kept: "Some copies of my letters to Mr. Churchill before I was married and not more than 15 years old," she wrote, folded them up and put them carefully away. She meant to burn them before she died; but in the last year of her life, in the shaky hand of extreme old age: "Read over in 1743 desiring to burn them, but I could not do it."

CHAPTER IX

Court Life and Home Life

I

WITH his private life and happiness now on a settled foundation, Churchill could go forward, with a more contented mind, on his career. At first the only home he and Sarah had in the country was with his parents at Minterne. We find him toiling up and down the dusty roads to his native Dorset in summer, going to and from Whitehall at the Duke's summons. Sarah was more at Minterne, with what consequences we can imagine. John's diplomacy was needed between the two women: he thanks Sarah for writing his mother: "if she takes anything ill that is in that letter, you must attribute it to the peevishness of old age, for really there is nothing in it that she ought to take ill. I take it very kindly that you have writ to her again, for she is my Mother, and I hope at last that she will be sensible that she is to blame in being peevish."[1]

Diplomacy was called for in every relation of what his descendant has well called John's "anxious, toilsome and troubled life," perhaps from the earliest days at Ashe. It came as more than "second nature" with him: it became his nature itself; so that by temperament he was exceedingly well fitted for the other half of his life's work.

These next years were filled with such labors: the chief confidant of James, going to and fro between the King and the Duke—he was the chief channel of communication between the two brothers when they were away from each other—between Whitehall and Versailles, James and Louis XIV. We may regard it all as his apprenticeship for the years when he was not only the military arm, but the diplomatic braincenter, of the Grand Alliance.

In March, 1678, he was summoned up from Minterne by the Duke: "I got to town by a little after three, very weary. However, I dressed and

132

went to the Duke for to know what he had to command me."[2] What was in question at this time, we remember, was this country's joining with Holland in the alliance to contain Louis' aggressions in Europe. Such was Danby's policy, and it would have united the nation behind the monarchy. Even James favored it; Charles kept his own counsel. Churchill was sent over to Holland to make the military arrangements for our intervention; Sidney Godolphin was sent to manage the political negotiations.[3]

Godolphin, who was five years Churchill's senior, was a coming man in politics: one of the "Chits," the three young men supposed to possess the King's confidence at this moment.[*] Of a Cornish Royalist family— Sidney had been called after his uncle, the Cavalier poet killed in the Civil War—Godolphin and Churchill had long been known to each other and they had much in common. They had both begun as pages in royal service; then their courses diverged: Churchill going into the army and serving abroad, Godolphin remaining always at Court. They had a similar West Country background, small gentry, not rich—though the Godolphins were of more consequence. They came from the house that still largely remains, with its gray granite colonnade at the northern foot of Godolphin Hill near Helston, out of which came their wealth. But Sidney's mother was a Somerset woman—one sees a portrait bust of another uncle of his, a splendid Caroline bronze, on the wall of the chancel in Bruton church.

Godolphin, too, had had a long and difficult courtship, of Margaret Blague—well-known to Sarah, since they were both maids of honor. In Margaret's case, the difficulties were chiefly made by John Evelyn, who was her spiritual mentor—and perhaps something of a satyr, since he wished to keep her away from married happiness for religion, and himself.[4] Evelyn's *Life* of Margaret Godolphin was a work of religious piety very popular with Victorians: we understand better the psychological nature of his relation to her and his motives. Margaret appears as no such

---

* Cf. R. North, *Life of Lord Guilford* (Bohn ed.), 230, for a portrait of Godolphin at this time. "Mr. Godolphin was a courtier at large, bred a page of honour; he had, by his study and diligence, not only all the classical learning but all the arts and entertainments of the Court; and being naturally dark and reserved, he became an adept in Court politics. But his talent of unravelling intricate matters and exposing them to an easy view was incomparable. He was an expert gamester and capable of all business in which a courtier might be employed. All which, joined with a felicity of wit and the communicative part of business, made him be always accounted, as he really was, a rising man at Court."

paragon in the pages of Hamilton, though she was a lady of virtue: she had that commodity in common with Sarah.* With great difficulty, and in secrecy, Godolphin married her and they were happy. In the autumn of this very year she died, leaving Godolphin and Evelyn alike disconsolate. The latter erected his memorial to her; Godolphin never married again. Later, he developed a platonic affection for James's young Duchess; and when they came to the throne, Godolphin was made Chamberlain to her household.

Godolphin and Churchill were both West Country Royalists by origin, Tories by conviction and affiliation. They had more in common. That shrewd judge of men, Charles II, said of Godolphin that he was "never in the way and never out of the way." He and Churchill were essentially servants of the state. There was a certain impersonality in their attitude to affairs; they were both reserved, prudent, dependable and loyal, and they were honest men. Churchill was more ambitious, and he had a not unworthy passion for money. Godolphin did not care greatly for power, and for money not at all; his passion was for horseracing. He was essentially an administrator, rather than a party politician; and though he spent a lifetime at the Treasury, he died a poor man.

We do not hear of Godolphin and Churchill together until this mission to Holland in 1678: it must have had the importance of cementing their friendship and alliance. Henceforth, their careers and lives became more and more closely interwoven; until, under Queen Anne, they achieved the famous partnership that brought Louis XIV low, Marlborough in command abroad, Godolphin as Lord Treasurer at home. Before this, they had achieved a closer tie: Godolphin's only son married Marlborough's eldest daughter, and their son, if he had lived, would have inherited Marlborough's dukedom. Except for Marlborough, Godolphin was the only person who had much sway with Sarah and who had her unreserved regard and affection. She recognized his goodness and disinterestedness, his unselfishness and care for her and hers. When he died, she wrote in her Bible that he "was the best man that ever lived."

The mission to Holland had the further importance that for the

---

* On December 15, 1675, Evelyn saw these two perform, along with the Princesses Mary and Anne, in a masque at Court, *Calisto or the Chaste Nymph*: "my dear friend, Mistress Blague, having the principal part, performed it to admiration. They were all covered with jewels." These, at any rate, *were* chaste nymphs. *Diary and Correspondence*, ed. W. Bray, II, 94.

first time Godolphin and Churchill were doing business with William of Orange. That young man, who was without the social graces of his ancestor William the Silent, nevertheless became by his achievement, like him, one of the grand figures of European history. All his life, from the time of the terrible threat to his country in 1672, he pursued unswervingly the aim of reducing Louis XIV; all his life the Dutch Stadholder fought the Grand Monarch; he was the architect of the alliance that accomplished his life's object. Nephew of the King of England, married to James's elder daughter Mary, who was the next heir to the throne, William was a factor of the first importance in English politics.

William was the same age as Churchill; though he had not Churchill's genius as a soldier, he possessed an even greater spirit, a lofty and indefeasible moral courage. Equally silent and farsighted, he must have welcomed the opportunity to make the acquaintance of these two young Englishmen, his future subjects, whose minds were ultimately ruled by the idea of the well-being of their country.

In the negotiations, the proposal was that James should be Commander in Chief. Perhaps it was as well that they came to nothing. Charles had no intention of intervening in the war: sufficient for him if the threat of it induced Louis to incline to peace. Churchill wrote to allay Sarah's anxiety: "You may rest satisfied that there will be certain peace in a very few days . . . therefore be not concerned when I tell you that I am ordered over and that tomorrow I go . . . I believe it will be about the beginning of October before I shall get back, which time will appear an age to me, since in all that time I shall not be made happy with the sight of you . . . So, dearest soul of my life, farewell. My duty to my Father and Mother." Later, when all these things were over, Sarah wrote on the treasured letter: "Lord Marlborough to ease me when I might be frighted at his going into danger."[5]

On his return, England was thrown into the panic of the Popish Plot, with all its incalculable political consequences. Charles was forced to send his brother into exile, and no doubt was glad to get him off his hands. James fixed himself at Brussels, with his intimate attendants, and there a small Court took shape. Churchill and Legge, whom old snobs like Reresby regarded as "scarce gentlemen," accompanied him. Then there were one or two ladies, of whom Lady Belasyse must have been a consolation—for she got twice Arabella's pension on the Irish establishment. The Princess Anne joined her father; Sarah was summoned over from Minterne and shortly afterward her beautiful sister arrived. So the ladies were happy; for James there was plenty of staghunting, and it looked as if the foxhunting would be very good too.

At this time, an attempt was made to make James to see reason on the religious issue: his obstinacy was rocking the throne, threatened to wreck his chances of the succession and was uniting the nation against him. It is not too much to say that at this time he was detested. It was no joke to be, with all one's belongings, in the boat with such a man, utterly dependent on him. All James's best friends tried to move him; it was left to Hyde to put the point directly, since he was his brother-in-law. The answer came back: "I assure you I will never try that way mentioned in yours to Churchill, and which also has been hinted to me by several of my best friends [they were, indeed], though I were sure it would restore me into the good opinion and esteem of the nation, which I once had; and therefore, I desire that neither you nor none of my friends will ever mention it to me, or flatter themselves that I can ever be brought to it: what I did was never done hastily, and I have expected many years and been prepared for what has happened to me, and for the worst that can yet befal me."[6]

He thus banged the door on his future in England: he got what he deserved.

At that moment Charles was struck down by his first stroke. Churchill was in England; it was agreed to send him over to bring James back hurriedly, in case the King died and the Whigs tried to set Monmouth on the throne. James came over in obvious disguise, in a black peruke and a plain suit without his Star and Garter, attended only by Lord Peterborough, Churchill and a couple of footmen not in livery; Churchill, "like a French officer in his scarf represented the best man in the company." And so to Windsor in the early morning, where James found his brother recovering; but the King did not dare to keep him in the country that was seething with anger and hysteria.

James had to go back to Brussels. Churchill was sent to Versailles, ostensibly to congratulate the Queen of Spain on her marriage.[7] The real purpose of the mission was to get Louis's support for James, on condition the latter identified his interests completely with Louis's. Louis did not think it worth offering an adequate sum. Nothing for James but continued exile, though he would not remain abroad. It was decided to send him to Holyrood, whence he could try his hand at governing Scotland.

That autumn James took the road to Edinburgh, with Churchill at his side. Sarah, expecting her first baby, had to be left behind in Jermyn Street, where her sister joined her to look after her. The child was born at the end of October, Sarah being then nineteen. John, on the road north: "You may guess by yourself how uneasy I have been since I left you, for nothing breathing ever loved another so well as I do you, and I do swear to you as long as I do live I will never love another . . . Mr. Legge leaves us this night, so that then I will write to you again; till when, my soul's soul, farewell."[8] The baby had arrived; John was weary with riding: from Stilton, "Pray kiss the child once for me."

At York, James was very coldly received, "which he never forgot afterwards."[9] John's thoughts were further south, on the house in Jermyn Street: "you cannot be truly sensible how much I desire to be with you. I swear to you the first night in which I was blessed in having you in my arms was not more earnestly wished for by me than now I do to be again with you, for if ever man loved woman truly well, I now do you, for I swear to you were we not married I would beg you on my knees to be my wife."[10] At the moment, he has been suffering from his violent migraine again: "which makes me melancholy, for I love you so well that I cannot think with patience of dying, for then we must part for ever, which is a dreadful thing to me that loves you above all expression." This does not say much for John and Sarah's hopes of a future state.

It is likely enough that John's recurring migraines were due to the increasing strain that he was under in serving James, the superhuman control that such a life demanded. He was anxious to obtain a post, a command, anything that would give him some independence, and his family some security. As it was, he had none: he was utterly dependent, all his fortunes embarked in that crazy vessel. As early as 1672 there was talk of his having the Vice-Chamberlainship of the Household: his friend, Harry Savile, was anxious to sell it and make the best of it, but of course John had no money and the Duke did not wish anyone else to have it.[11] Now there was talk of Churchill being made ambassador in Paris or at the Hague. Savile heard a rumor that Churchill was trying to supplant him, which much upset him for they had always been friends. Halifax assured him that this was untrue, with a marked tribute: "Churchill, whatever inclination he may have to be minister, will never give such a price for it as the supplanting of a friend."[12]

Then Barillon, the French ambassador, who knew everything and

everyone—many politicians on both sides were on his paybooks—
reported to Louis that the Prince of Orange wanted Churchill to be made
ambassador to Holland. "Mr. Churchill has the entire confidence of his
master, as your Majesty could see when he had the honour of presenting
himself to you last year." And then, with the professional's sense of
superiority: "he is not a man who has any experience of affairs."[13]

Churchill got none of these appointments: the truth was that he
was too indispensable to James. James confessed as much: "So long as I
am from him [i.e., the King], I would not willingly have Churchill from
me."[14] He could not get on without him. Churchill took no profit from
this indispensability: he was in part its victim. Among the numerous
politicians of both parties who appeared in Barillon's pay books, our
Sir Winston is quite right to point out: "one name is conspicuous by its
absence from these lists of shame—Churchill's."[15] In that age of unprin-
cipled men, who made all the more fuss of their principles, it was trimmers
like Halifax and Godolphin and Churchill who were remarkable for not
taking bribes. Of the "ubiquitous go-between," the ambivalent agent, who
made no such song and dance about high principle, Sarah wrote the
truth: "the Duke of Marlborough never took a bribe."

James was free to turn his accumulated resentment against the
temper of the Scots—a foretaste of what he would do in England, given
the power and the chance. It is true that the Covenanters were tiresome
and lugubrious fanatics; but so was he, on the other side. Torture was
no way to cure them of their illness: it merely aggravated the disease.
Reason, tolerance, skepticism are the only cure for such states of mind.
Of this James was totally incapable. The result was a parallel to Louis'
dragonnades of the Huguenots in France, which had James's enthusiastic approval. He brought in wild, but Catholic, Highlanders to hold
down the more civilized Lowlands; torture of the boot, hangings followed,
chasing the Calvinist *dévots* out of their homesteads with fire and
slaughter. The historical upshot was the creation of a saga of the martyrs,
a tradition, a legend; the practical consequence, an unquenchable spirit
of resistance: when the crisis came in 1688 all Lowland Scotland turned
against the King and went over to Dutch William.

What the sensible Churchills had to put up with while witnessing
James's fatuous conduct, Sarah has told us long after. Argyle, the
ablest brain in Scotland, was brought up before the Duke. "Marlborough told me he never heard a man speak more reason than he did to

the Duke; and after he had said what he first resolved, the Duke would never make answer to anything but 'You shall excuse me, my lord; you shall excuse me, my lord.' And so continued for a long time, whatever he said, without answering otherwise."[16] The fact was that the royal dunderhead was incapable of answering. What Sarah felt about James's rule, she has herself described: "for I saw it myself, and was much grieved at the trials of several people that were hanged for no reason in the world, but because they would not disown what they had said, that King Charles II had broke his covenant. I have cried at some of these trials, to see the cruelty that was done to these men, only for their choosing to die rather than tell a lie." All this had its influence in the end in making Sarah, with her rationalist frame of mind, into—what Marlborough never became wholly—a partisan Whig.

Nor was this wisdom after the event. We have evidence as to what Marlborough thought at the time in a secret letter to his cousin Legge: "I should make you both excuses and compliments for the trouble you have been at in sending my wife to me, but I hope it is not that time of day between you and I, for without compliment, as long as I live, I will be your friend and servant. My Lord Hyde, who is the best man living, will give you an account of all that is passed. You will find that nothing is done in what was so much desired, so that sooner or later we must be all undone . . . My heart is very full, so that should I write to you of the sad prospect I fear we have, I should tire your patience."[17] The rift was widening between the master and his servants, his best friends.

For Argyle's insistence that he took the oath of allegiance with the reservation "so far as it was consistent with the Protestant religion," James had him sentenced to death for high treason. Churchill deplored the sentence, and hoped, when Argyle escaped from prison, that no notice would be taken of it. Charles took no notice; when James became King, Argyle returned to raise rebellion.

Were James's private qualities much better than his public ones?

He showed up very badly in the episode of the sinking of the *Gloucester* in May, 1682. He was returning to Scotland for the last time, attended by Churchill; a small squadron and several yachts accompanied the vessel. Suddenly she struck a dangerous sandbank off Cromer and in an hour had foundered. There was plenty of time to get everybody off; but James's fatal obstinacy and hopeless judgment supervened. He was afraid to be thought a coward, so he would not give the order to abandon the ship until it was too late to save the people on board. He himself managed to get into the longboat—"so near was this poor kingdom to its deliverance," one might say, as Clarendon did of Cromwell's threat to leave England for America. James took with him his priests and his dogs, and a few of his friends, including Churchill. What Churchill thought of it all, we learn from Sarah years after, never from himself: "the truth of which I had as soon as Marlborough came to Scotland from his own mouth, (for I was there): who blamed the Duke to me excessively for his obstinacy and cruelty. For if he would have been persuaded to go off himself at first, when it was certain the ship could not be saved, the Duke of Marlborough was of the opinion that there would not have been a man lost. For though there was not boats enough to carry them all away, all those that were drowned were lost by the Duke's obstinacy in not coming away sooner. And that was occasioned by a false courage to make it appear as he thought he had what he had not; by which he was the occasion of losing so many lives. But when his own was in danger, and there was no hope of saving any but those that were with him, he gave the Duke of Marlborough his sword to hinder numbers of people that to save their own lives would have jumped into the boat, notwithstanding his royal Highness was there, that would have sunk it. This was done, and the Duke went off safe; and all the rest in the ship were lost."[18]

We may take it as an omen, with implications in several directions, of what happened in 1688.

These years of Popish Plot, Whig ascendancy, the King's first stroke and James's exile, were a time of constant negotiations and anxiety for Churchill. James was incessantly pestering the King with his advice: nothing but strong measures were any use against rebels; badgering him to allow him to come back to his side: how could Charles get on without him? Indeed the King could get on a great deal better without this nuisance on his hands. Churchill was sent south in 1681 to urge James's representations: not to allow Parliament to meet, an absolute monarchy and a French alliance, himself to be recalled from exile. But he cautioned Churchill not to communicate these matters to Halifax— the soundest brain of them all, who had saved James in the exclusion debates in the Lords—"as not likely to enter into such measures."[19] Certainly not; nor is it likely that they had Churchill's own agreement: his political line closely followed that of the wise and philosophic

Trimmer, and may well have been influenced by it. Their best friends sent him back with the advice to keep James out of harm's way at all costs. James merely registered resentment at the advice. Charles was engaged in a skillful rearguard action to save the prerogatives of the monarchy, and the succession, for his brother; taking full advantage of the excesses of the Whigs and their divisions, encouraging and exploiting the country's reaction against them, wearing them down with patience, waiting for the turn of the tide to come into haven at last.

Having won his last battle for the monarchy and its rights, supported by the Tory reaction, Charles could sink back into the peace and quiet he had achieved. In 1682 James was allowed to return from exile to his brother's side; in these last years he took full share in government as the second person in the kingdom, the accepted successor. Churchill received the reward of his labors with a Scottish peerage and, what was worth more, the command of the second troop of the Life Guards. He was spoken of for Secretary of State along with Sunderland. The Court said that this was grounded upon his having been learning to write lately. When the rumor came to Charles, he said pleasantly that he was not resolved to have two idle Secretaries.[20] It was true that Churchill was not well educated, certainly so far as book learning goes—though what an education he had received in more important matters!

It would seem that he was underestimated, like his father, by these gay, clever people. It was all taken in good part. The atmosphere had cleared: there was a *détente*: people could enjoy themselves. Churchill and Godolphin, both excellent players, were favorite tennis partners with the King, who tried to make up by excessive exercise for the ravages his other excesses made on his constitution. Then, one night at the end of January, 1685, he had his second stroke; after enduring tortures at the hands of his physicians, with his customary courtesy and philosophic resignation, he died.

James was King at last.

2

Meanwhile, a step had been taken in Sarah's fortunes which was more fruitful for the Churchills than anything in the relationship of John to the Duke, which was without an emotional element on either side. This was far from the case with the Princess Anne and Sarah: their relation was rooted in emotion, grew to a possessive intensity on one side and ended in a tragic breach—all of which exerted powerful effects upon history. The story has all the elements of a personal tragedy; what makes it the more exciting, and important, is that it was closely interwoven with public affairs and historic events.

We have noted the marked favor with which the Princess regarded Sarah from her early days at Court. It is not too much to say that Anne had a schoolgirl fascination for the companion who was five years her senior. Their characters and temperaments were complementary. There was a masculine element in the mind of the dazzling Sarah: forthright and fearless, she had a keen, incisive intelligence that was, as we have seen, more than a match for John, though he was ten years older. Though not well educated, she was a clever woman and by nature an intellectual: that gave her the advantage of inexhaustible resource, of constant interest and vivacity of mind that never failed her, when ordinary mortals faltered and paltered, and were dull, a prey to boredom. Sarah never: she had the indefeasible quality of the true intellectual: in herself she was never bored. I think this must have been a strong element in the unbroken fascination she had for John and in the intellectual ascendancy she came to exert over the most famous Englishman of the time. She was, as the late Duke of Marlborough says in his perceptive study of her, a maîtresse-femme.[21]

No one was a more feminine character than Anne; and, in spite of her plainness, her prosaic dullness, she is rather a touching figure. Left motherless by Anne Hyde's death, she was neglected and unloved all through her childhood: a pathetic little soul in that false and glittering Court. No one bothered to educate her; no one bothered to love her: these early impressions left their lifelong mark on her saddened heart. Like such children, she longed intensely for love: she rated it higher than anything else in the world. And she was very capable of returning it, with all the ardor of a sincere and simple nature. For she had a generous heart: nothing she would not give to those she loved. Then, too, she was truly religious—far more so than people who made a parade of their convictions: for her it took the place of a mental life, it was the consolation for loneliness. The most English of the Stuarts, she had a fund of common sense so conspicuously lacking in the line. In time, she developed a responsiveness to the moods and needs of her people that was wanting in cleverer and more intellectual persons: she was nearer them; it made her right when those were wrong. It was easy to underrate Anne, as Sarah—who had done so all her life—found in the end.

But now they were young, and they were complementary to each other: Sarah in all the pride and flourish of her spring; Anne still a girl, unsure of herself, but ready to give her heart unstintingly. All the more so to someone so self-confident and positive, where Anne was as yet so negative. Our Sir Winston says that there was "a romantic, indeed perfervid, element in Anne's love for Sarah," and thinks the affection "strangely intense." This is rather a masculine judgment: these things happen. And what more natural? Where Anne was silent and withdrawn, Sarah was lively and extrovert; Anne was reserved and restrained, Sarah was most unreserved and quite unrestrainable. She had the appeal that someone of high spirits and exceptional vitality has for the low-spirited and easily discouraged—especially, perhaps, when the latter is a person set apart by her birth for a position and a fate for which she lacks confidence.

It must be admitted that Anne had need of Sarah; Sarah no such need of her. Anne was in love, Sarah not: it is possible that, deep down, some sense of that rankled through the years and had its part in their eventual separation. Possibly even, love grew to detestation, as with Philip II and Antonio Perez; and in neither case could the long-privileged favorite of a sovereign believe the evidence of their senses or accept the verdict of time. Such are the tragedies of the human heart. For, in the end, Anne was—however dull and boring Sarah found her—a royal person, from whom all blessings flowed. When their differences were ineluctably revealed by time, and political exigencies rendered them acute and unbridgeable, they were wrenched apart with a loud noise that reverberated all over Europe and down the corridors of time.

In 1683 the Princess Anne was eighteen and marriageable. Her marriage was a matter of state, and even of European importance, since she was next in succession to the English throne after her sister Mary, married to William of Orange, and they had no children. Their cousin, Prince George of Hanover—son of that redoubtable woman, the Electress Sophia—had been invited over to England for inspection as a possible husband. Whether he did not like the prospect or Louis XIV—who took such a paternal interest in our affairs—did not approve, the young man departed without making a proposal. Anne was much mortified, and, with true Stuart temper, never forgave him. As Queen, later, she could not bear the thought of him as her successor and refused to allow him to come over and acquaint himself with the country he was to rule. It was a pity. George, though not a nice man, was an able one; the Hanoverian line more sagacious than the Stuart. It would have short-circuited a great deal of trouble, prevented the cruel scandal of Sophia Dorothea,* and provided a joint reign—after William and Mary—of Anne and George, 1702–27.

There remained the possibility of Prince George of Denmark, far better looking and much less intelligent. The Grand Monarch had no objection to him: a Lutheran who might at any time be converted to the true faith, perhaps carrying the Princess with him. (Pressure had already been brought upon her to become a Catholic, so far without effect. Her father's obstinacy, in her, stood her in good stead.) Prince George had already paid one visit to the country, in the company of Charles Churchill, who had been appointed a page of honor to the brother, King Christian of Denmark, ten years earlier. In June, 1683, John was sent over, with the royal yachts, to Glückstadt, to meet the King and Prince and escort the bridegroom to England.[22] Churchill's mission to Denmark was not purely ceremonial: several councils of war were held during his stay. The hesitation of the Elector of Brandenburg to commit himself was a check to designs for a northern alliance. On Churchill's departure the King presented him with a valuable ring and a sword set with diamonds.[23]

When a separate household was constituted for Anne on her marriage, the first thing she did was to get Sarah made a lady of her bedchamber: "the Duke came in just as you were gone, and made no difficulties, but has promised me that I shall have you, which I assure you is a great joy to me: I should say a great deal for your kindness in offering it, but I am not good at compliments."[24]

When the good-looking, heavy-feeding, stolid young Dane arrived, he found himself out of his depth in that sophisticated Court, where it was so easy to make a false step. Charles declared that he had tried him drunk and tried him sober and there was nothing in him. *"Est-il possible?"* was all that he could safely venture to say—or perhaps all he could think of—in that world of *sauve-qui-peut.* So they all called him *"Est-il possible?"* However, he settled down very contentedly with Anne, who became devoted to him; he gave her a child with uxorious regularity every year, all of whom died in infancy or Anne miscarried of them—except the little Duke of Gloucester.

---

* George I's wife fell in love with the fascinating Count Königsmark, was divorced and consigned to lifelong imprisonment at Celle.

Anne's feelings for Sarah were far too deep, and of too long standing, to be affected by marriage. Indeed, she needed her more than ever, with family and political difficulties thickening. "Kings and princes," Sarah wrote in her uncompromising way, "for the most part imagine they have a dignity peculiar to their birth and station, which ought to raise them above all connexion of friendship with an inferior . . . The Princess had a different taste. A friend was what she most coveted: and for the sake of friendship (a relation which she did not disdain to have with me), she was fond even of that *equality* which she thought belonged to it. She grew uneasy to be treated by me with the form and ceremony due to her rank; nor could she bear from me the sound of words which implied in them distance and superiority. It was this turn of mind which made her one day propose to me that whenever I should happen to be absent from her, we might in all our letters write ourselves by feined names, such as would import nothing of distinction of rank between us." No doubt they read the French and English romances of the time together, and this was in keeping with the tone of their world. "Morley and Freeman were the names her fancy hit upon; and she left me to choose by which of them I would be called. My frank, open temper naturally led me to pitch upon Freeman, and so the Princess took the other; and from this time Mrs. Morley and Mrs. Freeman began to converse as equals, made so by affection and friendship."[25] Though the Princess was well aware of her station, and never did anything to impair its dignity, this testified to the human need to have someone with whom she could relax and be as equals. Prince George became Mr. Morley, Lord Churchill Mr. Freeman; only one name was added to this very select circle: Lord Godolphin became Mr. Montgomery.

Sarah herself summed up their relations from the vantage point of later life, looking back upon their youth with a certain impersonality. She speaks of herself in the third person: "she now began to employ all her wit and all her vivacity, and almost all her time, to divert and entertain and serve the Princess; and to fix that favour which now one might easily observe to be increasing towards her every day. This favour quickly became a passion; and a passion which possessed the heart of the Princess too much to be hid. They were shut up together for many hours daily. Every moment of absence was counted a sort of tedious, lifeless state. To see the Duchess was a constant joy; and to part with her for never so short a time, a constant uneasiness—as the Princess's own frequent expressions were. This worked even to the jealousy of a lover. She used to say she desired to possess her wholly; and could hardly bear that she should ever escape, from this confinement, into other company."[26]

Sarah was an uncompromisingly or—one might equally well say— a compromisingly truthful woman. We do not need to corroborate her word; but if we did, here is the Princess: "if you will not let me have the satisfaction of hearing from you again before I see you, let me beg of you not to call me 'your Highness' at every word, but to be as free with me as one friend ought to be with another; and you can never give me any greater proof of your friendship, than in telling me your mind freely in all things, which I do beg you to do; and if ever it were in my power to serve you, nobody would be more ready than myself. I am all impatience for Wednesday, till when farewell."[27]

Marriage may be said to have added depth to the relationship; they now had each other's expectancies, each other's experiences, their joys and disappointments and sorrows to share. Anne continued to be emotionally dependent, the one demanding emotion. Sarah and John had at length achieved a secure and established family life. They even had a home. Had they not had to wait and work for it long enough? With the pay and perquisites of his posts, with the Colonelcy of the King's Own Royal Regiment of Dragoons and that of a troop of the Life Guards, he was at last well off. How magnificent they must have looked in their scarlet dress with gold lace; the chief officers' horses had their bridles gilded[28]— what a vivid, colored world it was, with its ceremoniousness only just covering the passions beneath! Often the passion broke through the crust of courtesy; but never, since his early days as a young officer, with John Churchill. Everyone noticed that it was impossible to penetrate his armor of good manners, of unfailing and distinguished courtesy.

In these years they extricated themselves from dependence on Minterne. Sarah succeeded to her share of her mother's property near St. Alban's. John was able to buy out her sister, and there they settled, at Holywell, and rebuilt the house. They made a pleasant place of it, laying out the gardens and walks, planting fruit trees, which the Duke saw in his mind's eye on battlefields abroad since they often appear in his letters, as with any other man much away from home. This was his home: "the pomp and magnificence of Blenheim were for his posterity."[29] Thither he sent the things he collected, tapestries, furniture, pictures, plate. A few evidences remain of their increasing wealth. In 1686, a hamper of china and other things arrives from the Hague, with a letter: "I could not get a skipper to take in the hamper, because they say they dare not bring tea in. What I have sent is the best of the kind of everything. There is but little good tea and all chaney [i.e., china] is very dear. I hope my lady will like the things. As for the chaney I have sent a full set for a desert for a large table . . . I have sent a few little things for fairings for the young ladies."[30]

Here the babies were arriving and growing into childhood. The first child had been born while John was in Scotland: "I hope all the red spots of the child will be gone against I see her, and her nose straight, that I may fancy it be like the mother, for as she has your coloured hair, so I would have her be like you in all things else."[31] For all his solicitude, the child died. She was succeeded by another Henrietta, to whose christening Arabella came as godmother: whether the godmother imparted an influence or no, Henrietta, who lived to be Duchess of Marlborough in her own right, ended up with a phase reminiscent of Arabella: though she did not entertain a King, she maintained a king among the wits, the dramatist Congreve. In 1684, another daughter arrived, named for the Princess, Anne, who lived to be the toast of the Whigs, "the Little Whig."

A charming side of John comes out in his tenderness to his children. He was always their favourite: "Malbrouck-s'en-va-t'en-guerre" could never be severe or even strict with them: he certainly spoiled them. He writes from Tunbridge Wells: "you cannot imagine how pleased I am with the children; for they having nobody but their maid, they are so fond of me, that when I am at home, they will be always with me, kissing and hugging me. Their heats are quite gone; so that against you come home they will be in beauty. Miss is pulling me by the arm, that she may write to her dear mamma." To gratify the child, he writes a post-script in her name: "I kiss your hands, my dear mamma. Harriet."

Time was to wreak a bitter irony upon that sentiment.

CHAPTER X

The Revolution

THE MEMBERS of this little circle of close friends needed all their resources of private happiness and of confidence in each other to face the storms that were bound to come with James's rule.

At first, all was deceptively fair. The new King met the Privy Council with the promise to maintain the established order in State and Church and to uphold the laws: "he recognised the members of the English Church as loyal subjects, he knew that the laws of England were sufficient to make the King a great monarch, and that he would maintain the rights and prerogatives of the Crown and would not invade any man's property."[1] We shall see how these promises were kept.

James, like Mary Tudor, got an unexpectedly warm welcome from his subjects. Some instinct of the English people told them that he had been hardly treated; and there were unexhausted reserves of sentiment—not to say sentimentality—that welled up to welcome a new King. The Tory reaction was still at the flood; but pains were taken to see that a favorable Parliament was returned. It was; to it James repeated his assurances, adding, "I have a true English heart, as jealous of the honour of the nation as you can be. I please myself with the hopes that (by God's blessing and your assistance) I may carry the reputation of it still higher in the world than ever it has been in the time of any of my ancestors."[2] This was improbable.

Parliament responded enthusiastically, and James received a grant of revenues for life, which had been granted to Charles grudgingly and only for a term of years. It was like the glad days of the Restoration again, with a Cavalier Parliament in a much more generous mood. Sir Winston came back to his former scene of action, after exclusion from the Parliaments of 1679 to 1681, now respected and listened to. His son was sent over to Versailles to negotiate the continuance of Louis's subsidies; before he arrived Barillon had laid half a million livres at James's feet. This was John Churchill's last call upon the Grand Monarch. All this made James financially freer than his brother—and he was a more careful manager. All would have been well if he could have responded fairly to the country's good will, and governed it in accordance with its wishes.*

Already indications of his unchanged intentions had been given. After his promises, loyal Anglicans were shocked when, the second Sunday after his accession, the King went in state to Mass in the Queen's chapel at Whitehall, the doors thrown open invitingly for all to follow. At his coronation, James promised once more to uphold the Church of England; but he refused to accept Communion at its hands, and the Communion service had to be omitted. After the coronation, John Churchill received an English peerage for his services: Baron Churchill of Sandridge. His mentor, Halifax, was kicked upstairs and shortly removed from the government altogether.

This was a significant pointer, even something of a danger signal. Halifax had saved the throne for James. He had fought for the life of the Catholic Lord Stafford against the fanatic Whigs, for the lives of the Whig Lord Russell and Algernon Sidney against the fanatic Tories. The most brilliant brain in English politics was also the most humane: the great Trimmer was not only the brain, but the heart, of England. Of course he was ambitious; but such are the men who ought to rule. He would not agree to the repeal of the Test and Habeas Corpus Acts, the two chief constitutional milestones of Charles II's Long Parliament. So he was dropped: the dropping of the pilot indeed.

In early June the Duke of Monmouth slipped away from Holland to raise rebellion in the West Country. Monmouth was the eldest and the handsomest of Charles's bastards, a favorite with his father. A soldier of dash, he was the candidate of the extremer Whigs for the throne. There could not have been a worse moment for his venture, with James's popularity at its height. How did he manage to slip off the leash under William's nose? That deep politician must have known: if Monmouth were (*per impossibile*) successful, William would have a Protestant England for ally in his lifelong struggle against Louis; if Monmouth were

---

* Cf. Ranke's judgment: "James II would have insured himself a peaceful and perhaps glorious reign, if he could have prevailed on himself to treat his religion as a private matter." *Op. cit.*, IV, 216.

defeated, a rival candidate for the throne would have been removed from his path. William would be all right in either case; and so it happened, for it is the intelligent, not the meek, who shall inherit the earth.

On June 11 Monmouth landed at Lyme—that town of Civil War memories and Puritan allegiance, now represented in Parliament by Sir Winston. At once the townspeople, who had not forgotten Blake and Lady Drake and their own heroic resistance for Parliament, joined the Duke's standard. He had some artillery and munitions with him, and he set out across country so familiar to the Churchills—especially Sir Winston, who had fought all over it—across Dorset and Somerset, toward Bristol, second city in the kingdom, fortress and seaport, full of Protestant sympathizers. On his march, hardly any of the gentry came in to him; but the simple folk, Protestant to the core, flocked to his standard. The militia, hurriedly mobilized, were disaffected and began to go over to the popular cause.

At once Churchill was given command and ordered to march West with what regular troops he had got—troops of the Blues and of his own Dragoons, with some horse. He marched with great rapidity, and on June 17 was at Bridport. Monmouth had moved north and now had greatly superior numbers. Churchill reported to the King: "I am sorry to send your Majesty this ill news; which is, unless speedy course be taken, we are like to lose this country [i.e., the West Country] to the rebels; for we have those two regiments run away a second time . . . I do humbly submit this to your Majesty's commands in what I shall do in it, for there is not any relying on these regiments that are left, unless we have some of your Majesty's standing forces to lead them on and encourage them; for at this unfortunate news I never saw people so much daunted in my life."[3] That shows where the sympathies of the people lay.

Those were the men of the militia, and half of them went to join Monmouth. Of his own regular troops, Churchill had no such fears: he wrote from Chard to cheer the Duke of Somerset, "I have forces enough not to apprehend [i.e., fear] the Duke of Monmouth; but quite contrary should be glad to meet with him, my men are all in so good heart this afternoon."[4] With his inferior forces, Churchill hung on to Monmouth's skirts while reinforcements marched West to hem him in. On June 18, Sunderland, now in chief power with James, announced that the King had appointed Churchill to the command of the forces against Monmouth.[5] The very next day the Frenchman Duras, Earl of

Feversham, was appointed Lieutenant General over Churchill's head. He had had no such experience of command in the field and, in addition to being twelve years older and fat and lazy, was a foreigner.

Churchill moved up to Bath, where—not far from his father's battlefields in 1643—he joined forces with Feversham. Thither, too, came his brother Charles with a train of artillery from Portsmouth. Headed off from Bristol, Monmouth fell back upon Bridgewater. Together, Feversham and Churchill countered the move by a more southerly route and arrived at Somerton. Sedgemoor, crisscrossed by its ditches and waterways, lay between the two armies.

From Somerton, July 4, Churchill wrote Clarendon—the King's brother-in-law, uncle to Princess Anne—a very revealing letter.[6] Perhaps we may cite it, for once, in his own spelling, just as he wrote. "I doe ashure you, that you waire very Just to me in the opinion you had of me, for nobody living can have bene more obsarvant than I have bene to my Lord feaversham, ever since I have bene with him, in soe much that he did tell me that he would writt to the King to lett him know how diligent I was, and I should be glade if you could know whether he has done me that Justice." In these phonetic spellings we hear the accents of that long-dead voice—how he pronounced the word "observant," for example. But we overhear a good deal more: the atmosphere of distrust, the King's distrust of Churchill, Churchill's uncertainty of the King's opinion, the correctness of his attitude under the slight put upon him, the anxiety that his correctitude be reported, the resentment beneath the submission and the courtesy.

He outlines his deductions as to Monmouth's plans, and then: "but of this and all other things you will have it more at large from my Lord Feversham, who has the sole command here, so that I know nothing but what is his pleasure to tell me, so that I am afraid of giving my opinion freely, for fear that it should not agree with what is the King's intentions, and so only expose myself. But as to the taking care of the men and all other things that is my duty, I am sure nobody can be more careful than I am; and as for my obedience, I am sure Mr. Oglethorpe [an inferior commander] is not more dutiful than I am. When you are at leisure, ten lines from you will be a great pleasure to me, who have not many things to please me here; for I see plainly that the trouble is mine, and that the honour will be another's: however my life shall be freely exposed for the King's service."

Everything is exposed in that letter: not only the atmosphere of suspicion, the King's distrust, the resentment at supersession, but the willingness to risk his life nevertheless, the care of his men.

Feversham took no care of anybody but himself. That evening, after a day's march, the royal army encamped on Sedgemoor, behind the shelter of the Bussex rhine, too deep to be crossed on foot. The General had a good feed and went to bed. Not so Churchill. He knew Monmouth and had divined his intentions: a surprise attack was his only hope. Though tired with a long day, Churchill visited all his outposts in person and posted strong pickets. In the darkness of the night, the rebel army was feeling its way across Sedgemoor to fall upon the royal camp asleep and unawares. The surprise might have been successful had not the rebels been halted by the rhine and Churchill awake and ready for them. He at once assumed command and took immediate action to prevent the royal forces being outflanked on the right, where the rebels had got round the ditch. Feversham, when awakened, approved the dispositions Churchill had made. This was the turning point of the action in the dark, for on the greater part of the front the armies could not come to grips across the waterway: there was a duel of the guns and indiscriminate firing exhausted the rebels' ammunition. In the gray light of dawn Monmouth saw that the battle was lost, and fled the field; the Puritan peasantry, stanch as their fathers, stood to the last by the ditch, fighting with the butt ends of their muskets and their scythes, charged by the regulars, battered by the guns.

Next day Churchill was in rebellious Bridgewater, whither Feversham followed more slowly.

He moved quickly away from his own West Country and the sickening scenes that followed there. In truth, he was lucky not to bear the responsibility for the last battle against Englishmen on our soil; while at the same time the army appreciated professionally that, had it not been for him, the battle might have been lost.

Judge Jeffreys, who got promotion by lending himself to James's purposes, was sent hotfoot down to the West on the Bloody Assizes. No amount of apologetics can get round the fact that nearly four hundred West Countrymen were strung up, and over a thousand sold into slavery in the plantations. The vindictive King showed himself in his true colors in that last unforgivable, unforgiving scene with his nephew. To a young West Country woman waiting to petition the King for her brothers' lives,

Churchill is reported to have said, "Madam, I dare not flatter you with any such hopes, for that marble is as capable of feeling compassion as the King's heart."[7] Improbable as it sounds, this represents the truth.

At last he had an opportunity of expressing openly what he thought. The extreme Whig, Lord Delamere, was sent for trial by his peers for complicity in Monmouth's rebellion, with Jeffreys as Lord High Steward. In the King's presence, it fell to Churchill as junior peer to give his vote first, "Not guilty, upon my honor!" and all the other peers followed suit. That should have been a warning to James: the open defection of his favourite servant, his ablest soldier.

James was not one to take warning; he belonged to the class of men who will hardly take "Yes" for an answer. But even the most loyal, the most Cavalier of Parliaments was not going to let him undermine the Protestant establishment. He saw that Parliament would interpose its veto upon the large dispensing measure he contemplated to suspend all laws against Catholics. So, suddenly in November, he dissolved Parliament: he never met another.

Led on by the insidious and insinuating Sunderland, and by the brazen Father Petre, his Jesuit confessor, James turned away all his best councilors. After Halifax, his Hyde brothers-in-law, Clarendon and Rochester, were thrown out. The control of Ireland was taken from Clarendon to be handed over to the Catholic adventurer, Tyrconnel, who was ready to execute James's scheme of providing Catholic Irish for an army to hold down England. An Ecclesiastical Commission was set up to dragoon the Church, though such a body was clean contrary to statute. It gave dispensations to curates who turned Catholic to hold on to their benefices. The Tory University of Oxford, which carried loyalty to the point of frantic absurdity, was affronted and wounded at its tenderest spot by James's proceedings: appointing a Catholic Dean of Christ Church, driving out the Fellows of Magdalen from their freehold to turn it into a Popish seminary, with Fellows appointed by Father Petre! The Archbishopric of York was kept vacant, it was said, in hopes of Petre's eventual succession. His claims to a cardinalate were pushed at Rome— in vain, for the intelligent Pope thoroughly disapproved of these rash and crazy proceedings. Petre had been allotted James's own lodgings as Duke of York in the palace; now he and Sunderland ran the government. Petre was given the dubious charge of Sunderland's spiritual welfare, and Sunderland duly bent the knee. He said afterward that he thought anybody who attempted to oppose a King's wishes a fool. The Jesuit priest was made Clerk of the Closet in place of its proper Anglican occupant.* The Bishop of London, the redoubtable Compton, was dismissed from being Dean of the Chapel Royal, brought before the Ecclesiastical Commission and suspended from exercising his diocesan functions. Evelyn tells us that this "very extraordinary way of proceeding was universally resented." The Jesuit priest was finally made a member of the Privy Council.

Catherine Sedley was the last hope of the Protestants with James. Under her influence he occasionally deviated into sense; under the influence of his wife and the priests, his feet were firmly back on the path of nonsense. On his accession he piously resolved to see her no more: she was packed off to Arabella's old house in St. James's Square, but with four times her allowance, i.e., £4,000 a year. In 1686 she was made Countess of Dorchester, an honor quite unsought by her; there were hopes of her return and the Catholic King saw her again, in secrecy. A sharp struggle for his virtue was put up by the Queen and the priests, and James was reduced to the scourge to subdue his inclinations. (This devout implement, a "curious love-token,"⁸ was subsequently bequeathed by the Queen to the nuns of Chaillot.) Virtue—or the Queen—triumphed; the Catholics at Court rejoiced; the new Countess was ordered to withdraw to Flanders. She replied that the number of convents there rendered the air too oppressive for her. She went off to Ireland, where she found the devout Irish "melancholy."

The good work could go on. Four Catholic peers were added to the Privy Council: Powis, Arundell, Belasyse and the disreputable young Harry Jermyn, now transmogrified as Lord Dover. What the Princess Anne thought of it we learn from a letter to Sarah: "I was very much surprised when I heard of the four new privy councillors, and am very sorry for it; for it will give great countenance to those sort of people, and methinks it has a very dismal prospect. Whatever changes there are in the world, I hope you will never forsake me, and I shall be happy."⁹

James proceeded on his crazy course, sawing off the bough on which

* Father Petre was sworn as Clerk of the Closet on November 5, 1687—Gunpowder Plot day: an ill omen. It should have been a warning to him. L. C. 3/30.

he sat as monarch: the passive obedience of the Anglican Church, the unquestioning loyalty of the Tory party. Anglican passive obedience began to turn into passive resistance; Tories began to question. The King took to making tours about the country, partly for devotional reasons—the pilgrimage to St. Winifred's was supposed to be good for making women pregnant (the Queen had no children)—partly to curry favor for his intending measures, to organize popularity. His public appearances, however, were apt to lack dignity: something always happened to put him in a false light and make him look ridiculous. He touched for the king's evil with great assiduity—in Anglican cathedrals, with his Catholic priests officiating. On one of these occasions, walking in the garden of the deanery after the ceremony at Winchester, James asked Churchill what the people thought, and got a very unsatisfactory answer.[10] What Churchill seems to have said was that the people in general disapproved, for they regarded it as intended to pave the way for Popery. After this, he was not spoken to during dinner; the King held forth to the Dean on passive obedience. He was determined to *make* people obey. He did not know his people: it is impossible to *make* the English obey.

What were the Churchills to do in this situation?

Evidently, not to make a false step, but to keep in close understanding with Princess Anne; to save money for a rainy day. For the rest, not to mislead the King, to serve him dutifully—with a saving clause of conscience not to forward his unconstitutional and religious measures. It was not the part of a servant to obtrude his disagreements, but, when asked, to answer with truth and candor. And that is exactly what Churchill did: it was a difficult line to pursue—everyone was thrown into difficulties by the King's folly—but it was a perfectly clear line, both honest and patriotic, in the best interest both of the country and himself. It is difficult to see why it should have been so misunderstood—except that people always seem to find anything but simple partisanship, on one side or the other, hard to understand: they never understand the virtues, or the advantages, of ambivalence. Certainly Churchill has not only been misunderstood, but cruelly misrepresented.*

Bishop Burnet, who was no friend to Churchill and saw everything from the point of view of William of Orange, yet observes: "as he never

---

* Above all, of course, by Macaulay, who riveted his crude and cruel caricature of Marlborough upon generations of readers of his *History*.

betrayed any of the King's secrets to the Prince, so he never set the King on violent measures, but on the contrary, as oft as he spoke to him of his affairs (which was indeed but seldom) he gave him moderate counsels. He had kept himself wholly out of the counsels and so set himself to manage his post in the army, in which he made great advantages, for money had as much power over him as he had over the King.* His wife is about the Princess and has gained such an ascendant over her, that there never was a more absolute favourite in a Court. She is indeed become the mistress of her thoughts and affections, and does with her, both in her Court and in all her affairs, what she pleases. Churchill is a very smooth man, made for a Court, and very fit for business, if his own interests prevailed not too much over him."[11] The tone of this is distinctly unfriendly, but one cannot but observe that it is a reluctant tribute to Churchill's essential honesty of conduct.

His financial affairs were, at last, prospering; though not opulent, he could save for the future of his family. For someone who had a peerage to provide for, with no foundation in land or money, this was doubly necessary. Fortunately it fitted in with his saving disposition. In addition to his lucrative army appointments, he was a Lord of the Bedchamber— along with the Duke of Beaufort, the Earls of Ossory, Lichfield, Feversham and others—at £600 a year.[12] His own private resources were exiguous—the famous annuity and anything that might come from his father's estate. Sarah had much more: her ultimate share of the Jennings estate may have been £2,000 a year. (Perhaps that consideration contributed to John's bondage to the girl so much his junior.) At any rate he was able, for the first time, in January, 1685, to lend £2,000 to the Exchequer at 6 per cent.[13] Further loans he made to the government, bearing interest at 6 per cent, were: in February, 1687, £2,000 and £3,000; in June, 1687, £2,000; and in February, 1688, £3,000.[14] In the absence of a Bank of England, as yet, the government was much the safest channel for investment. But it also meant that Churchill had a vested interest in seeing that government was not overthrown. He was no revolutionary and far from an extremist; he was an ordinary Englishman—save for his military genius, which had not yet had a chance to reveal itself— adhering to the middle way.

Not enough attention has been drawn to the significant fact that

* We have seen that he had no influence over James's policy.

Churchill, in spite of his lifelong service and favor with James, was promoted to no office by him during his reign. That speaks for itself. Legge, who was very much his junior in James's service, was made Master of the Ordnance, a very lucrative post, given an earldom and ultimately the command of the fleet. It is clear that James recognized that Churchill was opposed to his policy. Though he remained the King's servant, the foundation of his political position shifted, and his potential importance increased, as the confidant and adviser of the Princess Anne.

Anne kept discreetly in the background in this time of tribulation. But the eyes of the nation were upon the little Court at the Cockpit. James had not given up hope of his daughter's conversion. His daughter, however, had more sense than he; the influence of the Churchills went along with that of her favorite cleric, the Bishop of London, to fortify her Protestantism and ensure her prospects. It was from this time that the nation began to look to her and her popularity started. The country was prepared to put up with a good deal from James, provided it was temporary. The Queen had no children; his heirs, Mary and Anne, were firm Protestants: all would be well in time.

It is not to be supposed that the Churchills were very religious persons, as Anne was: England was Protestant and they were English. John Churchill's religion was that of a sensible Englishman; Sarah had less. On his last visit to Versailles, he had spoken his mind to the Huguenot Ruvigny, who left Louis to fight for William: "he said then to him that if the King was ever prevailed upon to alter our religion, he would serve him no longer, but would withdraw from him."[15] In 1687 William sent over a trusted agent, Dykvelt, to sound out opinion, gather assurances, make contacts, upon which William could form his plans. Fundamental was a good understanding between the Cockpit and the Hague. Anne entrusted the negotiations with Dykvelt to Churchill, who wrote to William: "the Princess of Denmark having ordered me to discourse with Monsieur Dykvelt and to let him know her resolutions, so that he might let your Highness and the Princess her sister know that she was resolved, by the assistance of God, to suffer all extremities, even to death itself, rather than be brought to change her religion, I thought it my duty to your Highness and the Princess Royal, to give your assurances under my own hand, that my places and the King's favour I set at nought, in comparison of being true to my religion. In all things but this the King may command me; and I call God to witness, that even with joy I should expose my life for his service, so sensible am I of his favours."[16]

The language was a little exaggerated; he was writing with emotion. There was no likelihood that the Princess Anne might have to stand by her religion to the death, or that it was religion only that was involved. Religion was, as so often in history, the convenient "platform," as we should call it: not in itself without significance, but of subordinate importance. More important matters were involved: the freedom of the English people, constitutional government and our liberties. Were we going to become an absolute monarchy, like France? That was what James intended. Would that have been a good thing, either then or looking forward into the future—to the French Revolution, or, for that matter, to the political system of France today? The English have followed an altogether better course, far more successful and fruitful, that still offers a better model for the world.

These things flow straight from the Revolution of 1688, moderate, conservative, responsible, humane.

While these contacts and understandings were being made, the more serious side to James's intentions was becoming apparent. He was building up a powerful army. It is not sufficiently realized that before the thing broke, he had an army of 40,000 men—the largest army that had ever been in England: larger than that with which Cromwell won the Civil War. He had placed a foreigner in command, Feversham; it contained large contingents of Catholic Irish, who would have had no compunction in fighting the English; it was officered, so far as possible, by Catholic officers. Arabella's son, the Duke of Berwick, was now put in command at Portsmouth; Catholics commanded at Hull and at Dover; in the summer of 1688 a Catholic was in command of the fleet in the Channel. The people of England would never have been able to resist, if William had not come over with an army and virtually the whole Dutch fleet to support it.

What were people in the situation of Churchill to do—true Englishmen—in the best interests of their country? The question became agonizing, as things grew to a crisis.

The Princess Anne thought of leaving the country. Permission to pay a visit to her sister in Holland was refused. She wrote secretly to warn William and Mary not to come over: "for though I dare swear the King could have no thought against either of you, yet since people can say one thing and do another, one cannot help being afraid."[17] Churchill tried to obtain the command of the English troops in Dutch service. That was too obvious a move: no hope of it. The net was closing round the small circle at the Cockpit. They were forced to declare themselves. Churchill was asked whether he would support the repeal of the laws against Catholics; like Halifax, he refused.

To gain support for altering the religious establishment of the country by his own authority, James was making up to the Dissenters. Not that he had anything but detestation for them. Barillon, who knew his mind, reported to Louis that his designs were "directed principally to the advantage of the Catholic religion, which he believes your Majesty has equally at heart, having worked with so much success for the destruction of heresy in France."[18] Some of the Dissenters took the bait; the Quaker, William Penn, lent himself to James's purposes. The bulk of the Dissenters stood firm by Protestantism: their common sense told them what to expect if James won. Barillon reported, "the King desires intensely that Catholics and Catholics alone should have freedom to practise their religion."[19]

In France, the *dragonnades* were going forward hotfoot. In Europe, the Grand Alliance to resist Louis's domination was taking shape; the Pope, who had himself been subject to Louis's bullying, joined it. Only England was being counted out. James, however, was too conceited to put himself entirely under Louis's protection. Besides, religion was more important than the facts of power. In May, James issued his grand Declaration of Indulgence, by his own authority suspending the laws and undermining the Establishment. His brother had recognized the impossibility of carrying this through in 1672 and accepted defeat. The attempt itself had been responsible for worsening the situation by the Test Act. Now James would carry it through by force, with the army behind him. The governing figures in the country at large, the Lords Lieutenant, were dismissed; the Catholic backwoodsmen who had had no experience of power for a hundred and thirty years were brought out, rather dazed, into the light of day. They were a tiny, ineffectual minority and, even with the Dissenters together, made no counterweight to the natural governing class of the nation backed by the people.

James not merely published his Declaration, but ordered it to be read in all the churches throughout the country. Those bishops who happened to be in London, led by the Primate, refused: they were the famous Seven. Furious that even these worms had turned, James—like his father with the Five Members of Parliament—determined to put them on trial. Sunderland and Jeffreys were alarmed by opposition from such a quarter; but James, fortified by his confessor, persisted. The reverend fathers were sent to the Tower: for the first, and last, time bishops became the heroes of the nation.

While they were awaiting their trial, a son was born to James: at last, a Catholic heir. The nation was consternated. Was this kind of thing to go on for good? The governing class awaited a clear indication where the sympathies of the people lay.

This came with the acquittal of the bishops: general rejoicings in London, bonfires, bell-ringing, people kneeling in the streets to receive the prelates' blessings—a very unwonted thing. The jubilation spread to the camp at Hounslow: the troops joined in; and so on throughout the country. The avalanche was set moving.

That night, June 30, 1688, the invitation was sent to William to come over and defend the country's liberties and his wife's inheritance. It was signed by such leading, and representative, figures as the great Danby, the Duke of Shrewsbury, the Earl of Devonshire; for the Church, the Bishop of London; for the navy, Admiral Russell. Churchill was not a signatory; but the little Court at the Cockpit must have been in touch with what was going forward. The legend that the child at Whitehall had been smuggled in in a warming pan was assiduously spread. Princess Anne wrote to her sister, "I shall never now be satisfied whether the child be true or false. Maybe 'tis our brother . . . Where one believes it, a thousand do not. For my part, unless they do give a very plain demonstration . . . I shall ever be of the number of unbelievers."[20] The legend was a lie; but it was a suitable response to people who believed the nonsense they did.

In August the national leaders sent over the handsome Sidney, who had already commended himself to William's attention; after the Revolution he was loaded with lands and favors. The clever men who were leading the nation were making no mistakes. Churchill was wholly with them. Sidney carried a letter from him to William: "Mr. Sidney will let you know how I intend to behave myself: I think it is what I owe to God and my country. My honour I take leave to put into your royal Highness's hands, in which I think it safe. If you think there is anything else that I ought to do, you have but to command me and I shall pay an entire obedience to it, being resolved to die in that religion that it has pleased God to give you both the will and the power to protect."[21]

Sunderland was now thoroughly frightened and urged James to retreat. William's preparations went forward. The European war was about to break out, and Louis made one of the many mistakes he made out of pride. He delivered an ultimatum to Holland: he took it upon him to declare William's military preparations a menace to England and to offer England his protection. Result: the Dutch, once more insulted, lined up behind William: James, humiliated publicly, refused France's protection. At that Louis made a further mistake: instead of going on to overawe Holland, he moved his forces south to attack Austria on the Rhine. William was free to move: the hour of the crowned fool in England had come.

Panic seized upon Whitehall. Sunderland persuaded the King to concede everything: abolish the Ecclesiastical Commission, restore the Fellows of Magdalen, put the Acts against the Catholics and Dissenters into force again. The Lords Lieutenant who had been dismissed were ignominiously asked back; the charters restored to the municipal corporations. These measures only revealed the weakness of James's position and his isolation. He now dismissed the reptilian Sunderland, who went over to William with all his secrets and all his information. With these he climbed on to the bandwagon.

In mid-October William set out on his combined operations: a small army in a large number of vessels, escorted by the Dutch fleet. They were scattered and blown back by a great gale. This was no surprise to James: "it is not to be wondered at," he said, "for the Host has been exposed these several days." Still his councilors pressed upon him the necessity of calling a Parliament. He refused. The comment of the profane Jeffreys, who was not without commonsense, was much to the point: "the Virgin Mary is to do all."

The wind changed again, into a Protestant wind—as in 1588, Armada year, exactly a hundred years before. It was an encouraging memory. William was able to sail down the Channel and landed at Torbay on November 5. When he was reminded that it was Gunpowder Plot day, William turned to Burnet and said, "what do you think of Predestination now?"

The landing in the West Country was a great disappointment to Danby, who had gone to raise the northern counties and hoped to control events from there. Moreover, now that things had come to the arbitrament of force, James preferred to have William in the West: the King had double the number of William's forces, and with this superiority hoped to coop him up in the southwestern peninsula. The royal army was ordered to concentrate at Salisbury; on November 7 Churchill was made Lieutenant General in command of a division. It was the best James could do for himself: to keep Churchill close to him under his own eye, while not giving him the command of the army.

Before setting out from Windsor, disconcerting news was reported to James: a significant pointer. His brother-in-law Clarendon's son and heir, Lord Cornbury, had gone over to William. Indeed, he had nearly carried over three regiments of horse: if it had not been for the immediate reaction and speed of young Berwick, who at once realized what was happening, dashed after him and prevented it—a remarkable debut for this lad of eighteen's military career. He clearly took after the Churchill side, not the dilatory Stuarts.

Lord Cornbury was a member of the circle at the Cockpit, cousin to Princess Anne. On November 18 she wrote to William: "I hope the Prince [i.e., her husband] will soon be with you, to let you see his readiness to join with you, who I am sure will do you all the service that lies in his power. He went yesterday with the King towards Salisbury, intending to go from thence to you as soon as his friends thought it proper. I am not yet certain if I shall continue here, or remove into the City; that shall depend on the advice my friends will give me; but whereever I am, I shall be ready to show you how very much I am your humble servant."[22] Evidently these moves had been prepared beforehand: their timing would depend on circumstances.

When the King arrived at Salisbury, the situation was one of touch and go. He contemplated arresting Churchill; but that would have advertised his insecurity to the world and been a shock to the morale of the troops. On the evening of November 23, there was a council of war. Churchill and the Duke of Grafton—Barbara's son—advocated an advance toward William; Feversham insisted on a retreat. Doubt, distrust, anxiety gnawed away James's nerve: he had a fainting fit and nosebleedings which took a long time to stop. He refused to go forward: he was convinced that it was a plot on Churchill's part to hand him over to William. That night, having failed to gain control of the situation—indeed, having been defeated by James's refusal to move—Churchill and

Grafton stole away from the camp, with some four hundred troopers, and rode through the night to join William.

Churchill left behind him a letter to the King, which exposes the dilemma in which he had placed his best servants: "though my dutiful behaviour to your Majesty in the worst times (for which I acknowledge my poor service is much overpaid) may not be sufficient to incline you to a charitable interpretation of my actions, yet I hope the great advantage I enjoy under your Majesty, which I own I can never expect in any other change of government, may reasonably convince your Majesty and the world that I am actuated by a higher principle, when I offer that violence to my inclination and interest as to desert your Majesty at a time when your affairs seem to challenge the strictest obedience from all your subjects, much more from one who lies under the greatest personal obligations to your Majesty."[23] This principle—or rather, interest—to which he appealed was that of Protestantism, with all that it implied in constitutional liberties, the liberty of the individual, the struggle for the liberties of Europe against the domination of Louis XIV. After all, to an English mind, kings were not ends in themselves, their service an absolute law to the individual's conscience: they were the guardians of their country's interest and well-being, the service they could command conditional upon their fulfilling their trust. Churchill said to Clarendon, in the George Inn at Salisbury where they met some days later, that he would never have left James, "but that he saw our religion and country were in danger of being destroyed."* It was as simple as that: James had made it so.

Churchill's conduct at this crisis for the nation needs no defending, and we need waste no time upon it. He was bound to suffer the charge of ingratitude, then and for ever afterward; but the responsibility was James's. In leaving him, Churchill was doing what was best for the nation.

What is far more fascinating, and what no one has penetrated, is the secret of his intentions at this decisive moment in history. What did he mean to do as between James and William? Neither then nor afterward did this reserved, inscrutable man, with the perfect command of himself, let fall one word as to what he had in mind. In consequence, historians have thought his conduct at the crisis very mysterious. It seems to me that if we put ourselves back into the circumstances of the

---

* *Corr. Clarendon and Rochester*, II, 214. It is pleasant to think that the George Inn still stands there in the High Street.

time he had lived through, from the Restoration to the Revolution, the explanation is simple. It is surprising that no one seems to have thought of it as a clue to his conduct.

We have seen the role played at the Restoration by that other West Countryman, Monk: it must have been very present to the mind of John Churchill, as to others. After all, the powerful Danby had hoped to control affairs by William landing in the North, which Danby was raising. Why should not John Churchill hope to control affairs from his position high up in the command of the army, with Princess Anne as a further pawn in his hand? What Monk had done was in the nation's interest, and what the nation wanted. He had well deserved the reward he had earned: a dukedom, the wealth to support it, command of the army for life. John Churchill was deeply ambitious; he had a serene confidence in his military star—Monk was no genius, just an ordinary competent general. If Churchill could have got the King in his control, he would have been the arbiter between James and William; he could have imposed the terms he thought best in the interests of the nation. We know what a humane and patriotic Englishman he was: he could have negotiated—a superb negotiator with a long and varied experience—a settlement that would have prevented any bloodshed. Actually, such a settlement would have worked out far better for James. James would have remained as King, nominally at least, with William perhaps as Regent. What William wanted more than anything in the world was that England should come into place in the Grand Alliance that was all he lived for. What Churchill cared for more than anything, we need not doubt, was the command of the English army playing its proper place in that alliance. Other things would follow, as they had for Monk: a dukedom, the wealth to support it, a name and fame to posterity.

All that had been *in posse* for a moment at Salisbury. But things did not work out like that: they rarely do so sensibly. James, by losing his nerve and taking fright, had really defeated Churchill. If James had had any real will power, instead of a fanatic's fatalism, he might still have kept control of the situation, or made William fight for it— the last thing the latter wanted to do. For Churchill, failing to gain control of the King, the only thing he could do was to go over to William. It must have been bitterly disappointing, even humiliating. William received him well; but that penetrating brain would realize acutely all that it meant for Churchill, as well as for himself. Henceforth, the Dutchman was in complete control of the national movement, with its prospects opening before him: he was in far more effective control on his side than the King on his: no Englishman could command him or hold up his designs. What adds corroboration to this view of it all is that it also provides the clue to Churchill's actions under William as King, accounts for his discontent and the nationalist form it took against the Dutchman.

These events set the avalanche in motion: the whole nation was turning against James. Danby had raised Yorkshire; the Earl of Devonshire, the county of Derby; Delamere, Cheshire. Opinion in the fleet was moving over to William; the faithful Dartmouth was distracted and in the end surrendered it to William. In that movement George Churchill had his part, carrying his ship the *Newcastle* over, and taking a hand in the submission of Plymouth, of which the most loyal of Cavaliers, Bevil Grenville's son, the Earl of Bath, was Governor. The King was on his way back to London. At Andover, Prince George and the Duke of Ormonde left him for William. Of two squadrons of horse, Brigadier Trelawny and Colonel Charles Churchill deserted with twenty or thirty of their soldiers.[24]

Clarendon's diary reports for us the state of affairs in London. Sunday, November 25: "In the evening I went to Court: great crowds in the galleries and consternation in all men's looks. 26 November. As I was walking in Westminster Hall, on a sudden was a rumour all about that the Princess was gone away, nobody knew whither; that somebody had violently carried her away. I went presently to the Cockpit. I found my Lady Frecheville and all the women in great consternation. All the light I could get was that last night after her royal Highness was in bed, the chamber doors locked, and Mrs. Danvers in bed in the outer room where she used to lie when in waiting, she rose again, went down the backstairs and, accompanied only by Lady Churchill, Mrs. Berkeley and a maid of Lady Churchill's, went into a coach and six horses, which stood ready at the street-gate."[25]

Clearly some move had been intended; but the news that the King was on his way back to Whitehall caught them by surprise.* There is no reason to disbelieve Sarah when she says that "this put the Princess into a great fright. She sent for me . . . and declared 'That rather than see her father she would jump out of the window.' This was her very expression." Sarah went to the Bishop of London, who was lying in

---

* When Churchill heard the news from Clarendon at Salisbury, he said he wondered that she had not gone sooner. *Correspondence of Clarendon and Rochester*, II, 214.

concealment, to make arrangements for their flight. "The Princess went to bed at the usual time to prevent suspicion. I came to her soon after; and by the backstairs which went down from her closet, her royal Highness, my Lady Fitzharding[26] and I, with one servant, walked to the coach, where we found the Bishop and the Earl of Dorset. They conducted us that night to the Bishop's house in the City, and the next day to my Lord Dorset's at Copt Hall. From thence we went to the Earl of Northampton's and from thence to Nottingham, where the country gathered about the Princess; nor did she think herself safe, till she saw that she was surrounded by the Prince of Orange's friends."[27]

The Princess left a letter to the Queen behind her, "to let you know that I am gone to absent myself to avoid the King's displeasure, which I am not able to bear, either against the Prince or myself: and I shall stay at so great a distance as not to return before I hear the happy news of a reconcilement . . . Never was anyone in such an unhappy condition, so divided between duty and affection to a father and an husband; and therefore I know not what I must do, but to follow one to preserve the other."[28] When James reached Whitehall that afternoon, all he could say was "God help me! Even my children have forsaken me!" Like his father, Charles I, he never understood what had hit him—the English people.

At Nottingham, where her grandfather had raised his standard in unpropitious circumstances, the Princess was royally received. The Earl of Devonshire had raised several hundred horse; the townsfolk trooped out to meet her. Fifty years later, old Colley Cibber, the dramatist, looked back on that day and the public banquet given her that night in Nottingham. What his romantic heart chiefly remembered was the dazzling figure beside the Princess, and the only words he heard Sarah utter as he waited at table, "Some wine and water." "Except at that single sound all my senses were collected into my eyes, which during the whole entertainment wanted no better amusement than stealing now and then the delight of gazing on the fair object so near me. If so clear an emanation of beauty, such a commanding aspect of grace, struck me into a regard that had something softer than the most profound respect in it . . ." in short the young Colley lost his head to the great lady, Sarah, in the prime of her beauty.*

* Colley Cibber, *An Apology for His Life* (Everyman ed.), 40-41. This work was published in 1740, when Sarah was still alive to reward him for his flattery.

A fortnight later, Anne made a splendid entry into Oxford, a regiment meeting her some miles outside. "The Earl of Northampton with five hundred horse led the van. Her royal Highness was preceded by the Bishop of London, at the head of a noble troop of gentlemen, his lordship riding in a purple cloak, martial habit, pistols before him, and his sword drawn; and his cornet had the inscription in golden letters on his standard, *Nolumus Leges Angliae Mutari* . . . The mayor and aldermen in their formalities met her at the North gate; and the Vice Chancellor with the heads of the university attended in their scarlet gowns, made to her a speech in English; and the Prince [i.e., George] received her royal Highness at Christ Church quadrangle with all possible demonstrations of love and affection, and they will be tomorrow at Windsor."[29]

Meanwhile, in London the issue was being settled. The day after his return, James had a meeting with such of the lords as could be assembled. He told them that he looked upon his bleeding at the nose to be a great providence; for had it not returned upon him the day he intended to view some of his troops at Warminster, he had great reason that Lord Churchill then designed to give him up to the Prince of Orange.[30] That was a great providence: no conception that what the Prince least wanted was to have his father-in-law on his hands. What he wanted was to have him out of the country.

There is no point in recounting the remainder of the story in detail, since Churchill had little hand in James's fate. Even in the hurry and scurry of his last days in England, James thought it worth while to discharge Churchill from his place as lord of the bedchamber, score through his name in the Lord Chamberlain's book of the household, and name someone else to the post.[31] After packing off his wife and child to France, James fled once and was fetched back from Faversham. From Windsor, William was giving his orders to the nation's forces; Churchill sent his commands to the Guards in London to assemble, and said he would unite with them in a few days.[32]

It is unlikely that Churchill had contemplated William's accession to the throne. Few people can have expected such an upshot—except William, and he kept his designs to himself. He was in no hurry to reach London and had no intention of parleying with his father-in-law. He wanted the coast clear and was ready to rely on James's fatuity, of which he had taken the fullest measure. James made the way easy by flight. With infantile vindictiveness, on his first going, he had sent orders to his faithful Feversham and Dartmouth to disband the army and the fleet; he had himself thrown the Great Seal into the Thames in the hope of bringing government to a stop and producing anarchy. Such a man was unworthy of the throne. Feversham's disbanding the army was a shocking piece of irresponsibility, throwing thousands of soldiers unpaid, but not disarmed, upon the population. Brokenhearted at his chief's desertion, Dartmouth surrendered the fleet to William. Fortunately William was there to step into the breach. James's mind was obstinately bent on flight: he feared for his life, and William did nothing to reassure him.

At last, December 19, "the King went off from Court, and this day about 3 o'clock the Prince arrived at St. James's with great acclamations of joy and huzzas."[33] Next day he went to Whitehall and from thence to Somerset House to call on his aunt, the Queen Dowager; on his return, hearing that the Princess Anne and her husband had arrived in town, he called to see them at the Cockpit. On December 23 James embarked for France; at once William gave the French ambassador twenty-four hours to leave the country. England fell into its proper place in the coalition against France: William's essential purpose in coming over was fulfilled.

But what next? The throne was vacant. Acute divisions of opinion, conflicts of conscience within men's minds, appeared. Had James ceased to be King? By what right? All the boring doctrines of political theory were trotted out by the doctrinaires. The pressure of events and the will power of the one man who held the key to the situation decided. Would William consent to act as Regent for James, government being carried on in His Majesty's name? This was the Tory solution; but it would not have worked, and Churchill did not support it. Would William act as Regent for his wife? He would not: he had no idea of being "his wife's gentleman-usher." He was willing to accept the throne for himself alone, leaving his wife on one side. This shocked his best friends, and the nation would not have accepted that. Common sense, expressing itself through the Commons, proposed the joint rule of William and Mary. Where common sense was to be found, there was John Churchill also: he supported the sensible compromise solution of the Commons.

It was not what the nation had expected or really wanted: it was the best that could be obtained in the circumstances. Churchill, at the very center of the nation and sharing its moods and apprehensions, must inwardly have been disappointed. The leading English soldier had failed to dominate the situation; the country had fallen under the control of a foreigner; nobody, and nothing, had been able to stop William. The instinct of an Englishman at such a juncture is to try and make things work. Churchill did his best by using his influence—still more, his wife's —with Princess Anne to surrender her right to succeed to the throne on Mary's death, so that William might enjoy the crown for life. Here, too, compromise was reached: any children there might be of William and Mary came first in the succession, then Anne's, then any William might have by a subsequent marriage.

It was not at all logical, let alone legitimist; it was very much of a compromise, in the English manner, and it worked.

CHAPTER XI

William III and Marlborough

NOT THE least part of the fascination that history exerts over us—especially if we belong to an old country with longer memories and perspectives—is to recognize the recurrence of similar situations, to watch the parallels that occur, the patterns that unfold in familiar shapes though never precisely the same. The game has an intellectual, no less than an aesthetic, interest: we should be able to learn from these recurring situations, these patterns of events and parallels of conduct, not to make comparable mistakes.*

The long struggle this country was engaged in against Louis XIV's domination of Europe covered two periods of war, separated by a truce. The Revolution of 1688 and William's accession to the throne committed us to the coalition which waged war with Louis for eight years, 1689 to 1697, until the peace of Ryswick; then followed the war of the Grand Alliance against him, from 1702 till 1713, when the Treaty of Utrecht re-established the balance of Europe for a period. Our long struggle with Louis XIV may be compared with that we waged against the aggressions of the French Revolution and Napoleon: two periods of war, 1793 to 1802 and from 1803 to 1815, separated by a truce. Or with the ordeal we have gone through in the twentieth century to save ourselves and the liberties of Europe from the intolerable aggressions of Germany: the two wars of 1914 to 1918 and of 1939 to 1945, divided by a longer period of peace.

Parallels between our earlier struggle with Louis XIV and that with Germany in our time were certainly forced upon the mind of Sir Winston Churchill in writing his masterpiece, *Marlborough, His Life and Times*.

---

* It will be seen that I do not subscribe to Sir Lewis Namier's view: "Possibly there is no more sense in human history than in the changes of the seasons or the movements of the stars." History is an extension of life into the past: there are lessons to be learned and people should learn them. They can, and sometimes they do.

It would have been better if they had been forced upon us: it might conceivably have saved many lives. There was the insistence of the Commons, immediately upon the peace in 1697 achieved by eight years of fighting, on disbanding the army: it weakened William's hand in dealing with Louis. There was the ignorance of the Commons as to European affairs that enabled Louis to go ahead with his designs and establish positions before the struggle—which only made it the harder to hold him later and prolonged the war. There was the readiness of the easygoing English—the same holds good for our kith and kin across the Atlantic—to throw away at the peace what we had won by courage and endurance in war.

There is a more particular parallel. At the height of his powers, in the prime of life, Marlborough—greatest of English soldiers—was hardly at all used by William III, kept on the shelf. Those were, for him, the years that the locusts had eaten—no less than the years 1931 to 1939 were for this country when his descendant, a man of equal genius and greater moral courage, was kept out.

I

From the first, William distrusted the English. Perhaps that was understandable in the circumstances of the Revolution. But he did little enough to commend himself to them. Evelyn's first impression of him at St. James's was: "he is very stately, serious and reserved."[1] A month later Evelyn says that to the general dissatisfaction must be added "the morose temper of the Prince of Orange, who showed little countenance to the noblemen and others, who expected a more gracious and cheerful reception when they made their court." The truth was that the great little man, with the heroic spirit, had the manners of a Dutch corporal. It was very different from the Stuarts: Charles II might betray his country and the cause of Europe, but he did it with an easy grace, an irresistible affability, that made him personally popular to the end of his life. Even James's formal manners were good: though rigid and haughty, he had a royal condescension and courtesy. William cared for nothing but politics and power, the convolutions and combinations of states, the army and action. He was like his precursor, the famous soldier, Prince Maurice. Like him, too, he did not much care for women—a striking enough contrast with the Court of Charles and James. He preferred men; and of them two Dutch favorites, Bentinck and the handsome young Keppel. To them, he added only one Englishman, the equally handsome—and rather lightweight—Sidney. It was said that his relations with these were intimate; and he rewarded them, and others among his closed Dutch circle, with a lavishness that outraged the English.

Within this closed circle he lived, not only protected by the Dutch guards he had brought over, but insulated by his Dutch servants and comrades. An observer of 1689 says that "he never saw English noblemen dine with the Prince of Orange, but only the Duke of Schomberg who was always placed at his right hand and his Dutch general officers. The English noblemen that were there stood behind the Prince of Orange's chair, but never were admitted to eat and sit."[2] The Earls of Marlborough and Clarendon were often in attendance, but "were dismissed when the dinner was half over." It was a bit too much.

At the very beginning Churchill was indispensable to William, and rendered him great service in reconstituting the army after the disorganization—Churchill knew all the personnel and all the ropes. Schomberg said that it was all "at my Lord Churchill's disposition . . . My Lord Churchill proposes all, I am sent for as to say the General consents, and Monsieur Bentinck is the Secretary for the write all."[3] Ailesbury tells us that the harvest Churchill made out of this was very large; he has a story of a footman holding a purse of a thousand guineas for his master, entering Churchill's lodgings at the Cockpit to obtain a regiment. He rendered an even more important service to William by obtaining Princess Anne's consent to the postponement of her right to the succession. Then there was Churchill's going over to William at the crucial moment at Salisbury.

For his services, he was rewarded with an earldom at the coronation. He took the title of Marlborough after his cousin (on his mother's side), the Royalist sailor Earl, who had been killed at Sole Bay—a very respectable association. William increased the salaries of the Gentlemen of the Bedchamber to £1,000 a year.[4] Then Marlborough had his pay as Lieutenant General,[5] his colonelcies, his perquisites and so on; Sarah, her salary as Lady of the Bedchamber to Princess Anne. At last the Marlboroughs were making money; and we find them lending to the government, investing £10,000 in the Bank of England when it was started, in the East India Company and in the Hudson's Bay Company.* Of the

---

* In 1697 we find Marlborough using Sir Benjamin Bathurst, a former Governor, of the East India Company, Treasurer of Princess Anne's Household, to invest his money in East India stock: "let the money be paid before Wednesday that I may not lose the ten shillings" (presumably a premium). *H.M.C., Bathurst MSS.*, 4.

last, Churchill had been made Governor in succession to James, when James became King. The Company thrived under its Governor's careful and painstaking management. Churchill was no sleeping partner: he threw himself into all the concerns of the Company. By 1690 it was able to pay a dividend of 75 per cent, and to treble the value of its shares by splitting the original stock. It is very right and proper that a settlement on Hudson's Bay, Fort Churchill, should be named after him.

Prosperity was in view at last—and how welcome it must have been after all the years of living on a shoestring! Even so, the Marlboroughs were the least well off among their class of peers; and they still had no land to speak of—indispensable to self-respect in such a society. Sarah told Ailesbury one day, walking alone with her in the garden at Holywell, "Lord [a common word with her], they keep such a noise at our wealth. I do assure you that it doth not exceed £70,000, and what will that come to when laid out in land; and, besides, we have a son and five daughters to provide for."[6] This was some years later: it makes Marlborough's opposition to William all the more courageous: he sacrificed a great deal for it. He came into harbor with Anne's accession. By 1728 Sarah was able to offer the Crown a loan of £700,000 at 3 per cent; and she and her daughter, Duchess of Marlborough, had near double that sum in land and money. It was certainly "Good Queen Anne" for the Marlboroughs.

In 1689 Marlborough was given the command of the English contingent of 8,000 men under the aged Prince of Waldeck in Flanders. They were in poor condition, and in three months Marlborough transformed them, paying particular attention, as he always did, to the comfort and well-being of the troops. The result was that when action came at Walcourt, the English won the honors in defeating the French assault on the town. The elderly Prince was generous in acknowledgments: "the English did marvels . . . Marlborough, in spite of his youth, displayed in this one battle greater military capacity than do most generals after a long series of wars."[7] He was thirty-nine, and had had an extensive experience of war by land and sea since youth. But it was an axiom with people on the Continent that the English were no good at fighting on land: they ought to have remembered Cromwell and the Civil War. (Just as in our time the Germans assumed that the Americans, because they are a civilian people, were no good at fighting: they should have remembered the American Civil War—one of the hardest fought in history.)

At the end of the year James landed in Ireland, which was under the command of the Catholic Tyrconnel and had not gone over to William. James had done his best to undermine the Acts of Settlement, and the Catholics now had the ascendancy. He had some hundred thousand indifferent Irish troops and a French contingent with him. William was forced to withdraw his attention from the European war and to lead an army in person to Ireland. He won the battle of the Boyne, and James fled, never to return to his refractory kingdoms. But Ireland was still full of troops and resistance continued; William was held up by the stubborn defence of Limerick. If Louis decided to send a French army, Ireland might still be lost. Marlborough realized that the southern landing ports were the key to the situation, and himself proposed an expedition.

William's Dutch generals, convinced that no English general could make a success of it, were against. The King saw the point and allowed Marlborough to undertake it. That September, with the minimum of fuss and the maximum of efficiency, Marlborough captured both Cork and Kinsale. Gone were the chances of a French invasion now. Field Marshal Wolseley says, "in twenty-three days Marlborough had achieved more than all William's Dutch commanders had done both in Ireland and abroad during the whole of the previous year."[8] The Churchills were much to the fore. Charles, whom Marlborough made a brigadier, took a leading part in the capture of Cork. At the conclusion of the operations, he was made Governor of Kinsale. Henceforth we find him lending to the government, building up his patrimony at Minterne.[9] Berwick, now nineteen, was left in command of James's forces in Ireland: this courageous and able young soldier was worthy of a better cause. He could do nothing to hold up Marlborough's operations: "he was the spectator, by no means for the last time, of his uncle's success."[10] Even William was gracious: "no officer living who has seen so little service as my Lord Marlborough is so fit for great commands."[11] That precisely expressed the inappreciative Dutch attitude.

The commands were not forthcoming. Next year William took the field himself in Flanders and carried Marlborough with him, inevitably subordinate. Nothing happened. There was a great deal of marching and countermarching, in which William was checkmated; when he retired, he handed over the command to Waldeck, who had qualified for it by getting himself badly beaten at Fleurus the year before. And this in spite of what William's cousin, the Prince of Vaudemont, had said to him about the English generals: "Kirke has fire, Lanier thought, Mackay skill and Colchester bravery; but there is something inexpressible in the Earl of Marlborough: all their virtues seem to be united in his single person."[12] This means the indefinable quality of genius. Marlborough was aware of it in himself; he was also aware that William, for all his invincible courage and resolution, was without it. William was a rarer spirit than Marlborough politically; but for all his much longer experience in the field, he was no match for him as a soldier. Here William was merely competent, plodding, safe and without imagination: the solid Dutchman, who had all the authority as King, beside the brilliant Englishman, with "something inexpressible" about him, who had had to make his way step by step for himself.

Without any doubt, there was an element of jealousy in William's attitude to Marlborough. Military glory was the one thing that that heroic spirit—caged in so miserable a carcase, asthmatic, hunched, tubercular—pined for; and it always eluded him. Beside him was the handsome Englishman, who knew all his secrets, understood every movement of his mind, who never gave himself away and had only to hold out his hand, it seemed, and all the fruits of life were his. No wonder a contemporary, watching the King's attitude to Marlborough, concluded that "at heart he never esteemed him."[13] William—watching these English aristocrats, with their smooth courtiers' manners, who had all betrayed their master—must have thought them all false; indeed, he never fully trusted any one of them, except Sidney, of whom he was fond.

Marlborough's legitimate ambitions were thus frustrated, his services insufficiently rewarded. It was rumored in London that he would be made a Duke—after all, Monk had been; that he would be given the Garter, appointed Master of the Ordnance, given the command in Ireland. Nothing came of any of these. He very much wanted to be Master of the Ordnance—a lucrative office—though at the Revolution he and Godolphin had generously joined in asking that Dartmouth might be continued in it. Now it was given to Sidney, a civilian with no qualifications whatever. Ginkel had been given the command in Ireland; the elderly and incompetent Waldeck continued to command the King's confidence in Flanders. A command was what Marlborough, with serene confidence in himself, wanted more than anything: an opportunity that would deploy his capacities, now at their prime, to the fullest. Was he to wait for ever? Under James, he had had to take second place for a third-rate

Frenchman, Feversham; under William, he was to play second fiddle, in his own country, to a lot of Dutchmen.

To these discontents were added the poison, the irreparable hurts, of a women's quarrel: of Queen Mary and her sister over money, politics and, above all, Sarah.

2

We must remember that the only account we have of this famous affair comes from Sarah and is necessarily biased: there must have been something to be said on both sides.*

Things were bound to be difficult between the two sisters in their position, as always between two royal persons set against each other by circumstances, with the constant pull of politics and rival Courts tugging them apart. Sarah believed that William was at the bottom of it; and no doubt there was the usual feeling between the occupants of the throne and the heiress presumptive waiting to step into their shoes. Moreover, Mary had no children; Anne was the mother of the little Duke of Gloucester and was still breeding. Though Mary was popular, William was decidedly not; he was jealous both of Anne's popularity and of her independence—for she had a party, as heir to the throne, at her service in the Commons, while the Tories and all the High Church people looked to her.

In addition, there was a complete incompatibility of temper between the royal sisters. "It was impossible they should be very agreeable companions to each other," Sarah said, "because Queen Mary grew weary of anybody who would not talk a great deal; and the Princess was so silent that she rarely spoke more than was necessary to answer a question."[14] Sarah gives an unflattering account of Mary; but in truth she was gay and lively, full of extrovert interests, modest about her own capacities and touchingly devoted to the great but inscrutable man, her husband, of whom she stood in awe and who gave her no children. We have seen what Anne was like—much more like her father: sullen and sad, capable of tremendous devotion, generous to those she took to, obstinate as a mule—but a common-sense mule.

The first clash took place with regard to the revenues to be settled on the Princess. William wanted these to be left to his discretion, to come

---

* There is a good account of it from Mary's side in Hester W. Chapman, *Mary II, Queen of England.*

out of his civil list, and expressed his wonder how the Princess could spend £30,000 a year, "though it appeared afterwards that some of his own favourites had more."[15] The Princess not unnaturally preferred a settlement on her by Parliament, which made her secure, rather than depend on William's grace and favor. Her friends were prepared to propose a grant of £70,000 a year. One night at Court the Queen asked the Princess what was the meaning of these proceedings in Parliament? "To which the Princess answered, 'She heard her friends had a mind to make her some settlement.' The Queen replied with a very imperious air, 'Pray, what friends have you but the King and me?' "[16] It was one of those sallies that are delicious to deliver and are never forgiven by the recipient. Anne had no answer, but she resented it all the more: she determined to accept no offer from William. Her friends answered for her: she got a Parliamentary grant of £50,000 a year.

A year after this, Sarah was surprised by a letter from the Princess: "I have had something to say to you a great while, and I do not know how to go about it. I have designed, ever since my revenue was settled, to desire you would accept of a thousand pounds a year. I beg you would only look upon it as an earnest of my good will, but never mention anything of it to me; for I shall be ashamed to have any notice taken of such a thing from one that deserves more than I shall be ever able to return."[17] Sarah consulted her confessor, Godolphin, whether she might accept the pension; he saw no reason in the world for her to refuse it, and neither did she.

Ill feeling between the royal sisters expressed itself in all sorts of ways: as to the Princess's lodgings at Whitehall, for she wanted to exchange hers at the Cockpit; as to the Queen's house at Richmond, which Anne wanted for the air for her children, and Mary would not let her have, though she did not use it herself. William treated Prince George worse. The Prince was anxious to serve in Ireland; William would not allow him to go in the coach with him: he had to tag along with the troopers behind, and during the whole campaign the King took no more notice of him "than if he had been a page of the backstairs."[18] Next year, the Prince asked permission to serve at sea, rather than on land, and, taking the King's silent embrace for consent, prepared his equipage and sent everything on board. At the last moment, he received the order that he was not to go to sea and that he was to make this appear as his own choice. It made Anne's husband, whom she adored, look still more of a fool. There was also policy in it: when William was so unpopular, it would not have done to give the Prince a chance of winning any laurels.

On top of this came Marlborough's disgrace. On January 24, 1692, Evelyn notes: "Lord Marlborough, Lieutenant-General of the King's army in England, Gentleman of the Bedchamber etc. dismissed from all his charges, military and other, for his excessive taking of bribes, covetousness and extortion on all occasions from his inferior officers."[19] This was the complexion it was given; but there was much more to the affair than this. Marlborough's extraordinary patience had at last given way. Resentful of the deliberate frustration imposed upon his military abilities, contemptuous of the futile conduct of the last campaign in Flanders, he became an outspoken critic of the King. He made himself the spokesman of the English resentment at being led by the nose by the Dutch: at his headquarters he made no bones about what he thought of them.* His indiscretions were calculated: he meant his remarks about the "wooden" Bentinck and others of William's intimates to reach him. He told the King to his face what he thought about his disposal, on an enormous scale, of the property of the English Crown to his Dutch favorites. The King turned his back on him. When William proposed to take him abroad again on campaign in a subordinate capacity—to witness similar futilities or worse—Marlborough refused: he never served William in the field again. For the whole of the rest of the war, for the five years 1692 to 1697, the genius of the most brilliant of English soldiers was given no chance to deploy itself, went unused. Meanwhile, William's third-rate commanders bumbled about and stumbled on disaster; he himself, though showing heroic tenacity in adverse circumstances, could never contrive victory.

It was like the years 1931 to 1939, during which the prescience and the experience, the courage and the talents, of Marlborough's descendant went unused, and the country stumbled into disaster. There is a further parallel: the mediocrity of the generalship in the first war 1689-97 may

---

* Burnet, who was in a good position to know from William's side, tells us that for his service at Cork and Kinsale, Marlborough hoped for an increase of title and to be made Master of the Ordnance. This was denied him, and "finding that he had not so absolute a disposal of all employments in the English army as he expected, he set himself to decry the King's conduct and to lessen him in all his discourses" and to decry the influence of the Dutch. This discourse was the constant entertainment at Marlborough's headquarters, the regular rendezvous of the English officers. *Supplement to the History of My Own Time*, 368.

be compared to that in the war of 1914-18. Just as the war of 1689-97 may have been a necessary apprenticeship to the brilliant achievements of Marlborough's war, 1702-13, so the war of 1914-18 may be regarded as a dress rehearsal for the more remarkable performance of 1940-45.

William was not the man to put up with insubordination, and Marlborough went further: he made himself the organizer of the opposition to the King. He set on foot moves both in the Lords and Commons for addresses to the Crown against the employment of foreigners. These might well have been carried in the unrest and discontent of 1692— and William would have been robbed of his Dutch guards, the guarantee of his authority. He had no intention of being a *roi fainéant*, dependent on the good will of the men who had thrown out James II. As part of his purpose of obtaining as wide support as possible, Marlborough was in touch with the Jacobites. Sir Winston, with his political instinct, has perceived, what historians have not, that it was not on this side that the danger to William lay. A nationwide movement in favor of the Princess Anne was far more dangerous than any that concerned James—and this was precisely the combination that Marlborough, with his strategic sense and his hold on the Princess through Sarah, was forming. William could see "Parliament, the Army and the Princess Anne—a fatal trident —in the hand of Marlborough, pointed at his heart. Macaulay says, 'William was not prone to fear, but if there was anyone on earth that he feared, it was Marlborough.' "[20] So like Macaulay's exaggerations: I do not think there was anyone on earth that William feared, not even Marlborough. But he was enraged: he said openly at Court that Marlborough had treated him so infamously that "had he not been a king, he would have felt it necessary to demand personal satisfaction."

Thus do human beings pile up *impasses* in their relations with each other. We may fairly observe that William was the more to blame for his treatment of Marlborough. On the other hand, since he was King, it was not for him to place himself at the mercy of his most menacing subject. Not that Marlborough would necessarily have removed William; but if he had been able to place the Princess Anne at the head of a combination of the army, the Church and the Tories, backed by the sentiment of the nation against Dutch rule, Marlborough would have been in the controlling position that he had missed so bitterly at Salisbury in 1688.

The heroic little man had not come to England for this consummation. Without a word of warning, Marlborough was dismissed from all his offices, civil and military, and forbidden the Court. Worse was to follow. Then, for the next three years, the King neither saw nor spoke to Marlborough.

Some weeks later, Sarah, who had refrained from appearing at Court, went to Kensington in attendance upon her mistress. The Princess was *enceinte*, and so the Queen spared her a scene; but she wrote her a letter next day: "seeing that you brought Lady Marlborough hither last night, makes us resolve to put it off no longer, but tell you, she must not stay . . . I must tell you, it was very unkind in a sister, would have been very uncivil in an equal, and I need not say I have more to claim. Which, though my kindness would make me never exact, yet when I see the use you would make of it, I must tell you I know what is due to me and expect to have it from you. 'Tis upon that account, I tell you plainly, Lady Marlborough must not continue with you in the circumstances her lord is."[21]

The Queen got a reply from Anne: "your care of my present condition is extremely obliging. And if you would be pleased to add to it so far, as upon my account to recall your severe command . . . I should ever acknowledge it as a very agreeable mark of your kindness."[22] To this the Queen did not reply, but sent a message by the Lord Chamberlain forbidding Lady Marlborough from continuing any longer at the Cockpit. The Princess was not going to give way to this. She determined to retire from Court and persuaded the Duke of Somerset to lend her Syon House for her approaching confinement.

The summer of 1692 was very critical for England. An invasion was at last being prepared by Louis in the Channel ports—and here were the central figures in the Revolution of 1688 divided and quarreling. At the height of the invasion scare, papers were laid incriminating Marlborough and others in a dangerous conspiracy: their signatures were very cleverly forged. Coming at such a moment, it looks like a frame-up. On May 4 Marlborough was sent to the Tower, on the dangerous charge of high treason. We must remember that this was the century of the Popish Plot and such things: those who were a danger to government were open to this kind of treatment. The enlightened twentieth century has not been without similar examples, or worse. Marlborough at least had powerful friends to protest against his being sent to the Tower on such dubious evidence. While he was there, a private grief assailed

John and Sarah: their younger son died, leaving only one boy to carry on the name and the line.

Anne's letters are full of solicitude: "I hear Lord Marlborough is sent to the Tower; and though I am certain they have nothing against him . . . yet I was struck when I was told it; for methinks it is a dismal thing to have one's friends sent to that place. I have a thousand melancholy thoughts, and cannot help fearing they should hinder you from coming to me; though how they can do that without making you a prisoner, I cannot imagine."[23] The Princess was expecting that a guard would be set on her the moment the French invasion fleet set sail. "But let them do what they please, nothing shall ever vex me, so I can have the satisfaction of seeing dear Mrs. Freeman; and I swear I would live on bread and water, between four walls, with her, without repining; for as long as you continue kind, nothing can ever be a real mortification to your faithful Mrs. Morley, who wishes she may never enjoy a moment's happiness, in this world or the next, if ever she proves false to you."

Alas, for the vanity of such assurances!—twelve years ahead and the breach between these two women was irreparable. Anne's passion for Sarah was too possessive, too overwhelming: Sarah could not requite it fully. She was really rather bored by it—husband and family were enough for her—and this must have been an element in the reaction that ultimately overwhelmed Anne's too passionate attachment and turned it, tragically, into detestation.

Now, Anne cannot see enough of her friend: every letter clamors for her dear presence. "I wish with all my soul . . . that it may be soon in our power to enjoy one another's company, more than it has been of late; which is all I covet in this world."[24] In the miserable situation in which the Princess was placed in relation to her sister, Sarah naturally offered again and again, as the obstacle between them, to remove herself. At once Anne replies: "there is no misery I cannot readily resolve to suffer, rather than the thought of parting from you. And I do swear, I would sooner be torn in pieces than alter this my resolution."

Whenever Sarah brought forward the idea of parting, to ease the situation between the royal sisters, the Princess "fell into the greatest passion of tenderness and weeping that is possible to imagine." Sarah said that if she could have known how long this was to last, she would have chosen to go to the Indies rather than endure it. That she was not exaggerating Anne's passion we can see from her language whenever

Sarah broached the thought of their parting: "I beg it again for Christ Jesus's sake, that you would never name it any more to me. For be assured, if you should ever do so cruel a thing as to leave me, from that moment I shall never enjoy one quiet hour. And should you do it without asking my consent (which if I ever give you, may I never see the face of heaven) I will shut myself up and never see the world more, but live where I may be forgotten by human kind." The accents of passion are unmistakable; Anne was a very single-minded woman, who could love only one object at a time, but with all the intensity of her nature. We also catch the very English Princess, though no reading woman, echoing her Shakespeare.

Dutch William was detested by these two women. After all, he had little to commend him to women; and, for his part, he took little notice of them. Anne and Sarah called him Caliban, or the Dutch Abortion. Used as they were to the polished manners of the Restoration Court, they were horrified by his ill breeding. We all know the story of the dish of new peas brought to his table when Anne was dining with him and her sister one day. The Queen dared not touch them; and Anne, to her horror—for she was pregnant and had a longing for them—had to watch William eat up every one himself without offering her any. This was all the more mortifying in that Anne, besides her pregnancy, was also a glutton.

In June Marlborough applied to the Council for his habeas corpus and asked for bail.* The great Trimmer, Lord Halifax, went bail for him. Anne wrote Sarah to ask if there were as yet "any hopes of Lord Marlborough's being soon at liberty. For God's sake have a care of your dear self, and give as little way to melancholy thoughts as you can . . . I will not fail of being with my dear Mrs. Freeman above five or six o'clock unless you are to go to the Tower." She followed this up with a spirited missive. "It is a comfort they cannot keep Lord Marlborough in the Tower longer than the end of the term; and I hope, when the Parliament sits, care will be taken that people may not be clapt up for nothing, or else there will be no living in quiet for anybody but insolent Dutch and sneaking mercenary Englishmen." That was the tone of the Cockpit

---

* Sarah writes, *Account of the Conduct*, 88, that "Lord Marlborough had friends who would bail him, but one of his best friends was a paper that lay upon the table, which I had often kissed, *The Act of Habeas Corpus*." We see that she was already a Whig and an emotional one.

circle: the assertion of a conscious English feeling against the foreigner ruling the country; and of course it appealed to national sentiment.

Marlborough was freed, indignant at his treatment and the King's ingratitude. He probably did not calculate that his tribulation rendered him a service in the long run. Hitherto, he had been regarded simply as a royal favorite, for whom things had been easy; human nature being constructed as it is, no one takes unalloyed pleasure in the success of others. The Churchills were disrespected and decidedly unpopular. This was the turning point. Marlborough had shown that he could speak out, that he was not afraid to take the sole responsibility for opposing a powerful sovereign—a very different matter from James. He had made himself the spokesman of national feeling; like all the best people in English history, like Queen Elizabeth herself, he had seen the inside of the Tower.

Perhaps, in accordance with the strange ironies of history, it was a necessary step in his becoming a national figure. Just as with his descendant: it turned out well for Sir Winston that he was kept out of power during the treacherous decade 1931-39 and had no responsibility for the fatal conduct of our policy. At the supreme moment, in 1940, he could come forward as the one leader of the nation, uncontaminated by the associations of false leads and hopes, appeasement and defeat.

While Marlborough was in the Tower, the decisive victory of La Hogue took place at sea—the Trafalgar of the age. English supremacy in the Channel was established, to last throughout those wars: all danger of an invasion was at an end. Tension was relaxed; Marlborough was free. But he was not employed. The feud continued. Anne was immovable and William considered bringing financial pressure to bear by curtailing her Parliamentary grant. This would not make her budge one inch: she and the Prince took up their position. "Can you think either of us so wretched that for the sake of twenty thousand pound, and to be tormented from morning to night with flattering knaves and fools, we should forsake those we have such obligations to, and that we are so certain we are the occasion of all their misfortunes? . . . No, my dear Mrs. Freeman, never believe your faithful Mrs. Morley will ever submit. She can wait with patience for a sunshine day, and if she does not live to see it, yet she hopes England will flourish again."[25]

It is evident that when that sunshine day came, and Anne was Queen of England, hers was a character that would have to be taken into account, if only for its monumental obstinacy.

At Syon House Anne gave birth to a child, which died immediately after. The Queen paid her a visit, but only to insist on removing Sarah. Anne trembled and went as white as the sheets, but would not give way. Small persecutions of a trivial royal character followed. Her guards of honor were taken away, and people at Court forbidden to visit her. When she went to Bath to recover, the mayor was instructed not to treat her with the usual ceremonies, attending the Princess to church in state, etc. The King and Queen would sometimes show an interest in Anne's child, little William, Duke of Gloucester; but whoever was sent was told to take no more notice of the Princess than if she was a rocker, and went straight to deliver messages to the boy. He was an intelligent child and one day embarrassed the King by observing that his mother used to have her guards too: why were they taken away? It was all the usual small change of futile human quarrels. Anne had a good friend at the Treasury in Godolphin: he resisted any attempt to cut down the revenue, and would have left the government if it had been attempted.

The stalemate was broken by the sudden illness of the Queen, who was stricken with smallpox—that scourge of all classes from highest to lowest: never were its ravages more striking than in the century from the Restoration onward. Anne at once wrote asking if she might come to her sister's bedside. Sarah received the reply saying that it was necessary to keep the Queen as quiet as possible; Lady Derby added a postscript, "Pray, madam, present my humble duty to the Princess."[26] From this Sarah, inured to the language of courts, concluded, "more than if the college of physicians had told it me, that the disease was mortal." The Queen died unreconciled to her sister: "nor, though she received the sacrament in her illness, did she ever send the least message to the Princess."

Mary's death transformed the situation for the Princess Anne, and for all her friends and dependents. Hitherto, Mary's life had seemed a much better one than Anne's: she had much greater spirits and vitality. There was little enough prospect that Anne would survive her and come to the throne. And that must be said for the loyalty of the Marlboroughs in sticking by her: Sarah does not fail to say it and to hint that Mary would have welcomed the transfer of her allegiance earlier. I dare say: actually, Sarah's Whig outlook would have been more in keeping with the royal circle than with Anne's.

Now the Princess was fairly certain to succeed to the throne: only the rickety life of William stood between her and it. Anne wrote a dutiful and sympathetic letter to the King; the King received her with extraordinary civility at Kensington. Everyone knew his (or her) duty in the changed situation. Crowds of people flocked to pay their respects to the heiress to the throne—with that heartless display of unmeaning civility, with an eye to the main chance, characteristic of an aristocratic society. The Princess's Court was more attended now than William's, growing more solitary and caring only for his boon companions. Berkeley House was too small for her. Old Lord Sunderland, whose manners were even more insinuating than his politics—Sarah tells us that "he had upon all occasions relating to her [Anne], showed himself a man of sense and breeding"—interposed himself to make things easy with William and persuaded him to give the Princess St. James's.[27] Here, in suitable state, the heiress to the throne could await with patience the "sunshine day" of which she had written to Sarah in the darkest of their troubles.

3

No one's prospects were more obviously transformed than Marlborough's: he could look forward to the future now with some confidence. William still did not employ him, and he continued to forgo the pay and profits of his offices—a very considerable sacrifice that has been overlooked.

Much as Marlborough loved money—a trait characteristic of a sensible man—he loved the proper exercise of his unique talents more; and this was denied him. The news of the near disaster at Steinkirk in the summer of his troubles, 1692, must have been bitter to him. Solms, the wooden Dutch general to whom William confided the command of Marlborough's troops, led them into a frightful carnage and stubbornly refused to send for help. Half their number, some three thousand of them, were killed or wounded. Even William was moved to tears, "*O, mes pauvres Anglais,*" as he witnessed their being cut to pieces, unable to control the battle. Marlborough would have done better if he had been there: he was never defeated in his life.

At home it was no longer Marlborough's business to make trouble for the King. Excluded though he was, his friends were in the inner circle of government: his best friend, Godolphin, always there, dependable, loyal, indispensable. Marlborough, entrenched at St. James's, exerted himself increasingly to give the King much-needed support, and to keep relations with Anne on a good footing. It was not always easy, for William was determined to keep all power in his hands and, like most monarchs, was jealous at the thought of a successor. Going on his last campaign, he proposed to appoint the whole household of the little Duke of Gloucester himself, though he had promised the Princess she should have her say, and on this she had engaged her word to several people. When Marlborough reminded him of this, "the King fell into a great passion and said, 'she should not be queen before her time.' "[28] It was very like Elizabeth I.

Marlborough continued his polite exchanges with the exiled Court at St. Germain. These had hardly ceased, any more than those of Godolphin, Shrewsbury and others among the government. William knew about them, and found them not inconvenient.* It was a way of obtaining information. One thing we can be sure of about Marlborough: he received more information than he gave. He never told St. Germain anything that it had not heard of already; and that seems to be the explanation of the famous case of the Brest expedition. In the autumn of 1694 Berwick came secretly to England to weave together the threads of a Jacobite conspiracy: there is no likelihood that he saw his uncle. When the Fenwick conspiracy burst upon the country, and Marlborough's old antagonist charged him with complicity, William took no notice. There could be no better sign of the understanding at length established.

At length, in 1697, peace was made at Ryswick—or rather a truce, as in 1802, for the issue of French supremacy, of Louis XIV's domination, was not settled. Everybody was glad of a breathing space. Tallard, whom Marlborough was to meet on a more famous occasion, came to England as the French envoy. Louis was ready to restore practically all his conquests; William to waive his demand for the extrusion of the exiled Court from France—indeed, he was so agreeable as to allow Mary of Modena £50,000 a year for her jointure, a polite way of making life easier for James in his last years.

In 1698 Marlborough was at last restored to his rank in the army,

---

* Ailesbury says that the King gave leave to Marlborough, Godolphin, Shrewsbury and Admiral Russell to correspond with Lord Middleton, the Secretary of State at St. Germain. "They infused into the King the great advantage that might arise to him by it, and on my conscience I believe it. Middleton was not to know anything of high secret moment that passed in England; but they four would wiredraw all out of my Lord Middleton, so that all the secrets of St. Germain would come to their knowledge." *Memoirs*, 391.

and to the Privy Council. A more significant mark of confidence and a recognition of the rôle he would necessarily play in the future came with the constitution of a household for the little Duke of Gloucester—promising in every way, except his health. Marlborough was made his Governor. Even William was gracious on this occasion: "my Lord, teach him but to know what you are, and my nephew cannot want for accomplishments."[29] The golden flow of favor was restored. In addition to his army pay as Lieutenant General and his colonelcies of regiments, Marlborough now received £2,000 a year as Governor and £1,200 a year for his table.[30] His own young son was made Master of the Horse to the little Duke, at £500 a year, quite a nice little sum for a playmate. Sarah obtained posts for her poor relations, the Hills: a younger daughter was made laundress at £200 a year, her brother Jack a groom of the bedchamber at something similar.[31] The little Duke was rather a favorite with his forbidding uncle, the King: the boy was mad about soldiers and that recommended him to that soldierly spirit. Then, one day in 1700, the boy caught smallpox and swiftly died. William, then in Holland, was much affected: "it is so great a loss to me, as well as to all England, that it pierces my heart with affliction," he wrote to Marlborough.[32] We can imagine how much more of a blow it was to Anne, her last remaining hope: it is from this time that she begins to sign herself in her letters to Sarah, "your poor unfortunate faithful Morley."

Marlborough's daughters were growing up, and of an age to be married. In 1698 the eldest, Henrietta, was married to Godolphin's only son: it seems to have been a love match between the young persons, but it was also another bond in the historic friendship between the parents. It was in every way a suitable match, except that the too-virtuous Godolphin had not the wherewithal to endow his son. The Princess Anne, in her constant rôle of fairy godmother to the Marlboroughs, weighed in; nor could it have been done with more tact and good feeling. "I have a request to make to my dear Mrs. Freeman. It is that, whenever dear Lady Harriet marries, you would give me leave to give her something to keep me in her thoughts . . . I beg my poor mite may be accepted, being from a heart that is without any reserve with more passion and sincerity my dear Mrs. Freeman's than any other can be capable of."[33] The mite proposed was £10,000. Sarah says, with some complacency, that it always had been the custom of the Crown to give portions to the daughters of their favorites, but that since the Princess had but £50,000 a year, she would accept no more than £5,000. It was on a par with Anne's constant generosity to the Marlboroughs, which Sarah took for granted and gave no very generous recognition of in return.

It is true that Sarah served Anne, both as Princess and Queen, with great competence and looked after the finances of her household with a firm and saving hand. And for the rest, great persons were apt to be served very ill, negligently, extravagantly, taken advantage of on all sides —Anne herself, to an extreme degree. On her side, Anne was very ready to recognize Sarah's service with generosity: "though it will be impossible for me to have everything done to my mind, unless I could meet with a Mrs. Freeman in every post of my family; but her fellow I do really believe is not to be found the world over, and I am sure I never can have any friend that will be so dear to me as she is." The Princess was touchingly pleased at the expression of gratitude on the loved one's part—she was "very kind in setting so great a value upon so poor an expression as I have made of my truth, which upon my word I am not satisfied with, it coming far short of what my heart is inclined to do."

We see that Anne is a much-underestimated woman, so far overshadowed by the figures that had dominated her life. But, observed under the powerful telescope of history, she emerges as a truly royal person, her breeding never failing her, or her tact, or her instinctive simple dignity; when the tremendous position of Queen of three kingdoms came to her, she added to her modesty and common sense an innate sense of responsibility and an immovable will power.

In 1698 Marlborough's favorite daughter, little Anne, vivacious and sparkling, was married to—of all people—Sunderland's son and heir. We have seen how Sunderland had retrieved himself from the shocking gamble for power into which he had plunged under James, and had wormed his way into William's confidence. He expressed a characteristic wish that his son would henceforth be governed in everything public and private by Marlborough. Of course he was not: such exaggerated wishes are always doomed to disappointment. The son was an extreme, a doctrinaire, Whig and became a liability later for Marlborough with Queen Anne—all the more so because he fortified Sarah's outspoken Whig propensities. In the end, his wife and son-in-law became too much for poor Marlborough. For the present, all was well: the Princess came forward with another portion of £5,000, and Marlborough, himself a Tory, gained the advantage of these important new Whig connections.

The last years of William's heroic, laborious life were spent in a quicksand of diplomatic activities on a European scale. His strength was ebbing; he felt Time's wingèd chariot hurrying near. But he would not relax his hold on power, or give up, till his last breath. All the subtle combinations of European politics, all the possibilities and alternatives, were in his brain as in no one else's. What he needed was a hand to execute for him in his failing strength. More and more he turned to Marlborough; he even began to make him confidences, of his troubles, his disappointments, his plans. William, with his European viewpoint, never could accommodate himself to the petty broils of English party politics: he was weary of them, weary to death, of their self-sufficiency, their ignorance, their irresponsibility. This was his great, though very understandable, weakness; it was where Marlborough, with his extraordinary patience, had an advantage.

As Sir Winston says, "the self-sufficiency of the House of Commons knew no bounds. Sagacious in all that fell within their sphere of domestic knowledge, they were ignorant or disdainful of the world issues which were shortly to invade their affairs."[34] As between the two great wars in our time, they were too ready to throw away, not merely the advantages, but the security which had been won at such a cost in lives and wealth.

It was sad, too, that for so long there had been no co-operation between William and Marlborough; that, when they had the same purposes at heart, the same common objectives, they should have been riven apart by the contrary pulls of affections and misunderstandings— alas for the tragedy implicit in so many human relations! Sir Winston sums it all up with the wisdom of a lifetime's experience: "these incomplete relationships were the King's own fault, and a misfortune to his reign. If in 1689 and 1690 William, with two kingdoms to govern and the diplomacy of half Europe in his hands, had treated Marlborough fairly and had not denied him his rightful opportunity upon the battlefields, he might have found that talisman of victory without which all his painstaking, adroit combinations and noble exertions could achieve but a mediocre result. He might have found across the differences of rank that same comradeship, never disturbed by doubt or jealousy, true to the supreme tests of war and fortune, which later shone between Marlborough and Prince Eugene."*

It is not our purpose to go into the diplomatic complexities that engaged William's last energies. The overwhelming problem that faced Western Europe was this: what was to happen to the vast inheritance of Spain, both in Europe and America, on the approaching extinction of the line of Spanish Habsburgs with the childless Charles II? The whole undivided inheritance could not be allowed to come to Louis XIV's grandson, the nearest male heir: it would overthrow irrevocably the balance of Europe, which William had fought all his life to maintain, was the only security for the lesser states of Europe, was the essential and necessary objective of British policy—as it always has been, when sensibly conducted.

In 1698 and again in 1700 William seemed to have reached agreement with Louis to partition the inheritance—in spite of the incomprehension of the House of Commons and their weakening the King's hand. But could Louis be trusted to keep his word? Again and again he had shown that he could not. When at last Charles of Spain died, Louis accepted the whole vast inheritance for his grandson, contrary to his engagements. There was no reaction to the menace in England, no realization of the danger in the Commons. Holland could not "go it alone." William was in despair; it looked as if his life's work were undone.

Then Louis came to his aid, as he had before, with a series of crashing mistakes, due to arrogant overconfidence: pride once more asserting itself and having to pay a heavy price. Without warning—a Hitlerlike move—Louis seized all the Dutch barrier fortresses along the frontier of the Spanish Netherlands, which were the line of Holland's security. The menace aroused the instinct of self-preservation among the Dutch, who now were ready to give William the complete support that had been wanting. At the same time, on James II's death at St. Germain, Louis recognized his son as King of England. This at last aroused the complacent English to what was in store for them; they, too, came into line behind the King, who had been prescient all along. How these themes repeat themselves, and how people in politics superfluously make the same kind of mistakes over and over!

It was now possible to knit together again the Grand Alliance of all

---

* Churchill, *Marlborough*, I, 505-6. Prince Eugene of Savoy was the most brilliant and successful of the commanders serving on the side of the Austrian Empire.

the powers of Western Europe whose security—and the existence of some
—was threatened by the domination, and the aggression, of Louis XIV.
William called Marlborough to his aid. At last he was to be engaged upon
a task that extended his fullest capacities, the work to which all his life
had led up. In the summer of 1701 he went over to Holland in state and
with full powers. Nothing was omitted to declare to the world that he was
the representative of the English state. He was appointed Ambassador
Extraordinary and Plenipotentiary for negotiations with the Empire, the
States-General and other princes at the Hague, and elsewhere, for securing the peace and liberty of Europe.[35] As such he was to receive £2,000
a year, £1,500 for his equipage and £100 a week for his ordinary entertainment. From the Jewel House went forth 5,893 ounces of white plate
and 1,066 of gilt plate—the proper allowance for such a mission.[36] At
the same time he was made Commander in Chief of all the English
forces serving in the Netherlands.[37]

All his life Marlborough had been negotiating; but when he first
appeared, a prime figure on the European scene, the world did not know
what a master was now taking a hand, subtler, more accommodating,
less autocratic than William. Swiftly yet surely, he drew together the
strands, winning people's confidence, never offending them, forming
the friendships that were to last through years of struggle, and beyond.
The treaties that Marlborough made were shaped and presented with
more Parliamentary understanding than William would have shown,
more patient forbearance for English foibles. The care that Marlborough took to marshal English opinion, the unfailing courtesy, may be
seen from a letter to a not very close supporter in the Lords, sending
him a copy of the treaties. "I take the liberty to send them as to a friend
whose judgment I much depend upon. I desire you will take no notice of
the having seen them, and when I have the honour of seeing you,
which I hope may be before the Parliament meets, I shall let you know
my reasons for what is done as well as acquaint you with all that shall be
done. For I call God to witness that I have had no thoughts but what
might be for the good of England."[38]

His strength failing, William gave helpful supervision from his
country house, Het Loo: after all, Marlborough had learned much from
him. When William got back to England, he was visibly dying. He
was worn out, his lifework done. At the same age—such are the injustices
of life and fate—Marlborough was just beginning upon his.

CHAPTER XII

The Duke

WE ARE all familiar with the outlines of Marlborough's military achievement, the unbroken record of success, the four great battles: the brilliant victories of Blenheim (1704), Ramillies (1706), Oudenarde (1708) and the bloody struggle of Malplaquet (1709). It may be well to ask at once, what were the qualities of Marlborough's generalship? To what did he owe his untarnished career of victory? It was a tremendous surprise to the Continent: the first time that an Englishman had given the French lessons in the art of fighting on land since Henry V. And it made an enormous impression in Europe: no wonder French school children still sing "Malbrouck-s'en-va-t'en-guerre."

That other soldier-Duke in our history, Wellington, was also never defeated. There could hardly be more of a contrast between him and Marlborough. Where the Iron Duke was cold, competent to the nth degree, a hard man, stoical and taciturn, Marlborough was *sensible* in the French sense, a most sensitive register of all the impressions that came to him, an artist by temperament in his ups and downs—the depressions he got before the precipitant of action, the headaches that racked him at all the obstructions he had to put up with, and the self-control he exercised so habitually that it became second nature to him. It exacted its price. Where Wellington, for all the edge to that remarkable personality, was a rather impersonal man, forbidding, a man of whom others stood in awe, apt to be silent, Marlborough was affable, of an extreme courtesy, talkative, willing to communicate what he wished his hearers to know and think. For he was, in fact, as an experienced observer saw, "brimful of policy"—and not only with regard to his immense European objectives, but in all the small change of personal life. Everything was calculated: personal attentions to a visiting Jacobite peer, the first lobster to his wife who is pregnant and longs for it; worn out after fourteen hours in the saddle after Ramillies and lying down on the ground to sleep in his cloak, then remembering to share it with some Dutch deputy who may be useful; offering empty *politesses* to the Court of St. Germain, but not hesitating to suggest two million livres for himself if peace should be made!

For what is exciting about John Churchill is that, beneath that handsome, polished, serene exterior, there was a most daring, far-ranging ambition. And that is characteristic of his generalship, as of the man as a whole. It is not for nothing that Blenheim Palace was his choice, his child, not Sarah's, whose common sense was affronted by anything so magnificent, so rhetorical—the nearest thing in England to Versailles. In John Churchill, there was a fascinating mixture of caution with extreme daring: we have seen it glimpsed and muffled in 1688, open and undisguised in his political action in 1692. We now see it displayed in warfare: in the Great Design of 1703, in the march to the Danube, the projects for a lunge into the heart of France, for another march across Europe to aid Prince Eugene in Italy, to be co-ordinated with the use of the Mediterranean for an attack on Toulon. In the first years of his supreme command, his allies—especially the Dutch—were terrified of his audacity: they thought it rashness and clung on to his coattails, clogging his operations, holding up action.

Certainly Marlborough took risks that Wellington would never have taken. In action, in strategy, on the field of battle, he had the confidence of a virtuoso: everything was brought into play, with a sure, deft instinct. There was "something inexpressible" about him—pure military genius. His old rival, Ginkel, after doing everything to hinder Marlborough's first campaign, declared breathlessly at the end of it, "the success of this campaign is solely due to this incomparable chief, since I confess that I, serving as second in command, opposed in all circumstances his opinions and proposals."[1] Marlborough brought a new spirit into warfare as William III and Louis XIV knew it, a rather static business of formal sieges, sedate marches and textbook battles ending in stalemate. In speed, flexibility, dash, Marlborough was the precursor of Napoleon; like Napoleon, too, Marlborough fought a battle to gain a decision. No wonder Napoleon made a special study of Marlborough: the only Englishman whom France, *mère des armes*, has ever thought worthy of that honor.

Marlborough, then, made war mobile.

There is something else to account for the consistent success of Marlborough's army in the field and the confidence it developed in itself, its faith in him—we must think of the army as his, for never more than one third of it was British: the rest were Dutch infantry of stubborn, fighting quality, squadrons of Danish horse, the rest Germans, who always make excellent mercenaries. The key to the superiority of Marlborough's infantry was that it was armed with flintlocks instead of matchlocks: the French were slow in catching up with this new weapon, which gave a much more effective volley. Marlborough exploited this advantage to the uttermost: he did not think of infantry as a static mass, but as a moving flame, and all his training of his troops was directed to increasing precision and weight of fire. In consequence, Marlborough could afford to advance his infantry in four-line formations against the French six or eight, with extended wings to outflank the enemy; while his use of man power was economical. The man who was so careful of cash was equally sparing of his men: he ended up the battle of Ramillies, completest of his victories, with a considerable number of fresh troops unused.

This enabled him to tackle superior numbers with confidence, and it helped to create the fluidity by which he gained a superiority of force at the decisive spot at the right moment. In the heat of the battle he calculated numbers, as he counted his cash. At the crisis of Ramillies, his most perfect work of art, he suddenly came out with, "I have five horses to two." Actually it was five to three; but it was sufficient to overwhelm the enemy. To obtain that preponderance was what he had been maneuvering for, like a chess player. As Sir Winston says of Blenheim, where Marlborough achieved the same result by taking advantage of the mistaken dispositions of the French: "there is a grand simplicity in two or three to one at the decisive point. To procure it—there lies the secret."[2]

Marlborough used cavalry, as Cromwell had done, as a shock weapon rather than a missile; and in those days of extended battle fronts, of four or five miles, as against Waterloo's three, cavalry was still the decisive force, giving the *coup de grâce*. Marlborough kept the artillery under his own personal direction, and used it in mobile fashion: at Ramillies, for example, he had the guns brought up against the French right that was crumbling, and from thence he rolled up the whole French army. His methods were distinctly unorthodox: that was what alarmed the Dutch textbook generals and caught out the French. At Blenheim he was thought to have taken an excessive risk: his attack in the center should have been overwhelmed by the enemy's wings. There were plenty of people who wanted to think that Höchstädt was a defeat from which Marlborough was only just saved by Eugene. Marlborough's risks were always well calculated and deep-laid; others fell into the traps: what seemed so risky was not so risky after all. In fact, his three greatest victories were won at a very low cost in casualties.

He was not only economical of his men, but very considerate of them, a humane man: not made of iron like Wellington, with his well-known contempt for "the scum of the earth." Often enough the Commander in Chief went the rounds himself to see to the comfort of his men, just as he never minded exposing himself in the thick of battle—in this case, to a fault. The tremendous six-hundred-mile march to the Danube was conducted with such forethought that the men enjoyed it like a picnic. The day's march always began at dawn, so that by the time it was really hot the troops had reached their next camp: "the remaining part of the day's rest was as good as a halt."[3] Provisions had been laid "before we arrived and the soldiers had nothing to do but to pitch their tents, boil their kettles and lie down to rest. Surely never was such a march carried on with more order and regularity and with less fatigue." It was something that the Commander in Chief had an economical mind.

Marlborough's natural good temper and unfailing tact were immense assets to the common cause: no one else, without the dual authority of William III, could have kept English and Dutch together. The Jacobite exile, Ailesbury, observed him at close quarters in the Netherlands: his information is valuable to us. "For his natural good temper he never had his equal. He could not chide a servant, and was the worst served possible; and in command he could not give a harsh word, no, not to the meanest serjeant, corporal or soldier."[4] This is very endearing in so great a man—though it certainly accounts for Sarah's getting so badly out of hand. There is a story of some Dutch officer getting in a rage and expressing himself very offensively in the Commander in Chief's presence: all that Marlborough did was to turn to someone and say peaceably, "Now I would not be of that man's temper for anything in the world."

He certainly would not have survived as Generalissimo if he had been. There were constant occasions for clashing between English and Dutch. Once when Athlone's (i.e., Ginkel's) men took the forage from Marlborough's in the field, many hard words passed, though fortunately no bloodshed. All that Marlborough said was, "Advertise my Lord Athlone's men to beware of doing that twice."[5] To his own men he explained, "the Dutch troops are in the wrong, but, for reasons, I will have you put up the affront." Ailesbury concludes, "if we had had a General of another disposition, the two nations might have come to hostilities." When there were troubles and disputes over the commissariat, he would say to the Dutchman in charge, "it is our business to look forward for the common cause, and"—putting his hand before his face—"let us wink at all this, and when we have a peace it will then be time to have a discussion." To difficulties that were objected against some enterprise or other, Marlborough would always say: "Done it must be, one way or the other: let us resolve on what way may be of less difficulty."

Along with this went a great deal of art and artifice. On his entry into Brussels, he was careful to make a good impression by paying a formal visit to the first lady of the land, the Countess of Egmont.[6] To the Archbishop à propos of the feast of Corpus Christi he said: "If I can contribute anything towards your solemnizing the festival with more lustre than usual, my brother shall receive my orders." (General Churchill had been made Governor.) The army stood to arms in a square where the procession would not pass, to avoid disturbance. In return the Queen's birthday was celebrated with enthusiasm, and Marlborough's state entry was performed with immense ceremony. "Brimful of policy" and, having made them every assurance as to religion and the laws, he had no trouble in getting them to pay large contributions to the war. In Belgium and Holland alike, he made himself popular—he was always more popular abroad than at home; and that was no disadvantage to one who aspired, as he did, to be made Governor General of the Netherlands, virtually an independent prince.

What ambition! It was like Wallenstein or Napoleon, quite unlike Wellington.

In fact, he was not in absolute command: he was never the master, but the servant, of the Grand Alliance. That added immensely to the complexity of the task, demanded all his powers of diplomacy, all his gifts of concealment, self-subordination, control. Sir Winston says truly, "no-one can read the whole mass of the letters which Marlborough either wrote, dictated or signed personally without being astounded at the mental and physical energy which it attests. The entire range of European affairs, all the intricate personal relations of the heads of states and governments, all the vital connexions with Holland, with the Empire, with Prussia, with the Archduke Charles and with a score of minor potentates, all the anxious and shifting combinations of English politics, all the ceremonious usage which surrounded the Queen, her husband and her Court, are disposed of day after day by a general maneuvering equal or smaller forces in closest contact with a redoubtable enemy, who often might engage in a decisive battle at no more than one hour's notice. After twelve or fourteen hours in the saddle on the long reconnaissances often under cannon-fire; after endless inspections of troops in camp and garrison; after ceaseless calculations about food and supplies, and all the anxieties of direct command in war, Marlborough would reach his tent and conduct the foreign policy of England, decide the main issues of its Cabinet, and of party politics at home. He thought for all, he acted for all . . . But for the life-effort and tireless scheming of Marlborough the whole structure which resisted Louis XIV would have fallen to pieces."[7]

In addition, there was the management of Sarah: a full-time job in itself.

The accession of Anne inaugurated a brilliant age. Whether we consider its literary distinction—with Swift and Defoe, Addison and Steele, the young Pope writing; or science, with Newton, Halley and Hooke still active; or architecture, with Wren, Vanbrugh, Hawksmoor all at work; or the military achievements of Marlborough—the age has left its imprint on England still. There are its visible memorials: St. Paul's and Greenwich Hospital, Castle Howard and Blenheim Palace. What brings the intellectual energies of a society to a finer point, what releases its artistic impulses and gives them fuller expression at one moment rather than another, is a subtle and perhaps not wholly decipherable matter. But it is worth noting that the epochs associated with the rule of a woman—Elizabeth, Anne, Victoria—gave expression to some deep feeling of satisfaction among the English or perhaps allowed that feeling to well up more easily into expression.

Certainly Anne's first appearance before Parliament gave the nation reason to rejoice: here was a lady of regal dignity, a recognizably English figure who could address her subjects in their own language, express their sentiments and their own prejudices in that well modulated voice— William did not speak his subject's language; he spoke the language of the enemy. "I know my own heart to be entirely English," the Queen declared, with an implied comparison with the dead William, and that thrilled the nation. With the Queen at the head, to symbolize the nation, and Marlborough at her right hand, there could be no question of jealousy or conflict: the relation would be one of chivalry and service, of a knight toward his sovereign lady. And something of that was always present in Marlborough's attitude, until the last sad phase, when the irresistible pressure of politics wrenched them apart.

Privately, the understanding between Mrs. Morley and Mr. Freeman, Mrs. Freeman and Mr. Montgomery, was complete: they four would stand against the world. In the autumn of 1703, when Marlborough was discouraged by the disappointments of the campaign, the Queen wrote him a remarkable letter. "The thoughts that both my dear Mrs. Freeman and Mr. Freeman seem to have of retiring gives me no small uneasiness . . . Give me leave to say you should a little consider your faithful friends and poor country, which must be ruined if ever you should put your melancholy thoughts in execution. As for your poor unfortunate faithful Morley, she could not bear it; for if ever you should forsake me, I would have nothing more to do with the world, but make another abdication; for what is a crown when the support of it is gone. I never will forsake your dear self, Mr. Freeman, nor Mr. Montgomery, but always be your constant faithful servant; and we four must never part, till death mows us down with his impartial hand."[8]

It is to be observed that in her serious thoughts, in regard to government and the country, Prince George was hardly a member of the party.

The Queen made Marlborough Captain General of her armies at home and abroad. She at once conferred the Garter on him—which William had not seen fit to confer in the thirteen years of his reign. The office of Master of the Ordnance, with all its lucrative appointments and perquisites, so long withheld from Marlborough, was now given him. William's favourite, Sidney, was turned out; his Dutch comrades brushed aside, to go home and serve their own country. The English were going to rule England.

The Queen showed her confidence by the generosity she always displayed toward those she loved. Within a year or two, Marlborough's pay and appointments came to some £60,000 a year, beside the percentages he was allowed on the bread contracts of the army abroad and the pay of foreign mercenaries for secret service, and beside the perquisites and gifts. By the time he died he was a millionaire. Sarah was at once made Groom of the Stole, Mistress of the Robes and Comptroller of the Privy Purse. As such, she managed the Queen's personal finances economically and well. She saved the Queen money, and thought herself worth the £5,600 a year (multiply by ten!) her appointments added up to.[9] In addition, her two married daughters were made Ladies of the Bedchamber, with their independent salaries. With Prince George as Lord Admiral, George Churchill became his right-hand man and head of the Admiralty. The Queen was surrounded by Churchills. It was natural enough in a way; but other people did not take unalleviated pleasure in the monopoly of favor enjoyed by the fortunate family. And so great were the rewards of power and favor in those days: what remains of the English aristocracy is founded upon such things.

So supported, with the government at home in the hands of his closest friend, Godolphin, Marlborough could go oversea with some confidence to conduct the war.

For some time it was not certain that the Dutch would give Marlborough the command of their army; they had generals of their own with far wider experience. To them Marlborough was a general by favor of the Queen of England: he had yet to prove himself. But he won the complete confidence—and, in the end, the true comradeship—of the Grand Pensionary, Heinsius; and this, from the leading figure in the Republic, was no small tribute. Marlborough was made Deputy Captain General. We may take this as marking the transition, in the long struggle against French ascendancy, from the leadership which lay with Holland, so long as William lived, to that of England henceforth. However, the Dutch attached two Deputies to him, "civilians with powers of obstruction as unlimited as their inability to understand war."[10] Perhaps we should add a rider—war as Marlborough understood it; for he proceeded to give them several turns that made them quite dizzy.

The situation, as usual at the beginning of any war the English take part in, was unsatisfactory. Louis' seizure of the Spanish Netherlands gave the French a powerful advantage; they were on the frontiers of Holland, the Meuse fortresses were in their hands; they were in a position to outflank the Dutch, with considerably superior forces. No static warfare would improve this situation. Marlborough was determined to seize the initiative and impose his will on the enemy. He proposed to invade Brabant: vetoed by the Dutch, who were afraid that it would expose them to invasion down the Meuse valley and the Rhine. Marlborough was confident that if he had had his way, the French "must then have had the disadvantage of governing themselves by our motions, whereas we are now obliged to mind them."[11]

Balked of this, Marlborough moved rapidly across the Meuse to place himself across the communications of the French army there and on the Rhine. This forced them to withdraw at a dangerous disadvantage. Marlborough had placed himself across their line of retreat in some disorder: the Dutch vetoed a battle. However, he gave himself the pleasure of taking their generals out with him "to see the enemy pass the heath . . . hurrying over it in the greatest confusion and disorder imaginable. Upon this they all acknowledged that they had lost a fair opportunity of giving the enemy a fatal blow."[12] A similar thing happened when Marlborough created another opportunity for catching the French on the wrong foot on the heaths of Peer. A Scots Fusilier wrote, "we had all the advantage a tired, disorderly and inferior army could give to good troops, but the States were against fighting," and the French slipped away in the darkness.[13]

Marlborough was exceedingly disappointed: he was out for decision. He sent a trumpet to Boufflers and Berwick, his own nephew, in command on the other side, to assure them with his compliments that it was not his fault that he had not engaged them—a charming touch, so true to that polite, formal age. To Godolphin he expressed his feelings, with a flash of patriotic spirit: "England, that is famous for negligence, should any they employ be guilty of half what I see here, it would be impossible for them to avoid being justly torn to pieces by the Parliament."[14] All the same, he had set things moving; and that autumn a series of successful sieges, Venloo, Stevensweert and Ruremonde, was crowned by the fall of Liège. The waterway of the Meuse was cleared from thence downward; the threat of Holland being outflanked was removed. With the capture of Kaiserswörth, the French were driven from the lower Rhine and the Electorate of Cologne taken by the Allies.

These successes aroused much enthusiasm and won the confidence of the Dutch people for Marlborough. They would have constituted a triumph for any campaign of William's; the only disappointed person was the Commander in Chief, who knew what had been missed. On his way down the river he was nearly lost himself. A night raid ambushed the Commander in Chief's boat. The Dutch Deputies had their passes on them, Marlborough none. While they were being held up, a clerk slipped into Marlborough's hand an out-of-date pass for General Charles Churchill, which he presented with his usual *sang-froid*. But a good deal else must have passed before the barge was allowed to go on its way. Marlborough gave that clerk a pension for life; the lieutenant who let the officers through deserted to Dutch service and was given a captaincy.

The rumor spread that the Commander in Chief had been captured and taken prisoner to France: it might have been the end of the war if he had been. His appearance in Holland occasioned a spontaneous outburst of feeling such as he had never received in his own country, and he was touched by it. "Till they saw me, they thought me a prisoner in France, so that I was not ashore one minute, before I had great crowds of the common people, some endeavouring to take me by the hands, and all crying out welcome. But that which moved me most was, to see a great many of both sexes cry for joy."[15]

The Queen was equally enthusiastic and determined to make Marlborough a Duke on his return. She wrote to Sarah, "I hope you will give me leave . . . I know my dear Mrs. Freeman does not care for anything of that kind nor am I satisfied with it, because it does not enough express the value I have for Mr. Freeman, nor nothing ever can how passionately I am yours, my dear Mrs. Freeman."[16] Sarah was not at all pleased; in fact she was very much against it: "there is no advantage in going in at a door; and when a rule is settled, I like as well to follow five hundred as one." A dukedom?—ridiculous without an appanage to support such useless grandeur. She wrote at once to John to refuse it. But this kind of thing was precisely where he differed from her: it is clear that he had every intention of being a Duke. He brought in the Grand Pensionary to argue for him: Heinsius was all for it, urging that it would increase Marlborough's standing among the European princes and strengthen his hand in dealing with them.

The Queen came to his aid financially, as so often before, with a grant of £5,000 a year from the Post Office. She wanted this to be in perpetuity; but there was strong objection in Parliament to this endow-

ment of a title, and the grant was confined to her lifetime. In compensation Anne wanted the Marlboroughs to accept £2,000 a year from her
Privy Purse; but this they generously refused. That winter there fell upon
them a blow which seemed to make Sarah right about the vanity of
dukedoms and to cheat John of his dynastic hopes: their remaining son
and heir was struck down by smallpox and died at Cambridge, aged
seventeen. When Ailesbury met him that spring in camp at Maastricht
and condoled with him for the loss, "the finest young man that could be
seen," the Duke said sadly, "I have lost what is so dear to me, it is fit for
me to retire and not toil and labour for I know not who: my daughters are
all married."[17] He certainly did not know for whom he would be
toiling.

The year 1703 was full of disappointment for Marlborough. He
began the year by bringing forward his Great Design: an ambitious plan
for converging movements on Antwerp, while moves were also being
made against Ostend in the northwest and the Lines of Brabant defending Belgium from the east. To execute such a masterly plan demanded
the closest co-ordination and supreme authority. That authority he could
not exert. The Dutch general Cohorn, who was to attack Ostend, went off
instead on a foraging expedition. Later, when Opdam tried to fulfill
his part of the attack on Antwerp, Cohorn left him with his flank
dangerously exposed so that Marlborough had to come up from the Lines
to the rescue. There was a rumor that Opdam was beaten: "he is very
capable of having it happen to him."[18]

In spite of his disappointment, with his usual resiliency Marlborough resolved on a second attempt to bring Villeroi to battle before
Antwerp. The French prudently withdrew behind their fortifications and
the Lines. Marlborough was all for an assault on these: he had probed
and found a soft spot, opposite Ramillies. Discussions raged, and this
time everyone was with him except the Dutch generals: we see him
gradually winning confidence. They maintained an obstinate refusal.
Marlborough wrote Godolphin that he would return to England early:
"I shall not be very fond of staying with an army that is to do no more but
eat forage."[19] Again: "the unreasonable opposition I have met with for
the attack of the lines has heated my blood so that I am almost maddened
with the head-ache." To Heinsius he delivered an ultimatum before
returning. "Even if I were given millions I would not again serve in the

field with such obstacles and forced to depend upon the unanimous consent of the generals. I would rather die than put up with anything like it again."[20] It seemed that he was bent on giving up the command, or perhaps handing it over to some royal prince—possibly Elector George of Hanover—who could command greater authority, while Marlborough acted as chief of staff.*

In this mood he returned to England for the winter to meet the equal frustrations of party politics. The basic fact of the political situation was that the Tory party, which commanded the bulk of the country gentry and therefore, normally, the Commons, was opposed to our intervention in the land war on the Continent. They would only fully support the war at sea. The Whigs, who continued William's policy, supported the war fully and with conviction. They had a majority in the Lords, they had the moneyed interest of the City and the Dissenters with them; their leaders were men of ability, who understood the realities of the European situation as the Tories did not. They knew what was necessary, and they were prepared to enforce it. But they were a minority. The Tories were far stronger, the majority party in the country and the Commons. They also had the sympathies of the Queen with them, and the Church: they were the Church party. How, in this intractable situation, to find a solid basis of support upon which to carry on the war? That was the problem. In the end, these intractabilities broke Godolphin and Marlborough, and the heart of Queen Anne.

The immediate situation was that the Tories were bringing forward, a second time, an Occasional Conformity Bill to stop the practice of Dissenters taking Communion occasionally, to qualify for Parliament and office. This was intended to destroy the strength of the Whigs, to make all Tories vote for it and thereby force the government to rest on a pure Tory foundation—with the corollary of a Tory conception of the war, inadequate and incompetent. There was the dilemma for Godolphin and Marlborough, who, though Tories in name, had become men of the center, caring above all for the nation's interest and the outcome of the war. Sarah, with whom her husband differed, was able to say "I told you so": only the Whigs could be relied on to prosecute the war. And this was the theme of the constant pressure to which she subjected the Queen, contrary to Anne's wishes, her beliefs and her prejudices.

---

* The Elector, it will be remembered, succeeded Queen Anne as George I. Through his mother, the Electress Sophia, he was the great-grandson of James I.

Now the Queen weighed in to help her faithful servants out of the dilemma. She waived her own sympathies in favor of the bill, to help the government get it defeated in the Lords. Previously she had made Prince George attend and vote for it. Now he was not to do so: "at the same time . . . I shall not have the worse opinion of any of the lords that are for it."[21] Her action, taken against her own Tory sympathies, was an impressive contribution. It shows how very far from negligible she was. She does not seem to have got much thanks from Sarah. The Tories were furious at their rebuff, and the way was clear for weighting the government further toward the Whigs, with the intention of a vigorous prosecution of the war.

When Marlborough went abroad in 1704, he had a solid foundation beneath him: Godolphin in undisputed control of the government, the subterranean, disingenuous, indispensable Harley to manage the Commons—a kind of Baldwin of the time, with an equal gift for private friendship and public humbug. Such men are always influential with the English. The Duke was in a stronger position now to demand a freer hand from the Dutch, and he got it. Heinsius favoured a Moselle offensive.

Though Marlborough's two previous campaigns had made Holland secure, the situation in Germany had grievously worsened. Bavaria had treacherously gone over to France; Hungary was in full revolt; Vienna was exposed and the Empire in mortal danger. A year before, he had warned the Queen what the consequences of the Empire's supineness would be;* now they were upon them: a Bavarian army in the field with a French army under Marsin to join it and strike down the Danube at Vienna. The Duke not only saw the strategy of the war as a whole, but was the only person on the allied side who felt each move intensely and reacted like an artist. We see the artist's temperament in the depression that accompanied each master plan: it is what happens with most artists in the process of gestation. He wrote to Sarah, "I am extremely out of

---

* In his letter, May 24, 1703, Marlborough is concerned with the consequences for England: "as long as the Empire and the Princes of Germany can have troops at the expense of England and Holland, they will never be at the cost of defending themselves by their own troops . . . They all hope by staying at home to draw money from England and Holland. If there can't be a method found to oblige the Emperor or Empire to defend themselves, I am afraid the consequence at last must prove fatal to England and Holland." H.M.C., *Ninth Report*, 467. This was very much the Tory point of view.

heart . . . for in all the other campaigns I had an opinion of being able to do something for the common cause; but in this I have no other hopes than that some lucky accident may enable me to do good."[22]

The plan for the march to the Danube was germinating. It demanded elaborate planning and co-ordination: an army out of the Dutch and deceiving them as to its destination; providing for their safety during his absence; moving his army up the Rhine and through Germany; counteracting French moves and deceiving them as to his own; providing for supply on a six-hundred-mile march—the whole army was to be reequipped with shoes, for example, at Frankfort; opening new communications with his advance along the Danube; arranging for a junction with Eugene; smashing Bavaria out of the war. All these, in the event, he accomplished; and it astonished Europe. He had one advantage: he would be moving on interior lines of communication; of this he would make the utmost advantage: "if they should let me get ten days before them, they may come too late."[23]

Like a wise man, he did not tell Sarah where he was going; merely that he intended to go "higher up into Germany." Twice he assured her, "whatever becomes of me," "whatever happens to me . . . my heart is entirely yours." As the great adventure went forward, doubts and hesitations past, his confidence grew. "The troops I carry with me are very good, and will do whatever I will have them." According to the number of reinforcements the French send into Germany, "I shall have the more or less success where I am a-going." Then: "Let them send what they will, I have great hopes God will bless this undertaking." He has now arrived in the Palatinate, and from a country house there has a splendid view of the Rhine and the Neckar, "but would be much better pleased with the prospect of St. Albans, which is not very famous for seeing far."[24]

The march in itself was a triumph, in strategic conception, in organization and execution. "The annals of the British Army contain no more heroic episode than this march from the North Sea to the Danube. The strategy which conceived, the secrecy and skill which performed, and the superb victory which crowned the enterprise have always ranked among the finest examples of the art of war."[25] The French were thoroughly deceived, first by a feint toward the Moselle; second, along the Rhine frontier, where he had boats constructed as if for an attack on Strasbourg. That he was a deceiving sort of man served his country well: "the French had been deluded and could not now prevent the concentration of his army in the heart of Southern Germany."[26] There was his constant thought for his troops; on the Danube it was cold and rainy: "the poor men, I am afraid, will suffer from these continual rains." Later, "I am extremely pleased to know that I have it now in my power that the poor soldiers shall not want bread."[27] The news of Marlborough's march roused excitement and expectation in England: even William Penn came out with, "he will be Xenophon and Cyrus too if he beats the great Duke of Bavaria, so great a captain and a sovereign prince."[28]

Nothing interfered with his determination to inflict a decision. The key to the entry to Bavaria was a strong position, the Schellenberg, above the Danube. It was immensely strong by nature, and the Margrave of Baden was aghast at Marlborough's determination to storm it. But time pressed: the Bavarians had neglected to fortify it and were only now throwing up defences; Tallard was on his way with an army to join the Bavarians. Marlborough was right to order an assault, though it was a bloody business and the losses fell heaviest on the English. "Many weary feet that had trudged from the Thames to the Danube here came to rest."[29] It may be regarded as the first British victory on the Continent, though it was unfavourably reported because of its heavy losses. The Bavarians, however, lost twice as heavily, and this key position was in Marlborough's hands while he proceeded to subjugate and devastate Bavaria.

This was a necessary operation of war; as he wrote to Sarah, "You will, I hope, believe that my nature suffers when I see so many fine places burnt, and that must be burnt if the Elector will not hinder it."[30] His aim was to drive the Elector out of the war, to remove the threat to the Empire. But Tallard was now approaching with his army to join up with Marsin and the Elector. They would have an overwhelming preponderance, if Eugene, marching along a parallel route from the Rhine, did not arrive in time. The anxiety revealed itself in one of Marlborough's violent headaches, lasting for days: "I depend very much on the vigilance of Prince Eugene." Armies were converging on a Napoleonic scale.

At last Eugene, whose movements had been concerted with Marlborough, arrived with 18,000 men. Those two allowed the Margrave to go off on a siege with as many men: they must have thought his absence was worth such a heavy price. The Franco-Bavarian army was approaching, with a slight superiority in numbers: 60,000 and more guns against 56,000. "Deserters" were planted on Tallard and the Elector to give them the information that Marlborough was retreating. In consequence, when the armies were within range on August 12, the French did not attack. That night, the Duke spent some time in prayer and received the Sacrament. (He was a more conventional person than Sarah and had a simple faith—she had as good as none.) Early next day, instead of a retreating army, the French found that they were going to be attacked. It was a complete moral surprise, and contrary to the experience of a generation of war: by the rules, finding himself countered by a superior army, Marlborough should have retired. More marching and counter-marching would have followed, as in the former days of the Grand Monarch and William.

That was not Marlborough's conception of war. There followed a tremendous battle, which blew much of the Grand Monarch's scheme for Europe sky high. It was also a most complicated battle, impossible to describe here: only a soldier of genius could keep all the operations in his head—as there is the best of evidence that Marlborough did. The simple outline is this. The French had a good position on ground rising from a marshy stream that ran into the Danube on their right. Forward on their right was the village of Blenheim. On their left, four miles away was the village of Oberglau, with Marsin and the Elector behind, forming the French left; Tallard in command of the center and right. To their surprise, they found that they were going to be attacked in the center and that Marlborough's lines were crossing the marshy stream to reform in novel formations on the other side: the first line of foot, the next two or three of horse, another of foot in the rear. With some complacency Tallard allowed them to reform, sure that a cavalry charge would throw them back into the stream. But he had weakened his own center of infantry, of whom twenty-seven battalions were concentrated in Blenheim.

Marlborough's dominant idea was simple: to hold or mask the very strong French flanks, while *he*, not Tallard, delivered the assault in the center, concentrating everything on that. On our left, Cutts advanced with sixteen battalions to pen the twenty-seven French battalions within Blenheim; and was able to do it—though not to subdue them—since the space they were cooped up in prevented them from deploying their strength or playing anything like a proper part in the general action. On the right, Eugene had difficulty in getting across the stream, but attacked Marsin and the Elector with extreme tenacity; and though he no more than Cutts could gain the upper hand, he held back superior forces. In the center Marlborough was locked in struggle: "from one end of the armies to the other, everyone was at grips and all fighting at once—a feature very rare in battles," wrote a French eyewitness.[31] At the critical moment, when his second assault was wavering, Marlborough asked Eugene for the help of a brigade. Eugene was having a very tough struggle and could make no headway; but he sent the brigade at once, and this turned the scale in the center. Up till this time, having taken the offensive everywhere, the Allied losses were perhaps double the French. No matter: a decision was being reached.

In mid-afternoon there was a lull while the Duke brought into play the immense superiority he had accumulated—like the saving man he was. He now had nearly eighty squadrons of horse against Tallard's sixty, and twenty-three battalions of foot against his nine. Tallard could get no help from the twenty-seven battalions penned within Blenheim, and was now himself rolled back and penned against Oberglau. Marlborough brought up his guns to mow down the French squares that would not give way, and ordered forward a general advance of the Allied cavalry under which the French center now broke and gave way. They streamed off the field in two directions, some falling back on Marsin and the Elector, the others rushing to the right: these were pushed down the steep slopes of the bank into the Danube, where many hundreds perished. In the moment of victory, Marlborough, with his usual command of himself, checked the pursuit of Marsin and the Elector's undefeated wing, to make sure of the twenty-seven battalions in Blenheim. Marshal Tallard was captured trying to make his way into Blenheim, which was now encircled.

At this moment of the evening the Duke paused to write his famous message to Sarah—first in his thoughts—penciling it on the back of a bill of tavern expenses: "I have not time to say more but to beg you will give my duty to the Queen, and let her know her army has had a glorious victory. Monsieur Tallard and two other Generals are in my coach and I am following the rest. The bearer, my aide-de-camp Colonel Parke, will give Her an account of what has passed."[32] From the coach, Tallard could observe the agony of his men in Blenheim: he offered to command them to stop firing if the poor fellows might retire. The Duke, astonished at this piece of French arrogance—Tallard had, of course, been received with every courtesy—gave a sharp reply: "Inform Monsieur Tallard that in the position in which he now is, he has no command."[33]

While Marsin and the Elector withdrew in order, Blenheim surrendered. The grief and fury of these famous regiments knew no bounds: they burned their flags; their officers would not sign the convention. By the time the Duke arrived, they were disarmed prisoners. Two thirds of this large French army had been either destroyed or captured.

Orkney described Blenheim as "the greatest and completest victory that has been gained these many ages"; and he attributed it, very properly, to the Duke who had "been everywhere from one attack to another and ventured his person too much."[34] No doubt about his generalship now. The effects of the victory were tremendous. The remnants of the French army were quite demoralized and retreated from Germany to behind the Rhine. "If they had not been the most frightened people in the world," he wrote, "they would never have quitted these parts."[35] The fabric of Louis's schemes for Germany fell to the ground: henceforth France would be fighting on the defensive. Louis gave orders that in future "the best troops should be placed opposite the English." Gone were the days of Charles and James when the French monarch could interfere at will in our internal affairs and, externally, offer to take England under his protection. Marlborough's war was the first round in the long struggle that ended at Waterloo.

When the news of the glorious victory reached the Queen at Windsor, she was sitting, that summer's day toward the end of August, in the bay overlooking the terrace, playing a game of dominoes with Prince George—so tradition says. All is unchanged there in that bay; there are the dominoes still.

At once Mrs. Morley began planning a suitable reward for her faithful Mr. Freeman, who had raised the British name to such heights and shed such luster thus early upon her reign. Already the Emperor was suggesting that he might make Marlborough a Prince of the Empire, with a principality and a vote in the College of Princes. This would need the Queen's permission. Sarah's attitude was one of disgust at more nonsense of this kind: Princess of the Holy Roman Empire was the last thing to commend itself to her rational spirit. She made no impres\

sion on John: he was bent on getting every recognition of his service and his genius. The Emperor, in the Austrian manner, was now going back on his generous impulse: perhaps the title without the principality would do? It would not: Marlborough was not going to accept an empty title. So the little principality of Mindelheim was constituted for him: an estate of a few square miles in Swabia, worth £2,000 a year. At the peace, this Imperial generosity was subtracted, and there remained but a hollow name after all.

The strain of that summer told upon Marlborough's health and spirits; and there still remained much to be done. As after the storming of the Schellenberg, he gave the care of the wounded his own special attention. To Godolphin: "I have been so employed about our own wounded men and the prisoners, that I have not one hour's quiet, which has so disordered me, that if I were in London I should be in my bed in a high fever."[36] Of all the leading figures on the field at Blenheim, we must remember that Marlborough was the oldest: he won his first great battle at fifty-four. By then, Wellington had won his last and Napoleon was dead. To Sarah Marlborough wrote: "for thousands of reasons I wish myself with you. Besides, if I were with you quietly at the Lodge [in Windsor Park], I should have more health; for I am at this time so very lean . . . that your care must nurse me this winter, or I shall certainly be in a consumption." He found the pressure on his brain relieved by bleeding, and decided to journey back to the Rhine more comfortably in his own coach.

There was still much to be done before he could return. He had to obtain the assurances of aid from the states of North Germany if the war were to be finished next year. His personal prestige would clinch his diplomatic persuasions. The news of Blenheim had given universal joy at Berlin: now was the time to strike.[37] So off he rumbled in his coach on his eight-hundred-mile tour of North Germany, jolted and shaken fourteen or fifteen hours a day on the bad roads. At Berlin he gained all he wanted: a sizable contribution of troops, subsidized by England and Holland. On his return, he visited the Court of Hanover, where he made a strong impression and conquered the very intelligent Electress Sophia, granddaughter of James I: the thought of whom Queen Anne could not bear, since that tough old lady was next in succession and might easily outlive her. It was a useful visit: the Duke made the acquaintance of his future sovereign and his family.

When Marlborough got back to England in December, he got, at last, the reception his labors had deserved. He brought back with him Marshal Tallard and sixteen French generals, a score more of high-ranking officers, a mass of standards and colors captured at Blenheim. These were paraded around London before being deposited—where he had been himself twelve years before—in the Tower. There were votes and addresses of the Lords and Commons; processions, bell ringing, fireworks; receptions, banquets in the City. The question was in what more permanent form could the nation's gratitude be given? Parliament now voted the grant of £5,000 a year, which had been restricted to the Queen's lifetime, in perpetuity.

The Queen came forward with her own well-considered plan, making over to the Duke and his heirs the historic royal manor of Woodstock, with its offices and perquisites. There on its site, with all its memories of the English royal house—of Henry II and his fair Rosamond, of Queen Elizabeth as Princess, confined there under her sister Mary—was to rise a great building, the Castle of Blenheim, to be a reminder of that glorious victory to Englishmen for ever. It was an act not only of princely generosity, but of historic imagination.

Godolphin had done his best, too: he had called in the talent of the promising Whig poet, Mr. Addison, to celebrate the campaign in verse.[38] To encourage the young man's muse, the Lord Treasurer had made him a Commissioner of Appeal in Excise, in succession to the philosopher Locke. An aristocracy takes the arts seriously. Rarely has a government been so rewarded by a poem it has subsidized. Addison's *The Campaign* was published on the day the Duke landed; it expressed perfectly the mood of the moment, the mood of the nation, the spirit of national self-satisfaction, the objectives and the purpose of the war.

> Our British youth, with inborn freedom bold,
> Unnumbered scenes of servitude behold,
> Nations of slaves, with tyranny debased,
> (Their Maker's image more than half defaced)
> Hourly instructed, as they urge their toil,
> To prize their Queen and love their native soil.

> But see the haughty Household troops* advance!
> The dread of Europe and the pride of France . . .
> Vain insolence! with native freedom brave
> The meanest Briton scorns the highest slave.

---

* The troops of the Maison du Roi who had been shattered in the center of the line at Blenheim.

The roving Gaul, to his own bounds restrained,
Learns to encamp within his native land . . .
Scared at his near approach, great Louis fears
Vengeance reserved for his declining years,
Forgets his thirst of universal sway,
And scarce can teach his subjects to obey.

We may not respond to this national self-esteem now; but that is partly because it has won its battles for the nation. What Addison's poem said was true enough.

Most admired was his description of the Duke, with the two lines that became among the most often quoted in the language:

'Twas then great Marlborough's mighty soul was proved,
That, in the shock of charging hosts unmoved,
Amidst confusion, horror and despair,
In peaceful thought the field of death surveyed,
To fainting squadrons sent the timely aid,
Inspired repulsed battalions to engage,
And taught the doubtful battle where to rage.
So when an Angel by divine command
With rising tempests shakes a guilty land,
Such as of late o'er pale Britannia passed,
Calm and serene he drives the furious blast;
And, pleased th' Almighty's orders to perform,
Rides in the whirlwind and directs the storm.

The poem won not only immediate success, but for more than a century was looked up to as the model of its kind. It was a favorite with Washington, as Addison was his favorite poet. Strangely, too, the poem won admiration abroad. Voltaire, that professional Anglomane, described it as a *"monument plus durable que le palais de Blenheim."* In fact, it has been forgotten, while Marlborough still stands on the top of his column in the park at Blenheim, with the trees grouped in battle formation beneath him, still

Rides in the whirlwind and directs the storm.

CHAPTER XIII

Summit and Fall

I

THE YEAR 1705 was a disappointing one for Marlborough, according to the rhythm that was establishing itself: a series of successes as in 1702, or a great victory as in 1704, 1706, 1708, followed by countercheck, a year of disappointment and frustration. It is the rhythm of life itself.

After Blenheim, Louis withdrew his outlying forces from Germany and concentrated them behind the Rhine. Marlborough was full of confidence, at the height of his genius, and was preparing to attack across the river: it was always his idea to carry the war into France and teach Louis upon his own soil what his aggressions meant for other people. With their concentration of forces, the French were able to take the offensive down the Meuse valley. Perhaps, after all, Blenheim was a fluke, due to ill luck, a mere exception in Louis' long career of glory? The Dutch reacted to the threat at once: appeals, Deputies, commands to the Duke to return and give up his plans. Finally, the threat to make a separate peace made him give way. All his life he had been having to give way: he never had the sovereign authority of a Napoleon to do what he thought best; always conflicting demands to reconcile, his own ideas how best to finish the war frustrated. No wonder it became second nature with him to give way: it had its effect on his character and must have sapped his will power.

He opened his heart to his friend, Godolphin: "I may assure you that no one thing—neither for the troops nor for the subsistence of the Army—that was promised me has been performed . . . These considerations and the knowledge I have that it is in this place [i.e., on the Rhine] where we can do most hurt to France, vexes me so that I have made myself sick . . . I have for these last ten days been so troubled by the

213

many disappointments I have had that I think if it were possible to vex me so for a fortnight longer it would make an end of me. In short, I am weary of my life." To Sarah: "my dearest soul, pity me and love me."[1]

A piece of German treachery now surrendered Trèves to the French: "the loss of Trèves and its stores ended all chances of Marlborough's return to the Moselle. He never returned there in any of the campaigns, and the surest road to Paris was never trodden by the Allied armies."[2]

Back in the Netherlands, Marlborough was confronted by the immensely strong Lines of Brabant—a sort of Maginot Line—which extended all the way from Antwerp to Namur, from the Scheldt to the Meuse. Faced with a problem like this, Marlborough's chess-player mind comes visibly into play. He had not only to cheat the enemy, but to deceive his masters, the Dutch. After some weeks of waiting, threatening now in the north, now in the south, there followed a series of dizzy marches and countermarches, punctuated by feints—and behold, Marlborough was through and across the celebrated lines and the enemy in full retreat from Louvain. Marlborough led the charge himself, riding like a trooper with the front rank—like the young man of thirty years before, fighting under Turenne. The Commander in Chief never seems to have minded taking these risks. Sir Winston says penetratingly of him: "sometimes he was over-daring and sometimes over-prudent; but they were separate states of mind, and he changed from one to the other in quite definite phases."[3]

Now there occurred one of those curious lapses of the will that bring home to one, more than anything, how much Marlborough's temperament was that of an artist. He could have marched on Louvain, but somehow failed to: he lost a chance. Perhaps he was exhausted by the excitement of the maneuvers, the demand they had made on sheer brain power. It was only human: anyone less statuesque and impassive among soldiers would be hard to find. He was not a piece of seasoned oak, still less iron; his was a willowy nature, always resilient. Anyway, he had outwitted the French and by-passed the Lines.

He was just as pleased at having outwitted the Deputies: "I was forced to cheat them into it." His chaplain wrote, with an ecclesiastic's appreciation, that he had "perfectly bubbled them into it."[4] What gave him more intense pleasure was his discovery of his troops' enthusiasm for him. "The kindness of the troops to me had transported me."[5] He had had only his own troops with him at the break-through, no reinforcements; "but this gave occasion to the troops with me to make me very kind expressions, even in the heat of the action, which I own to you gives me great pleasure, and makes me resolve to endure anything for their sakes." He owned as much only to Sarah: "my dearest soul, my heart is so full of joy for this good success, that should I write more I should say a great many follies." Emotion must not be allowed to disturb his classic composure: this is the Augustan age of good sense and reason; no romanticizing, above all, no enthusiasm.

All the same, "those who know the army and what soldiers are," wrote one of his officers, "know very well that upon occasions like this, where even the common soldier is sensible of the reason of what he has to do, and especially of the joy and success of victory, soldiers with little entreaty will even outdo themselves, and march and fatigue double with cheerfulness what their officers would at other times compel them to."[6]

Later that summer, he led them to the plain of Waterloo. By his masterly maneuvers he had caught Villeroi's army at a decided inferiority—the only occasion, apart from the Schellenberg, when he had a large superiority of numbers. The Deputies would not allow him to engage. There followed an extraordinary scene: the Dutch Deputies arguing, while the Commander in Chief pleaded and sometimes burst out in anger, and the French dug themselves in. An eyewitness gives us a vivid close-up of Marlborough at that moment. Slangenberg flatly refused to undertake the attack: it would sacrifice too many men, he said. The Duke replied that he would lead it himself. " 'C'est donc là, Monsieur, où je veux aller moi-même, c'est là où je vous mènerai.' Then, turning to all their generals, 'Messieurs, vous ne saurez pas répondre ni à Dieu, ni à vos maîtres, si vous laissez échapper cette belle occasion, et je vous assure que c'est pour la dernière fois que je vous mènerai à l'ennemi.' I write you as near as I can the very words of my Lord and in the language he spoke them. I do not remember ever to have seen him so stirred and speak with so much heat."[7] "Had Marlborough won the unfought battle of Waterloo in August, 1705, all the French power in the Netherlands would have been thereby annihilated. The French stood with their faces toward France, just as the Dutch looked toward Holland. In such a situation there could have been no recovery in the Low Countries for the defeated side. Marlborough would have acquired that supreme authority which he always lacked to plan the campaign of 1706 . . . The year of victory, 1706, might also have been the year of peace."[8]

The frustration of his plans in 1705 enabled the French to take the offensive both on the Rhine and in Italy. Marlborough worked out complete plans and went far in his preparations for a march to the rescue of his comrade, Eugene, in Italy. Godolphin did not like the thought of his going so far away; still less the Dutch. The threat made them amenable. They would agree to a large reinforcement for Eugene, provided that the Duke would remain to command their armies in the Netherlands. He should be free from the hampering restrictions of the Deputies, to conduct the campaign as he wished. Marlborough thought this a good offer, and it was. It enabled him to give the Dutch the completest and most artistic victory of his career.

The tactical situation on the battlefield of Ramillies closely resembled that at Blenheim. Villeroi had a good position above the slope down to the marshy Geet that covered his left, and to the little Mehaigne on which his right rested, protected by two villages, Tavières and Franquenay. Ramillies was just in front of the center of his line. Marlborough began with two powerful thrusts upon the flanks. The Dutch Guards gained surprisingly quick possession of the two villages and opened up an immediate threat to the whole French right. The French sent fourteen squadrons, dismounted, to retake Tavières and fend off the danger. At that moment a powerful charge of the Danish cavalry descended on them: the dismounted French dragoons never saw their horses again.

Meanwhile, on the right, the British infantry had succeeded in crossing the marshes and were attacking the French left. There was a tough struggle here, but the British troops under Orkney made unexpected—and, apparently, unintended—progress. For Marlborough was contemplating a maneuver like that which had decided the issue at Blenheim. On the left center, he observed the Dutch cavalry and the rest of the Danish crash into the Maison du Roi. On the right center his infantry was attacking Ramillies and its defenses. But Villeroi was alarmed by the progress the English were making against his left flank, and just before the crisis of the battle began altering his dispositions, sending reinforcements from his center to his left. That is to say, Villeroi was doing exactly what Marlborough wanted him to do: the Duke was imposing his will on the enemy, making them conform to his intentions. At this moment, the Duke ordered all his remaining cavalry reserves to the left and himself rode into the whirlpool.

"The mile and a half space between Ramillies and Tavières had now become the scene of the largest cavalry battle of which there is any trustworthy account. In all nearly twenty-five thousand horsemen were brought into collision hand to hand."[9] Here the decision was to be forced: Marlborough had brought about the superiority he intended. He led two charges of the Dutch himself at the crisis, a conspicuous figure with his staff in scarlet and gold amid the sober blue and grey of the Dutch. It was not right—any more than Nelson's pacing the deck of the *Victory*, a very recognizable figure, was right. A dead set was made at the Commander in Chief; he was thrown from his mount, and disappeared from view in the scrimmage. His faithful aides-de-camp closed in round him and at last got him mounted again. As he changed to a second charger, the Colonel holding the horse's head had his own struck off by a cannonball.

Regaining control, the Duke sent order after order to the British to break off their attack on the right. Here he had difficulty in making his will prevail, and Orkney was furious, just when he had good prospects of capturing the French strongpoint in front of him. Marlborough saw that the battle was being won in the center and on the left, and the entire French line being rolled back. As at Blenheim there was a pause, while he and Auverquerque wheeled the whole of the allied cavalry— some hundred squadrons—round to practically right angles from its original attack. It was a tremendous operation, and must have been a wonderful spectacle. Not even the Maison du Roi could stand it, let alone withstand it. The French army was broken in two, before the final assault was delivered; it streamed from the field, while Marlborough still had reserves in hand, including the British infantry, which he had had to force to break off.

The victory was essentially a Dutch victory: won by their splendid, stubborn fighting qualities and by Marlborough's brain. He himself, with his retinue, remained with them in the center the whole time. The allied losses were some 4,000, against 15,000 French; 5,000 prisoners, all the French guns and baggage, fell to the victors. The French army, shattered by the battle, was dissolved by the pursuit that followed. Where after Blenheim there had been none, and the French left got away, the pursuit after Ramillies was mercilessly effective: it "may well rank among the great pursuits of history, with Napoleon's after Jena or Blücher's after Waterloo."[10]

The political consequences of the victory were even more spectacular. Town after town, for each one of which William III had fought a slow and stubborn campaign, fell to the more fortunate Marlborough. He soon saw, as he wrote to Godolphin, that "the consequence of this battle is likely to be of greater advantage than that of Blenheim; for we now have the whole summer before us and, with the blessing of God, I will make the best use of it."[11] He certainly did: practically the whole of the Spanish Netherlands, i.e., Belgium, fell to the allies. The authorities of the capital and the chief towns, disillusioned with French rule, declared for the Austrian candidate for the Spanish throne, Charles III, against Louis's grandson, Philip V.

From England came congratulations and thanks. St. John, better known to posterity as Bolingbroke, whose interests Marlborough had promoted and who was now Secretary at War, wrote: "every man that wishes well to the common good of Europe, must be transported with the glorious action of Sunday last; but those who are particularly devoted to the service may pretend to a greater degree of joy. The vast addition of renown which your Grace has acquired, and the wonderful preservation of your life, are subjects upon which I can never express the thousandth part of what I feel."[12] Marlborough had been very good to him and even intervened to help him financially, for he was always an extravagant gambler, which did not prevent him from expressing his gratitude to the Duke by sabotaging him later. The poet Prior wrote: "my wishes for the continuance of all good to my patron and protector may properly be the contents of a private man's letter: the conquests and honours of the Duke of Marlborough must be the subject of our historians and the theme of our orators and poets." He went on to add, "since I dare not trouble your Grace often by letter, I take this occasion to thank you most humbly for having mentioned to my Lord Treasurer an affair so small as my fortune." Marlborough had taken an interest in helping the indigent poet, which did not prevent him from materially helping Marlborough's enemies later. Such is the small change of politics.

From Godolphin came the sincere, unforced words of an honest man: "the Queen is come to town to give God thanks next Thursday for your victory. I assure you I shall do it from every vein within me, having scarce anything else to support either my heart or my head. The animosity and inveteracy one has to struggle with is unimaginable, not to mention the difficulty of obtaining things to be done that are reasonable, or of satisfying people with reason when they are done." Godolphin was now engaged in a more difficult campaign than Marlborough's, caught in a political situation that was intractable: between the Whigs, who were the only people whose heart was in the war and who were willing to give it priority, and the Queen, who loathed the Whigs and would not have them in the government. Godolphin was under constant pressure from the Whigs, being attacked by them while he knew that they must have a larger share in the government if the war was to be won. In consequence, he had to put pressure on the Queen, who resisted every step of the way, with all her father's obstinacy and much more sense. The struggle was ruining the friendship, and indeed all good feeling, between Mrs. Morley and her faithful Mr. Montgomery. Nor did Sarah's ceaseless vexation of the Queen help: it was turning Mrs. Morley's love into detestation.

All these worries were transmitted regularly to Marlborough, who henceforth had to conduct his campaigns and fight his battles under this sense of strain and insecurity: the political support for the war threatening to cave in, the personal friendship of the intimate Cockpit circle breaking down, the atmosphere poisoned, their happiness in each other ruined.

For the present, the Queen wrote him in her usual generous style: "it is impossible for me ever to say or do much as I ought in return of your great and faithful services to me, but I will endeavour by all the actions of my life to show you how truly sensible I am of them."[13] The future was to add its irony to that assurance. "I want words," she said, "to express my true sense of the great service you have done to your country, and I hope it will be a means to confirm all good and honest men in their principles, and frighten others from being troublesome." There was a note of warning in that remark. She added kindly, "I must repeat my earnest request that you should be careful of yourself." Godolphin added his: "I am very sensible you could not avoid exposing yourself upon this occasion; but where so much consequence turns upon one single life, you must allow your friends the liberty to think and say it ought not to be done without an absolute necessity."

In Brussels, now, Marlborough was suffering the usual effects of such exertions. To Sarah: "I have been in so continued a hurry ever since the battle of Ramillies, by which my blood is so heated that when I go to bed I sleep so unquietly that I cannot get rid of my headache . . . My dearest soul, I have now that great pleasure of thinking that I may have the happiness of ending my days in quiet with you."[14]

When Brussels had capitulated and the Estates of Brabant trans-

ferred their allegiance, there was no source of authority to take over the
government of these rich provinces. The Duke had had to take everything upon himself. It was then that Ailesbury saw him making his
solemn entry into the capital, in immense state and, as usual, exploiting
every circumstance—his handsome presence, his familiar courtesy, his
fame and prestige—to win the favor of the people. It was obvious policy
and, as usual, entirely successful. He guaranteed all the religious and
civil rights of the country; he was particularly careful of Catholic sus-
ceptibilities; he laid down stringent orders to prevent any molestation of
the inhabitants by the military. The result was even better than might
be expected: food and forage poured in; the country came into the war
alongside the allies. It wanted no better Governor than the Duke.

At this point, the Emperor made him the formal offer of the Governor Generalship in the name of Charles III. At once Marlborough informed Godolphin: "I beg you to assure the Queen that I have in this
matter, nor never shall have in any other, any desire of my own, but
with all the submission in the world, be pleased with what she shall think
is for her interest."[15] The Queen and the English government were
wholly in favor. The Duke was already most acceptable to the inhabitants. His rule there would, more effectively than anything else, knit
together England and the distant Empire, make it more easy to co-
ordinate the war and control the peace.

At once the Dutch were alerted, and jealous. This was their most
sensitive spot. Since the breach in the unity of the Netherlands, a century and a half before, some elements among the Dutch had perhaps
never given up hope of restoring it. It could only come about now as the
result of the ascendancy of North over South, of Dutch over Belgians.
The Dutch saw no objection to that: they felt that the burden they had
borne in the war, their tremendous efforts and sacrifices, Ramillies itself,
entitled them to it. There has always been an element of obtuseness in
the tough Dutch character. The truth was that the South would rather
be governed by anybody than the North; the Belgians, as we may call
them, by anybody but the Dutch—as Europe proved a century later
again, after Waterloo, when it was tried.

No: Marlborough would have been by far the best solution. But the
best solution rarely comes about sensibly and directly in history: it comes
about more often the way of mutual erosion and disenchantment, people
wearing each other out with their efforts; after long conflict and much

bloodshedding, the sensible solution sometimes steals in upon the scene, deviously, almost surreptitiously.

Marlborough intensely desired to accept. He saw all its advantages to the common cause; even apart from his own personal interest, he knew it was best. For himself, it would be a tremendous elevation among the princes of Europe, where by nature and achievement he belonged. The appointments of the Governor Generalship, the richest in Europe, were worth another £60,000 a year. Since he saw that the Dutch were against it, without any hesitation he declined the offer: the common cause was more important. He wrote to the Grand Pensionary: "I infinitely prefer their friendship before any particular interest to myself; for I thank God and the Queen I have no need nor desire of being richer, but have a very great ambition of doing everything that can be for the public good . . . And let me, on this occasion, assure the States that I serve them with the same affection and zeal that I do my own country."[16]

He had proved himself a worthy successor of the heroic Dutchman who had been King of England, worthy of the confidence William had been so reluctant to give him. His renunciation, without any resentment—so far as one can decipher so indecipherable and secret a man—was not without grandeur. "Ramillies, with its prelude and its sequel, was the most glorious episode in Marlborough's life. Whether as the victorious commander, the sagacious Minister, or the disinterested servant of the Allied cause, his personal conduct was noble."[17] And Sir Winston adds the reflection that would be so salutary to the more cynical among contemporary historians, if they had the perceptiveness to see its truth and the humility to take it home to themselves: "how vain are those writers in many lands who suppose that the great minds of the world in their supreme activities are twisted by sordid or even personal aims." These, of course, are present; they are part of the ascent; but at the summit, they are transcended: in the moment of vision, the elect see pure and clear.

This was Marlborough's summit. If he had become Governor General of the Netherlands, he would have had the authority, and the unity of direction, to finish the war. In the malign manner that is mixed into, but does not altogether govern, human affairs, things from this moment began to go wrong. Though Marlborough continued to win victories, his military genius to shine forth as brilliantly as ever, the seed of distrust between the Dutch and him, sown by the grand offer, grew evil fruits. The confidence between them, so hardly won, was broken; the understanding no longer complete; and this put peace further off than ever.

2

The year 1707 repeated the rhythm of 1705 in its disappointments; indeed the situation worsened. The Habsburgs, selfish as ever, made a separate peace on the Italian front, releasing a large number of French troops for service elsewhere. This enabled them to mount an offensive on the Rhine and break into Germany again. Meanwhile, the British were left to bear the brunt of supporting Charles's cause in Spain, and here their inadequate army suffered a complete defeat at the hands of Berwick at Almanza. (Berwick was granted a Spanish estate in gratitude; his son settled in Spain and the Berwick title came ultimately to the house of Alba, bringing a trickle of Churchill blood into that famous line.) On the Flanders front, the French had been reinforced, and Vendôme, a much abler general than Villeroi, dispatched to hold Marlboro in check behind the fortresses of the French frontier. He had strict orders not to let himself be engaged in battle. As if this were not sufficient, the Dutch on their side vetoed a battle too.

> There is a tide in the affairs of men,
> Which, taken at the flood, leads on to fortune;
> Omitted, all the voyage of their life
> Is bound in shallows and in miseries.

That tide had been missed: all that Marlborough could do this campaigning season was to catch Vendôme's rear and some four thousand prisoners.

In the midst of these discouragements, and in the intervals of being badgered and appealed to on all sides by Sarah, Godolphin and the Queen, his consort saw fit to send him regular bulletins on the troubles about the building at Blenheim. "Your expression of the ice-house, that it can't be of use this three years, is a very melancholy prospect to me, who am turned on the ill-side of fifty-seven."[18] In his troubles, Marlborough took comfort in the thought of retirement to the splendid place he was creating—monument to his achievements—which his services had earned, and where he might live his last days in quiet with his still-golden-haired Sarah. Ten days later: "my head is full of things that are displeasing, that I am at this time a very improper judge of what would be best for the work at Woodstock; for really I begin to despair of having any quietness there or anywhere else . . . My greatest concern is for the Queen, and for the Lord Treasurer. England will take care of itself, and not be ruined, because a few men are not pleased. They will see their error when it is too late."

That winter the political issue in England was resolved, for the time. Godolphin caught Harley out in underhand intrigues against the government. By this time—with the aid of his cousin Mrs. Masham's favor with the Queen, in which she had supplanted Sarah—Harley was sure of the Queen's support. Godolphin and Marlborough both tendered their resignations. Anne was prepared to accept them. It was the Privy Council that was not, and would not hear Harley when he proposed to take over the government. There was a deadlock. Still the Queen would not give way; it was Harley who gave in his hand and resigned. St. John and the rest of the Tories went with him into opposition; the Whigs were in control. The Queen was defeated and never forgave the affront. With something of her father's vindictive spirit, she went underground and bided the time of her revenge. The circle of old friends was irretrievably broken.

The victory of the Whigs meant that Marlborough and Godolphin —the men of the center—were no longer in control either. Had Marlborough had an independent source of authority in the Netherlands, he might have forced a decision and put a term to the war. But the Whigs, who represented the commercial and imperial interests of England, were committed to wresting Spain and the Spanish Empire out of the hands of the Bourbons. The Spanish people had opted for the Bourbon Philip V. Was the war to go on for ever? From now on Marlborough lost control over the high political direction of the war: he became the military executant of Whig policy.

The Whigs gave themselves enthusiastically to its winning. Returned with a majority at the election, they voted large sums speedily for its financing. With this support behind him, Marlborough delivered his best: a great victory at Oudenarde, followed by a series of successes that more than retrieved the situation and left him poised for the invasion of France.

Oudenarde was quite different from Marlborough's previous battles in that it was an encounter-action, almost a running battle, touched off by chance, with the main armies coming piecemeal into action as and when they could. It was not at all a formal set piece such as was dear to the heart of that classic world, like its cotillions and stately dances. Sir Winston describes it as a twentieth-century battle, with its looseness and flexibility, its improvisations and the wide encircling movement foreshadowing Tannenberg. In consequence, the element of chance and risk was much higher, while at the same time training, mutual confidence, skill, precision of movement, paid even greater dividends.

Marlborough had spent that rainy spring in constant reviewing and training his veteran army, which had reached a high degree of perfection. Louis had concentrated a larger army than ever before against him, 90,000 men, under Vendôme and the heir presumptive, the Duke of Burgundy; with them was James II's young Prince of Wales, the pathetic Pretender. On the other side served the Elector of Hanover who was to occupy *their* throne. All the brilliant young men of Versailles were there: there was not much love lost between them and the rough, violent Vendôme. Of this Marlborough, whose intelligence service was always of the first order, was well aware. It enabled him to take calculated risks that no one could take with him and Eugene, so perfect was their understanding.

When campaigning became possible, very late that season, Eugene was on his way to reinforce Marlborough, against whom alone the French had a weighty superiority. Berwick made a parallel move to Eugene's, north from the Moselle; but Marlborough and Eugene were already in strategic touch, their moves achieving an instinctive co-ordination. The season began with the loss of Ghent and Bruges to the French: the citizens disliked Dutch rule so much that they simply surrendered the towns. The Dutch, thoroughly alarmed, were now prepared to allow Marlborough's army alone to attack the French. Fortunately he and Eugene joined arms in time; for the French were making for the Scheldt crossing at Oudenarde. Marlborough's army now made one of its swift marches to head them off: fifty miles in some sixty hours. The French moves were hesitating: there were differences in the high command, between the royal prince and the elderly Marshal. Marlborough himself was getting elderly, two years from sixty: he had had fever that spring and was so weak from it that he could hardly sit his horse. He arrived, nevertheless, at the Scheldt crossing first; once he was in contact with the enemy, no sign of weakness, no hesitation: perfect clarity, the artist keyed up for action.

It was already afternoon and the troops had marched fifteen miles that day. Marlborough pushed Cadogan's redcoats across the pontoons, where they entirely mopped up the small advance forces of the French, unaware of what they had blundered into. The Hanoverian cavalry with Cadogan scattered the French squadrons behind, and then found themselves engaged with the vast mass of the whole French left. Fortunately the ground was broken and marshy, and Burgundy held his punch. Marlborough fed the Prussian horse on to Cadogan's right to give him some protection; in danger as he was, Marlborough did not withdraw him: Cadogan's business was to engage the enemy in a holding action as long as he could stand, while the rest came up. He did this with dogged tenacity and to Vendôme's fury, who hurled brigade after brigade from his center against the redcoats. The Marshal now ordered the entire French left wing under Burgundy to advance; and that could have overwhelmed Cadogan, while Marlborough's army was still not half across the Scheldt. For some reason, the French left did not advance: conflict of opinion about the state of the ground, still more conflict of pride between the prince and his courtiers and the rugged Marshal.

Cadogan was now being overlapped on his left by Vendôme's right advancing. But the pontoons and bridges were disgorging their men and Argyll moved up to join him with twenty more battalions. The center of each army was now in close grip: "always the French brought up superior numbers and reached round the Allied left. Always Marlborough's infantry poured across the bridges and advanced to make new head against them."[19] Now the entire Dutch army, 25,000 men, was crossing by the two bridges in Oudenarde: these could decide the battle. At this moment Marlborough sent Eugene off to command the right, including all the British troops, while he went left to concert the decisive junction of left with center. There was a delay at the bridges: they could not deliver so many men so fast. At this juncture, Eugene had to bear the full strain of the attack of Vendôme's center. Marlborough sensed his comrade's stress and stripped himself of twenty Hanoverian battalions, which he withdrew from his own attack to send to Eugene. It was a generous gesture, and at the same time characteristically economical: for it gave those hard-pressed troops a rest from the firing line while they marched to the right to Eugene. Marlborough left himself with only eighteen battalions, as compared with Eugene's fifty-six.

The delay in Oudenarde held up the immense enveloping action the Duke was projecting by an hour; but the moment Auverquerque was in touch, Marlborough sent his remaining regiments to join Eugene to resist the threatened onslaught of the French left. Here was a second gesture of confidence and selfless generosity at the height of action: "It is these qualities of perfect comprehensive judgment, serene in disappointment or stress, unbiased by the local event in which he was himself involved, this fixing with untiring eye and absolute selflessness the problem as a whole, that deserve the study and respect of soldiers of every age."[20] The French right, fighting a confused action down in the valley, had not observed the immense turning operation of Auverquerque, now in full swing. Vendôme had lost all control of the battle, and even any conception of what was happening, in spite of the tremendous advantage of the position he had enjoyed all along, with the greater part of the allied forces employed in crossing while the battle was joined. The whole French right and center were now bent back into a vast horseshoe, in which were 50,000 Frenchmen struggling in confusion. Up there on the ridge above was the French left wing, under the command of the royal princes, surrounded with a glittering retinue, taking no effective part in the battle at all.

Vendôme rode up to them to demand a last effort, or at least that they should remain in place to try to recover their fortunes next day. There was no point in it: two thirds of the French army were surrounded. As after Blenheim, the left wing sought refuge in flight, the young dandies of Louis's Court trundling along with the rest. In the dark, large numbers managed to slip through the allied cordon in all directions. But many battalions and regiments surrendered whole. Eugene sent Huguenot officers out into the dark to call them in, "À moi, Picardie," "À moi, Roussillon": hundreds of prisoners were collected this way; it was a nice revenge for the idiocy of the revocation of the Edict of Nantes. The prisoners taken were more than 9,000; there were more than 6,000 casualties, and more than 2,000 deserters. "If we had been so happy to have had two hours more of daylight," the Duke wrote, "I believe we should have made an end of this war."[21]

Queen Anne's first words, on hearing the news of yet another glorious victory, were: "Oh, Lord, when will all this dreadful bloodshed cease?" In fact, the allied casualties were remarkably small: only three thousand altogether; and, strangely enough, as John was able to assure Sarah, "I thank God the English have suffered less than any of the other troops; none of our English horse having been engaged."[22] The Queen was a humane person: her sympathies were not confined to her own nation. Her young brother—whom she sometimes hoped against hope might succeed her—had been present on the other side. She had to tear herself away from the sickbed of her dying husband to ride in state to St. Paul's to give thanks for the victory. On the way took place an open quarrel with the Duchess.

To the Duke, however, she wrote graciously and sincerely. She had not broken with him, as she had with Sarah and Godolphin. All that summer she bombarded him with letters, putting her own point of view, appealing to him against his wife and his friend. "If you were here, I am sure you would not think me so much in the wrong in some things as I fear you do now."[23] What could he do, for her or for himself? He was responsible for the war; only the Whigs would fight it. He was as much the prisoner of the Whigs as the Queen was. But she had no intention of enduring it: a time would come . . . meanwhile she took refuge in Stuart dissimulation. Marlborough could only reply to her—be advised by Godolphin, follow his advice. To Sarah: "we are now acting for the liberties of all Europe, so that, though I love the Queen with all my heart, I can't think of the business of England till this great affair is decided, which I think must be by another battle."[24]

He was thinking out his most original and daring project: it was for the invasion of France by land and sea, combined operations: a strong task force from the Isle of Wight and himself with his victorious army converging upon Abbeville and marching upon Paris. It might have ended the war: the project at least disproves those people who later argued that he had prolonged the war for his own advantage. His enemies in England were already saying—because he had had the magnanimity and the confidence to hand over the command on the right at Oudenarde to Eugene—that the Prince had won the battle for him. There will never be wanting such persons to detract from the achievements of great men, or to fail to understand their greatness. Never a shadow ruffled the complete understanding between the two comrades or disturbed the admiration of the younger for the older and greater man.

The invasion project was vetoed by the Dutch: far too risky, far too imaginative. (What an artist he was! and how the thought of his thwarted plan must have recurred to his descendant's mind in 1942, 1943, 1944!) Marlborough was now raiding across the French frontier, deep into Artois and Picardy for forage, hostages, provisions. Louis, unable to protect them, authorized them to compound with Marlborough for a million and a half livres—quite a *renversement* from the days when such sums had enabled his cousin to keep England neutral on the sidelines.

A more terrible task than Oudenarde awaited Marlborough: the reduction of Lille, the great double fortress that was the hinge of the line of fortresses protecting the French frontier. It was the richest city in France, after Paris, and certainly the strongest, with its inner pentagon within the enormous fortifications: Vauban's masterpiece. The city was indeed "the most splendid fruit of Louis XIV's lifelong aggressions."[25] Marlborough, like the man of genius he was, would have much preferred the flexibility of movement, the art and skill, the invasion project would have demanded and where his genius would have told most. The commonplace, conventional minds, who govern human affairs, preferred slogging at Lille—like the second-rate generals who preferred a war of attrition on the Western Front in 1914-18 to the flexibility, the imaginative possibilities, of the Dardanelles project.

Marlborough embarked on the siege of Lille: it exacted a ghastly toll in blood—like the Western Front.

Louis had given orders that a decisive battle should be fought rather than allow Lille to fall; and he had built up a superiority of forces to this end. Marlborough got ahead of the enemy, as usual, and encircled Lille. Vendôme and Berwick joined forces and together deployed 110,000 men against Marlborough's 75,000, on the position he took up south of the city. This is the only occasion on which we can study Marlborough on the defensive. He took up a position such as Tallard threw away at Blenheim and Villeroi at Ramillies. He posted his army on the top of a slope, flanks protected by streams and villages ahead to serve as strong points. Where he differed was that, with his much inferior strength, he placed it on a narrow front, with his artillery posted along the whole front. He clearly meant to break the much more numerous French cavalry by artillery fire, then to charge downhill upon it in confusion. The French command studied the position. The more they looked at it, the less they liked it. Berwick, now Marshal of France for his splendid services—the capture of Nice, the victory of Almanza—knew his uncle's mind better than anyone: *cet animal est méchant, quand on l'attaque* . . . He persuaded the French command not to attack. It drew off, leaving Lille to its fate.

The reduction of Lille proved a bloody business: the first big assault cost the allies as many casualties as Oudenarde had done. There followed a long struggle of attrition. At one stage a large convoy was passed into the city. Then Eugene was wounded and Marlborough had to bear the entire burden of the siege, providing for the army, keeping open communications, parrying threats himself. "This was a period of incredible strain. The besiegers were in extremities. The batteries were approaching the end of their ammunition."[26] Then a heavy convoy on its way through to the besiegers was threatened by much superior forces, which were successfully fought off by the British at Wynendael. This was the turning point: Lille was forced to surrender, but the price had been a terrible one in total casualties.

Anyone but a supreme artist would have been satisfied with the immense achievements of this campaign. Not so Marlborough: "he was set on rounding off the campaign by recovering all that treachery had handed over to the French earlier in the year."[27] Frost made it easier for the allies to surmount the water defenses of Ghent; at the turn of the year both Ghent and Bruges surrendered. "I cannot express enough the importance of these two towns," the Duke wrote, "without them we can neither be quiet in our winter quarters or open with advantage the next campaign."[28]

That winter there fell upon Louis XIV retribution for his long career of aggression. Addison's words came true. A prolonged frost held France in its grip: we remember the vivid impression from the pages of Saint-Simon, the courtiers at Versailles roasted on one side in front of the blazing fires, on the other freezing. Outside in the streets, in the exhausted countryside, bled white by so many years of war, poor people were frozen to death. The Great Frost was followed by famine: people died of hunger in the streets of Paris, bands of starving men roamed the country pillaging markets and châteaux, the women of Paris marched on Versailles demanding bread and peace. This was the end of sixty years' pursuit of glory.

There is no doubt that the vainglorious Louis, Le Roi Soleil, was at last touched, smitten to the heart. It is a pity that it takes such eventualities to reduce people to common sense. He was prepared to consider almost anything in the way of peace terms.

Tentative discussions about peace had been going on for some time—the most important of them through the secret correspondence of

Marlborough with his nephew, Berwick. They were now taken up again, with the renewal of the offer of two million livres to the Duke. He was not to be bribed. If peace came about, with himself as intermediary, he would accept—or even expect—recognition and reward for his services. He always did: he was building up a ducal patrimony, a monument to posterity. It may not, in modern times when the most eminent service is expected to be its own reward, be thought very *chic*, but one must observe that there is a difference.

Louis was prepared to give up the whole Spanish inheritance for which he had fought so long. This is where the fatal touch of pride betrayed the Whigs. They were fighting for the destruction of France; they were out for the trade of the Spanish Empire—what Britain did not corner till a century later with the end of that empire. They were determined that it should not fall to France, and that was reasonable enough. Louis humbled himself to renounce Spain and her empire for his grandson and to accept that it should all go to the Habsburg candidate. There was a snag: the Spanish people had rejected Charles III; they wanted the Bourbon, Philip V. The Whigs demanded that Louis himself should extrude his grandson from Spain. It is possible that the old and tarnished king might even have accepted that; but his son and heir would not: he rose in council and refused such a demand.

This was the climax of the war. Here was the one chance of the allies to secure the complete defeat of France—thrown away by overplaying their hand. It is a recurrent theme in history, and perhaps the most valuable moral to be drawn from its study. Again and again in human action, one observes leaders who cannot stop in their career of victory—and finish by hitting on disaster. The rarest quality of statesmanship seems to be the sense of moderation and balance, of knowing when and where to stop—perhaps of not even beginning—such as we see displayed so notably, over so many years, by Elizabeth I and Burghley. On the whole, this quality has been remarkably characteristic of the conduct of the English-speaking peoples in modern times, by contrast with Spain, France, Germany: hence their long record of success. The Whigs provided a striking exception: they paid for it, and profited later by the lesson.

Louis threw himself, for the first time, upon his people—as the leaders of the Dutch had done in 1672. He appealed, no longer to glory, but to their patriotism, the sense of their country in danger—a more worthy sentiment. And not in vain: one more large army was got together and concentrated on the frontier against Marlborough; France's ablest soldier, Villars, was brought out against him. We see what the strength of the most powerful nation in Europe was, and how hard it was to get her down.

There is no reason to doubt the sincerity of Marlborough's wish for peace, "which upon all accounts I long for, being extremely weary of the life I am obliged to live, for my spirit is so broke that I am become fit for nothing else but a lazy and quiet life."[29] He was weary and ill—as we can see from his symptoms, with high blood pressure. The offer of the Governor Generalship of the Spanish Netherlands was again being pressed on him by Charles III. It was rendered impossible for him to accept now, not only by the Dutch but by his embattled Duchess; though, speaking for himself, he saw no reason why he would not do as well as another. He still hoped that at the peace, perhaps his claims might be considered. This naturally did not incline him to favor a Barrier Treaty which the Dutch were attempting to negotiate. Marlborough feared that if the Dutch were given the barrier fortresses in the Spanish Netherlands, for which they had poured out their blood and treasure, they would have no motive for continuing in the Alliance. And why should he aid them to antagonize the Austrians who were willing to confer a principality upon him?

These jars continued to disturb the Alliance to the end.

The French refusal of the allied ultimatum came as a shock to Marlborough: "is there, then, no counter-proposal?" There was not—merely the continuance of the war, when he had assumed that there would be peace. Marlborough concluded that only a victory inside France and putting its government on a constitutional basis, with the three estates functioning as a Parliament, would stop the aggressive tendencies of absolute government.[30] In this he showed himself very prescient—as we can see from the career of Napoleon and other dictators. It also reveals his strong conviction in favor of English constitutionalism, in which he had been consistent all along, in spite of having been placed in a false light by his career as a royal favorite.

The responsibility for the breakdown of peace negotiations rested fairly with the Whig government. Perhaps if Marlborough had realized that this would happen, he would have exerted himself more. There is a limit to the exertion of a man's will power, and the Duke no longer had his former authority: he was the executant of Whig policy. In return, the Whigs gave him all he could want for the next campaign. They poured out supplies and subsidies: he took the field with 25,000 men more than the previous year; for the first time he had a superiority over the French.

The character of the war was changing: the French were defending their homeland from invasion; the fighting became more desperate, more murderous. The ground that was being fought over was that so familiar, so bloodsoaked, in 1914–18. It was not less difficult terrain: in Marlborough's time a lot of it was tangled woodland, cut up by canals and rivers, starred by fortresses. The reduction of Tournai cost 5,000 casualties. No wonder the Queen by now hated the war: she thought in the terms in which Elizabeth I had prayed, for "the least expenditure of English blood."

The battle that followed, Malplaquet, was the bloodiest of the age. Villars had taken up a strong position behind two woods; the gap between he had fortified with entrenchments, redans, batteries. Marlborough and Eugene had some 100,000 men to Villars' and Boufflers' 80,000. The allied right had to fight its way through the wood, and suffered severe losses in doing so. In its depths, the Royal Irish met the "Wild Geese"— the Irish regiment fighting in the French army. In the gap in the center there raged a bitter infantry struggle, and no quarter was given on either side. Here Marlborough was able to bring up a strategic reserve, as at Blenheim and Ramillies. There followed a vast cavalry battle in the open ground they had won. Marlborough in person led up the British and Prussian squadrons. The Maison du Roi charged again and again, and were only pushed back by the arrival of the Imperialist cavalry under Eugene.

On the left flank, the daredevil young Prince of Orange had mounted three assaults and suffered shocking losses, until Marlborough countermanded any more. The French might have launched a counter-attack along the whole line if Villars had not been dangerously wounded at the crisis of the battle. Now the French position was being turned on their extreme left by Withers' division marching right round the wood and bearing down on the exposed flank. The French left was broken and began to retreat; a general retirement was ordered. The allies were too exhausted to pursue: their losses that day had been far heavier than the French, over 20,000 to the French 10,000 or 12,000.

Europe was appalled by the carnage: not until Borodino was it equaled. Marlborough was deeply affected by it, and what with that

and his exertions he was rendered ill: to that is attributable his failure
to pursue the French over the frontier. To Godolphin: "in one of yours
you lament the killed: in so great an action it is impossible to get the
advantage but by exposing men's lives; but the lamentable sight and
thoughts of it has give me so much disquietude, that I believe it the
chief cause of my illness; for it is melancholy to see so many brave men
killed with whom I have lived these eight years, when we thought ourselves sure of a peace."[31] Actually the British losses were relatively small,
some 1,800 killed and wounded out of 14,000 men—less than at Blenheim. Marlborough's enemies in England and the opponents of the war
fanned public feeling about the carnage of Malplaquet and blamed him
as a "butcher." The nation was turning toward peace; the Whigs, in
turn, were to pay the forfeit for their tempting of Providence.

In 1710, in the interests of peace, the Queen took the offensive.
She was advised secretly by Harley, supported and consoled by Abigail.
She had ceased to see—or hear—Sarah. She waited until the Duke had
gone abroad to face another campaign, and then she embarked on hers.
She began with small strokes and proceeded to heavier ones: one by
one the blows descended that summer on Marlborough's patient back.
After all, it was her duty as Queen to interpret the will of the country,
and she was not sure of that: she was feeling her way until it crystallized.
From the dark corners of her palaces, up the back stairs and into her
closet, came Harley to hold one hand, Abigail the other.

The moves were well concerted; every advantage was taken of the
hesitation and division among the Whigs. Abigail's incompetent soldier
brother was promoted brigadier; to put him there all the colonels of
1705 had to be made brigadiers. This was a direct affront to the Duke at
a sensitive spot: his sense of professional propriety and efficiency. The
Whigs, foolishly, did not support him: he had to give way. So, in June,
his son-in-law, Sunderland—whom the Queen had always detested—was
turned out of office: a Tory took his place as Secretary of State. The
allies began to take alarm: did this change portend a separate peace? Four
directors of the Bank of England waited on the Queen to express their
fears of a financial panic. She replied that she did not contemplate any
more changes at present. Harley began to organize opinion, making use
of writers such as Swift and Defoe—like Baldwin he was an artist at
maneuvering opinion; surreptitiously he encouraged attacks on the
two grand figures.

Godolphin now made a mistake: in an attempt to stop libelous traducers of himself and his government in the pulpit, he embarked on the prosecution of the loud-mouthed Tory clergyman, Sacheverell. The cry, "The Church is in danger," was at once raised and effectively propagated. Harley had not yet completed his preparations, however. When the Lord Treasurer sought a showdown with the Queen, he ended his harangue by asking whether it was her will that he should continue in office. She replied unhesitatingly "Yes." Next morning he received his dismissal by letter brought by a servant. "The uneasiness which you have showed for some time has given me very much trouble, though I have borne it," wrote the Queen; "and had your behaviour continued the same it was for a few years after my coming to the crown, I could have no dispute with myself what to do. But the many unkind returns I have received since, especially what you said to me personally before the lords, makes it impossible for me to continue you any longer in my service; but I will give you a pension of four thousand a year, and I desire that, instead of bringing the staff to me, you will break it, which, I believe, will be easier to us both."[32] Godolphin broke his white wand of office into pieces, threw them into the fire—and refused the pension.

Such was the background at home against which Marlborough had to fight the campaign of 1710—fight his way through the barrier of frontier fortresses into France. Should he give up his command? That would be to betray the allies, the loyalties, the comrades of many years' standing; it would probably mean the break-up of the Alliance—certainly the stultification of all his efforts, his planning, his life's work, denying it of its proper end. No artist could support the thought of that. He began to doubt whether he would be allowed to complete his life's work: "I am not so fully pleased with those sanguine thoughts as formerly, that God would protect and bless us."[33] He was now poised on those plains, "where two lucky hours might decide the fate of France."[34]

He was not to be given that chance: Villars had strict orders not to engage France's last army. The politicians in London were coming to Louis's rescue, as Marlborough felt acutely: "the King of France is so encouraged by what passes in England that he has taken a positive resolution for the continuation of the war, and reckons upon my not being employed this next campaign."[35]

What remained for Marlborough was the costly business of reducing the frontier fortresses one by one: it was a race for time between him and Louis, with the new English government keeping time for Louis. The war was getting more and more like that on the Western Front in 1914–18, and being fought over the same ground: Béthune, Vimy Ridge, in front of Arras. Marlborough moved as quickly, and maneuvered as skillfully, as ever: first upon Douai, no easy fortress to attack, protected by its river and inundations. It held out for two months and cost the allies 8,000 casualties. Next Béthune, which took a month to reduce; St. Venant, a fortnight; Aire, which held out unexpectedly long, in miserable weather: "our poor men are up to the knees in mud and water which is a most grievous sight and will occasion much sickness."[36] It was like 1917. Such were the achievements of a disappointing campaign: a serious breach of the fortress barrier that barred the road to Paris had been blasted. But there had been no hope of a battle that might have ended the matter. Instead, Villars was engaged in constructing an elaborate system of field fortifications, making use of every natural feature—rivers, canals, woods, inundations—stretching practically from the Channel to the Meuse: the *Ne Plus Ultra* Lines.

The new government at home, headed by Harley, won the election with a large majority and proved that the Queen was right in interpreting the nation's will as being for peace. The size of the Tory majority was a handicap to Harley, who was a man of the center, and found himself in turn under the pressure of their extreme wing. In the way that often happens in human relations, the two enemies, Harley and Marlborough, now stood in need of each other. For Harley, the Duke's command of the allied armies became his chief asset in bargaining with France; moreover, Marlborough had the support of both Hanover and Prussia, which threatened to leave the Alliance if he laid down his command. Both interest and duty indicated an accommodation. Marlborough could remain the General of the Tory government until peace was assured; he could not have supposed at this stage that they would go so far as to make a separate peace and let down the allies. That would force a decision. For the time, he remained; relations with Harley were conducted on a basis of mutual civility. As a testimonial to this, the payments from the Treasury for the works at Blenheim, which had been suspended, were resumed.

The Duke started on his tenth campaign in a bad way: he complained to Sarah of much "giddiness and swimmings in my head, which also gave me often sickness in my stomach." This was his last campaign: another might well have brought on the stroke that partially incapacitated him five years later. A grave disappointment was added to oppress him. Before the campaign started, he was counting on concentrating 140,000 men to Villars' 120,000, and on Eugene's comradeship. With the Emperor's death, Eugene was ordered back to Germany with his army. Marlborough now had 90,000 with which to pierce the *Ne Plus Ultra* Lines and invade France, in face of a superior army, and with his health failing.

Actually, once he got going, never did his military genius shine more brilliantly than in this last campaign. It was like Napoleon's last campaign in 1814—except that Marlborough was still on the offensive. There was the problem: to get across those lines in the face of a stronger army, commanded by the best of the French generals, with whom one could not afford to make a single mistake. Marlborough judged that the best place to pierce the line was at Arleux, near the fortress of Bouchain. To get his army across the river and the inundations there, he would have to get Villars moving westward away from Arleux. He decided to practice a double bluff, on the principle of telling your opponent the truth: he will not believe it. In the event, he accomplished more: he got Villars to do his work for him.

As a preliminary, Marlborough captured Arleux and strengthened its defences. He then marched in full force west, as if to mount his intended full-scale attack toward Arras. Villars followed him by a parallel march behind the lines, leaving a detachment to recapture Arleux and demolish its defences. Marlborough closed up to the lines as if to attack—while secretly sending his artillery in the opposite direction. It was a risk. At the end of his career, it is nice to think, he was as daring and as ready to take (calculated) risks as at the beginning. Other detachments he sent off to the rear. The men were dumfounded: had the "Old Corporal" taken leave of his senses? Still they trusted him; only the Duke's chaplain knew what was in the wind. On the intended night, when the moon was at the full, the whole army was set in motion back to Arleux. "We had the finest night in the world to march in," wrote the chaplain: everything, as usual, had been thought of. "His attention and care was over us all," wrote a corporal.

It was a tremendous march, far longer than that before Oudenarde: nearly forty miles in sixteen hours. Villars discovered that Marlborough was missing three or four hours after the start; the French were on interior lines with a good road, ten miles fewer to go; Marlborough marching across open country. So that it was a most exhausting race; half the infantry fell out on the way. But by that afternoon Marlborough's army was across the river at Arleux and behind the enemy lines. The furious Villars, riding anxiously ahead of his army with his staff, was nearly captured. He had to accept the fact that the *Ne Plus Ultra* Lines had been turned—and with no casualties. Even the government at home was pleased. Eugene, away from the scene, was delighted: he understood, better than anyone, all that it involved. The excitement over, the work of art accomplished, the Duke was ill again: "I must confess to you the last six weeks have given me frequent and sensible remembrances of my growing old."[37]

Still there was no battle: Villars dared not risk one with France's last army; his men were in poor condition, the country war-weary: *"Je ne trouvais plus le caractère national."* Nothing for it but for Marlborough to force open the road to Paris, fortress by fortress: it was another race for time, with the home government irrevocably committed to its secret peace negotiations. The Duke turned to the reduction of Bouchain, the strongest fortress in his direct road. It was protected by its river and practically surrounded by the inundations to which the French were reduced to defend their country—by historic justice—like the Dutch in 1672.

Bouchain was a very tough proposition; and one of Marlborough's captains describes him contemplating it—a last close-up of the Duke in action. "The Duke of Marlborough (ever watchful, ever right) rode up quite unattended and alone, and posted himself a little on the right of my company of Grenadiers [his own regiment from early days], from whence he had a fair view of the greater part of the enemy's works. It is quite impossible for me to express the joy which the sight of this man gave me at this very critical moment. I was now well satisfied that he would not push the thing, unless he saw a strong probability of success; nor was this my notion alone: it was the sense of the whole army, both officer and soldier, British and foreigner. And indeed we had all the reason in the world for it; for he never led us on to any one action that we did not succeed in."[38]

It is wonderful to have this tribute to him at the end, telling us what his men thought and felt about him; the world's greatest soldiers have all had this quality of inspiring the illimitable devotion of their men. Marlborough remained there for a few moments more in that exposed position: "we were in pain for him while he stayed, lest the enemy might have discovered him and fired at him; in which case they could not well have missed him." No sooner had he gone than orders came to them to retire.

He had judged that Bouchain could be taken, and taken it was, in the presence of a French army of decidedly superior strength. Sir Winston describes it as "an amazing operation"; and so it would appear, if Marlborough had not accustomed his own time and posterity to expect nothing but victory from him. This was his last operation: but for two minor fortresses, he now had the road clear down the Oise to Paris. Posterity, however, was to be cheated of that last and grandest spectacle. The Tory government at home was too far down its own road to peace to make any more sacrifices for further advances into France. In Marlborough's ten campaigns, "he had broken the military power of France, and reduced the first of military nations to a condition in which they were no longer feared by any country . . . During the whole of these ceaseless operations of war on the largest scale the world had seen, or was to see for several generations, confronted by the main armies of France and their best generals, he had never sustained a defeat or even a serious check . . . The annals of war contain no similar record."[39]

That winter of 1710-11 the campaign for the peace was decided in London. When all is said, in the complexities of politics, the personal issues, the struggles, the feuds and hatreds, it is the simple overriding facts that matter. England wanted peace; so did France. The question was whether, in these circumstances, it was worth going on fighting any more. With the death of the Emperor, a transformation had taken place that profoundly affected the political objectives of the war. The Austrian candidate for Spain was now Emperor himself: to combine Spain and her empire with all the possessions of the house of Austria was as much of a danger for Europe as to have Louis's grandson enthroned in Madrid.

This consideration much strengthened the Tories in pushing forward with the peace negotiations. They needed every ounce of their strength, for they had embattled against them the allies—particularly Hanover, and that was very important for everybody's future—the reunited Whig party with its majority in the Lords; Marlborough and, behind him, the heir to the throne, the future George I. Against this formidable array there stood the Queen and the Tory party, with their majority in the Commons. Harley thought of trying to come to terms with Marlborough, but his party was too strong for him. In any case, Marlborough embodied the Grand Alliance: he was the power engaged in rallying the allies; he was the most dangerous enemy in the way.

In the debate on the Queen's speech in the Lords, in the presence of the Queen—sitting there *incognita* in her box—Marlborough vindicated himself, replied to the aspersions that had been cast upon him and stated his view with a last challenge. "I can declare with a safe conscience, in the presence of her Majesty, of the illustrious assembly, and of that Supreme Being, Who is infinitely above all the powers upon earth, and before Whom, according to the ordinary course of nature, I must soon appear, to give an account of my actions, that I was ever desirous of a safe, honourable and lasting peace; and that I always have been very far from any design of prolonging the war for my own private advantage, as my enemies have most fasely insinuated. My advanced age, and the many fatigues I have undergone, make me earnestly wish for retirement and repose, to think of eternity during the remainder of my days; the rather, because I have not the least motive to desire the continuance of the war, having been so generously rewarded, and had honours and riches heaped upon me, far beyond my desert and expectation, both by her Majesty and her Parliaments."[40] At the same time, he would not consider a separate peace without the allies, "for I am of the same opinion with the rest of the Allies, that the safety and liberties of Europe would be in imminent danger, if Spain and the West Indies were left to the house of Bourbon."

The Queen herself was shaken and hesitated to take the last step. The atmosphere of crisis continued; the friends of the new ministry wondered how it would resolve itself. The ministry was in a minority in the Lords. At this juncture, Harley—now Earl of Oxford—did not hesitate; like a true leader, he calculated his steps and coolly took them. Proceedings were on foot against Marlborough in the Commons for malversation of funds; the press campaign against him was redoubled— Swift lent himself to these purposes and was much the most effective penman. With Harley to guide the Queen, and with Abigail to warn her of the consequences of defeat—namely, the hated Duchess back in her presence, ruling her household—Anne took the last steps. She created twelve peers at once, one of them Abigail's husband, to secure a majority for the government, and the peace, in the Lords. She dismissed Marlborough: we do not know in what terms, for, moved beyond endurance and losing his habitual self-control, he threw her letter into the fire. But, resuming his serene manner, he replied to her with dignity: "I am very sensible of the honour your Majesty does me in dismissing me from your service by a letter of your own hand, though I find by it that my enemies have been able to prevail with your Majesty to do it in the manner that is most injurious to me . . . I wish your Majesty may never find the want of so faithful a servant as I have always endeavoured to approve myself to you."[41]

The comment of Louis XIV, on hearing the news, was much to the point: "The affair of displacing the Duke of Marlborough will do all for us we desire." There needs no further tribute to what Marlborough had accomplished.

CHAPTER XIV

Sarah and the Queen

I

WE MUST retrace our steps to tell the extraordinary story of the relations between Sarah and the Queen.

When William was dead and Anne was Queen, the Cockpit circle came into its own: nothing was too much, nothing was too good, for Sarah. She was at once made Groom of the Stole (i.e., the Stool, in actuality), Mistress of the Robes, Keeper of the Privy Purse. As such, Sarah's emoluments, independent of her husband's, came to £5,600 a year (multiply by ten or twelve). Her two married daughters, Henrietta and Anne, became ladies of the Bedchamber at £1,000 a year each.[1] Not content with this, the Queen wanted to give Sarah a grant of Windsor Lodge for life, since she had once expressed a wish, when riding by, to live there. The air was good; no doubt, also, it would help to attach her adored Mrs. Freeman to the vicinity.

Anne made the offer with her usual delicacy: "mentioning this . . . puts me in mind to ask dear Mrs. Freeman a question which I would have done some time ago; and that is, if you would have the Lodge for your life, because the warrant must be made accordingly; and anything that is of so much satisfaction as this poor place seems to be to you, I would give dear Mrs. Freeman for all her days, which, I pray God, may be as many and as truly happy as this world can make you."[2] As things turned out, it was lucky for Sarah that the grant was for life: it became a favourite residence with both her and John for many years.

While the going was so good, Sarah looked after her poor relations. Her mother's sister had married a Nonconformist merchant, named Hill, in the City and fallen upon bad times. Sarah afterward said grandly that she "never knew there were such people in the world"; but she was not

241

without kindness of heart and she took the fortunes of her young cousins efficiently—as was her way—under her wing.[3] The elder daughter, Abigail, she took to live with her at Holywell, "and I treated her with as great kindness as if she had been my sister." That may not have been Abigail's impression of the matter and, anyway, such relationships are apt to breed resentments. Before Anne's accession, Abigail had been advanced to the post of a bedchamber woman (not lady) to the Princess. The younger daughter was given the job of laundress to the little Duke of Gloucester; when he died she got a pension and, later, she too became a woman of the bedchamber. The elder brother, at Sarah's request, was given a job in the Customs House by Godolphin; the younger, "whom the bottle-men afterwards called *honest* Jack Hill, a tall boy, whom I clothed (for he was all in rags) and put to school at St. Alban's," was taken into the army and given a regiment by Marlborough.

Sarah never learned what a mistake it can be to do people a good turn; but she had a warmer heart than her husband, and she sometimes burned her fingers by her good actions. For the moment, all was well: it was "good Queen Anne" for the Hills as well as for the Churchills. To quote the phrase of Castlereagh to Metternich, à *propos* of the Emperor Alexander I, the Queen was effectively "grouped"—one might almost say insulated.

Anne apparently did not mind, or even notice: love covered all. The endearments that passed give us the tone, and the temperature, of the circle: "My dear adored Mrs. Morley," and Mrs. Morley in reply, "I am so entirely yours, that if I might have all the world given me, I could not be happy but in your love."[4] It was the language of the sentimental French romances, Mademoiselle Scudéry and the rest, on which the ladies of the Restoration Court had been brought up. But that there was strong emotion we may see from an occasional sentence that throws a shaft of light upon present or past stresses. Sarah expresses concern, at the rumor of some plot, for the Queen's safety. "Certainly, if I were never so weary of the world," Anne replies, "I would take care of myself because you desire it . . . What you say to convince me of Coupas being false was not at all necessary, for, if you remember when you adored her to that degree that it had almost broke my heart, I always thought her a jade."[5]

Now it is Sarah's fondness for Abigail that arouses Anne's jealousy. Sarah has been away two or three days without writing, and the Queen must write if only to get a line or two. If Sarah is in town, no doubt she will be tempted to see the Opera: "I should be so too, if I were able to stir, but . . . my fever is not quite gone, and I am still so lame I cannot go without limping. I hope Mrs. Freeman has no thoughts of going to the Opera with Mrs. Hill, and will have a care of engaging herself too much in her company; for, if you give way to that, it is a thing that will insensibly grow upon you. Therefore give me leave once more to beg for your own sake, as well as poor Mrs. Morley's, that you would have as little to do with that enchantress as 'tis possible, and pray pardon me for saying this."[6]

From this we learn that Abigail had already been a subject of contention between Sarah and the Queen and that Abigail had her own share of the Jennings charm.

Sarah gives the Queen a ring. "Ten thousand thanks for the dear ring, which, methinks, is very pretty; but 'tis a little too big. I have given it to Mr. Murar to do something to and he promises to let me have it again tomorrow. When I have once got it on my finger, we will never part; and Oh! that my dear Mrs. Freeman could imagine how much I value any mark of her favour, but that's impossible."[7]

So far the Cockpit circle remained firm. What neither of them realized was the profound change that was bound to come from the fact of Anne's accession to the throne. So long as William lived, the Cockpit circle was united in opposition to, and detestation of, him. With him removed, their own differences of temperament and opinion were bound to come into play: they were open to be forced apart by the pressures of politics.

Anne was devoted to the interests of the Church. The new Queen dismissed William's Parliament with the declaration: "My own principles must always keep me entirely firm to the interests and religion of the Church of England, and will incline me to countenance those who have the truest zeal to support it." This was a declaration of war upon William's coalition of Latitudinarians, Dissenters, Rationalists—the Whigs. All Anne's associations and predilections were Tory: her family principles were those of passive obedience and divine right (as channeled through the Church of England); her uncles were high Tories; the Church was the Tory party at prayer. Sarah tells us that the Queen really hated the Whigs: she associated them with the injuries she had received in William's reign; she regarded their principles as antimonarchical. As a sovereign—and perhaps no less as a lady—she regarded her prerogative as a very personal matter, and any demeaning of it as a personal affront.

For Sarah's part, "I had not the same prepossessions. The *word* 'Church' had never any charm for *me*, in the mouths of those who made the most noise with it; for I could not perceive that they gave any other distinguishing proof of their regard for the *thing*, than a frequent use of the *word*, like a spell to enchant weak minds."[8] In short, the temper of Sarah's mind was that of a rationalizing Whig. She had no patience with the humbugging cry of "The Church in danger," with such a "nursing mother" as the Queen—Sarah turned the Tories' cant phrase against them. Still less had she any patience with "the high church nonsense of promoting religion by persecution." And she scores a shrewd point with her remark: "the gibberish of that party about non-resistance and passive obedience and hereditary right I could not think to forbode any good to my mistress, whose title rested upon a different foundation."

One cannot but sympathize with Sarah—I sympathize with her as few have done. It was Sarah's lacerating candor that so frightened people; they are somehow afraid of naked truth: they prefer to cushion themselves with illusions and—if they are English—they take refuge in humbug. It was this, in turn, that so shocked Sarah in Harley, who—like Baldwin—was a ripe purveyor of what the English like best in this line. Sarah had a blistering contempt for it; as for the Tory attitude to Marlborough's victory at Blenheim as "an unfortunate accident . . . by the visible dissatisfaction of some people on the news of it, one would have imagined that, instead of beating the French, he had beat the Church."

One recognizes the familiar disingenuousnesses of party politics.

The Queen, however, thought herself above party: a Whig government was a party government; a Tory government was not. This fixed idea Sarah set herself, from the beginning of the reign, to eradicate from the Queen's mind. She apparently protested against that minatory phrase in the Queen's speech, for Anne replied: "I know the principles of the Church of England, and I know those of the Whigs; and it is that, and no other reason, which makes me think as I do of the last. And upon my word, my dear Mrs. Freeman, you are mightily mistaken in your notion of a true Whig: for the character you give of them does not in the least belong to them, but to the Church."[9]

One would have thought that this was warning enough of the Queen's temper. But Sarah was never one to take warning, and, moreover, she regarded it as her duty to make the Queen's mind more receptive to the rest of her subjects who deserved as well as the others. In former days, the Princess had adjured her to speak her mind freely and with candor on all subjects: how was she to know the truth, if surrounded, like her father, with flattery and dissimulation? "I did therefore speak very freely and very frequently to her Majesty upon the subject of Whig and Tory, according to my conception of their different views and principles." We may be sure that she did. Here, again, comes in a difference: it was all very well for her to regard the diffident, taciturn Princess as in tutelage, but a change had overtaken the situation now that she was Queen.

This change is the sort of thing that clever people often understand less well than ordinary ones—and Sarah, though far more intelligent than Anne, was not gifted with tact or imagination. The same woman who had had little confidence in herself as Princess was now, as Queen, the source of sovereign power and authority: its very exercise was bound to strengthen the will. It would not be so easy to speak so very freely to the sovereign; and if one insisted, it would be certain to lay up against one stores of resistance and accumulated resentment that might one day overwhelm ancient friendship. One could hardly expect to batter at the Queen all day and every day with impunity; and that was what Sarah proceeded to do. To some extent the exigencies of politics, the overriding need to support Marlborough's war, forced Sarah to it. This was bound to ruin their friendship; the element of necessity, which was present in it, gives it the character of a true tragedy. After more than a year of such battering, even after Blenheim, the Queen could still write: "I have the same opinion of Whig and Tory that ever I had. I know both their principles very well, and when I know myself to be in the right, nothing can make me alter mine."[10]

Perhaps it is more remarkable that their friendship lasted as long as it did than that it should have ended so grievously. The Queen sought to keep her intimate relationship with Sarah on the old private footing, while Sarah as relentlessly pushed her views in the political sphere. Everything with her became acutely personal—we may say, was reduced to the personal: friendships became exclusive, hatreds implacable. In private matters the Queen was as kind as ever. Griefs and joys still drew them together. When Sarah's only remaining son died, the Queen was all sympathy and would have gone down to Holywell to console her. "It would have been a great satisfaction to your poor unfortunate faithful Morley, if you would have given me leave to come to St. Albans, for the unfortunate ought to come to the unfortunate."[11] Sarah had nursed the boy struck down with smallpox: "Give me leave once more to beg you for Christ Jesus' sake to have a care of your dear precious self, and believe me with all the passion imaginable your poor unfortunate faithful Morley." This way of referring to herself went back to her own loss of an only son, the extinction of her hopes of her blood inheriting the throne.

His son's death was a grievous blow to Marlborough's dynastic sense, his profoundly masculine instinct to found a family. For a time he hoped that Sarah might bear him another: "whilst you are kind . . . I cannot but hope we shall yet have a son, which are my daily prayers."[12] Full of solicitude as ever for Sarah, he confided, not to her but to Godolphin, how much he missed his son: "since it has pleased God to take him, I do wish from my soul I would think less of him." Now he learned from Sarah that his hopes were vain and that she was ill: "you and I have great reason to bless God for all we have," he consoled her, "so that we must not repine at his taking our poor child from us, but bless and praise him for what his goodness leaves us."[13]

There were the four daughters, all married now. At the marriage of the third, who became Lady Bridgwater, and of the last, who became Duchess of Montagu not long after—rather to her mother's annoyance— the Queen repeated her generosity: £5,000 each, though the Marlboroughs were now rich.

In these early years of her reign Anne's attitude was a perfectly intelligible one: "never let difference of opinion hinder us from living together as we used to do."[14] In reading her letters, one is struck by the consistency with which she attempted to preserve their friendship by keeping politics out of it: "my dear, dear Mrs. Freeman, who, though she has sometimes hard thoughts of me, yet will never find in all the search of love a heart like her poor, unfortunate Morley's, that will be for ever yours." "Give me leave to add that whatever professions you may have made to you by any sort of people whatsoever, you will find very, very few that are sincerer at bottom besides her that ever was and ever will be, with all truth and tenderness, dear Mrs. Freeman's."

In 1704 and 1705 circumstances came to the aid of Sarah's too-insistent arguments, with the mistakes of the Tories. To make trouble and split the government, which rested on the moderate men of the middle, the extremer Tories were prepared to do a deal with the Whigs. The Queen grasped this firmly and sent two of the Tory *frondeurs* packing. She reported this, with some satisfaction, to Sarah and with curious Stuart deviousness: "I am told by a very good hand that the Queen has sent a message to Lord Jersey and Sir Edward Seymour which they will not like. Sure this will convince Mrs. Freeman that I never had any partiality to any of these persons; for if that had been so, this would certainly never have been done. Something more of this nature, it is believed, will soon happen, that will not be disagreeable to Mrs. Freeman."[15]

We observe the Queen anticipating the approbation of her adored friend; yet the situation is a little subtler than this: she remains, and is determined to remain, mistress of her actions: she is the Queen.

Next year the Tories made a further mistake: some of them raised the project of bringing over the Elector of Hanover, or his son, to take his seat in the House of Lords. Nothing could be more disagreeable to the Queen: she disliked the thought of the Hanover family as her successors, and could not bear the idea of one of them being in the country for a week. Godolphin's increasing co-operation with the Whigs delivered her from this horrid specter. Anne was grateful: "I believe dear Mrs. Freeman and I shall not disagree as we have formerly done, for I am sensible of the services those people have done me that you have a good opinion of, and will countenance them, and am thoroughly convinced of the malice and insolence of them that you have always been speaking against."[16]

Alas, for these hopes! The Whigs in turn now clamored for their recompense, a greater share in power. This renewed the Queen's alarm. She wrote to Godolphin: "I must own to you I dread the falling into the hands of either party, and the Whigs have had so many favours showed them of late, that I fear a very few more will put me insensibly into their power . . . I know my dear unkind friend has so good an opinion of all that party that, to be sure, she will use all her endeavour to get you to prevail with me to put one of them into this great post, and I cannot help being apprehensive that not only she but others may be desirous to have one of the heads of them in possession of the Seal."[17] From now on, Sarah becomes Anne's "dear unkind friend"—in itself a sufficient warning, especially with someone who could take refuge in the Stuart capacity for dissimulation. Sarah was totally without any such capacity—perhaps too much so for a tolerable life: everything about her was naked and exposed. She was, like people of her type, far too proud of her candor—it was really a self-justification for her bullying, overbearing ways. It was no use the Queen's appealing to her Lord Treasurer: he was on Sarah's side, and anyway, as a politician, needed the Whigs' support for the war. They got the Privy Seal for one of their leaders.

Next year, 1706—the year of Ramillies—the Whigs demanded further representation in the government: they pressed for the key post of Secretary of State for Lord Sunderland. The Secretary of State would be in constant contact with the Queen, and Anne detested Sunderland: he was the incarnation of all that she hated in pure Whiggery—an arrogant intellectual, tactless and inconsiderate, an oligarch whom Anne regarded, not without reason, as having no great respect for monarchy and meaning to subordinate the sovereign to the oligarchy. The Queen put her point of view forcefully to Godolphin: "All I desire is my liberty in encouraging and employing all those that concur faithfully in my service, whether they are called Whigs or Tories, not to be tied to one or the other; for if I should be so unfortunate as to fall into the hands of either, I shall look upon myself, though I have the name of Queen, to be in reality but their slave; which as it will be my personal ruin, so it will be the destroying of all government, for instead of putting an end to faction, it will lay a lasting foundation for it."[18]

This passage is of striking interest to the historian, for it points to the transition in government to a party basis. For Parliamentary government, party organization is indispensable; when that evolution was complete, real political power would inevitably shift from the sovereign to Parliament and party government. We have observed an earlier phase of this development in the reign of Charles II; the reign of his niece constitutes a second chapter. The Queen was naturally a conservative; she had a profound sense of her duty as Queen, and was equally conscious of her prerogative and her rights. To her, parties were factions: why could they not pull together for the country's good, leaving it to her to choose those who would govern best in the interests of the country as a whole? "Why, for God's sake, must I, who have no interest, no end, no thought, but for the good of my country, be made so miserable as to be brought into the power of one set of men, and why may I not be trusted, since I mean nothing but what is equally for the good of all my subjects?"

We see that Anne—invalid as she was, crippled with gout—was a force not to be disregarded; and indeed she has been much underestimated. She proceeded to put up a strong resistance to Sunderland's appointment. She appealed to Marlborough, whose own sympathies—chivalrous as ever—were with the Queen: he did not want his son-in-law forced upon her. But he could not go against Godolphin, who was himself under pressure from the Whigs. The Queen returned to him: "you say yourself they will need my authority to assist them, which I take to be the bringing more of their friends into employment, and shall I not then be in their hands? If this is not being in the hands of a party, what is?"[19] She proposed a compromise: making Sunderland a member of the cabinet council, without office. "If they are not satisfied with so reasonable a thing as this, it is very plain, in my poor opinion, nothing will satisfy them but having one entirely in their power. This is a thing I have so much at heart, and upon which the quiet of my life depends, that I must beg you, for Christ Jesus' sake, to endeavour to bring it about."

The Queen held out for months. But they were all under the inevitable pressures of politics. The Whigs were obdurate and from their point of view they were right: they were the people whose heart was really in the war; they were the most competent and able to wage it; why should they not have their proper share in the government? Godolphin could not now maintain his government without their support; Marlborough could not conduct the war without Godolphin and the Whigs.

But Sarah? She might at least have sympathized with the Queen's agony of mind. Not a bit: she was herself much under the intellectual influence of her son-in-law; she really shared his point of view, rationalizing, debunking the *mystique* of monarchy, libertarian and leveling. She took a passionate part in the controversy, bombarding the Queen with letters, arguments, interviews. To her, the Queen's resistance was mere obstinacy and stupidity. The tone of her communications was coldly offensive: the incessant wrangling was killing all affection, and in these circumstances the appeal to old memories and endearments simply poisoned feeling. We can only say on Sarah's side that the situation was becoming disagreeable enough for her; for she was under pressure from the Whigs to exert her influence with the Queen, and the more she tried, the more resistance she encountered. The situation had to be resolved one way or the other; on her own responsibility Sarah forwarded to the Queen a letter from Marlborough assuring Godolphin that he could not go on without him: the effect was to coerce the Queen.

"I must in the first place beg leave to remind you of the name of Mrs. Morley, and of your faithful Freeman, because without that help I shall not be well able to bring out what I have to say . . . I will tell you the greatest truths in the world, which seldom succeed with anybody so well as flattery . . . Upon recalling everything to my memory that may fill my heart with all that passion and tenderness I had once for Mrs. Morley I do solemnly protest I think I can no ways return what I owe her so well as by being plain and honest."[20] When love is dead, this kind of language leaves a most unpleasant taste. Sarah then proceeded to say something unpardonable: "as one mark of it, I desire you would reflect whether you have never heard that the greatest misfortunes that have ever happened to any of your family had not been occasioned by having ill-advice and an obstinacy in their tempers."

This was a shocking thing to say, to remind the Queen, at such a moment, of her father's fate, to wound her at her conscience's most sensitive spot. Sarah had indeed forgotten herself, as she often enough did with other people: this was not only her friend from girlhood, the loved one of many years, to whom she and her husband owed everything—this was her Queen.

The insult was beyond apology and it was never forgiven. The Queen had to give way, since government had to go on: Sarah's son-in-law became Secretary of State—in what conditions! The Whigs were on their way now to dominate and monopolize the government. The Queen bided her time and went underground. There was always the refuge of dignified dissimulation: courtesy on the surface, alienation at heart. One observes the new tone set in her letters to Sarah. At the same time, the Queen found that she was not without resource. Mr. Harley discovered that he, too, was a cousin of Abigail's: he was ready to come up the backstairs with his information and advice. The Queen's relation to her bedchamber woman became a matter of the first political importance.

2

It took Sarah longer than it would have done most people to discover the footing upon which Abigail was with the Queen: she was so used to domineering over everyone that she could not believe her place in Anne's affections might be taken by another, least of all by her own poor relation "whom I took out of a garret." And now one observes with fascination how helpless the strong overbearing character was—as often happens—in dealing with the disingenuousness and dissimulation of weaker natures: she had not the weapons to deal with Anne or Abigail. Her only chance would have been to try and retrace her steps, recover something of Anne's affection, even if the passion of love were over.

Offended pride made this impossible: she would not give way. Instead of going to the Queen, renewing her attentions, surrounding her with solicitude, she absented herself from Court for weeks at a time. Anne's was a lonely life, rendered doubly so by her position and her temperament. Sarah had often been bored, at the height of their intimacy, by the duties of attendance. Anne had no conversation, was low spirited and preferred to be alone in a crowded Court. Sarah's vitality had cheered her up and supported her spirits when she had the spleen or was in actual pain. Now she chose to absent herself. It was unwise, as her daughter, Lady Sunderland, warned her. It played Abigail's game for her: the coast was clear.

It is certain that the Queen never intended Abigail to occupy the position of near equality on which Sarah had been with her from girlhood; and for some time she labored to keep relations with Sarah on a friendly footing. "If I have not answered all my dear Mrs. Freeman's letter (as indeed I should have done) I beg she would not impute it to anything but the apprehensions I was in of saying what might add to the ill impressions she has of me . . . I have the misfortune that I cannot agree exactly in everything, and therefore what I say is not thought to have the least colour of reason in it, which makes me really not care to enter into particulars."[21]

The strain of all this had its effect upon Anne, who found it difficult to express herself in words at all times. In another letter she explains why she had denied that she was in the spleen, when she really was feeling low and dispirited at the way things were with Sarah. "My poor heart is so tender that I durst not tell you what was the matter with me, because I knew if I had begun to speak, I should not have been fit to be seen by anybody."[22] There is pathos in this avowal: the Queen has to maintain control of herself; appearances must be kept: there are ministers and courtiers coming and going, business to be transacted, audiences given.

In the summer of 1707, Sarah learned news of her cousin and protégée that astounded her: Abigail had been married secretly to Samuel Masham, groom of the bedchamber to Prince George. Masham, of course, owed his promotion to Sarah; but the news had been kept from her. He was a gentleman of good birth, having a Plantagenet descent: a respectable marriage for the daughter of a Baptist merchant, no longer young. Sarah went to the Queen for confirmation of this; all that Anne would say was, "I have a hundred times bid Masham tell it you, and she would not."[23] Sarah suddenly saw the hold her cousin had upon the Queen and that there was some mystery in the affair into which she was not being admitted. She set inquiries on foot, "and in less than a week's time I discovered that my cousin was become an absolute favourite; that the Queen herself was present at her marriage in Dr. Arbuthnot's lodgings, at which time her Majesty had called for a round sum out of the Privy Purse; that Mrs. Masham came often to the Queen when the Prince was asleep, and was generally two hours every day in private with her. And I likewise then discovered beyond all dispute Mr. Harley's correspondence and interest at Court by means of this woman."

Sarah now called to mind several passages over a long period that indicated the intimate relations established between the Queen and Abigail. She recalled one night in particular when, having gone by a secret passage to the Queen's bedchamber, "on a sudden this woman, not knowing I was there, came in with the boldest and gayest air possible, but, upon sight of me, stopped; and immediately changing her manner, and making a most solemn curtsy, 'Did your Majesty ring?' And then went out again."

Henceforth there was to be no quarter between Sarah and Abigail: the affair bore all the extremism of a women's quarrel. We know what Abigail felt toward her former patron from her correspondence with Harley. "The 22nd day I waited [i.e., on the Queen], and in the evening about eight o'clock a great lady came and made a visit till almost ten. I was in the Drawing Room by good luck, and as she passed by me I had a very low curtsy, which I returned in the same manner; but not one word passed between us, and as for her looks, indeed they are not to be described by any mortal but her own self."[24]

The Duchess determined on a showdown with "this woman." She wrote reproaching her with keeping her marriage secret from her; to this she received an artful, obsequious, insincere reply. She demanded an interview, at which she reproached her cousin with doing her ill offices with the Queen. To this Mrs. Masham "very gravely answered that 'she was sure the Queen, who had loved me extremely, would always be very kind to me.' It was some minutes before I could recover from the surprise with which so extraordinary an answer struck me. To see a woman, whom I had raised out of the dust, put on such a superior air, and to hear her assure me, by way of consolation, that the Queen would be always very kind to me!" No doubt its effect had been calculated: Abigail was an intelligent woman. She must have hated Sarah: it was intended to madden.

Sarah could not let it rest there. She had once before protested to the Queen, and got a cool rebuttal of the "suspicions you seemed to have concerning your cousin Hill, who is very far from being an occasion of feeding Mrs. Morley in her passion, as you are pleased to call it, she never meddling with anything. I believe others that have been in her station in former times have been tattling and very impertinent, but she is not at all of that temper; and as for the company she keeps, it is with her as with most other people. I fancy that their lot in the world makes them move with some out of civility rather than choice; and I really believe, for one that is so much in the way of company, she has less acquaintance than anyone upon earth."[25] This was true; Abigail was a great contrast to Sarah: a discreet, secret woman, who never raised her voice, a woman of confidences and *chuchotements*, who melted easily into the background.*

Now the Queen replied to Sarah with a finality that showed it was useless to raise the subject any more. "I beg you would not mention any

---

* This autumn of 1707, we come a little closer to Mrs. Masham in the Lord Chamberlain's accounts: we find a note of the furniture of her lodgings at Kensington: "four banister-back chairs, black frames with crimson damask seats and green fringe, two window curtains of red taffeta for her bedchamber, in her dressing room and dining room five taffeta window curtains of the colour she shall direct; likewise three table-beds with bedding." L. C. 5/70, f. 401. In 1711 we come a little closer still to this retiring backstairs lady, with the order to the keeper of the Privy lodgings at Hampton Court to deliver "a close-stool covered with Russia leather for Mrs. Masham." We watch her progress up in the world with the orders next year for the fashionable new umbrellas to be delivered at Lord and Lady Masham's lodgings at Kensington. L. C. 5/71, ff. 57, 75, 90.

more that person who you are pleased to call the object of my favour; for whatever character the malicious world may give her, I do assure you it will never have any weight with me, knowing she does not deserve it, nor can I never change the good impressions you once gave me of her, unless she should give me a cause, which I am very sure she never will. I have nothing further to trouble my dear Mrs. Freeman with at this time, but that whatever opinion she may have of me, I will never deserve any that is ill, but will always be her faithful Morley."[26]

All this was duly retailed by Sarah to Marlborough abroad, in the midst of all his other worries, the intricacies of European diplomacy, fighting his campaigns: she spared him nothing. He had judged the situation pretty correctly all along: he knew that the Queen would not give in. "The account you give me of the commerce and kindness of the Queen to Mrs. Masham is that which will at last bring all things to ruin; for by all you write I see the Queen is determined to support, and, I believe, at last own her. I am of the opinion I ever was of, that the Queen will not be made sensible, or frightened out of this passion."[27]

These quarrels would not have had their importance, or been so bitter, if they had not been inextricably interwoven with the struggle of men for power. Sarah felt it incumbent on her to fight her husband's battles at home—actually he would have done better without her; but as long as the war went on, it was necessary to support him. The Queen longed for peace: as early as the summer of Ramillies she wrote, "I having no ambition . . . but to see an honourable peace, that whenever it pleases God I shall die, I may have the satisfaction of leaving my poor country and all my friends in peace and quiet."[28] The Tories were the peace party, and it was this, in addition to Anne's determination to free herself from the Whigs, that gave Harley so much influence with her; Abigail was his intermediary and his instrument. Their correspondence, with its code references to "my aunt" (i.e., the Queen) and "my Lady Pye" (i.e., Sarah), leaves an unpleasant taste; still more, Harley's hypocritical and sycophantic letters to Marlborough at the same time as he was undermining him and trying to supplant Godolphin. He was a good politician, of Puritan origin: he spoke the language.

The quarrel between the Queen and the Duchess was becoming public property, and Sarah did not restrain herself from talking about it.*

---

* Cf. such a letter as that to Sir William Trumbull, November 13, 1707: "Tis plain you live in the country by your writing to me to ask a favour of the Queen,

The Queen saw its unwisdom and approached Marlborough in a letter which shows how much more sense she had. It also reveals a perfectly respectable conception of how their relations could continue: Sarah keeping to the exercise of her offices, showing courtesy and discretion, and ceasing to try and oust Abigail. "I have had a great mind to speak to you this week [February, 1708], but when I have met with an opportunity I have found such a tenderness coming upon me on the thought of the subject I was to speak of, that I choose rather to trouble you this way with my complaints than any other. You know I have often had the misfortune of falling under the Duchess of Marlborough's displeasure, and now, after several reconciliations, she is again relapsed into her cold, unkind way . . . and I find she has taken a resolution not to come to me when I am alone, and fancies nobody will take notice of the change. She may impose upon some poor, simple people, but how can she imagine she can on any that have a grain of sense? Can she think that the Duchess of Somerset and my Lady Fitzharding, who are two of the most observing, prying ladies in England, won't find out that she never comes near me as she used to do; that the tattling voice will not in a little time make us the jest of the town? Some people will blame her, others me, and a great many both. What a disagreeable noise she will be the occasion of making in the world besides, God knows of what ill consequences it may be."[29] The Queen appealed to Marlborough to dissuade Sarah from making the breach an open one. But the great soldier never had had his wife under proper control; it was now too late.

That summer there was an open altercation between the two women on, of all days, the Thanksgiving for Marlborough's victory at Oudenarde and, of all places, in the state coach on the way to St. Paul's.[30] In the exercise of her office Sarah had laid out the jewels that the Queen was to wear in the accustomed way. The Queen chose to wear no jewels. Sarah was beside herself with rage: she was convinced that this was Mrs. Masham's doing, a fresh example of her insolence, and that it was intended as a humiliation on the very occasion of returning thanks for her dear lord's victory. Reproaches, recriminations poured forth all the way to St. Paul's. We know the difficulty the Queen had in speaking her mind

---

to whom I never have the honour to speak of anything but what concerns my own offices, and in that I can't prevail to recommend according to custom: all which is compassed by the black ingratitude of Mrs. Masham, a woman that I took out of a garret and saved from starving and all her family." H.M.C., Downshire MSS., 855. Observe that the Queen in her replies always insists on referring to Abigail as Sarah's cousin.

immediately: it was not until they were in the Cathedral that she began
to reply—and then Sarah commanded her to keep quiet, she afterward
explained, "for fear of being overheard." When, after this, Sarah forwarded a letter of Marlborough's, on her own responsibility, backing her
up, she received a cold and cutting reply from the Queen. "After the
commands you gave me on the Thanksgiving day of not answering you,
I should not have troubled you with these lines but to return the Duke
of Marlborough's letter safe into your hands, and for the same reason do
not say anything to that nor to yours which enclosed it."

Sarah felt that she had put herself in the wrong: she now wrote a
dignified letter, in a different tone, which she would have done well to
adhere to. "Though I have always writ to you as a friend and lived with
you as such for so many years, with all the truth, honesty and zeal for
your service that was possible, yet I shall never forget that I am your
subject, nor cease to be a faithful one." This was one of the few occasions
when Sarah condescended, quite simply, to touch the Queen's heart. The
memory of their former love, if no longer love itself, softened their hearts,
and from a renewed meeting both Anne and Sarah withdrew in tears.

Unfortunately the Duchess was one of those women on whose good
resolutions one cannot rely from one moment to another. The next
moment she was sending the Queen copies of the ballads and lampoons
that were being circulated about her and Abigail. She could not resist the
cutting remark that it was not to be expected that Mrs. Masham would
acquaint her with them, "though the town and country are full of them."[31]
We may be sure that Sarah did not discourage their appearance. She
dared to remind the Queen that her father had been "sung out of his
kingdom by silly ballads" and warned her not to risk everything similarly
for a woman incapable of giving her any good advice, "nobody but a
chamber-maid, whom I took from a broom as the ballad says rightly."
Clearly, hatred of Abigail was making Sarah quite unbalanced. The
wrangles, altercations, scenes continued.

That autumn the Queen, a sick woman herself, was nursing her
dying husband. Prince George was always a good friend to the Churchills.
Sarah now wrote, with repellent self-justification at such a moment:
"though the last time I had the honour to wait upon your Majesty your
usage of me was such as was scarce possible for me to imagine, or for
anybody to believe, yet I cannot hear of so great a misfortune and affliction to you as the condition in which the Prince is without coming to

pay my duty, in inquiring after your health."[32] When Sarah presented herself, she was very coolly received; but she came back next day and was present when the Prince died. On this occasion, mindful of appearances, the Duchess knelt to the Queen and prevailed on her to withdraw from the death chamber to her own closet. She took charge of the situation, as was her right, and persuaded Anne to leave Kensington, where the preparations for the funeral were going forward, for St. James's: Sarah would take her in her own coach.

At this moment of her grief, all that Anne wanted was Abigail to console her. She gave Sarah her watch and, pointing to some little time later when she should come back, asked her meanwhile to send Abigail to her. Sarah felt humiliated and did not give the message; but when announcing that the carriage was ready, she added, "your Majesty may send for her at St. James's, when and how you please." Anne acquiesced and passed out through the gallery, leaning on Sarah's arm for support. As Abigail's sister put on her hood, the Queen whispered a commission; shortly after, Abigail appeared to see her off; and the Queen turned leaning toward her, though neither spoke. At St. James's, Anne wrote Sarah a touching little note. "I scratched twice at dear Mrs. Freeman's door, as soon as Lord Treasurer went from me, in hopes to have spoke one more word to him before he was gone; but, nobody hearing me, I wrote this, not caring to send what I had to say by word of mouth; which was to desire him that when he sends his orders to Kensington, he would give directions there may be a great many Yeomen of the Guards to carry the Prince's dear body, that it may not be let fall, the great stairs being very steep and slippery."

This was the last kindness that passed between them. If only Sarah could have left matters here, if only she attended to Marlborough's words of wisdom: "it has always been my observation in disputes, especially in those of kindness and friendship, that all reproaches, though ever so reasonable, do serve to no other end but the making the breach wider. I can't hinder being of opinion, how insignificant soever we may be, that there is a power above which puts a period to our happiness or unhappiness; otherwise, should anybody, eight years ago, have told me, after the success I have had, and the twenty seven years' faithful services of yourself, that we should be obliged, even in the lifetime of the Queen, to seek happiness in a retired life, I should have thought it impossible."[33] If only Sarah had acted on his advice: "be obliging and kind to all your friends, and avoid entering into cabals, and whatever I have in this world, if that can give you any satisfaction, you shall always be mistress of, and have the disposing of that and me."

Instead of that, the intolerable woman—perhaps the only extenuation of her conduct may be her change of life, and an element of hysteria—went on tormenting the Queen about Mrs. Masham. In 1709 the disreputable Mrs. Manley—who later became Swift's understrapper on the *Examiner*—published her *New Atlantis,* which drew attention to the situation at Court. It was intended to curry favor with Harley and Abigail; but it gave Sarah an opening to write to the Queen, for it commended Abigail's efforts as making for peace, "and there is stuff not fit to be mentioned of passions between women."[34] The prim Sarah found it a disagreeable subject, but perhaps not so disagreeable to let the Queen know what she was opening herself to. It was a case of the characteristic Stuart infatuation for their favorites, like James I's and Charles I's for Buckingham. Even when Sarah was still supreme at Court, a mere man could write, "but the Queen's fondness for t'other lady is not to be expressed."[35] Now, Sarah's clever confident, Maynwaring, wrote: "since you have lost nothing but her passion, which it is plain you never cared for,"[36] and that may let us into the secret springs of Anne's resentment against the beautiful, and more masculine, Sarah.

Anne at last, all kindness gone, replied in kind, charging the Duchess with inveteracy against her cousin and "having nothing so much at heart as her ruin."[37] She told Sarah outright that it was impossible for her to recover her former kindness, though she would behave to her as the Duke of Marlborough's wife and her Groom of the Stole.

At this the Duchess drew up a long narrative of her services to Anne during the past twenty-six years, which she presented to her to read. The Queen replied that, when she had the time, she would. The Duchess added the directions given by the author of the *Whole Duty of Man* in regard to friendship, the instructions given in the Prayer Book in regard to reconciliation, together with Jeremy Taylor's rules on the matter. The Queen's reply to that was, when passing by to receive the Communion, to smile very graciously upon Sarah; "but the smile and pleasant look I had reason afterwards to think were given to Bishop Taylor and the Common Prayer Book, and not to me." To Marlborough, the Queen wrote: "you seem to be dissatisfied with my behaviour to the Duchess of Marlborough. I do not love complaining, but it is impossible to help saying on this occasion I believe nobody was ever so used by a friend as I have been by her ever since my coming to the Crown. I desire nothing but that she would leave off teasing and tormenting me, and behave herself with the decency she ought both to her friend and Queen, and this I hope you will make her do."[38]

This was the year of Malplaquet, 1709. The Queen took no notice of Marlborough's victory. Impelled by a sense of insecurity, wanting to shore himself up to see the war through to a finish, he made a grave mistake: he asked to be made Captain General for life. This corroborated his enemies in their accusation that he was aiming at a monopoly of power. The Queen had no difficulty in refusing his demand. Then the Whigs failed to make peace—which made the Queen right, at any rate more certain that she was right in relying upon Harley's advice. Mrs. Masham's influence inevitably grew, even if the Queen did not rely on it in political matters as people supposed: Harley was the real figure in the background, on his way into the foreground now. Rumors flew around of Sarah's disrespectful talk about the Queen and Mrs. Masham: she wrote demanding to be heard in her own defense. The Queen desired that she would do it in writing. "Believing by what you said to me tonight you are very desirous to go out of town, I cannot help giving you this trouble to desire you would not stay a minute longer than you have a mind to, upon my account; for whatever you have to lay before me may be as well done in a letter, and more to your ease as well as to mine, I believe. Therefore pray gratify yourself in going into the country when it is easiest to you, and me in letting me know your thoughts in writing, which *shall be answered without delay.*"[39]

One cannot but notice the accents of real detestation: the long love had at last been turned to hatred. It was like that between Philip II and Antonio Perez: the favorite could not bring himself to believe that the man who had once adored him, who had been so much under his influence, had at length come to hate him.

Sarah wrote again asking for an audience: no doubt she thought her presence would be more effective than mere writing. The Queen, a few days later: "whatever you can have to say to me may certainly be as well writ as said, I *desire* you once more to put your thoughts in writing."[40] Without permission, Sarah announced that she was coming to Kensington that afternoon and would wait every day till the Queen would grant her an audience. Arrived there, the Duchess sat down in a window of the long gallery "like a Scotch lady with a petition, instead of a trusted and lifelong confidant."[41] She was kept waiting outside a long time— which must have given her bitter thoughts of the days when she was always within, when the Queen could not see enough of her.

At last she was called in. The Queen said that she was just going to write to her. When Sarah began to speak, Anne interrupted again and again, repeating, as her manner was, the phrase, "whatever you have to say, you may put it in writing."[42] Sarah said that Her Majesty never did so hard a thing to any as to refuse to hear them speak; and she assured her that she would not trouble her upon the subject she knew to be so ungrateful to her. At this Anne turned away: she must have been so sick of the subject; she had been through it all so many times before. In the next breath, Sarah went on to say that there were those about Her Majesty who had made her believe that she had said things about her which she was no more capable of saying than of killing her own children. (This was an unfortunate image, for Sarah was not on good terms with two of her children.) Anne said, with justice, to this: "Without doubt there are many lies told."

Sarah took advantage of this to ask the particulars of which she had been accused, that she might clear herself. The Queen, laying hold of a phrase in Sarah's letter, replied that she would give her no answer. Characteristically, Sarah pressed again and again and would not desist; she said, with the so-familiar implication, that she did not ask the names of the authors of these calumnies. To every attempt Sarah made Anne replied, "You desired no answer, and shall have none." The Queen made a move toward leaving the room; Sarah followed. "When she came to the door, I fell into great disorder; streams of tears fell down against my will and preventing my speaking for some time." Sarah poured out passionate protestations, asking the Queen whether she had ever in the course of their long friendship played the hypocrite, or offended except by pressing too zealously what she thought necessary for her service. To everything Anne opposed, "You desired no answer, and you shall have none."

The repetition of a phrase like this was very characteristic of Anne: it was a defense against her own lack of confidence, her hesitation to speak and, perhaps in the present instance, to maintain her self-control against the solicitations of hysteria. Sarah appealed to Anne's own knowledge whether she was capable of disowning anything she knew to be true—always Sarah's first and last gambit: her candor, her sincerity. "You desired no answer, and you shall have none." "This usage was so severe, and these words, so often repeated, were so shocking . . . that I could not conquer myself, but said the most disrespectful thing I ever spoke to the Queen in my life . . . and that was 'I was confident her Majesty would suffer for such an instance of inhumanity.'" To this the Queen answered, "that will be to myself."

These, to my mind, are the most tragic words spoken in the course of that famous altercation—their last, for they never saw each other again. Those words reveal the Queen's full sense of the responsibility she was taking home to herself, the suffering that would be her lot, which she was ready to accept and endure. Nor was it long now in coming.

After Sarah emerged from the private apartments, she sat down again in the long gallery to wipe her eyes before confronting the world. One cannot but admire the stoicism, the courage, of these women, worthy of their exalted position: never giving away appearances, always putting on a brave face to the world. But O the pity of it, the heartbreak beneath!

A few days later, the Queen wrote asking for the return of her letters: "all my strange scrawls, it being impossible that they can now be agreeable to you."[43] Sarah neither complied nor replied.

There was a latent threat that she might publish them, with all their revelations of Anne's feelings toward her predecessor. When Marlborough came home that winter, he persuaded Sarah to make a complete submission to the Queen. His own position as Commander in Chief was in jeopardy, and Sarah, who would make no submission for herself, was willing to humble her pride for his sake. She wrote the Queen a letter of contrition and apology, promising never to raise the old topics of controversy, and abjectly begging that she might retain her offices.[44] Marlborough himself bore this letter to the Queen; he had written, before coming home: "I would go upon all-four to make it easy between you."

It was too late. He could hardly get the Queen to open the letter, and then she said, "I cannot change my resolution." Her steps were resolved, her plans made. She demanded that Sarah's gold key of office be delivered up within three days. Marlborough begged for ten days' respite. Anne, now implacable like her father, cut it down to two; and she would discuss no business with him till she had the key.

The tradition is that when he delivered the message, Sarah flung the key on the floor and told him to take it back at once. Her offices were divided: the Duchess of Somerset became Groom of the Stole, but Abigail Keeper of the Privy Purse.

Perhaps the saddest thing of all is that this long and famous friendship should end in the squalor of money. In the noonday of friendship and favor, the Queen had offered Marlborough £2,000 a year out of the Privy Purse to support his dukedom: Sarah had refused it. Now she claimed the arrears of it for the past nine years; the Queen—in contempt, we may be sure—made it good. Sarah was left to clear her things out of St. James's Palace: the Queen sent a message that she might take a lodging for ten shillings a week to put her lord's goods in. Sarah commented savagely, "it sufficiently shows what a good education and understanding the wolf has, who was certainly the person who gave that advice."[45] The lodgings were wanted for someone else: Sarah had them stripped of every mortal thing that belonged to her, down to the locks on the doors, leaving a desert behind.

CHAPTER XV

Exile and Return

MARLBOROUGH was dismissed from all his employments December 30, 1711. Next day twelve peers were created—Abigail's husband being one—to give the Tory government a majority in the Lords to carry the peace. This did not resolve the crisis: indeed, we may regard the last years of the Queen's reign, until the safe realization of the Protestant succession with George of Hanover, as one prolonged crisis. Nor did it mean that the European figure of the Duke ceased to be dangerous to the Tory ministry. It was necessary to damage him in the eyes of the public, direct against him what is only too well known in contemporary politics as a "smear campaign."

In the art of maneuvering opinion Harley was a past master: Sarah described it, for once with some justification, as "that wonderful talent Mr. Harley possessed, in the supreme degree, of confounding the common sense of mankind."[1]

All the wits were Whigs by origin: Addison and Steele, Prior and Swift, and that unattractive, camouflaged figure, something apart on his own, Defoe. Harley had recruited Defoe to his intelligence service, bought him for the Tories. And he bought Jonathan Swift, no less, though not with cash: with a little influence and less power, which Swift valued even higher than money. Godolphin, who was too old-fashioned or too Philistine to care for such things, or too lofty to notice, lost both Prior and Swift. The Marlboroughs were made to smart for this.

Sarah had been responsible herself for alienating the poet Prior; in nothing do we see so much the contrast between her and the Duke. Prior had written a verse "Letter to Monsieur Boileau" to celebrate the victory, and the victor, of Blenheim. He had composed the inscription for the fountain, with effigies of the Queen and the Duke, which ornamented the celebrations with a display of the chief rivers of the world:

Ye active streams, where'er your waters flow,
Let distant climes and furthest nations know,
What ye from Thames and Danube have been taught,
How Anne commanded and how Marlborough fought.

Sarah, however, had got it into her head that Prior had written some lampoon against the Duke; though Prior denied it, she returned the packet containing the "Letter to Boileau" unopened. The Duke, on the other hand, assured him that "though some people may have endeavoured to give him wrong impressions of you, it has not had the least effect with him, and that he is sure if your heart had not gone hand in hand with the poet, you could not have said so much in his favour beyond his merit, and that he will endeavour to deserve your friendship and that you may rely entirely on his upon all occasions."[2] How charming this was from the great man: we cannot but find such manners irresistible.

It meant, perhaps, more: Marlborough wished his victories to be sung by the poets: artist spoke to artist. Not so with Sarah: she hated poetry—so contrary to common sense. She left a binding instruction in her will that in the official life of the Duke, for which she had both arranged and paid—the work was never written—not a line of verse should be quoted. When the Duke came home from Blenheim, Prior complained of the Duchess's ill usage of him; he replied peaceably that, though Prior was not a married man, he could not but know that women would have their humors and that he should receive no prejudice. This throws a shaft of light upon how Marlborough dealt with Sarah and what he had to put up with.

After Ramillies Prior addressed a long Spenserian ode to the Queen, for which the Duke gave him "particular thanks." The Queen also was pleased with the Ode. Not so Sarah: she pursued her vendetta. When the Commission of Trade and Plantations was reformed, Godolphin, who was more under Sarah's influence than Marlborough was, left Prior out of his job. The poet would have had nothing but his Cambridge fellowship to live on if the Duke had not come to the rescue with a pension. It is surely remarkable in this avaricious, careful man that it should have been a poet to whom he opened his bounty. Nevertheless, when the Tories came in, Prior went over to them; he became one of the group of writers in the *Examiner* who attacked Marlborough, and the trusted agent of the Tories sent over to Paris to conduct the secret negotiations for peace. Marlborough may be said to have owed that to Sarah.

Godolphin was responsible for losing Swift. Swift was born and bred a Whig; but, balked of anything better, poor and without prospects, he took orders. The Church was his regiment, and though it may be doubted—as Queen Anne doubted—whether he had any belief in God, he had unquestioning belief in himself and a determination, rendered savage by long frustration, to advance his own prospects. He had been sent over by the Church of Ireland to obtain the grant of first fruits from the Crown. Godolphin, who had other things to think about, put him off and cold-shouldered him. Swift rewarded him with a satire, "Sid Hamet the Magician's Rod," and did not hesitate to hint that Sarah was Godolphin's mistress. No one else sank so low—anyone who knew Sarah or Godolphin knew how impossible such a relationship was. It is to be feared that the misanthrope of genius himself makes a mean figure in all this. He went wholly and savagely, as was his way, on to the other side.

Harley caressed and nursed the great satirist, who put his incandescent powers at the service of the new ministry. Never was a political tractate more immediately effective than his *Conduct of the Allies,* which came out a month before Marlborough's dismissal. This brilliantly written pamphlet argued, persuasively enough, that the other allies had a greater stake in the Grand Alliance than we and then suggested, untruly, that we had borne a greater burden than they. "Ten glorious campaigns are passed, and now at last, like the sick man, we are just expiring with all sorts of good symptoms."[3] Swift argued the Tory case for a sea war, as against taking part on the Continent, and put the point of view of the country gentry, who paid the land tax, as against the moneyed interest and the stockjobbers who were doing well out of the war. At the head of these stood out, above all, the Marlboroughs: "so that whether this war were prudently begun or not, it is plain that the true spring or motive of it was the aggrandizing a particular family, and in short, a war of the General and the Ministry, and not of the Prince or people."[4]

This was a *suggestio falsi.* It was true that Marlborough had made an immense fortune out of the war; it was not true that that had been either the spring or motive of it. Ordinary people would be incapable of distinguishing between the two propositions, and no line of attack on the Duke was so damaging as this, however unwarranted. It would appeal to people's jealousy and envy—always on the alert against any singular degree of eminence—to people's cupidity and suspicion, as Swift, with his precise knowledge of the baser side of human nature, knew well. He went on to describe the exemplary partnership of Marlborough and Godolphin, really a national union of moderate nonparty men, "as a conspiracy founded upon the interest and ambition of each party."[5] We know what to think of that: we know that Godolphin had no ambition at all, and no wish to be where he was, except to serve his friend, and that that friend's overriding ambition had been to serve his Queen and country. Swift ended on the note of peculation, the suggestion of fraud, always grateful to common ears, which was bound to have the widest and most popular reverberation.

This was the note that was constantly struck in the campaign that was let loose week by week in the *Examiner*, directed by Swift, in pamphlets, squibs, satires, epigrams—for this was an exceedingly literate society and a literary age. It was as if Swift could not get away from Marlborough, as if he had a fixation on him: again and again he comes back to the theme of his avarice, his covetousness—almost the only thing that could be urged against the Duke—and the interesting thing is that Swift was fairly avaricious, pretty covetous, himself. Then, too, Swift wanted power more than anything: all his life, though conscious of his own capacity, he had been frustrated. Marlborough had reached the summit of power, and was still not done for: he was a living danger to the ministry, a threat to the peace. Swift did not draw back from hinting that Marlborough was aiming at the Crown—for which there is no shadow of evidence, or the least likelihood. Though certainly Marlborough intended his weight to be felt in the matter of the succession, which was becoming more urgent with each year and the sinking health of the Queen.

The pamphlet and press campaign did its work: it undermined the Duke's credit with the people and prepared the way for measures against him in Parliament. One week the *Examiner* would come out with the observation that some subjects' palaces were more splendid than those of the Queen herself; another week, that Marlborough had more ready money at his disposal than all the monarchs of Christendom. An issue of the *Examiner* had been devoted to an effective balance sheet, showing an account of Roman gratitude compared with British ingratitude.[6] A statue, a trophy, a laurel wreath, a triumphal car, valued as a modern coach, etc., came to no more than £994.11.10. On the other side, the capital value of Woodstock, Blenheim, the Post Office grant, Mindelheim, the Duke's emoluments, came to £540,000—and the figure was not inaccurate. Trevelyan comments that never had the nation received better value for every guinea spent on Marlborough. But every argument of Swift had its value and its effect; and when that pure, remorseless prose had done its work, he could vary the dose of poison by his verse—such verses as "A Widow and her Cat," or "The Fable of Midas."

> This tale inclines the gentle reader
> To think upon a certain leader,
> To whom from Midas down, descends
> That virtue in the fingers' ends:
> What else by Perquisites are meant,
> By Pensions, Bribes and Three Per Cent?
> By Places and Commissions sold,
> And turning dung itself to Gold?
> By starving in the midst of store,
> As t'other Midas did before?[7]

Then Sarah took a hand. Nothing of all this daunted her: she was guns for any of them, spoiling for a fight. She employed her own scribes to attack the Ministry: the obvious result was to redouble the attacks on the Marlboroughs. It is possible that she enjoyed the fight, for all her life she managed to be in the thick of one row after another. In some ways she was a more masculine spirit than her husband, far more aggressive and altogether less sensitive. "She had herself all the qualities of a successful man."[8] John had the more feminine qualities of sensitivity and intuition; his gift as a soldier was something apart, it was pure genius, unfailing and inspired. In the ordinary commerce of life he was a man of infinite accommodation, not at all aggressive.

To this heroic soldier all this was unbearably painful, and he wrote touchingly to Harley, now Earl of Oxford, to deliver him from it. "I do not know whether your lordship looks into such papers, and I heartily wish they had been kept from me. [Sarah saw to it that nothing was kept from him.] I am sure you cannot hear of one without the other, and when I protest to you I am no way concerned in the former, I doubt not but you will have some feeling of what I suffer from the latter . . . All the remedy, all the ease I can at present expect, under this mortification, is that you, my lord, would do me the justice to believe me in no way an abettor or encourager of what has given me a mortal wound."[9]

He received an exceedingly disingenuous reply: "I hope my senti-ments are so fully known of that villainous way of libelling, I need say little to your Grace upon that subject." The campaign continued.

Swift was not the worst of the vilipenders, and sometimes he had his doubts. Even St. John felt sorry for the Duke, he looked so worn out at this time with his lifetime of labors, his fatigues and misfortunes.[10] He had denied that he was covetous or ambitious to the Queen; in vain: she said, according to St. John, that if she could have conveniently turned about, she would have laughed and could hardly forbear to in his face. St. John told Swift that "the Queen and Lord Treasurer mortally hate the Duke of Marlborough and to that he owes his fall, more than to his other faults."[11] Swift began to question "whether ever any wise state laid aside a general who had been successful nine years together, whom the enemy so much dread; and his own soldiers cannot but be-lieve must always conquer; and you know that in war opinion is nine parts in ten."[12] He wondered how far his dismissal might not encourage the French to play tricks with us. For Louis, it had been an almighty deliverance: Marlborough in Paris might have given the *ancien régime* the necessary propulsion toward liberty and constitutional government. We know that he had it in his mind: who knows what the consequences might have been for France in an orderly evolution making the Revolu-tion unnecessary? There was no limit to Marlborough's profound ambi-tion to leave an immortal name in history. The fact that the artist in him was defrauded of the proper end of his life's work, the march on Paris—which he could certainly have accomplished in 1712—is enough to account for his personal hatred of Harley. There was no one else in his whole life against whom Marlborough felt so deeply or so bitterly.

St. John told Swift that the Duke was saying he desired nothing so much as to find some way to soften Dr. Swift. (If Marlborough had had a bishopric to dispose of, he could have done it easily enough.) This was very flattering to Swift's vanity, his inflamed inferiority complex, always on the alert. "He is mistaken; for those things that have been hardest against him were not written by me. And I'm sure now he is down, I shall not trample on him; although I love him not, I dislike his being out."[13] The Doctor comments, sagely, "I do not love to see personal re-sentment mix with public affairs." Really, the obtuseness of the satirist with regard to himself—as if the whole of his work did not spring out of personal resentment!

On the night of Marlborough's dismissal, Swift wrote boastingly to Stella that he was at Court in the bedchamber, where he was pointed out to Marlborough's daughter, Lady Sunderland: "I desired Lord Roche to tell Lady Sunderland I doubted she was not as much in love with me as I was with her; but he would not deliver my message."[14] In January, 1712, Marlborough's daughters, Lady Rialton and Lady Sunderland, resigned their posts as Ladies of the Bedchamber. Next month, Prince Eugene arrived, too late to save Marlborough. At the fete in honor of Eugene, Swift observed three of Marlborough's daughters at St. James's looking out of the window in undress.[15] Not one Whig lady was there, the Tory ladies monstrous fine. We see what a small society this was, and how acutely personal its quarrels therefore were.

In March, 1713, Swift went to sit with Lady Clarges and found Marlborough's eldest daughter, now Lady Godolphin, playing whist. "I sat by her and talked of her cards etc. but she would not give one look, nor say a word to me. She refused some time ago to be acquainted with me. You know, she is Lord Marlborough's eldest daughter [this for the benefit of Stella]. She is a fool for her pains and I'll pull her down."[16] What a scene it presents—these ladies, with the insolent parson persisting at the elbow of the one whose father and mother he had vilified. There were some people, we have to admit, who needed Sarah to deal with them; and she dealt with Swift as he deserved. "The Rev. Mr. Swift and Mr. Prior quickly offered themselves to sale (besides a number of more ordinary scribblers); both men of wit and parts ready to prostitute all they had in the service of well-rewarded scandal, being both of a composition past the weakness of blushing or of stumbling at anything for the interest of their new masters. The former of these had long ago turned all religion into a Tale of a Tub, and sold it for a jest. But he had taken it ill that the ministry had not promoted him in the Church for the great zeal he had shown for religion by his profane drollery; and so carried his atheism and his humour into the service of their enemies."[17]

The government found that the most effective way of damaging its opponents was to keep charges of financial peculation on the boil. The able young leader of the Whigs in the Commons, Robert Walpole, was got out of the way and sent to the Tower for some small misdemeanor committed by a subordinate. Ground was made for an attack on Marlborough. He had received some £6,000 a year from Sir Solomon Medina, the contractor for bread for the army, and a deduction of 2½ per cent on the pay of all the foreign troops, which yielded large sums. These perquisites had been regularly permitted, to constitute a secret service fund; and all who knew recognized that Marlborough's intelligence service throughout the war had been superlative—one clue to his unbroken success, never caught out. Harley offered to let the Duke off any severe censure if he ceased to oppose the government's resolutions on the subject. For once, Marlborough refused point-blank; he was deeply wounded and indignant. He had made a vast fortune, but it was honorably made out of his employments; he had not needed to resort to fraud: all his accounts were in order, he refused to besmirch himself to help his enemies, even though they held hostages of his—above all, his unfinished Blenheim.

The government resolution that the taking of an annual sum from the bread contractor was "unwarrantable and illegal" was passed in the Commons by 276 to 165. It was a pure party vote. The Tory ministers proceeded to authorize the Duke of Ormonde, whom they had appointed to succeed Marlborough as Commander in Chief, to draw the same deduction upon the bread contract and the same 2½ per cent on the pay of the foreign troops, for precisely the same purposes as Marlborough had used it. So much for the humbug of politics. Meanwhile, Harley—now Earl of Oxford—accepted £10,000 from the Queen for his services.[18]

Far more important than any of this were the Restraining Orders which the Tory government gave its new Commander in Chief, not to hazard any battle or engage in any siege. In the Netherlands, Eugene found himself fighting with one arm tied behind his back. The British troops, after their long career of victory and glory, were mutinous at the humiliation of their position. The egregious Jack Hill, whose incompetence had produced a complete fiasco in his Quebec expedition, was made Governor of Dunkirk: Swift was able to compliment Abigail as governess thereof. St. John had made several thousands out of fraudulent contracts for the Quebec expedition, and done even better by taking Abigail away from Harley and capturing her—or rather her ear—for himself.

Against this background of the Tory conduct of the war, the egregious Earl Paulett insulted its hero in the Lords: "Nobody could doubt of the Duke of Ormonde's courage and bravery; he was not like a certain general who led troops to the slaughter to cause a great number of officers to be knocked on the head in a battle, or against stone walls, in order to fill his pockets by disposing of their commissions."[19] As against this shocking allegation, we know what Marlborough's men felt about his care of them all. The Duke was so roused that he sent Paulett a challenge. The Queen had to interpose her command against his fighting a duel. This Paulett was the grandson of the one who had burned down Ashe over Lady Drake's head—so long do these family resentments continue. We may take the opportunity to observe that, at length, his grandmother's blood had prevailed in Marlborough, the Villiers over the Churchill in him, the Whig over the Tory.

In the Netherlands, the war, without him, went not so much badly as disgracefully. Villars knew that Ormonde was not allowed to fight. Some 12,000 British troops were withdrawn. For the first time in the long war, there was a mutiny provoked by the badness of the bread. A corporal writes, "Sir, what can be the meaning that all our garrisons are disturbed in this manner? It is an instance that never happened during the time of the Duke of Marlborough . . . O the Duke of Marlborough that gained the love of all men, knew better than to put it in any one's power to upbraid him; for all his men in general were obsequious. Now they are become refractory and neglect their duty."[20] Villars was able to win a victory at Denain which, Napoleon said, saved France. Marlborough's captures, Douai and Bouchain, were lost. Louis XIV was saved from himself and France able to make peace on far better terms than were justified by the course of the war.

The peace terms presented to Parliament were a disappointment to many of the government's supporters. Marlborough, Godolphin and the Whig Junto registered their solemn protest at what they regarded as inadequate terms and a shameful desertion of our allies. But the terms were accepted by large majorities in both Houses. The fact was that the nation wanted peace: the Queen, that woman of ordinary composition and abilities, proved a more correct interpreter of her people than those Lords of very superior parts and the one man of genius. The courage and determination with which she had fought, and at length defeated, them were anything but ordinary.

On Blenheim Day the Duke gave a feast to his old companions and the Whig leaders at Holywell. The magnificent tent, in which so many historic decisions had been made on his campaigns, was pitched on the bowling green, and all that summer crowds visited it. The attacks on him were redoubled. The aftermath of the war would be a dangerous period, for Marlborough's veterans were returning in no good mood, either at his treatment or theirs. The Duke offered a vulnerable target, if quite unjustly. After the resolution in the Commons he might at any moment be sued for the repayment of all the money he had spent on his intelligence service. Work at Blenheim was stopped; a suit to make him repay at least £30,000 was threatened. The government wanted him out of the way, and Marlborough was glad to go.

This summer of 1712 Godolphin was at Holywell, nursed by Sarah in his last illness. On his deathbed, he recommended the young Walpole to her care as a future leader; it will be seen how she carried out his wishes. Her tribute to her friend was sincere: "Lord Godolphin had conducted the Queen with the care and tenderness of a father or a guardian through a state of helpless ignorance, and had faithfully served her in all her difficulties before she was Queen, as well as greatly contributed to the glories she had to boast of after she was so . . . He was a man of few words, but of a remarkable thoughtfulness and sedateness of temper; of great application to business . . . of wonderful frugality in the public concerns, but of no great carefulness about his own. He affected being useful without popularity; and the inconsiderable sum of money which he left at his death, showed that he had been indeed the nation's treasurer and not his own."[21] In fact, it transpired that Harley's administration of the Treasury cost more than Godolphin's at the height of the war.

Godolphin's death removed Marlborough's last objection to going abroad. He transferred £50,000 to The Hague for all eventualities, and on December 1 embarked with a small retinue: a couple of gentlemen in waiting, three valets, a cook, etc. Sarah was to follow. The Queen approved of his going into exile: "the Duke of Marlborough has done wisely to go abroad." At this moment of dejection, Addison paid him a deeper-felt tribute than the more famous verses on his prime victory:

> Go, mighty prince, and those great nations see,
> Which thy victorious arms before made free;
> View that famed column, where thy name engraved
> Shall tell their children who their Empire saved:
> Point out that Marble where thy work is shown
> To every grateful country but thy own.

O censure undeserved! Unequal fate!
Which strove to lessen *Him* who made *Her* great;
Which, pampered with success and rich in fame,
Extolled his conquest but condemned his name . . .

At once the alarm was set going in England. Swift: "Here is the Duke of Marlborough going out of England (Lord knows why), which causes many speculations. Some say he is conscious of guilt and dare not stand it. Others think he has a mind to fling an odium on the government, as who should say that one who has done such great services to his country cannot live quietly in it, by reason of the malice of his enemies."[22] What was he up to now? His enemies found that he was up to a great deal in the twenty months before the Queen's death and his return.

In the Netherlands, where he might have ruled, he was received with almost sovereign honors. He was anxious not to give the Queen cause for complaint, so he traveled quietly by byways, across the scenes so familiar to him, to Maastricht and Aix-la-Chapelle. He asked that his old comrade in arms, Cadogan, might be released from duty to travel with him. The Queen gave him permission, and shortly after dismissed him from all his appointments. In the New Year Sarah went to join him. Swift tells us: "the Duchess of Marlborough is leaving England to go to her Duke, and makes presents of rings to several friends worth £200 a piece. I am sure she ought to give me one, though the Duke pretended to think me his greatest enemy and got people very mildly to let me know how gladly he would have me softened towards him. I bid a lady of his acquaintance and mine to let him know that I had hindered many a bitter thing against him, not for his own sake, but because I thought it looked base; and I desired everything should be left him except power."[23]

It does not seem that Sarah had ever been abroad before, and in her letters home a new character appears, which helps one to understand something of the charm that must have existed underneath so much that was intolerable. The schoolgirl stands before us, very innocent and much surprised at what she saw; sometimes shocked, excited by the newness of it all, corroborated in her insular prejudices; a very English figure, patriotic among all those foreigners, in the end longing for home. Here she is at Maastricht, writing with all the authority of a few weeks abroad, to homekeeping Mr. Jennings, yet another relation. "All the places one passes through in these parts have an air very different from London. The most considerable people I have seen have but just enough to live, and the ordinary people, I believe, are half starved. But they are all so good and so civil that I could not help wishing (if it were possible to separate the honest from the guilty) that they had the riches and the liberties that our wise citizens and countrymen have thrown away, or at best put in great danger, and that *they* were punished as they deserve to be by an arbitrary prince and war, as these poor people have been for fifty years . . . The honours they have done me in all places upon the Duke of Marlborough's account is not to be imagined, which is not disagreeable now, because as it cannot proceed from power, it shows he made a right use of it when he was General."[24]

It was not long before Sarah's strong Protestant common sense was affronted by what she saw "in visiting nunneries and churches, where I have heard of such marvels and seen such ridiculous things as would appear to you incredible if I should set about to describe them."[25] At Frankfort, Sarah watched Eugene's troops pass by from a window. "They paid all the respects as they went by to the Duke of Marlborough, as if he had been in his old post . . . To see so many brave men marching was a very fine sight, but it gave me melancholy reflections and made me weep. But at the same time I was so much animated that I wished I had been a man that I might have ventured my life a thousand times in the glorious cause of liberty."[26] Sarah shed tears whenever she thought of Godolphin, the best friend she ever had in her life, who managed most of her money for her. In the country round about, there are no houses with nice clean gardens, "the sand that goes over one's shoes is so disagreeable that I love to walk in the road and fields better, where the Duke of Marlborough and I go constantly every day in the afternoon, and stop the coach and go out wherever we see a place that looks hard and clean."[27] All the same, if she were at home, "I am confident that I should have been the greatest hero that ever was known in the Parliament House, if I had been so happy as to have been a man." As to the field, she cannot brag that she has much of that sort of courage; but again, a week later, "if I were a man I should struggle to the last moment in the glorious cause of liberty."[28] It seems that Sarah was much given to wishing that she were a man; no doubt there were occasions when the Duke wished he could claim the privilege of being a woman.

Soon, Sarah's thoughts were turning homeward: she could not believe that she would be content to live the rest of her life in "these dirty countries . . . I think 'tis much better to be dead than to live out of England."[29] On another occasion, "as dismal a condition as England is in, I know of no other country where one can place money that one can be sure of having in again."[30] Her mind rattles on and on: "I know one must die some time or other, and I really think the matter is not very great where it happens or when; but if I could have my wish it should be in England, in a clean house, where I might converse with my children and friends while I am in the world. But if that must not be, I submit; and I will own to you that I am not so much to be pitied as some people, having never seen any condition yet that was near so happy as 'twas thought. When I was a great favourite, I was railed at and flattered from morning to night, neither of which was agreeable to me; and where there were but few women that would not have poisoned me for the happiness they thought I enjoyed, I kept the worst company of anybody upon earth . . ."[31] Still, she reflected, thinking of home, "we are like a sort of banished people in a strange country."

We may be sure that the Duke was a good deal more contented: he had spent so much of his life abroad, one way or another, that he was used to it. Besides, after a lifetime of exertions and fatigues, he was enjoying a rest, not even putting pen to paper. He had plenty to turn over in his mind. "I wish he would write himself sometimes because his hand would not trouble you so much to read; but he is intolerable lazy, and has not writ once to any of his daughters since he left England."[32] Early in 1714 came the news of the death of one of these daughters, Lady Bridgwater—a favorite with her father, for she was gentle and took after him. Not a word passed those reserved lips, though, it is said, when the news came he leaned against the marble chimneypiece, losing consciousness. For Sarah there was always the release of words: "the loss of my poor dear child is very terrible to me, though I know there is a great many reasonable and true things to be said upon such sad occasions, and that one ought to remember the blessings which are yet left."[33] Two of the remaining daughters Sarah was already in the way to find very far from blessings: they took after her.

All the time, at the back of Sarah's mind, she was wondering what would happen when the Queen died: "for let the sorcerers give out what they will of Mrs. Morley's good health, it is next to impossible that one with such a complication of diseases can last long."[34] Would the villains at home bring in the Pretender? Sarah's mind ran much upon this theme as the year 1714 advanced. She was inclined to think they would bring in the Prince of Wales—as she often referred to him. If so, she agreed with Mr. Steele, "Farewell Liberty, all Europe will soon be French."[35] It is fairly clear that, on these matters, the Duke kept his own counsel.

Sarah hardly remembered two days together what she wrote: her pen came back to the inconvenience of living abroad. "Indeed one must have suffered a good deal to make one find any ease or satisfaction by being here; and I am full of wonder every day to see countries that have been so long civilised want all the conveniences of life. We are now in one of the best houses, I believe, in this town [Frankfort] and yet there is but one place that one can make a fire in, and the weather is so cold that we are half starved, for their manner is stoves, which is intolerable and makes my head so uneasy that I can't bear it."[36]

It is a familiar strain; it was time to go home.

There, things were going badly with the Tory government. It had held together well enough to put through the Peace of Utrecht; and we must admit that, though the manner of doing it was ill, it provided very well for the interests of this country. In the curious way in which things are apt to work out unexpectedly advantageously for us, we did far better than we should have done by William III's partition treaties. Louis XIV would have done vastly better to be an honest man and keep his word.

Once the peace was out of the way, the government had to confront a still more dangerous issue—that of the succession to the throne. The Queen's health was visibly precarious: she was seriously ill in 1713 and again early in 1714. She detested the Hanover family, and they were unknown in England. She wanted her brother—no more nonsense about the warming pan now—to succeed her. Both Harley and Bolingbroke, the Tory leaders, would have preferred James's son, if he were prepared to become a Protestant. He was not. His refusal left the Queen and the government with no policy but to drift with events.

The difficulties of the political situation were exacerbated by the overwhelming Tory majority in the Commons, with its powerful wing of extreme Tories, who were the foundation of Bolingbroke's strength and to whom he appealed. Harley—Earl of Oxford and Lord Treasurer—

was a moderate; the Queen was no more inclined to be the catspaw of a Tory government than she had been of a Whig one. At the end of 1712, she is writing to him, "you cannot wonder that I who have been ill used so many years should desire to keep myself from being enslaved; and if I must always comply and not be complied with, is [sic], I think,very hard and what I cannot submit to."[37] In August, 1713, she writes, "I desire you would not have so ill an opinion of me as to think when I have determined anything in my mind I will alter it."[38] At the end of the year: "now that I have a pen in my hand I cannot help desiring you again when you come next, to speak plainly, lay everything open and hide nothing from me, or else how is it possible I can judge of anything?"[39]

This woman, ailing as she was and within sight of her end, was determined to remain mistress with all the prerogatives of the sovereign. What a way she had come from those earlier days of submission to the adored Sarah—a more remarkable transformation than anything that had happened to Sarah, who remained singularly unchanged. Here was the effect of the exercise of sovereign authority. Perhaps, as we watch her more closely, we appreciate the better that Anne was worthy of the place she occupies in our history.

No one knows the trouble that Harley had with her; he, in turn, could now appreciate the difficulties Godolphin had had to contend with. And Swift with his sharp nose for any humbug, except his own, observed after Godolphin's death, " 'tis a good jest to hear the Ministers talk of him now with humanity and pity, because he is dead and can do them no more hurt."[40] Nor was the Queen unaware of the failings of her beloved Abigail, as we can descry from a little note to Harley: "my Lady Masham told me she heard one of the chaises that are come out of France was intended to be given to her. Do not take any notice of it to her but find out if it be so and endeavour to prevent it; for I think it would not be right."[41]

When the pamphleteers had not hesitated to charge Sarah with fraud in her accounts as Keeper of the Privy Purse, the Queen herself had given them the answer: "Everybody knows cheating is not the Duchess of Marlborough's crime."[42] We cannot say as much for Abigail. She was in league with Bolingbroke to get money out of the Asiento contract, for trade with Spanish South America, provided for by the Treaty of Utrecht. Bolingbroke had made a good £3,000 out of the grants of passports to France upon the peace, besides abstracting sums from secret service funds to pay off his mortgages. Tory finance was by no means incorruptible, as Godolphin's had been—but then, they had been kept away from the trough a long time.

Harley's veto on Abigail's sharing in the Asiento contract earned him her hostility: she went over to Bolingbroke. The last months of the reign were riven by the factions within the government. Swift describes it all with despair in his heart. "That whole period was nothing else but a scene of murmuring and discontent, quarrel and misunderstanding, animosity and hatred, between him [Harley] and his former friends. In the meantime the Queen's countenance was wholly changed towards him; she complained of his silence and sullenness; and, in return, gave him every day fresh instances of neglect or displeasure."[43] All the while there was the prospect of ruin opening before them if the Queen died and no steps had been taken to make themselves secure: the House of Hanover would come in and the Whigs would be there for ever. The Lord Treasurer himself said to Swift, "Whenever anything ails the Queen, these people are out of their wits; and yet, they are so thoughtless, that, as soon as she is well, they act as if she were immortal."[44] The Tory ministry was ruining itself by its intestine quarrels, which made any policy impossible; the party would go down into the night.

What was Marlborough up to abroad? What were the steps he was engaged on—of which Sarah was plainly kept in ignorance?

Like the strategist he was, he first made sure of his rear. The communications with St. Germain that had never been completely dropped were taken up again through his nephew Berwick. Dividends might always accrue from courtesy, politeness, assurances. His wealth, estates, Blenheim itself, were at the mercy of the government at home: could not St. Germain influence the French government to moderate the hostility of the ministry to him? This was a cosmopolitan society—the world was small; in it everyone knew everyone else; anyone might be at another's mercy by a sudden turn in affairs. Perhaps his nephew Berwick would obtain a pardon for him in the event of James III's restoration? Berwick was not deceived by these protestations; but neither was he so impolite as to allow it to appear that he was not deceived. He passed them on, without enthusiasm, but with no reluctance: blood is thicker than water.

These intelligences did not disturb the confidence of Hanover in him: all his real preparations were made on that front. He gave his advice that on the Queen's death, George of Hanover should at once go over to England; in the same contingency he and Cadogan were given authority, in the name of the King, to take command of all the troops. Marlborough and his commanders, colleagues of the war, drew together, made their preparations. In England, all depended on a dying woman. Marlborough moved slowly toward England with the cool deliberation with which he had moved on objectives in the field. He sent a message in mid-June to Hanover: "my best friends think my being in England may be of much more use to the service than my continuing abroad, *upon which I design to return as soon as the Parliament is up.*" Observe these words. He arrived at Antwerp. "We had a very inconvenient house," wrote Sarah, "and before we could remove from thence the Duke of Marlborough was so weary that he took a resolution to go for England."[45] Sarah seems to have been much in the dark.

That last week of July took place the last struggle around the Queen. Harley had really given up hope and wanted to resign: he knew the chasm that was opening under their feet for the Tory party with the accession of the House of Hanover. It was far too late for them ever to put themselves right. Bolingbroke was trying all in all to oust the Treasurer and take his place. The time came when Abigail refused to carry any more messages for the latter to the Queen—she had carried so many in the years before—and when she said to her "cousin": "You never did the Queen any service, nor are you capable of doing her any." The time came when the Queen dismissed him, as she had done Godolphin; but telling all the Lords, with contumely, her reasons: that he neglected all business, that he was seldom to be understood, that she could not depend on the truth of what he said, that he never came to her at the time she appointed, that he often came drunk, that he behaved himself toward her with ill manner, indecency and disrespect.[46] Well might the wise Godolphin say, "Things change, and times change, and men change."[47]

The Lord Treasurer was out, but could the Queen put the staff into the hands of a man whom, however brilliant, she knew to be a debauchee, a dissolute adventurer? Her sense of duty forbade. On July 27, 1714, the struggle raged for hours in the cabinet council, in the presence of the Queen, determined to abide it to the last. Before the end she was mortally stricken and had to be carried from the room.

Abigail wrote to Swift, who had fled in despair to the country, cautiously as ever, "my dear mistress is not well, and I think I may lay her illness to the charge of the Treasurer, who, for three weeks together, was teasing and vexing her without intermission"; she appealed to Swift to come back and help, of "your charity and compassion for this poor lady, who has been barbarously used."[48] It was all too late, as Swift had seen all along it would be. "At the time I am writing, the breath is said to be in the Queen's nostrils; but that is all. No hope left of her recovery. Lord Oxford is in Council; so are the Whigs."[49] The whole Council was in constant session. In her last moments the Queen's hand was guided into giving the staff into the hands of Shrewsbury, Marlborough's friend of many years, one of the grandees at the Revolution, one of those men of the center who really rule England.

Swift took leave of Abigail with dignity: "I pray God to support your ladyship, under so great a share of load, in this general calamity . . . I most heartily thank your ladyship for the favourable expressions and intentions in your letter, written at a time when you were at the height of favour and power."[50] The town was less dignified in what was said. "The town tell a world of stories of Lady Masham now; as that a Friday she left the Queen for three hours to go and ransack for things at St. James's."[51] And again, "Lady Masham and Mrs. Hill are cried out upon for their behaviour; though they roared and cried enough whilst there was life, but as soon as there was none they took care of themselves."[52] Abigail's lodgings at St. James's, where Swift had so often enjoyed himself at night reading a new squib or a poem to the company, were searched by the Hanoverian envoy. Abigail withdrew into the country, where, with her talent for noiselessness, she lived in such obscurity that not a breath of her existence reached the world.

Of the Queen, the most humane, the most perceptive words were spoken by her own physician, dear Dr. Arbuthnot. "My mistress's days were numbered even in my imagination, and could not exceed such certain limits; but of that small number a great deal was cut off by the last troublesome scene of this contention among her servants. I believe sleep was never more welcome to a weary traveller than death was to her."[53]

Marlborough was on his way to England and would have been present at that last scene if contrary winds had not detained him. There were rumors, before the Queen died, that he was to take over the government. The day after her death he landed at Dover. His home-coming was a triumphal progress such as he had never had in the days of his victories. At Rochester, August 3, "today, about 12 o'clock, the Duke and Duchess of Marlborough passed through this city; they were received with great expression of joy from the people, especially those at Chatham, who strewed their way with flowers, as they adorned their houses with green boughs, and welcomed them with repeated shouts and acclamations."[54] Everywhere they passed, they were given an official reception. On entering the City, they were received and escorted by the civic authorities, a train of coaches and a troop of militia with drums and trumpets. This welcome was not much appreciated by the Tories; but the future was not with them. At this moment of uncertainty, when people could not see their way, with a spontaneous movement they turned instinctively to the Duke for confidence, as never before.

When the King landed later that summer, Marlborough was first to receive him: "My lord Duke," George I said graciously, "I hope your troubles are now all over."* Marlborough was at once restored to his offices—Captain General, Master General of the Ordnance, Colonel of the 1st Guards—by the first warrant the King signed. As before, in 1702 when Anne came to the throne, as in 1689 when William became king, Marlborough was there at the right hand of a new monarch, in this case a new dynasty, still happily with us.

---

* George I, great-grandson of James I, succeeded by virtue of the Act of Succession of 1701—which is still in force—limiting the succession to the English throne to Protestants.

CHAPTER XVI

Blenheim Palace

DURING all these years of struggle and victory, setbacks and dis-appointments, exile and return, the great house that was the nation's monument to an unexampled English victory in the heart of Europe was taking shape—and with a similar rhythm. It too had its prodigious beginnings, its gathering difficulties, criticism and spreading disparage-ment, a crisis when all the work was stopped; then continued slowly upon political contingencies; at last finished quietly under changed auspices, a new reign. In all this Blenheim Palace offers an eloquent parallel to, almost a physical expression of, Marlborough's career.

Never was a house carried on with such difficulties, under such cumulative vexation and trouble, carrying into stone the hazards, the ups and downs, of politics. But rarely has there been such an under-taking. It is the English parallel to Versailles—intended as such by Marlborough, that reserved, inexpressive man who thus expressed both his profound ambition and his sense of art. At last it stood forth, the noblest, the most splendid conception of a house in the island, to cele-brate the noblest victory, the unbroken splendor of his feats of arms.

Blenheim has hardly ever been understood, or properly appreciated for what it was intended to be. It was not much liked in its own time: too vast, too grandiose, that "wild unmerciful house" Sarah called it, who could not bear it. Shortly after, when Palladian standards ruled, it was disapproved of: too rhetorical and declamatory, too dramatic and unrestrained. The Victorian Age detested such an immense, classic pile. Perhaps in this age, we are beginning to descry its true meaning at last. In the first place, it is a national monument, a building of state, and always has been intended as such; only secondarily is it a house, intended for the posterity of John, Duke of Marlborough, victor of Blenheim. The private apartments in the east wing, the Duke's Grand Cabinet, his study, and so forth are on a reasonable, modest scale—like Philip II's at the Escorial.

Then there is all the drama of the site and the composition, the complex changing masses, the rhetoric of the roofscape, the astonishing grandeur of the layout. As one enters Sarah's Triumphal Arch—an expression of her love for the Duke—and looks across the crescent of lake with its monumental bridge, to see the skyline dominated by the Palace with spreading wings reaching out toward the bridge, one reflects that not for nothing was Vanbrugh a dramatist: there is the scene set in stone. If St. Paul's Cathedral is the *Paradise Lost* of our architecture, Blenheim Palace is one of Dryden's heroic poems or heroic plays.

Imagine the private citizen, however, the subject of Queen Anne, who meant to rival Louis XIV! Only as one stands in the middle of the grand saloon and grasps that one is on the center of an axis extending a couple of miles or more—from Bladon's classical church tower, where the later Churchills are buried, through the house and portico across the bridge, to Marlborough standing on his Victory Column and the avenue beyond—does one realize the heroic grandeur of the conception and that one is in touch with the spirit of John, Duke of Marlborough, who conceived it.

The response of the ordinary uncritical person has always been one of incomprehension and of a certain dumbfounded awe. And that is right in a way, since no one has understood the spirit of Marlborough: not even Sarah, though she accepted his incomprehensible genius, and what she did for this house—she recognized it as "his passion" and thought it his greatest weakness—is the ultimate evidence of her submission.

Perhaps least of all has the rational critic understood it, as we see from Pope's clever epigram:

> See, sir, here's the grand approach;
> This way is for his Grace's coach:
> There lies the bridge, and here's the clock,
> Observe the lion and the cock.
> The spacious court, the colonnade.
> And mark how wide the hall is made!
> The chimneys are so well designed,
> They never smoke in any wind.
> This gallery's contrived for walking,

The windows to retire and talk in;
The council chamber for debate,
And all the rest are rooms of state.
    Thanks, sir, cried I, 'tis very fine,
But where d'ye sleep, or where d'ye dine?
I find, by all you have been telling,
That 'tis a house, but not a dwelling.

Of course, Pope was being deliberately obtuse for the sake of the joke; but his poem does represent what people said at the time. Moreover, Pope's genius was nondramatic: he was out of sympathy with the drama of the house, which, for the rest, was on too big a scale for him.

On successive visits to Louis XIV, on missions for Charles II and James II, Marlborough was able to see Versailles rising upon its ungrateful site. Blenheim Palace was his Versailles, rival to the great monarch he at length defeated. About this Marlborough never said a word. We have already seen what an impersonal sort of man he was, and he seems to have held to a distinction between himself as an individual person and his achievements which were public property, for the country and for posterity. It is the tradition of his family that has best preserved the sense of this, and that thus offers us the truest guide to the understanding of the man. Sir Winson Churchill says justly, "about his achievements Marlborough preserved a complete silence, offering neither explanations nor excuses for any of his deeds. His answer was to be this great house."[1]

So, too, the late Duke of Marlborough, than whom no one has written more perceptively about John and Sarah and the national monument they raised. "It was his achievements, not himself, that were to be recognized by a grateful country. For this reason he determined that the stately palace which his countrymen intended to build should be named after the first and most dazzling of the victories that it recalled. But he felt that his fame would be the special heritage of his descendants, and he determined that they should be in a position to maintain it. For them he saved money and for them he collected pictures and tapestry in his travels through Europe."[2] That Blenheim became a more personal memorial to him was really due to Sarah, to whom the task of completing it was left after his death. "It was not by any desire of hers that Blenheim was planned on so gigantic a scale; and she never quite understood what was in her husband's mind when he planned it. But she obeyed his wishes the more closely because she did not understand them; and, as she was incapable of drawing the distinction, of which he was so conscious himself, between his personality and his genius, she converted the house he had projected into the stateliest personal memorial that has ever been raised to any Englishman." The Triumphal Arch and the Victory Column are entirely hers. She and her descendants accepted their duty: "Blenheim, as they have maintained it, is the most splendid relic of the age of Anne, and there is no building in Europe, except Versailles, which so perfectly preserves its original atmosphere, and so adequately enshrines the memory of the man for whom and for whose victory it was called into being."[3]

Blenheim, then, is a monument to their love, too. There could be no more striking tribute that, disliking it as she did, Sarah acted as the Duke's agent throughout. For it went clean contrary to her spirit and convictions. She wanted something smaller, less extravagant and more manageable: this lion of a house was contrary to common sense and rationality. Hers was a prose spirit, allergic to this kind of thing—though, strangely enough, at the moment of completion, it conquered her. The Palace was in keeping with the deeper layers of John's spirit. He saved for it, he slaved for it; nothing was too good for Blenheim; so careful a man about money, he never grudged a penny he spent on it; anything that Vanbrugh wanted, for its completion or its furnishing, he was ready to buy. All this throws the most revealing light upon this extraordinary man: the deep, latent poetry, the romanticism concealed beneath the external formality—it is a very ceremonial house—the absolute determination to make his place in history, as absolute as anything in Louis XIV.

No one knows why Sir Christopher Wren was not chosen to build Blenheim, or why it should have been Vanbrugh. It must have been Marlborough's own choice. There is a historic propriety that it should have been an artist of Dutch extraction and French training who was chosen. Wren, one would have said, was obviously much closer to Marlborough's personality: the classic form, the calm courtesy, the romanticism underneath, the subtlety, the elegance and coolness. But that was not all that Marlborough wanted: he wanted the clash of battle, the drama and bravura of magnificence, military glory in stone. Vanbrugh, too, had been a soldier. There was an instinctive understanding between them— even apart from Vanbrugh's deep admiration, a real hero worship, for the Duke. They would have been friends for life if it had not been for that *femme fatale,* the Duchess. Never a cross word passed between the two men, in all the campaigns, lasting longer than Marlborough's in the field, before the palace was finished; while the quarrels that raged between Sarah and Vanbrugh created a complex on both sides. In the architect's correspondence with the Duke, we note a tone of entire confidence, the assumption of mutual understanding; the Duke never criticizes or crabs, or suggests cutting down the design—his only suggestions are for more. In Vanbrugh's letters to Sarah, he is constantly on the defensive, having to explain himself, observe caution or he will be taken up: the boisterous dramatist becomes a cat on hot bricks. Never can an artist have had such an experience as he had with Sarah.

Woodstock was already a legendary place, full of memories and fables, when the Marlboroughs took over. It was an ancient possession of the Crown, a royal forest from Norman times where the kings came to hunt, and where a manor house had been erected for their convenience on the edge of the forest, high above the steep ravine made by the little Glyme winding through its marshy valley, not far from the town. Here Henry II brought Walter de Clifford's daughter, Fair Rosamond, and kept her as his mistress. The well in which Rosamond bathed her pretty self still springs, not far from Vanbrugh's bridge spanning the ravine. It seems that there was a labyrinth of winding, twining walls between this and the castle, which looked down—the ground was higher then—upon what is now Queen Elizabeth's Island with its slender columns of Lombardy poplars that sway in the wind coming up the drowned valley from the west, leaning together toward their native east.

Here the Black Prince, eldest son of Edward III and Queen Philippa, was born, and their youngest son, Thomas of Woodstock. Something of those late medieval days remains in the church, and the house of Chaucer's son, when he was Ranger of the Forest, at the entrance to Sarah's forecourt and Triumphal Arch. The Princess Elizabeth was rusticated here from Court, when in disgrace with her sister, Queen Mary, from May, 1554, to April, 1555. Indignant and protesting, she inhabited the Castle, which, with its gatehouse and dependencies, was still not large enough for her suite: the young woman, up to every trick, led her Catholic keeper, Sir Henry Bedingfield, trusty and stupid, a dreadful dance. On a windowpane in the gatehouse were scratched the words, which people came long distances to see:

Much suspected, of me
Nothing proved can be,
        Quoth Elizabeth, prisoner.

And that was the long and the short of her confinement there. In happier days, as Queen, she came there once and again to hunt with Leicester, the whole Court in attendance.

Of all this, nothing remains. The Marlboroughs have laid so powerful an imprint upon the landscape as to obliterate even that vital and idiosyncratic shade.

When Queen Anne gave Marlborough, after Blenheim, the royal manor of Woodstock with the forest and its appurtenances, the place was in considerable disrepair.* Much of the castle had been a ruin since the Civil War; only a few of its rooms were at all habitable. The forest was rough, scraggy ground, with magnificent oaks and a deer park; the course of the little River Glyme was very marshy; the manor house looked down on a picturesque swamp. All the same, it was a princely gift, with its several thousand acres, and what a scene to challenge the imagination, the will power and art, of John, Duke of Marlborough and John Vanbrugh!

To build a house worthy of Blenheim, a monument for the nation to all posterity, to subjugate the wilderness and bring it into order like a battle formation, a work of art—there was the task that lay before them. Neither of them had any idea of the years it would take before it was done, the gigantic struggle that lay before them, the separate battles waged, both private and public, individual and governmental, the quarrels and lawsuits, the oceans of paper upon which it now floats serene— though not even the historian, let alone the reader, can wade through it all.

Vanbrugh produced his design in the spring of 1705, and it was an inspired site that he selected. Not that of the original manor house, where the space was confined by the steep slopes of the hill, but across the ravine from there: a vast expanse of level ground looking to the south, while on the west there was the sharp fallaway to the valley giving magnificent prospects to all this side of the house. Vanbrugh

---

* £12,000 was granted from the Treasury for buying in the incumbrances on Woodstock, the offices of Lieutenant, Ranger, Controller, etc., within the royal honor, with the tithes on the park, to settle them on Marlborough and his heirs. *Cal. Treasury Books*, 1704-5, 505.

already had the experience of designing Castle Howard to go on—a sight
of the design may have decided Marlborough that this was the architect
he wanted. And now Vanbrugh was in a position to improve upon even
that superb and lovely house. Blenheim, as it emerged, has a much higher
degree of integration in its composition, with the raising of the central
mass to dominate the whole and, even so, reinforced with its tremendous
corner pavilions. So imposing a centerpiece can easily ride the spreading
wings, joined by the segmental colonnades that remember Bernini's
colonnade at St. Peter's. Where Castle Howard has the dispersed
grace of a feminine composition, Blenheim—it was originally thought of
as the Castle of Blenheim—has a more masculine strength and concentration. There is something Michaelangelesque about it.

We see that Blenheim is more than an extrapolation of John
Churchill's spirit. If it were merely that, charm would have to be a
leading element. But Blenheim is not out to charm; it is there to strike
with awe: it is the most daring genius among all English soldiers whom
it commemorates, the loftiest exploits, the most difficult mind to comprehend.

On a pleasant June evening, the light falling across those swards
from the valley, the foundation ceremony took place. Vanbrugh laid a
polished stone with the inscription: *In memory of the battle of Blenheim,
June 18, 1705, Anna Regina.* (We remember that, a hundred and ten
years later, this was the day Waterloo was fought.) "There were several
sorts of music, three morris dances; one of young fellows, one of maidens,
and one of old beldames. There were about a hundred buckets, bowls and
pans filled with wine, punch, cakes and ale. From my Lord's house all
went to the Town Hall where plenty of sack, claret, cakes etc. were
prepared for the gentry and better sort; and under the Cross eight barrels
of ale, with abundance of cakes, for the common people."[4]

Both Godolphin and Sarah wanted a more modest scheme. Not so
the Duke: it was no objection, to his frugal mind, that the nation was
paying for it; the house was planned to cover, with its courts, seven
acres. The boy from the roofless house at Ashe had traveled a long
way: it was no wonder his enemies said that he was as covetous as Hell
and as ambitious as the Prince thereof! It is indeed a Lucifer of a house:
pride and ambition are its keystones. Vanbrugh at once hurried on the
foundations for the whole thing; and, all through, we see his determination, as an artist, to carry up the building as a whole, without finishing

any part of it, for fear that the Duchess might intervene, once the living part were finished, and countermand the rest. This motive of Vanbrugh's has not been realized by any of the writers on Blenheim; and yet it might easily have happened, had the Duke been killed or died. Vanbrugh knew that the Duchess was well capable of it: she hated the thing and thought it all madness.

We must in justice allow that there was a good deal to be said for her—she said so much for herself that her case has usually been discounted. And yet, look at her position. She was under constant pressure from the Duke abroad to get the house finished for him to inhabit when peace came. It was all very well for him to urge, but she was in the thick of her troubles with the Queen, and she could not get Vanbrugh to finish any one part of the house for the Duke to live in. The vast quarry of a place, with acres of stone lying about and forests of scaffolding, was either rising together or at a stop together—there was trouble with the winter frosts and the stone flying, then trouble about the carting of stone from considerable distances. The quarries in the park had early failed to provide such enormous quantities as were needed: this greatly increased the initial costs and delayed the building. Then the architect was full of ridiculous schemes for grottoes and temples, for a great orangery on the western side, for a vast bridge which was to contain a house in itself; and now he was repairing the ruinous manor house as a residence for himself. Was the man mad? He must be deliberately misleading her, no doubt he was cheating her; worst of all, perhaps he was laughing at her? He was not a dramatist for nothing; but, really, the thing went beyond a comedy. After a lifetime's experience of architects, Sarah concluded that they were all mad, and that the sensible thing to do was to build what you wanted yourself. She always fancied her skill as a doctor; for very little, she would have left us an example of her powers as an architect.

A more serious threat to the completion of Blenheim, and what gave rise to difficulties of all kinds and to complicated legal proceedings, was a certain ambivalence in the initial financial arrangements. The house was the nation's gift to the Duke and to be built at its expense. Marlborough accepted no financial responsibility for it and was careful to interfere in no part of the financial arrangements. Godolphin, however, issued a warrant to Vanbrugh to make agreements with the contractors, who had no direct dealings with the Crown: their money was issued from the Treasury as to the Duke. This provision was probably intended by Godolphin to protect the Crown from spoliation and keep rates down; but it had the effect of making either the Duke or Vanbrugh liable when work outran the Treasury payments and large liabilities were incurred. In the end the Duke had to meet a portion of this—contrary to the original intention, contrary to his wishes—and this was the result not so much of the size of the building, for the sums paid out were vast, but of the intolerable delays in its completion. To the Duchess, with whom patience was not a strong point, it was all maddening.

That very summer of 1705, Marlborough was bidding Sarah "Pray press on my house and gardens; for I think I shall never stir from my own home, being very sensible that it is impossible to serve with any satisfaction, where it is in so many people's power to do mischief."[5] Sarah sent on a draft of house and gardens, which fell into the hands of the French, who politely forwarded it unopened. "I hope some time this summer you will go down to Woodstock for three or four days, and that you will let me know if Mr. Wise be still of the opinion that he shall be able to make all the plantations this next season, which would be a great pleasure to me at my return."[6] Vanbrugh promised that the gardens should be formed and planted in a year from their beginning; to form the grand parterre alone some 17,000 yards of earth had to be removed, and good earth, and dung dug in. Plants, fruit trees and trees were bought and planted on an equally colossal scale: scores of junipers, laurels, cedars, apricots, quinces; hundreds of peaches, pears, vines, apples, wych-elms, sycamores, limes; flowering shrubs, espalier limes, hedge hollies, hornbeams and sweetbrier in thousands. Flowers were bought in scores of thousands: irises, hyacinths, narcissi, Dutch yellow crocuses, tulips, jonquils. Henry Wise was the gardener who planned and planted it all, and he made a splendid job of it.[7]

On campaign abroad the Duke had something pleasant to think about, to look forward to, in such interstices of time as he could switch his mind to, from the innumerable calls upon him. Ailesbury, when visiting him this autumn at Tirlemont, asked him "who was his architect (although I knew the man that was), he answered 'Sir John Vanbrugh.' On which I smiled and said, 'I suppose my Lord you made choice of him because he is a professed Whig.' I found he did not relish this, but he was too great a courtier for to seem angry. It was at my tongue's end for to add that he ought as well to have made Sir Christopher Wren the architect,

Poet Laureate. In fine, I understand but little or nothing of this matter but enough to affirm (by the plan I saw) that the house is like one mass of stone, without taste or relish."⁸ People who know little or nothing of the matter are always ready to give this sort of opinion: Ailesbury was a very ordinary person.

It is touching to find Marlborough writing, immediately after Ramillies, "I am so persuaded that this campaign will bring us a good peace, that I beg of you to do all you can that the house at Woodstock may be carried up as much as possible, that I may have a prospect of living in it."⁹ A month later he reproaches her with not going down to Woodstock: "I find your heart is not set on that place as I could wish."¹⁰ Thus propelled, Sarah went down for a few days, finding fault as she went. Difficulties were already accumulating, but Marlborough would not have Godolphin worried about them: "though Woodstock is extremely at my heart . . . upon my word, I had rather never be in the house than put any difficulty upon him."¹¹

Hawksmoor, an artist hardly less original than Vanbrugh, was now collaborating happily with the latter; and Hawksmoor made important contributions to the design of the interior, the conception of the rooms and details in them, cornices, chimney pieces, doorcases. As the great house gathered wing, it is most impressive to watch the concentration of talent and craftsmanship upon it: a forum for the best craftsmen of the time. The St. Paul's men were here, headed by their redoubtable contractor, Strong. Much of the carved stonework was done by Grinling Gibbons; above his princely doorcases rose the frescoes of Laguerre, the painted ceilings of Thornhill. The clocks and sundials were by Langley Bradley and John Rowley, the plaster work by Weatherill and Isaac Mansfield. Nearly all of them had had their apprenticeship at St. Paul's. Wren himself was called in to advise about the approach, though his characteristic suggestion of compromise was rejected and Vanbrugh's uncompromising bridge across the ravine prevailed. When it came to completing the statuary of the house, Rysbrack was called in. Indeed, it was a national monument. It would take all Marlborough's fortune to carry it on safely to posterity.

In the hot summer of 1707 in the Netherlands, the Duke's mind turned to Woodstock and the icehouse he was planning there. "It is true what you say of Woodstock, that it is very much at my heart, especially when we are in prosperity, for then my whole thoughts are of retiring with you to that place."[12] Three weeks later, "as this is the third year of the trees at Woodstock, if possible, I should wish that you might, or somebody that you can rely on, taste the fruit of every tree, so that what is not good might be changed. On this matter you must advise with Mr. Wise, as also what plan may be proper for the ice-house; for that should be built this summer, so that it might have time to dry."[13]

This year took place one of the major interruptions in the building of the house, due to Vanbrugh's drastic alteration of scale and consequent replanning of the façades and towers at the corner pavilions. For this he must have had the Duke's approbation; though there is nothing to show that the Queen was informed of what the alterations amounted to: she had taken much interest in the original model, which was deposited in the Gallery at Kensington for her to study. Now—though Vanbrugh said nothing about it—it was departed from drastically: nothing less than raising the main block by perhaps a third in height, and changing the whole order from Doric to Corinthian. It would have the effect of making the house less austere and forbidding, more of a triumph and a festival: turning it from a castle into a palace. It necessitated pulling down many yards of existing building and altering the level of the windows already built in the south front. At the same time, stone was more difficult to get and payments were coming in more slowly from the Treasury.

That autumn Vanbrugh found the Duke "out of patience about it; for this morning, telling him I feared it would be three weeks yet before the scaffolds could be struck about the great tower, he was quite peevish upon it, being resolved to go down by that time."[14] A month elapsed before his visit: Vanbrugh ordered "the clearing of every place about the building that can be, both within and without, to show it to the best advantage; for my lord Duke comes down full of expectation." In April, before setting out on campaign, the Duke went down again to gaze upon his darling house—a more respectable Henry II with a more recalcitrant Fair Rosamond. From camp he wrote to Sarah, "You say nothing of going to Blenheim, but the weather is so fine I could wish you there, by which the finishing within doors, I believe, would go on the faster. If it were possible, I would flatter myself that I might be so happy to see it the next summer."*

And what, meanwhile, was Vanbrugh doing? Pushing forward the

---

* Coxe, II, 515. This is the first time that we observe Marlborough calling the place Blenheim; hitherto it has always been Woodstock.

building of the bridge: it was not possible to inhabit that (could he really intend to make a habitable house of it?); repairing and doing up the ruined manor as a very nice residence for himself. When Sarah came down, he rigged up a temporary ceiling to her bedroom and a temporary door, to give her the impression that things were further advanced than they were; but she was not taken in. She was furious about the work going on at the manor: had she not told him again and again that making the main body of the house habitable for the Duke was what mattered? It was all very well for Vanbrugh to plead that he haunted the building like a ghost, from six o'clock when the workmen left off till it was dark— that was literature; his claim that he was studying "to make this the cheapest as well as (if possible) the best house in Europe, *which I think my lord Duke's services highly deserve,*" was a pretence and an insult to the meanest intelligence.[15] (The Duchess never thought meanly of her intelligence.)

Sarah was in favor of pulling the ruins of the manor down. "Sir John Vanbrugh having a great desire to employ his fancy in fitting up this extraordinary place, had laid out about £2,000 upon it . . . Mr. Travers* let this thing go on (I will not call it a whim because there has been such a struggle about it) till it was a habitation; and then came and complained of the great expense of it to me, desiring me to stop it."[16] Vanbrugh appealed to Godolphin, with a most persuasive paper: "Reasons for Preserving some Part of the Old Manor." "There is perhaps no one thing, which the most polite part of mankind have more universally agreed in, than the value they have ever set upon the remains of distant times, nor amongst the several kinds of those antiquities are there any so much regarded as those of buildings . . . If travellers many ages hence shall be shown the very house in which so great a man dwelt, as they will then read the Duke of Marlborough in story; and that they shall be told, it was not only his favourite habitation but was erected for him by the bounty of the Queen, and with the approbation of the people, as a monument of the greatest services and honours that any subject had ever done his country: I believe, though they may not find art enough in the builder to make them admire the beauty of the fabric, they will find wonder enough in the story to make them pleased with the sight of it."[17] He proceeded to apply what might be said of Blenheim to the remains of the historic Woodstock.

The historian must sympathize, and Vanbrugh was before his

---

* Travers was the government's agent for Blenheim, handling the money.

time in his love of the picturesque. Even Sarah allowed, in her endorse-
ment of this paper, that though it had "something ridiculous in it to
preserve the house for himself, ordered to be pulled down . . . I think
there is something material in it concerning the occasion of building
Blenheim." Marlborough and Godolphin went down together to decide
the matter. The old manor stood a little to the right of the bridge as
viewed from the portico of the Palace, "in the way of the prospect down
the great avenue, for which a bridge of so vast an expense is made to go
into . . . and I remember the late Earl of Godolphin said, that could no
more be a dispute than whether a man that had a great wen upon his
cheek would not have had it cut off if he could." Godolphin, we observe,
was a true Augustan. Marlborough was something different, more
incalculable; his sympathies were with Vanbrugh. He directed that no
more work should be done on the manor; Vanbrugh went on occupying
it. Not until Sarah got the finishing of Blenheim into her hands was it
pulled down. Nor can one say, here either, that she was wrong; for
though one misses the medieval and the picturesque, it would have
broken the ordered symmetry, the uniformity, of the majestic scene.

In 1709 a new distraction came to complicate the family building
operations. For some time Sarah had been desirous of a town house, and
while Godolphin was still in power she obtained a Crown lease of the
land next door to St. James's Palace, to build Marlborough House. She
would show the Duke and Vanbrugh how to do it. The first condition
was that Vanbrugh should have nothing whatever to do with *her* house.
She went to Sir Christopher, who would have been her choice for
Blenheim. She laid down two conditions: that the contracts should be
reasonable and not as Crown work, that the house was to be "strong, plain
and convenient . . . and not have the least resemblance of anything in
that called Blenheim, which I had never liked but could not prevail
against Sir John."[18] The agreeable Sir Christopher obliged with a very
sober design, the only nonsense being four statues in niches on the front
and decorative figures along the roof. The Duchess was convinced that
her building operations would proceed without trouble.

The Duke was not so sanguine. "I do wish you all happiness and
speed with your building at London, but beg that may not hinder you
from pressing forward the building at Blenheim, for we are not so much
master of that as the other."[19] Notwithstanding her dislike for Blenheim,

Sarah saw no objection to drawing on the craftsmen there for her own operations: the Strongs, the Bankses, the Hopsons, Henry Wise were all mobilized. The Duke was unhappy about it: "I am so desirous of living at Woodstock that I should not much care to do anything but what is necessary anywhere else . . . But I would have you follow your own inclination in it. You know I never liked to build it at all. And I am confident you will find 'twill cost you much more money than the thing is worth. You may build a better apartment than you have now, but you will never have as many conveniences as in your lodgings. And you may depend on it, 'twill cost you double the money they have estimated. 'Tis not a proper place for a great house; and I am sure, when you have built a little one, you won't like it."[20]

Having said his say, the Duke gave way to her, as he usually did, and made arrangements to advance the money. He never grudged money for this kind of thing; and shortly he was asking for the measurements of the rooms to have tapestry woven for them. Sarah was able to assure him that *her* house met with general applause. The Duke was glad, since it gave her pleasure, and "for the same reason be not uneasy that it costs more money than you thought it would, for upon my word, I shall think nothing too much for the making you easy."[21] Of course, it did cost too much. Instead of the Blenheim way of going on, Sarah agreed upon a sum, £30,000, which—woman of her word, as she was—she paid over before the house was finished. But, in spite of her efforts and her tantrums, it cost nearer £50,000. Was Sir Christopher no better than Sir John? To admit as much offended her pride: the poor old man— Wren was seventy-eight—must have been imposed upon.

Sir Christopher was sacked. Sarah took the finishing of the house upon herself, and was persuaded that it was done to everybody's satis-faction. At any rate, it was ready for her occupation by 1711, when she herself was sacked and had to remove from St. James's: so perhaps, as usual, she could consider herself to have been right. Even if it had cost £50,000: "almost incredible, but not really as extravagant as it appears, because it is the strongest and best house that ever was built."

She had built it herself. The horrid Sir John observed maliciously that Wren had paid higher prices than would have been paid at Blen-heim: "'tis true she would have gone to law with them, but the Duke would not let her." But then, she consoled herself with the thought, *all* architects were mad.

While the roof was not yet on at Blenheim, Vanbrugh was planning a further grand addition: a superb orangery on the western side, "having a very beautiful situation (the west end of it coming to the very brow of the hill and so looking directly down the valley and the river) may perhaps be thought proper for a distinct retired room of pleasure, furnished with only some of the best greens, mixed with pictures, busts, statues, books and other things of ornament and entertainment. These kind of detached buildings have ever been extremely valued, where there has happened anything particularly fine for their situation, and I believe there is not in Europe a finer than this."[22] The Duke could not find it in his heart to reject this, much as Sarah protested.

Vanbrugh tried to enlist the support of Godolphin's son, Lord Rialton—who, as Henrietta's husband and coming next in succession, took a close interest in Blenheim and regularly visited the works—for his projected orangery. But Sarah killed it: "the second greenhouse, or a detached gallery, I thank God I prevented being built; nothing, I think, can be more mad than the proposal, nor a falser description of the prospect."[23] No doubt it was too much; but we have lost thereby one of the noblest rooms in Europe.

The work was advancing faster in 1709, when two circumstances befell to hold things up worse than ever. The summer proved a wet one and building was impeded. Plenty of stone was at last lying waiting at the quarries, but the carriage was more expensive. The Duchess would not allow a penny more to be offered: the stone could stay there, the building wait. Meanwhile, Vanbrugh could "wish your Grace joy at the outside of yours at St. James's being quite completed, which I hear it is."[24]

Though his roof was still not on, the Duke had long been collecting furnishings, fabrics, treasures from all over Europe for his Palace. A very fine set of hangings at Antwerp had been bespoken for William III. They were offered to Marlborough for £1,800: worth much more. Should he buy them?[25] He was "so fond of some pictures I shall bring with me, that I could wish you had a place for them till the Gallery at Woodstock be finished."[26] Vandyke's famous equestrian portrait of Charles I was among these: it had been given by the Elector of Bavaria to the Emperor. Marlborough took as much interest in the furnishing of the house as Sarah did. "I have been to see the hangings for your apartment and mine; as much as are done of them I think are very fine . . . I should be glad, at your leisure, you would be providing everything that may be necessary for furnishing these two apartments, and that you would direct Vanbrugh to finish the breaks between the windows, in the great cabinet, with looking glass; for I am resolved to furnish the room with the finest pictures I can get."[27] Splendid tapestries, depicting scenes from his battles, were being woven at Brussels; marble from Alicante, silks from Genoa, pictures, busts, statuary, gems. The Duke spared no expense for the temple of his glory, did not even complain. Two suites of hangings made at Brussels cost £800. William III, just before his death, had been negotiating for four fine statues from a palace at Florence; Marlborough ordered their purchase for the niches designed for the Grand Saloon. Unfortunately, he was disappointed and the scheme never took effect. He was in treaty for bronze figures to be cast at Florence, which cost £1,000, and the Spanish ambassador in Rome presented him with a full-scale model of a Bernini fountain in the Piazza Navona. At the siege of Tournai, chance offered him a many-ton marble bust of Louis XIV over the gateway: the very thing to set his great opponent's head on the roof of his house. There it stands, with its reference to Versailles, high above the garden front, looking out across what were once the hunting grounds of medieval English kings, now subjugated to Augustan order, where everything remembers Marlborough.

By the end of 1709, when the position of the Marlboroughs was thoroughly undermined, the Palace was getting on fast. Vanbrugh assured the Duchess that the whole house would be covered that year and the bridge finished; the chapel should be left alone. He, too, had his troubles: Banks's men were cutting up the best big Portland blocks for paving, when smaller stuff would do. Pebbles to pitch ten thousand yards would be necessary. That winter, his mind full of disquiet, the Duke came down to gaze upon his house. Would it ever be finished? Would he ever live in it? His hold was running out: it was becoming a race between the finishing of the house and the retention of his position at the head of the allied armies. He was still ordering materials: hundreds of yards of stuff from Dutch looms, velvets, designs for his coat of arms for the hangings. The canopy of state which he had ordered for the peace negotiations was to be made in such a way that it could be used for a bed at Blenheim. Alas, there was no peace.

Next year came the thunderclap of the change of government, of which there had been premonitory rumblings, disturbing the workmen at Blenheim and causing alarm among the tradesmen of Oxford. The debts on the building were very large and the new Tory government had reason to question the position. By 1710, £134,000 had been spent and the house was still not half completed. The Treasury stopped payments, which were already far in arrears. This was a critical moment for the house, and for the Marlboroughs. If they admitted the slightest financial responsibility, they might be charged with the debts and the arrears, and still have to complete the building themselves: that would make a heavy inroad into even their fortune. At Oxford the rumor was that the debt to the workmen was some £60,000, of which that to Strong, the contractor, was over £10,000: "it will go hard with many in this town and the country who have contracted with them. Their creditors begin to call on them, and they can get no money at Blenheim."[28]

There were scenes at Woodstock, since there was no money to pay the men and they were in want. A mob assembled—somebody advanced a few hundreds to pacify them: not the Marlboroughs. This was to be a monument of the nation's gratitude: it looked like turning into a monument of ingratitude, said Vanbrugh. The government sought to inveigle the Duke into taking steps that would involve him in financial responsibility. Sarah was furious and disposed to intervene. The Duke was wiser: "it is not our best way to give any orders, but to let the Treasury give what orders they please, either for its going on or standing still."[29] Sarah sent down an order stopping all the work on the building till the Treasury should direct money for it. The Duke was alarmed: "it no way becomes you or me to be giving orders for the Queen's money. You know my opinion, that neither you, nor I, nor any of our friends ought to meddle in their accounts, but to let it be taken by the Queen's officers, as they always ought to be. She is the mistress of her own money, and consequently of the time of finishing that house." Now that he had lost the Queen's favor, he said that he had grown very indifferent; but this may be doubted. As for Vanbrugh, on the Duchess's stopping the work: "I think she has given orders she'll repent of, but be it as she thinks fit. If she orders the house to be pulled down, I desire you'll comply with her."[30] Even the Duke, Vanbrugh said, was angry with Sarah for meddling in the matter. Godolphin went down to view the distasteful scene: "Let them keep their heap of stones!" he said. Tempers were rising all round the tempestuous building.

Sarah was more strong-minded than the men: she was quite unmoved by threats. "Pulling down the house will be of no great use to the workmen, or to the towns about that have so much reason to hope to live by it, neither am I apprehensive that the people of Oxford should head a mob to take down one of the Queen's houses—that is a thing to frighten children."[31] Besides, did this not prove that she had been right all along? "Every friend of mine knows that I was always against building at such an expense . . . I always thought it too great a sum even for the Queen to pay . . . I never liked any building so much for the show and vanity of it as for its usefulness and convenience, and therefore I was always against the whole design of Blenheim as too big and unwieldy, whether I considered the pleasure of living in it, or the good of my family who were to enjoy it hereafter."[32]

The Queen did not wish it to go to ruin and let the nation's money be thus wasted. Harley asked how much it would cost to cover it in and protect it from damage until a resolution was taken. Vanbrugh replied £8,000. Harley allowed £7,000—the implied condition being that Marlborough would not lay down his employments and thus weaken the government's hand in making peace. Luckily, the building suffered no injury during the stoppage; and next year a further £20,000 was allowed by the Treasury, with the same implied condition that the Duke would not withdraw from his post. This enabled the work to be pushed forward so far that henceforth, though it was still unfinished when the Marlboroughs went into exile, it might be regarded as safe.

While they were away the building went slowly on, in Vanbrugh's fashion, not Sarah's: that is to say, not finishing the main pile, but on everything else. She was incensed to hear that the new money was to go on the kitchen court, two grand acroteria on the bridge and the formal walls that blocked the view from her windows to the east. The interiors of the private apartments were constantly being raised or lowered or altered: they were still not ready for furniture. Vanbrugh continued to live in the manor in great jollity, as he had done for years, and now made himself a closet in the middle, complained Sarah, "as if he had been to study the planets." Surely, she was not unreasonable in her view that "painters, poets and builders have very high flights, but they must be kept down." From his eyrie Vanbrugh took a hand in local politics in the Whig interest, much to the distaste of Tory Oxford. A letter of his to the mayor of Woodstock was betrayed to Harley, in which he referred to the "continual plague and bitter persecution" with which the Duke had been most barbarously followed; and for this he lost his job as Commissioner of Works.[33] Sarah made this up to him with £200 a year for his traveling expenses.

On George I's accession, the Duke got Vanbrugh one of the first knighthoods of the reign. Marlborough was anxious to know how much fresh money would be necessary to finish the building, over and above the debts which were Crown liabilities; Vanbrugh replied some £54,000 and, on the understanding that the Duke would meet that himself, the last stage of the works was undertaken. But the legal difficulties that flowed from the ambivalent conditions upon which the house was begun continued to dog all parties: Strong, the contractor, now began proceedings for the large debts owing him, not against the Crown, but against the Duke.

Sir John was in high spirits, however, and able to tease the Duchess. "I do promise your Grace I will have the homely simplicity of the ancient manor in my constant thoughts for a guide in what remains to be done, in all the inferior buildings . . . Even that frightful bridge will at last be kindlier looked upon, if it be found (instead of twelve thousand pounds more) not to cost above three; and I will venture my whole prophetic skill, that if I live to see that extravagant project complete, I shall have the satisfaction to see your Grace fonder of it than of any part whatsoever of the house, gardens or park."[34] Sir John was contriving a surprise for her: "if at last there is a house found in that bridge, your Grace will go and live in it." But she was contriving a surprise for him.

In 1716 the Duke had his first stroke and Sarah took complete charge. Now came the time of reckoning for that rascal, Sir John: she was free to quarrel with him to her heart's content; for years she had been storing up her complaints against him. In accordance with what had become a habit with her—for she was really a writer *manquée*—she drew up a thirty page narrative of all her grievances. Vanbrugh's defense was that he had never done anything at Blenheim without the Duke's approbation. But the Duke was now in the hands of Sarah; without compunction she pushed Vanbrugh out of Blenheim and took over herself. In later years she said it was a "terrible undertaking," which she would not have ventured on without encouragement; at the time she did not quail.

She was fighting on two fronts: there were the legal liabilities and complexities, which were almost inextricable; there was the house to be finished, decorated and furnished. She was the less successful in dealing with Sir John. Here she found herself up against a professional writer who could give as good as he got. He described her narrative as "so full of far-fetched, laboured accusations, mistaken facts, wrong inferences, groundless jealousies and strained constructions, that I should put a very great affront upon your understanding if I supposed it possible you could mean anything in earnest by them, but to put a stop to my troubling you any more. You have your end, madam, for I will never trouble you more, unless the Duke of Marlborough recovers so far to shelter me from such intolerable treatment."[35] Her treatment of him was intolerable, for she did not propose to pay him for his work: he had the prospect "of losing (for I now see little hopes of ever getting it) near £6,000 due to me for many years' service, plague and trouble at Blenheim, which that wicked woman of Marlborough is so far from paying me that the Duke, being sued by some of the workmen for work done there, she has tried to turn the debt due to them upon me, for which I think she should be hanged."[36] To all which the Duchess had the simple reply: he should have finished the house long ago.

Vanbrugh's complaint against her was true. She was not going to accept the liability for Strong's debts: they properly belonged to the Crown. In 1721 Vanbrugh reported joyously: "my Lady Marlborough has been cast by the workmen—the cause held three days—she's outrageous at it, she accuses the Judges, and says I have foresworn myself."[37] So he had: Vanbrugh had withheld testimony to the Crown's liability for the debts in Blenheim, partly because he did not want to do the Duchess a service, partly because he did not wish to risk his post as Commissioner of Works again. This failure to tell the truth was very shocking to Sarah: "he has been more wicked to me than all the enemies that ever I had put together (which is saying a great deal)."[38] The case left her dangerously exposed for a series of claims and lawsuits might now be expected from workmen whose debts were still unpaid. The Duchess immediately appealed, and also filed a suit "against everybody that had been concerned in the building"—some four hundred persons from Vanbrugh downward to workmen whose descendants are still living at Woodstock. It was like one of the Duke's own battlefields, outsize like everything to do with Blenheim.

When the smoke of action cleared away, and the Crown accepted proper liability, the Duchess and Vanbrugh were still found confronting each other. Libels and squibs circulated; she handed round papers against him; he invented lampoons upon her. In the end the Duchess was forced to pay him some £1,700 he claimed as owing to him, for his expenses; and everybody must be glad, for he had been shabbily treated. "Being forced into Chancery by that B.B.B.B. Old B. the Duchess of Marlborough and her getting an injunction upon me by her friend the late good Chancellor, who declared I never was employed by the Duke of Marlborough and therefore had no demand upon his estate for my services at Blenheim, since my hands were tied up from trying by law to recover my arrears, I have prevailed with Sir Robert Walpole to help me in a scheme I proposed to him, by which I have got my money in spite of the hussy's teeth, and that out of a sum she expected to receive into her hands towards the discharge of the Blenheim debts, and of which she resolved I should never have a farthing. My carrying this point enrages her much, and the more because it is of considerable weight in my small fortune, which she has heartily endeavoured so to destroy, as to throw me into an English Bastille to finish my days, as I began them in a French one."[39]

These redoubtable combatants were not ill matched; perhaps we may adjudge Sir John the victor, since, in addition to getting his money, Blenheim came through, in spite of everything, as he, not Sarah, meant it. The money became an article in her indictment against Walpole, her last long quarrel. It was provoking that, for all her money and her will power, she could not get her way.

All the same, we owe it to Sarah's will, perhaps, that Blenheim was finished and furnished at all. In 1715 she writes to her crony and man of business, Mr. Jennings: "I am employed every morning at least four hours in cutting out, and ordering furniture for Woodstock. My next bed will be for the room you chose, where I hope to see you often, and dear Mrs. Jennings."[40] To her Sarah writes, "I shall want a vast number of feather beds and quilts. I wish you would take this opportunity to know the prices of all such things as will be wanted in that wild unmerciful house."[41]

Sarah exerted herself for the Duke's sake. In these quiet last years of his life, a shadow of his former self, nothing delighted him so much as to ride about the grounds, contemplating what he had called up out of the rough ancient forest of Woodstock: his child, his amusement, the temple of his glory. He loved the theatricals that Sarah—an unexpected role for her—arranged for him: acted by Mr. Jennings and the grandchildren, Anne and Di Spencer and Anne Egerton. There was *Tamburlane*, with a prologue written to celebrate the Duke's achievements, a tribute he did not decline. There was Dryden's *All for Love*, with its episcopal prologue, written by Bishop Hoadley, flattering the graces of the Duchess. Not all the speeches passed the test of that prim censor. Her own girlhood passed at the Court of Charles II, she was not going to have her granddaughters corrupted by its most splendid poet. "The Duchess scratched out some of the most amorous speeches, and there was no embrace allowed, etc. In short, no offence to the company. I suppose we made a very grand appearance; there was profusion of brocade rolls etc., of what was to be the window curtains of Blenheim. Jewels you may believe in plenty; and I think Mark Antony wore the sword that the Emperor gave the Duke of Marlborough. The old Duke was so pleased that we played it three times . . . the third time at the Duke's request."[42]

After his death Sarah went on with the works. She erected the Victory Column in his memory, the inscription reciting his achievements from the pen of his old disciple and then antagonist, Bolingbroke. "Times change, and things change, and men change." To the Triumphal Arch she put up, with its enclosed forecourt—the design by Hawksmoor —the townspeople objected: "I have had a very ridiculous petition from several of the inhabitants of Woodstock who desire not to have the door made up I ordered; but nobody of that town has merit enough to put me to any inconvenience upon their account, and I desire you to proceed without loss of time and do as you are directed."[43] Then came the chapel, to which her dear Duke's body was transferred from Westminster Abbey, the magnificent tomb by Rysbrack, "upon the wall of one side the chapel. The rest of it is finished decently, substantially and very plain. And considering how many figures and whirligigs I have seen architects finish a chapel withal, that are of no manner of use but to laugh at, I must confess I cannot help thinking that what I have designed for this chapel may as reasonably be called finishing of it, as the pews and pulpit."[44] Lastly, as the years rolled away and old resentments gave way to new, the past appeared to her in a mellower light: she commissioned a fine statue from Rysbrack so that the familiar, once loved, figure should dominate the gallery: "To the memory of Queen Anne, under whose auspices John, Duke of Marlborough conquered, and to whose munificence he and his posterity with gratitude owe the possession of Blenheim."

At length even Sarah could be proud of the place. "I have had a letter lately from a very good judge who says he has been at Blenheim and that the lake, cascade, slopes above the bridge are all finished and as beautiful as can be imagined, the banks being covered with a most delightful verdure; the canals are also finished the whole length of the meadow under the wood, and there are a hundred men at work sloping the hill near Rosamond's Well. And when all the banks are done in the same manner, and the whole design completed, it will certainly be a wonderful fine place, and I believe it will be liked by everybody, and I am glad it will be so, because it was the dear Duke of Marlborough's passion to have it done."[45]

Sir John had said it would be so, years before. "The beauty of this place at this time [in high summer] is hardly to be conceived, which all strangers and passengers will be ten times more sensible of when the house is inhabited . . . The garden, now the trees are in full vigour and full of fruit, is really an astonishing sight. All I ever saw in England or abroad of the kind are trifles to it."[46]

One day in this summer when Sarah first perceived its beauty, some passengers drew up at the gate: they were Lord and Lady Carlisle, for whom Vanbrugh had built Castle Howard and with whom he had become fast friends, with Sir John and his lady. During the couple of days they stayed at Woodstock, the Duchess gave strict instructions that Sir John was not to enter anywhere, house, gardens or park. Blenheim was what, after all, lay nearest his heart. He had to be content with what he could see by looking over the wall at his noblest creation, that fabulous and incomparable house.

CHAPTER XVII

The Three Brothers

I

THE CAREERS of Marlborough's two brothers in the services—George in the navy, Charles in the army—naturally followed their famous brother's star: their fortunes rose and fell with his. But they were very independent personalities, each of them men of ability, decision and weight. They made contributions to the success of Marlborough's war that were very important in themselves. That of the Admiral was the more weighty: as the right-hand man of Prince George at the Admiralty from 1702 to 1708—really in the position of a First Sea Lord—it fell to him to press forward Marlborough's policy of sea power, sometimes against the incomprehension of the seamen, and to carry the main burden of the administration of the navy. To do this, he made a sacrifice of his career at sea; otherwise, we need not doubt, he would have left as familiar a name as Rooke or Cloudesley Shovell in the annals of the navy, for he was more able and spirited than the one, and more intelligent than the other. Precisely because of this, he was kept at the Admiralty. His sacrifice gained him no credit: it was used to discredit him by jealous rivals and by enemies of Marlborough. At the head of the Admiralty in his brother's best days, he was an obvious target for detraction, much (and unjustly) maligned.

The Churchills were indeed too successful: flesh and blood could not stand it: pull them down! In the curious way in which fate has dealt with the Churchills, the Admiral has been even more unjustly treated than the Duke: he has come down in history, if at all, with his work totally unappreciated, himself disconsidered and traduced.* Again, it

---

* Cf. J. K. Laughton's quite unworthy notice of him in *D.N.B.*, biased, unfair and inaccurate in several respects. It should be rewritten.

is only in our time that justice is being done to this long-dead sailor, the detractions of the envious rectified.

The latest historian of the war at sea records the dashing Peterborough's judgment: "in the little acquaintance I have had with him, I find Admiral Churchill has a very just and quick apprehension of naval affairs; and though Admiral Mitchell is a very good man, I can find nobody so able to assist the Prince and the Queen as Mr. Churchill in cases of dispatch and difficulty."[1] A jealous rival, however, wrote, "if Churchill have a flag, he will be called the flag by favour, as his brother is called the General by favour." On this, our naval historian comments justly, "he was certainly far out in his judgment on the elder brother, and I think he was far from right about the younger." He points out that the system of convoys employed in William's war had been foreshadowed in proposals put forward years before by Admiral Russell and George Churchill, when an active captain, who had both "worked out detailed stations for cruisers engaged in the defence of trade. It is worth notice that Churchill's proposals agree more closely than Russell's with the scheme adopted by Parliament and with later developments, particularly in furnishing a substantial force to cruise in the Channel Soundings and off the south coast of Ireland, the forerunner of the long famous Western Squadron of later days which Barham in 1805 called 'the mainspring from which all offensive operations must proceed . . .' Whatever his share in framing the policy, he [Churchill] worked hard to supply the means and direct the ways by which the Navy played its great part in a continental war."[2]

In reward for this, he was a constant target of abuse. He was accused in his own time—and the charge has been constantly repeated since—of making a fortune out of his post. This is untrue. The legitimate perquisites of such a post at that time were large; but the Admiral, unlike his famous brother, was not interested in money. Unmarried, and with no family to support, he left only a moderate fortune of some £20,000 to his natural son and a nephew between them.

The truth is that the Admiral was not a popular personality; he had no charm: he was a Churchill, not a Villiers. One has only to look at his portrait at Greenwich—enormous, full-bottomed wig, luscious velvet coat with gold facings, hand forcefully upon his baton of command— to see that he was exactly like Sir Winston. There he is, heavy-jowled, double-chinned, forceful, uncompromising; the eyes give one a direct, unsmiling stare: a simple, self-willed personality, all of a piece. His portly figure affords a contrast with John, who was if anything too slim—perhaps in both senses of the word. It fell to the Duke to push his brother out of office in the end because of his forthright, unaccommodating Toryism: a sacrifice to the clamorous, monopolizing Whigs.

The Admiral—a strong figure of a man, erect, with the fine hands of his family, a more sensitive nostril than his father—was as unyielding as he. There was this difference: like all those children born in the ambivalent household at Ashe, he was reserved and taciturn. He presents the teasing paradox of a man of strong personality, who yet has a hard impersonal core. The strong man, who knows his own mind and does not give his inner self away—that is always unpopular.

Both of the brothers left an illegitimate son. We have no letters from either of them. It is a fair inference that the youngest, Charles Churchill, the General, presents also this figure of an impersonal man, with yet a marked personality. For he was a fine fighting soldier, who lived a hard life. He bore a distinguished part at Blenheim, where as General of foot he was responsible for getting the infantry across the marshes of the Nebel. In the Duke's absences from the Netherlands, he was left in command of the British troops there—with complete confidence. Few letters passed between the brothers: it is extraordinary how impersonal their relations were with each other. All that must have been induced in them by the circumstances of their early life, the shabby insecurities, the galling dependence, the callousness of Courts in which they received their first training.

Neither of these brothers lived to be really old: the Admiral died at fifty-seven, the General at fifty-eight. They wore themselves out in the service of their country; they served it well.

With the Court background of impecunious Sir Winston, all three boys began as pages: John to the Duke of York, George to the Earl of Sandwich at sea, Charles to the King of Denmark, whence he returned to Whitehall with Prince George. In those days there was no exclusive distinction between land service and sea service, especially since the corps of Royal Marines was not established till Marlborough's war. We have seen that, as a soldier, he served several times at sea; later on, he had an insight into the character and potentialities of sea power such as no soldier, except William, had—far superior to most of the seamen. Conversely George, who was a sailor by training, was made an ensign in his brother's company in the Duke of York's Regiment in 1676, and a lieutenant two years later.[3]

George's first service was at the age of thirteen* with Sandwich on his mission to Spain, 1666 to 1668: a start for his subsequent appreciation of the importance of the Mediterranean which marked his administration of the Navy. All three brothers had experience of the Mediterranean when young, and this gave them wider horizons than their more *borné* colleagues. During the Dutch war of 1672–74 George served as lieutenant in the *York* and then the *Fairfax*. In 1678 he was made captain of the *Dartmouth;* he was now twenty-five: nothing unusual at that age in such a promotion. In 1680 he commanded the *Falcon,* in charge of convoy, as far as the Canaries; in 1682 on the coast of Ireland.[4]

He first became a member of Parliament on James's accession; no doubt, as a good Tory, a seat was found for him: St. Alban's, which he represented in every Parliament for the rest of his life, until his last (1708), when he was returned for Portsmouth.[5] In 1688 he was, in command of the *Newcastle,* in the Channel fleet awaiting William that stormy autumn: in November he put in at Plymouth, very leaky, and went over to William with everybody else.[6] He commanded the *Pendennis,* 70 guns, at the engagement at Bantry Bay. He was promoted to the *Windsor Castle,* 90 guns, in which he fought at Beachy Head; and in 1692 to a first rate, the *St. Andrew,* 100 guns, in which he served with distinction at La Hogue, "serving as Lord Torrington's second in the line of battle in the first two actions and as Russell's in the third."[7]

This post was in the direct line of succession to a chief command: Churchill was clearly an able sea officer, who inspired people's confidence and so far had had no setback. It was rumored that he had been made a flag officer. Instead of that he was involved in his brother's disgrace by William; when Marlborough was forbidden the Court, George surrendered his commission and for several years was out of active service with him.[8] So he, too, made a big sacrifice. The flag was given, instead, to Aylmer, Churchill's rival, several places junior to him on the list of captains. Aylmer ended up as a peer; Churchill was never even given a knighthood, for all his privileged position with Prince George. One can hardly say that the rewards of favor, for him, were excessive; but

---

* He was born at Ashe February 29, 1653, not 1654 as *D.N.B.* states. Wolseley, *op. cit.,* I, 23.

he was not ambitious in this line, and was content for the family honors to be concentrated on John. Younger sons, in those days, knew their place.*

When Marlborough came back to favor George Churchill was appointed a Commissioner of the Admiralty at a salary of £1,000 a year[9]—the same figure as Arabella received for her (past) services. With Anne's accession, the sun shone: only a few days after, he was given the flag, for which he had been made to wait ten years. He was promoted Vice-Admiral of the Red and appointed to the Council of the Lord Admiral, Prince George. This Council performed the functions of the Board of Admiralty.[10] Within a week he had himself made, at one bound, Admiral of the Blue. Another little *douceur* came Churchill's way: Deputy Ranger of Windsor Little Park (where Sarah was Ranger of the Great Park), with £65 a year and a pleasant villa to reside in.[11] He owed this to his intimacy with Prince George: it was convenient to have him in the Park. At St. James's he was equally accessible: he lived in St. James's Place in one of the new houses looking into Green Park.[12] George was, at length, in clover.

Like the greatest of naval administrators, Lord Barham, Churchill never went to sea as an Admiral: his was a full-time job of hard work at home—the main burden of the administration fell on him—and coping with the flights of other admirals. The first job was to draw up the principles and detailed schedules for the armaments of the Queen's ships for the war.[13] Then Admiral Fairborne—a very handsome sailor, as we see from his Greenwich portrait—refused to accept the conditions of command of the West Indies fleet; insisting upon his own terms, he was dismissed. Upon this a duel was threatened between him and Churchill; by order of the Queen they were confined to their houses to prevent it.[14]

Much more trouble was given by the leading Admiral, Admiral of the Fleet Sir George Rooke. He could not be so easily dealt with: he was top dog. He had been William's choice among sailors, and of course he was a competent seaman. He had, however, no strategic imagination: William had supplied all that. With William's wonderful strategic

---

* Ailesbury tells a story (Memoirs, 413) that at the time of Sir John Fenwick's conspiracy, when the Churchills were pushing his attainder hard—there always had been bad blood between them—George Churchill said in the hearing of an acquaintance, "Damn him! Thrust a billet down his throat. Dead men tell no tales." This would not be out of character for such a man at such a time.

brain, he had grasped all that the Mediterranean meant for the struggle with France, for the balance of power, for the support of our allies, for the division of France's energies. Marlborough was the heir of his invention: he grasped all that too, and added, so like him, something else: the possibilities for an attack on France, a lunge at Toulon, an invasion—combined operations with Eugene—from the southeast. Before he died William's mind had been set on Cadiz, as the key to the Straits and the best base for Mediterranean communications. Marlborough took over these plans, wove them into his immense and flexible strategic schemes and was bent on carrying them out.[15]

The Admiral of the Fleet was opposed to these plans: his mind was hidebound by the responsibility of getting the fleet safe home again through winter seas. Marlborough's bland reply was that once it had a satisfactory base there, it need not come home. George Churchill's chief service was to do all he could to advance his brother's strategic plans at the Admiralty. Rooke's objections were met one by one, with tenacity and shrewdness. A large fleet was got to sea in 1702 for an attack on Cadiz—it was like Howard's and Essex's expedition of 1596 come again. At Cadiz Rooke did absolutely nothing: a complete fiasco, only partially retrieved by the scuppering of the Plate Fleet in Vigo harbor—and this was largely the work of the Admiralty in running it down and making it impossible for it to escape. Rooke got all the credit for this with the mob: he was always popular, because stupid. Churchills not: too intelligent.

Next year, 1703, Marlborough pressed forward the Mediterranean objective: he saw that the chance of gaining Lisbon as a base was so important—for, with the extension of our naval power southward, Portugal could emancipate herself from French pressure—that he offered to sacrifice his campaign in the Netherlands that year and remain on the defensive for the sake of a Lisbon expedition.[16] That shows what Marlborough was capable of—sacrificing his own show for the general good of the war. It also shows what Rooke was not capable of. He obstinately held back from putting to sea; the rumor was that he was ill. The government threatened to replace him, and Churchill was sent posting down to the Isle of Wight to take the command.[17] That cured Rooke, who put to sea; but keeping the main fleet in the Channel was needless and wasteful: it accomplished nothing. Meanwhile, Marlborough was writing, "everybody is so much out of humour at the great disappointment we have long laboured under for want of their Mediterranean squadron."[18]

In 1704 Marlborough brought forward the grand scheme that showed the full extent of his strategic imagination. At the same time as he was secretly planning his march to the Danube, he was projecting a blow between the wide-extended wings of Louis's southern domain, at the center—Toulon. It was to be a combined attack, co-operating with the Austrian forces penetrating from Italy. The Toulon expedition failed of its objective because the Austrians were unable to play their part by land. Gibraltar, however, was taken as an afterthought: not much credit in the operation, but henceforth we had not only our base, but the command of the straits. The command of the Mediterranean was abandoned to the Allies.

Sir Julian Corbett pays an enthusiastic sailor's tribute to the soldier. "When we think of all its wide results, when we see how far it went to fix the European system on its still existing lines, it seems too brilliant a jewel to add to Marlborough's crown."[19] It is good to see such generosity in an historian; even if we reduce it a little to suit our meaner minds, it corroborates our view of Marlborough as without question the prime spirit among the nation's soldiers, and it forces the conclusion upon us that, if Marlborough had had the full power and authority of William, he would have brought the war to an earlier end.

Sir Winston holds the view that "in the war of the Spanish Succession the energies of the fleet were devoted to fighting purposes and the main war-plans in a far higher degree than ever before or since."[20] For this Marlborough and his brother were primarily responsible. Concentration on the proper strategic objectives of sea power, however, gave ground for increasing complaints from the merchants that the protection of trade was neglected, convoys inadequate. Further, as Louis gave up the hope of sending fleets to sea, France's maritime effort went into commerce raiding—as with Hitler in the last war. Seamen like Duguay-Trouin and Forbin made their name and fame by preying on commerce in the Channel. Churchill was the prime force behind the strategic use of sea power; he was also primarily responsible for the convoy system. Whatever fell victim to French raiders, he was held responsible for. It was his job to arrange the sailings of the convoys with the different bodies of merchants: Baltic and North Sea, East and West Indies, North America, Guinea Coast, Levant. He was a hard-pressed, hard-worked man;* it does not seem that he was tactful in handling the merchants—a Sir Winston (old style), rather than a Marlborough. Anyway he was a Tory; the merchants were more Whigs.

In 1707 the losses from commerce raiding at sea reached their height—following a similar pattern in the two wars of our time, the worst fell beyond the halfway line through the war. The legitimate complaints from the merchants grew louder, the cabals of the Whigs sharpened, against the Tory conduct of the Admiralty. Anyone who was responsible for naval affairs in such circumstances was bound to be unpopular: there was a great outcry and Admiral Churchill was the obvious target. Sarah sent off delighted news of this to the Duke, worried as he was by her quarrel with the Queen and everything else. That sensitive register at once responds: "I see that I am to be mortified by the prosecution of my brother George. I have deserved better from the Whigs; but since they are grown so indifferent as not to care what mortifications the Court may receive this winter, I shall not expect favour. My greatest concern is for the Queen, and for the Lord Treasurer. England will take care of itself, and not be ruined, because a few men are not pleased. They will see their error when it is too late."[21]

Marlborough humbled himself to write to one of the leaders of the Whig Junto to spare his brother: Halifax did not deign to reply to the Duke.† (They were an arrogant lot, as the Queen thought them.) Events did not come to his rescue: this very year French raiders were at their most effective: "they had raided three trading fleets, and taken a heavy toll off Brighton, off the coast of Holland and between Scilly and Ushant, capturing or destroying six battleships of the escorting squadrons."[22]

The Whig war in Spain, which the Tories had never liked, had hit upon disaster, with the complete defeat of Galway at Almanza, at the hands of the Admiral's nephew, Berwick. Churchill did not fail to rub this in, with caustic comments on the conduct of the operations by the Whig Galway—and with all the more pleasure since his own sympathies were Jacobite, like his father's, not his clever brother's.[23] What a liability this was for Marlborough, who was having to rely more and more on the

---

* He seems to have had no time for social life. One of the few public events we find him attending was a professional duty—the funeral of Sir Cloudesley Shovell in Westminster Abbey, December 17, 1707. Owen, 192.

† This was not the great Trimmer, but Charles Montagu, Earl of Halifax. Marlborough speaks of "the contempt of Lord Halifax, not answering my letter I meant with all the kindness imaginable." Ibid., 274.

Whigs for the support of the war; and what a handle it gave Sarah in her campaign with the Duke against his brother!

In November, 1707, Admiral Churchill laid the Navy Estimate for 1708 before the new Parliament with its Whig majority.[24] He gave them a complete account of the state of the Navy—numbers of ships, complements of men and guns; he added a record of the losses and gains throughout the war, ships captured or destroyed by the enemy, enemy ships destroyed or taken. An Act, of no value in itself, was passed by Parliament for better securing trade by cruisers and convoys. Actually, from this deadline, the situation began markedly to improve: the destruction of the French fleet in Toulon freed forces from the Mediterranean for the Channel and the North Sea.

The reconstitution of the Admiralty Board, to admit Walpole and other Whigs, did not please the Admiral, and he made difficulty about taking the new oaths with them, which confirmed people in thinking that he was a Jacobite. There could not be a worse moment for such suspicions at the Admiralty; for at Dunkirk a large expedition was being assembled to land the Pretender in Scotland. The port was blockaded, but gales drove the squadrons away and the fleet slipped out. The young man was landed in Scotland, which did not rise, and he got back again without being captured. The escape was laid at the Admiral's door.

The more hardly he was pressed, the less he gave way: like his father, not his brother. He engaged himself stoutly on the Tory side, taking a hand against the Whigs in the elections, and, through his influence with the Prince, shoring up the Queen in her obstinate refusal to admit Whigs into the government. This meant that the Admiral was now pulling clean contrary to the Duke, and had become more than a liability—an encumbrance, virtually an opponent. Since he continued to enjoy the Prince's complete confidence, his removal became an affair of state. The Whigs were preparing an attack on the Prince, who was very ill, and his conduct of the Admiralty, through an attack on Churchill.

Something had to be done to forestall the situation. Marlborough was appealed to: from the sadness of his tone, one sees his kindness toward his brother, his essential gentleness. "I am sorry that my brother George is gone to Oxford, fearing he may do what I shall not like. I can't hinder being concerned for him, though I find he is not at all sensible for the trouble he is like to have this winter, so that I shall have mortifications upon his account."[25] He appealed to Godolphin to tell him the truth.

Godolphin's reply gives further evidence, if any more were needed, of the delicacy of feeling between these two men, in addition to their entire mutual confidence. "You may do me the right to observe that I never trouble you with stories from hence, being sensible I ought not to make you uneasy, upon whom all our hopes and safeties depend. But since you required an account of the noise about your brother George and Mr. Walpole, I cannot but think he was very much to blame in that whole affair from the beginning to the end . . . I must needs add, upon this occasion, that your brother does certainly contribute very much to keep up both in the Prince and in the Queen the natural, but very inconvenient, averseness they have to the Whigs in general . . . and nothing is more certain than that the general dislike of your brother in that station is stronger than ever, and much harder to be supported; but nothing less than your express command should have made me say so much to you upon so disagreeable a subject."[26]

The Duke turned this over and over in his mind. It was several months before he could bring himself to write his brother a letter of dismissal. "Finding you still in the Prince's Council, and the Parliament now so near, I cannot be so wanting either to you or to myself as not to tell you plainly, with all the kindness of a brother and the sincerity of a friend, that if you do not take an unalterable resolution of laying down that employment before the Parliament sits, you will certainly do the greatest disservice imaginable to the Queen and Prince, the greatest prejudice to me, and bring yourself into such inconveniences as may last as long as you live, and from which it is wholly impossible to protect you." Marlborough assured him it should be to his advantage, "doubly to what you do now, both in profit and quiet."[27]

Marlborough thus hoped to spare the Queen the distress of a Parliamentary attack upon her beloved Prince. To avoid it, she gave way at the last moment and accepted a Whig administration. What made that all the more bitter was that, in the event, it did the Prince no good. The actions of both the Queen and Marlborough were rendered superfluous by the Prince's death, upon which the Admiral's appointment lapsed. The Whigs appointed Aylmer as Commander in Chief, who did not at all well and was displaced when the Tories came in.

After the Prince's funeral, the Admiral retired to his villa at Windsor and the solace of his remarkable aviary. He must have been a rather solitary man. His will reveals that he was on friendly terms with the well-known bookseller and publisher Awnsham Churchill and his nephew William.* Awnsham was a kinsman, one of the Churchills of Dorchester and Colliton, who not only prospered in, but made a valuable contribution to, the book trade in London. It is a fair inference that their best-known publication, *A Collection of Voyages and Travels*—a kind of Hakluyt of Queen Anne's reign—which began to appear in 1704, owed something to the Churchills' friendship with the Admiral. Having made a fortune in London, Awnsham eventually went back to Dorset, where he bought an estate which continued in the family.

The Admiral made Awnsham and William Churchill his executors, leaving each of them £100 to buy mourning, and to the latter "the picture of the Duke of Buckingham's family," which must have come to him from his mother, "my diamond ring and my striking gold watch to keep in memory of me." The bulk of his property was to be divided equally between his natural son, George Churchill, who was serving, perhaps at sea, and was not yet of age, and his nephew, Francis Godfrey, Arabella's son.

He was on good terms with Arabella. Only a few months of life in retirement remained to him. On May 12, 1710, he was buried in Westminster Abbey, at the upper end of the middle aisle, on the right hand going into the choir.[28] Twenty years later, practically to the day, Arabella was buried in the same grave. There they are together.

2

The memory of this breach at the end must not blind us to the immense service the Admiral gave in the conduct of the war, to the country and to his brother. No such *contretemps* disturbed the relations between the Duke and his youngest brother Charles, with whom he was in constant touch throughout the campaigns of 1702 to 1708.

Charles began his military career at the age of eighteen as an ensign in his brother's company of foot in the Duke of York's Regiment.[29] In January, 1681, he was involved in a duel fought behind Arlington's house, as second to a Captain Richardson, who was run through the body: the young bloods had quarreled over their wine.[30] Next year he was off to Tangier as lieutenant colonel: he served in Colonel Trelawny's regiment and must have remained there a couple of years. We next hear

* P. C. C. Smith, 106. Awnsham evidently represents the old pronunciation of Anselm.

of him serving at Sedgemoor, having brought the siege train up from Portsmouth. At the Revolution he went over to William at Andover, with Prince George and the Duke of Ormonde, and with his senior officer, Brigadier Trelawny.

Thenceforward, we follow his regular promotion, step by step—a most competent officer—with no setbacks. Since he was abroad fighting at the time, he was not involved in his brother's disgrace. He had fought under him in Ireland, leading the infantry across the tidal estuary at the siege of Cork. He was left as Governor of Kinsale. At the battle of Landen in 1693, we have seen that he had the good luck to capture his nephew, Berwick; for this William allowed him 20,000 guilders of ransom. Of this £1,205.15.3 in English money, he was able to invest £1,000 in government loans in the autumn.[31]

In 1694 he was promoted to Major General, and continued to serve under the uninspired Waldeck in the Netherlands. With the return of Marlborough to influence, Charles was returned to Parliament for his father's old seat, Weymouth, and represented it in every Parliament up to 1710.[32]

With the accession of Anne he, too, shared in the favor, and the solid advantages, that accrued to his family. Promoted Lieutenant General, he was made Lieutenant of the Tower of London.* We must remind ourselves that this meant work—to which none of the Churchills objected. His appointment as Master of the Queen's Buckhounds must have been practically a sinecure, with a small salary. In the Prince's regiment which he commanded, his illegitimate son, another Charles, served under him. A humbler member of the clan became bookseller and stationer to the unreading Queen, and made a good thing out of it.

For the war Marlborough asked that his brother be made General in command of all the English infantry; he wanted him as his right hand: and his confidence was not misplaced. Charles never at any time failed him: his service was of the highest order. He obeyed his brother's wishes implicitly, carried his instructions into execution, and took his place at the head of the English troops—not, of course, of the allies— as his brother's deputy in his absence. Their collaboration is seen at its best in the Danube campaign.

Churchill sailed with the Duke and Orkney from Harwich that fate-

---

* *Cal. S. P. Dom.*, 1702-3, 485. This corrects the date in the notice in the *D.N.B.*, as in one or two other particulars.

ful year, 1704, on April 19.[33] A month later he assembled the army at Bedburg for the Duke to review at the outset of the long march.[34] Marlborough had set out later but, traveling faster with the horse, caught up with his brother and went on ahead.[35] He keeps in daily touch with Charles, in command of the infantry and artillery, advising him of the difficult and mountainous passages to avoid, the road to take, the villages where to bivouac. On June 3 the Duke sends an express to him to know the condition of the troops and artillery, and advising Charles to take the route to Heidelberg, since his own via Ladenburg "will be too difficult for you."[36] He wishes to be informed where Charles is camping each night. A little later, having passed through hilly country, thinking of everything, he sends back instructions: "you must take care beforehand to ease your artillery horses all you can, and if in the rest of your route . . . you find any difficulty in reaching to the place appointed, in case it can be done conveniently and the forage brought to you, you may encamp a little short, provided you do not come more than one day later to Gieslingen than the route directs."[37] Next day follows a letter about the shoes to be bought at Frankfort and sent on to Nuremberg, and about distinguished persons whom the Duke wants his brother to entertain at his headquarters in passing; then, "I hope this warm weather you take care to march so early as to be in your camp before the heat of the day."[38] Never anything more personal—but how it brings back the hot summer of 1704, the dusty roads, the campfires at night, those trudging feet along the routes of southern Germany!

Toward the end of June the weather broke. At once Marlborough is "very sensible the foot must have suffered by the great rains we have had."[39] He has ascertained that the best place to nurse the sick men is Heidenheim, "which is not far from you, and therefore I desire you will forthwith send them thither in carts with an able chirurgeon and a mate or two to look after them . . . giving them at the same time money for their subsistence." The thought of the sick men must have pierced beneath the Duke's customary formality; for, in place of his usual impersonal subscription, he suddenly ends, "I long to have you with me, being your loving brother, Marlborough." Those were the feelings beneath the polished exterior.

It is fascinating to have this internal correspondence from the army as the well-drilled machine rolled on to its ordained rendezvous. Nothing in it detracts from—everything goes to support—the high standards of

duty, public spirit, care and consideration for the men which we expect
from Marlborough and his brother. The result was that when Charles
crossed the Danube with twenty battalions of foot, and the Duke passed
the rest of his troops across that and the Lech to join up with Eugene
before Blenheim, the troops were all in fine fighting trim.[40] That they
were so was as much due to Charles's silent hard work as to the Duke's
vigilant care over them all.

In the battle he bore a foremost part, getting his infantry safely
across the swamp of the Nebel, when Tallard had judged it not possible
and regarded its accomplishment with dismay. Later, Churchill was responsible, with Orkney and Cutts, for the reduction of the twenty-seven
battalions shut up in Blenheim, assaulting the besieged village again
and again. After the battle, he was given the honor of escorting Tallard
and the captured French officers back to England and to their comfortable
quarters at Nottingham and Lichfield.

Churchill's reward was to be made full General of foot, which gave
him seniority over Slangenberg, the Dutch General who detested Marlborough, had a poor opinion of his generalship and impeded his operations. The year 1705, we recall, was that when the Dutch placed the
greatest obstacles in Marlborough's way, the year of the unfought Waterloo. What Slangenberg said about the Duke was too much for Charles's
brotherly loyalty: he sent "Brigadier Palmes to him to tell him that if
these things were as he was informed, he expected to meet him and find
satisfaction; and if it was otherwise, he expected he should show his
letters to Mr. Palmes."[41] Slangenberg denied that he had traduced the
Duke, but he was not employed again in command: an effective showdown.

The General was in command of the British infantry, under the
Duke, through all the operations of these years: at the forcing of the Lines
of Brabant in 1705, in the splendid achievements of the year of victory,
1706—Ramillies, the crossing of the Dyle, the capture of Brussels (of
which he was made Governor), the siege of Dendermonde, which he
directed. For his services he was given the governorship of Guernsey,
upon which he resigned the Lieutenancy of the Tower. Such a life of
strain brought on a stroke, which incapacitated him, in March, 1708.[42]
Marlborough was just leaving England for the campaign. He put it off
until he had seen his brother. It does not seem that his brother was able
to play any active part in the war thereafter: their best days together

were over. Charles Churchill continued nominally to hold his appointment, and no doubt to draw its emoluments, until the Tories came in: in February, 1711, he was replaced by General Erle.[43]

Charles Churchill spent his declining years at Minterne. He was, we have seen, the appointed heir of Sir Winston. In the year of his good fortune, 1702, he married Mary Gould of Dorchester, who was something of an heiress. This enabled him to complete the work his father had begun and build a substantial, if plain and unassuming, Queen Anne house, which survived until rebuilt at the beginning of this century.

The General's marriage, it seems, was a happy one, though there were no children of it. On his death in 1714, he left his property to his widow, who left it to her own relations, the Goulds. By Charles Churchill's will, there was charged upon his estate an annuity of £50 for Elizabeth Dodd, who was probably the mother of his son. To "my natural son, Colonel Charles Churchill," he left £2,000.[44]

This son, a Charles the second, served under his father in the Netherlands—there is a reference in the Duke's dispatches to his nephew. He was a soldier of merit and lived a life of much gaiety. He was for a time Governor of Plymouth and finished up as a Lieutenant General. When Sarah's friend, Arthur Maynwaring, died at Holywell—the Duchess often in tears by the deathbed of that cherished companion—he left his scanty property to the beautiful Miss Oldfield, the actress, by whom he had a son. Miss Oldfield's acting in the part of the virtuous Marcia had contributed greatly to the success of Addison's *Cato*; it was only her inability to hold out any longer that compelled the ending of its run: for the last performances she was said to have a midwife in the wings in case of necessity.[45] After Maynwaring's death she did not remain long unconsoled; Brigadier Churchill came to comfort her. "He made it his sole business and delight to place her in the same rank of reputation (to which her own natural deportment greatly contributed) with persons of the best condition."[46] By him she had a son, the third Charles Churchill. When she died, in 1730, she was given a funeral in Westminster Abbey; the General wished to erect a monument to her memory: this the Dean refused. She left her not inconsiderable property to her two sons, making the General, as a tribute of respect, her residuary legatee.

When George I came in, Marlborough did his best to get this gallant soldier placed as Groom of the Bedchamber to the Prince of

Wales, but "could not prevail upon the account of his birth, so that my Lord Marlborough came out and told the Duke of Argyle they must insist no more on't for it would not do."⁴⁷ No wonder George I asked if there was not something wrong with the Archbishop of Canterbury, since he had spent half an hour with him without his asking anything for his relations. Later, Churchill seems to have got some such Court appointment: his birth presented no serious impediment to his career.

The General's devotion to what Louis XV admiringly called *le beau sexe* made him a butt for clever young men like Hanbury Williams. The old beau still moved gallantly about in society, a popular figure: the young wit thus describes him:

> The General one of those brave old commanders,
> Who served through all the glorious wars in Flanders,
> Frank and good-natured, of an honest heart,
> Loving to act the steady friendly part:
> None led through youth a gayer life than he,
> Cheerful in converse, smart in repartee.
> Sweet was his night and joyful was his day,
> He dined with Walpole and with Oldfield lay.
> But with old age its vices came along,
> And in narration he's extremely long;
> Exact in circumstance and nice in dates,
> On every subject he his tale relates.
> If you name one of Marlborough's ten campaigns,
> He tells you its whole history for your pains:
> And Blenheim's field becomes by his reciting
> As long in telling as it was in fighting.⁴⁸

There is the customary rhythm of life: the heroic actions of one generation become the bore of the next.

Not all the young men were bored by him: Horace Walpole loved him for his sense of fun, his puns and his jokes. "If you have a mind to know who is *adored* and *has wit*," he wrote in 1742, "there is old Churchill has as much God-damn-ye wit as ever—except that he has lost two teeth."⁴⁹ When young Horace went to a masquerade, dressed appropriately as an old lady, he teased the General, saying he was ashamed to be there till he met him, "but was comforted with finding one person in the room older than myself."⁵⁰ The General was a favorite with the

Walpoles, through whose influence he sat in Parliament as member for
Castle Rising for thirty years.

No doubt it was through this close association that the General's
illegitimate son, the third Charles, married Sir Robert Walpole's illegitimate daughter by his charming Irish mistress, Maria Skerrett.* Horace
did not take much to this match to begin with, but he shortly became
great friends with this gay, untidy couple and remained on excellent
terms with them all their long lives. They never had any money, but
this did not cramp their good humor or their enjoyment of life. When
Horace grew old, they were the faithful ones who did not fail to come and
spend an evening with him. Lady Mary Churchill, as she was called in
spite of her birth, was at length provided for by being made housekeeper
in charge of Kensington Palace, and subsequently of Windsor Castle.
Their daughter Sophia married Sir Robert Walpole's greatnephew, the
second Earl of Orford of the third creation.[51] It is pleasant to think
of these marriages between Churchills and Walpoles, after Sarah's last
and longest feud, that with Sir Robert, which filled her declining years
with vexation, interest and joy.

3

In 1714 the Hanoverian dynasty began its prosperous career—perhaps we may say, in the circumstances, its *glückliches Fahrt*—with the
most famous soldier in Europe at its right hand. And that, when we think
of his career—his long attachment to the Stuarts, his experience with
William and again with Anne, the equivocations of fortune—was both
an achievement and a happy augury. Perhaps the upshot of it all was less
extraordinary than it seems, when we reflect that John Churchill was a
very English figure in his ambivalence and reserve, his combination of
subtlety and common sense. He was extraordinary only in his ambition
and his genius.

Once more his family surrounded the throne. Of his sons-in-law,
young Godolphin was cofferer to the royal household, Bridgwater Lord
Chamberlain to the Prince of Wales; the Duke of Montagu was given
a regiment, the Duchess made Lady of the Bedchamber to the Princess
of Wales, the intelligent, redoubtable Caroline.[52] (She had been chosen
for wife to the heir by clever old Sophia, the Electress, who had only

---

* Not the second Charles, as the *D.N.B.* notice mistakenly says: cf. *D.N.B.*
notice of Sir Robert Walpole, which gets this right.

just failed by a head to inscribe on her tomb "Queen of Great Britain.")
Sunderland came back to power again. Marlborough's earlier protégés,
Walpole and Cadogan, were at the head respectively of the Treasury
and the active administration (under the Duke) of the army.

Marlborough was the least vindictive man in the world; but, almost
by accident, he took an effectual revenge upon Bolingbroke, against whom
he had no ill will, though plenty of reason for it. Bolingbroke's nerve
broke under the strain of the events of 1714. His gamble had failed; the
Tory party was broken. He came to Marlborough, of all people, to ask
his advice. The Duke advised him to leave the country: his life was in
danger. It must have been a source of wry amusement to the Duke when
his former disciple, later enemy, acted on it. No one could have foreseen
that Bolingbroke would ruin himself in this way. Oxford pursued a more
honorable course. He remained in the country and defended himself
in the Lords against the attacks upon him for the desertion of the allies
and the peace. He was the only person against whom Marlborough felt
resentment: Harley had prevented him from making the peace in Paris.
The Duke pressed his impeachment; but once the excitements of 1714
and 1715 were over, moderation asserted itself and Oxford was discharged.
Marlborough was much moved, and recorded his protest in the Lords.
It was in regard to this that Dr. Johnson wrote his famous line in "The
Vanity of Human Wishes":

> From Marlborough's eyes the streams of dotage flow.

He was too much exhausted and worn out for serious application
to business, though he was consulted over appointments and had his
say in decisions. He presided over the arrangements to suppress the
Jacobite Rising of 1715, the landing of his old patron's son, the Pretender,
in Scotland. In 1716 we find him engaged in an important consultation,
along with Stanhope and Townsend, with Bernstorff, the Imperial
envoy, from which the Triple Alliance resulted.[53] That spring he had
a stroke. At the time of his illness he was taking a hand in a new political
combination, which would bring in some of the Tories.[54] It is fascinating
to see that at the very last he reverted to what he had been all along: a
moderate, a man of the middle, a trimmer. And who can doubt that this
line would have been better for the dynasty, and for English politics,
than the rigorous monopoly of power by the Whigs, the rancorous exclusion of the Tories? For him, it was now all too late.

Marlborough's first stroke followed close upon the death of his favorite daughter Anne, the only one who could keep the peace with her mother. She left a touching letter behind for her husband. "I have always found it so tender a subject to you, my dear, to talk of my dying, that I have chosen rather to leave my mind in writing."[55] She wanted to warn him "to be careful (as I was) not to make your circumstances uneasy, by living beyond what you have, which I could not, with all the care that was possible, quite prevent . . . You will ever be miserable by giving way to the love of play [i.e., gambling]. As to the children, pray get my mother, the Duchess of Marlborough, to take care of the girls and if I leave any boys too little to go to school . . . for a man can't take the care of little children that a woman can. For the love that she has for me, and the duty that I have ever showed her, I hope she will do it and be ever kind to you, who was dearer to me than my life."

Sarah more than fulfilled her child's wishes. "I send you enclosed that most precious letter which you sent me yesterday. You will easily believe it has made me drop a great many tears, and you may be very sure that to my life's end I shall observe very religiously all that my poor dear child desired . . . I have resolved to take poor Lady Anne Egerton, who, I believe, is very ill looked after* . . . I will send for her to St. Alban's, as soon as you will let me have dear Lady Dye; and while the weather is hot, I will keep them too and Lady Harriet, with a little family of servants to look after them, and be there as much as I can. But the Duke of Marlborough will be running up and down to several places this summer . . . and I don't think his health so good as to trust him by himself . . . I desire when it is easy to you that you will let me have some little trifle that my dear child used to wear in her pocket, or any other way; and I desire Fanchon will look for some little cup that she used to drink in."[56]

Here we see Sarah at her best. It was a good thing that she was a woman of competence, able to take command at such junctures. We see too that she had kindness of heart: these grandchildren became her favorites, with whom she was happier than with her own children.

Shortly after, the Duke suffered a lesion of the brain which deprived him of speech and paralyzed his limbs; but under the care of Sarah, who was a devoted nurse, and the excellent Dr. Garth, a good friend of the family, he made a quick recovery. He was able to go down

---

* The child of her dead daughter, Lady Bridgwater.

to Bath for the summer, where he was received by the civic authorities, a long train of nobility and gentry, bell ringing and multitudes—not very good, one would have thought, for a man recovering from a stroke. On his way back he paid a visit to Blenheim, where he was at length pleased with the progress made: he had entered upon another race, the completion of the house before his death. Sarah described herself as "working like a pack-horse" in these years to get it finished. She had plenty besides to do. The Duke was getting better, but now she was nursing one of her grandchildren through smallpox: the child recovered, and "I think her life is owing to her having had no doctors, and in my persisting in not letting her blood, which I think generally damps and lessens the fever which is natural to bring them out."[57] Sarah was certainly justified in her general disbelief in eighteenth-century doctors.

In November, 1716, Marlborough had a second and more severe stroke. Again he recovered; but now he was much more frail and, though he retained his faculties as clear as ever, his speech was somewhat affected—he had difficulty in finding the words he wanted. In May, 1717, the weather was so bad that Marlborough "could not go into the gardens at St. Alban's; he was tired with it in one day and he fancied he should be better here"—at Windsor Lodge, whence Sarah wrote to good Mr. Jennings to visit them: "you shall ride and walk and be alike free as if you were at home; if I could think of anything more to tempt you I should be glad to say it, for I think the Duke of Marlborough will be much the better for company."[58] In August Sarah and pleasant Dr. Garth—an exception to her strictures—took the Duke to Tunbridge Wells. Here Steele, who had won the hearts of the Marlboroughs by his stout defence of the Duke, both in Parliament and the press, when things were at their worst in 1712, visited them and made one of the party.[59] His famous pamphlet, *The Crisis*, had been the only effective counterblast to Swift, and Steele was sued for it. It was not only this that endeared Steele to the Duke: his gaiety and good humor made him a welcome guest at Blenheim. In the autumn of 1718, they were at Windsor: "notwithstanding the winter is come, he has set no time for leaving this place, but says he will continue here as long as he can, and as long as he likes it and finds any good by going out to take the air. But at this time of year we can't stay long, and the Duke of Marlborough's humour always was to remove of a sudden without giving much warning."[60]

Such was the habit formed by a lifetime of moving here, there and

everywhere. He was used to having company about him, too, and wherever he went he moved in considerable state—as befitted the most famous
figure in Europe, now that his old rival, Louis XIV, was dead. What the
Duke liked best was to be out every day on horseback, or walking round
his grounds, especially at Blenheim where Sarah at length got them in-
stalled in 1719. A favorite spot was Vanbrugh's bridge, about which there
had been so much fuss. Here the Duke would post himself to survey the
operations, no less a field of battle than Blenheim or Ramillies—one sees
that lean and graceful shade resting against the parapet, looking up at
the Palace of his creation. Here too victory was in sight.

As the Duke's hold on life slackened, Sarah came into her own and
took control. She may indeed be said to have taken the field. Within a
short time she was on the worst of terms with Sunderland, who had
married again—Sarah considered beneath him and to the prejudice of
her daughter's children. By the time he came into power in 1718 there
was a complete breach, and she blamed him for the South Sea Bubble,
of which she thoroughly disapproved and from which she profited
hugely—a very sensible attitude. She was as much of an asset from the
business point of view as she was a liability from the political: Sarah
should have been confined to business, for which she had a flair, and not
allowed to interfere in politics, where her touch—though not always her
judgment—was fatal. She took up the cudgels with Cadogan, whom she
accused of misappropriating money from the £50,000 with which the
Duke had entrusted him before leaving England in 1712. This must
have been painful for Marlborough, who was forced to stand aside and
witness Sarah's operations. Still, Cadogan had been more than careless:
he had made use of Marlborough's money and Sarah made him pay up.
It crippled him financially to do it; but Sarah had not been his fellow
campaigner, so why not? At the height of the South Sea fever—Sarah
said that it was all madness, and it was—she forced the Duke out of the
market and added a round £100,000 to their enormous fortune.

Even so, it was a high price to pay for the squabbles and quarrels
with which she made him uneasy—worst of all, those with her daughters.
Henrietta Godolphin and the Duchess of Montagu were too much of
their mother's disposition to get on with her: they had all her positive-
ness without any of her wit and vivacity. She had been unwise and un-
affectionate in her treatment of them, and when they grew up they gave
as good as they got. Henrietta ignored her mother as much as she could:

the heir to the dukedom, she was very lofty—at the same time compromis-
ing herself, in her mother's view, by her association with a "low poet,"
the dramatist Congreve. (His company was of the most enchanting kind.)
Mary Montagu took pleasure in flouting and tormenting Sarah, who
allowed herself to be tormented very easily, though she was not unaware
of her failing. She admitted as much to her dear Mr. Jennings: "I am
sure you have often heard of my passions and assaultments":[61] she did
try to rein them in when she remembered. The trouble was that she was
one of those women with whom one never knows what they are going
to do next—nor did she, very often.

She was, I have suggested, a frustrated writer: she would have
been far happier, if only she could have written—but she had never been
educated. She was a naturally clever woman, with genuine interests of
mind that ran into the sand. This must have been a source of insatisfac-
tion and restlessness, which her practical capacity did not provide for.
With pen frequently in hand, she confided her troubles to her Green
Book.* "After the great illness that the Duke of Marlborough had in
1716, I was determined to bear whatever she [the Duchess of Montagu]
would do rather than hinder any of the Duke of Marlborough's children
from coming to my house when he was sick. And this was so great an
encouragement to all manner of ill behaviour, that what I had hid so long
they made public; for they never came to see their father in a morning,
but at the hours when company was there, going up towards him without
taking any notice of me, as if they had a pleasure in showing everybody
that they insulted me."[62] We need not suppose that Sarah had taken
much trouble to keep these family wrangles "hid": years before, Marlborough had warned her against giving the town an opportunity to take
part in them. In vain, of course.

Marlborough loved taking a hand at cards. In his last year we find
his daughter, Mary, writing him: "if you could have the least pleasure in
the variety of coming here any afternoon, it would be a great one to me,
and to anybody, I am sure, that you would let meet you. My Lord Sunderland is a very good whist player, and my sister Godolphin can play and
would be pleased with it (I know) in your company." It was very provoking: not one word of her mother; the party would be more like a
cabal of her personal enemies. The Duke replied, gently as always, but

_____

* A narrative of some one hundred pages, summing up all her grievances against
her daughters.

with such sadness: "I thank you for your letter, my dear child, but I observe that you take no manner of notice of your mother; and certainly when you consider of that, you can't imagine that any company can be agreeable to me who have not a right behaviour to her. This is doing what is right to yourself as well as to your affectionate father."

Mary Montagu did not give way: she wrote at once, justifying herself and charging Sarah with having done "what no mother did." Infinitely weary, her father went into it but could not find "that you had any reason for your complaint, but she had a great deal. Praying God Almighty to turn your heart to what is certainly most just and what has always been my earnest desire." Later still, in a trembling hand he wrote: "I am not well enough to write so long a letter with my own hand; and I believe I am the worse to see my children live so ill with a mother for whom I must have the greatest tenderness and regard."

He was at Windsor Lodge in the high summer of 1722 when his last illness fell on him. Sarah recounts this last sad scene. "The afternoon before her father died, I was mightily surprised and troubled at what I did not expect, that the Duchess of Montagu and my Lady Godolphin were without . . . At the time I thought my soul was tearing from my body and that I could not say many things before them, yet I would not refuse them to come in, for fear I should repent of it . . . They stayed a great while and, not being able to be out of the room longer from him, I went in though they were there and kneeled down by him. They rose up when I came in and made curtseys, but did not speak to me, and after some time I called for prayers. When they were over, I asked the Duke of Marlborough if he heard them well, and he answered, 'Yes, and he had joined in them.' "[63]

Thus do people break their hearts.

When it was getting dark, the Duke was carried on his couch into his own room, and there at dawn on June 16 he died.

The Duke's body was embalmed and borne to Marlborough House, where he lay in state. On August 9 a funeral procession of semiregal magnificence bore him to Westminster Abbey, where he was buried among the kings of England. The Abbey Registers have the entry: "9 August 1722. The most noble Prince John, Duke of Marlborough, Marquis of Blandford, Baron Churchill of Sandridge, Baron of Aymouth in Scotland, Prince of the Roman Empire, Knight of the most noble Order of the Garter."[64]

Those titles are familiar milestones to us in his full and toilsome life: he had come a long way from Ashe.

Marlborough's will made a great sensation, though there is nothing in it to surprise us.[65] His two chief cares were Blenheim and Sarah. He left Sarah £15,000 a year for life—she was already immensely rich herself—and £10,000 a year for five years for the completion of Blenheim. The estate at St. Alban's was at her own disposal; she was to have all the furniture, plate and jewels there, except the gold plate given him by the Elector of Hanover, the Emperor's diamond sword and the George and collar of the Garter, which were to go as heirlooms with the title. Sarah was to have Blenheim and Marlborough House for life; after, they were to go with the dukedom. The succession to the remaining estates was provided for, along with the title: first, Henrietta's children, the Godolphins; after them, if they failed (as they did), Anne's children, the Spencers (who did not). No less than £400,000 was set aside in trust to buy estates to settle on his right heirs, and, by an exceptional provision, an Act was to be obtained from the legislature for settling future purchases on his representative in the title.[66] We see his determination not only to leave his name in history, but to provide for his posterity in supporting it. We need not go into the complexities relating to its contingent provisions, the details of lands and moneys. We know that Arabella was not forgotten—nicely provided for, in fact. He expressed his wish to be buried "in my chapel in Blenheim house" at Sarah's direction, i.e., when completed.

On the news of Marlborough's death, Swift, who could not forgive him his fame and power and wealth, distinguished himself with a mean poem, "A Satirical Elegy on the Death of a late Famous General":

> His Grace! impossible! what dead!
> Of old age too, and in his bed!
> And could that Mighty Warrior fall?
> And so inglorious, after all! . . .
>
> Come hither, all ye empty things,
> Ye bubbles raised by breath of kings;
> Who float upon the tide of state,
> Come hither and behold your fate.

Let pride be taught by this rebuke,
How very mean a thing's a Duke;
From all his ill-got honours flung,
Turned to that dirt from whence he sprung.[67]

There could be no better evidence of how contrary Swift's feelings were to those of common humanity.

Chesterfield, for all his brilliance, was more in keeping with the ordinary sense of human beings. "Of all the men that ever I knew in my life (and I knew him extremely well), the late Duke of Marlborough possessed the graces in the highest degree, not to say engrossed them; and indeed, he got the most by them, for I will venture (contrary to the custom of profound historians, who always assign deep causes for great events) to ascribe the better half of the Duke of Marlborough's greatness and riches to those graces . . . The Duke of Marlborough, who was at least as able a negotiator as a general, was exceedingly ignorant of books, but extremely knowing in men. Military men have seldom much knowledge of books, but what makes great amends for that want is that they generally know a great deal of the world; they are thrown into it young; they see variety of nations and characters; and they soon find that to rise, which is the aim of them all, they must first please: these concurrent causes almost always give them manners and politeness. In consequence of which, you see them always distinguished at Courts and favoured by the women.

"The Duke of Marlborough studied the art of pleasing, because he well knew the importance of it: he enjoyed it and used it more than ever man did. He gained whoever he had a mind to gain; and he had a mind to gain everybody, because he knew that everybody was more or less worth gaining . . . He had an inimitable sweetness and gentleness in his countenance, a tenderness in his manner of speaking, a graceful dignity in every motion, and an universal and minute attention to the least thing that could possibly please the least person. This was all art in him: art, of which he well knew and enjoyed the advantages; for no man ever had more interior ambition, pride and avarice than he had."[68]

We observe that there are some things besides that the mere intellectual never understands.

CHAPTER XVIII

Sarah in Old Age

————————

SARAH was now free—and rich enough—to indulge her likes and dislikes, her loves and hates, her feuds and quarrels, her prejudices, whims, opinions, propensities for building, politics, cards, decorating her own (and other people's) houses, interfering, moving about the country, giving advice (often sound) where it was not asked, laying down to the law to everybody, though most people took no notice. Not that the Duke had ever seriously cramped her style in these ways—as he ought to have done from the beginning; but I dare say she would have walked out on him if he had tried. As long as he lived, her vagaries were kept within some bounds; his life and care gave polarity to her existence. With him gone, her life lost its centricity; she was free to become a rich and glorious eccentric.

Her indefatigable energies of mind and body boiled over: sometimes usefully, as in business affairs, where she continued to pile up money and landed estates; sometimes to no purpose whatever, as almost always in politics—for which she had a hopeless itch, for ever meddling and for ever checkmated and defeated. In personal relations her touch varied: sometimes successful, more often hopeless. There was no middle way with her: she either took to a person, and then was apt to be warm and generous, or she took against them, and then nothing they did was any good.

And yet, intolerable as Sarah was, she was not a bore: she had too much vivacity and wit. Anyway, with pen constantly in hand, tongue never still, crawling upstairs and downstairs on crutches, or having herself carried in a chair between two poles when she grew too gouty to walk, she has left us a portrait of herself more complete than any other

330

woman of the age. The ninth Duke of Marlborough, who had a *tendresse* for her—at the safe distance of a couple of centuries—understood her well and wrote of her with perceptive sympathy: "hers was a dominating character which, for the last thirty years of her life, lacked scope for action, and therefore asserted itself violently in the narrow field left open to it. But in the last resort it is not as a mother, nor even as a wife, that she must be judged. She belongs to history. No woman not of royal rank has ever held before, or is ever likely to hold again, such a position as was hers during the critical years of the early eighteenth century, when the map of Europe and the constitution of England were in the making."

It did not take her long not to be on good terms with the Hanoverian Court and its peculiar denizens.

To begin with, all was deceptively well. Her family were provided for, and Sarah had no wish to return to the drudgery of office: "for though the Princess [i.e., later Queen Caroline] is very easy and obliging, I think anyone that has common sense or honesty must needs be weary of everything one meets with in Courts. I have seen a good many and lived in them many years, but I protest I was never pleased but when I was a child, and after I had been a maid of honour some time I wished myself out of the Court as much as I had desired to come into it before I knew what it was."[1] Her relations with the clever Caroline were, at first, good. While Sarah was at Bath with the Duke in 1716, the Princess wrote her affectionately: *"J'ai reçu, ma chère Duchesse, avec beaucoup de joie votre obligeante lettre et suis ravie de voire que les eaux ont déjà fait un si bon commencement. Le Duc de St. Albans écrit à la Duchesse que vous allez souvent à la comédie. Vous voulez, Madame, savoir l'état de ma santé, qui est, Dieu merci, très bonne mais très grosse et je vous paraîtrai une boulle à votre retour que j'espère sera en parfaite santé, ce qui fera beaucoup de plaisir à celle qui vous aime tant que Caroline."*[2] The new rulers of England did not speak English: the language of the Court was French.

In spite of the victory of her side, Sarah was politically as restless and factious as ever. She was now at daggers drawn with her son-in-law Sunderland, who was at the head of the government; which did not prevent her from being on equally bad terms with his rivals, Townshend and Robert Walpole. Secretary Craggs, she had quarreled irretrievably with; Cadogan she had sued in the courts. Here was the whole of her party alienated: what a woman, what a lesson! When she made a fuss about a ridiculous charge of aiding the Pretender and wrote a passionate vindication of herself and Marlborough to the King, she got an almighty snub that ought to have done her nothing but good. "Whatever I may have been told upon your account, I think I have shown upon all occasions, the value I have for the services of the Duke your husband . . . Upon which I pray God, my Lady Marlborough, to preserve you in all happiness. George R."[3] But then, nothing of this kind ever did her any good.

When the Duke died, Caroline wrote Sarah a kind letter of consolation; but there was no longer affection. It was perhaps impossible for these two women to get on: each so positive and self-willed, especially since the younger was an educated woman with both intellect and political judgment. One of her first acts on arrival was to buy the complete works of Bacon. The girl who had been brought up by the Electress Sophia and shared the conversation of the philosopher Leibniz was more than a match for Sarah. Sarah was jealous—one detects the familiar accent: the reverend Dr. Clarke had once told Sarah that "her Majesty knew as much as he did, but that was when he hoped to be a bishop."[4] At Scarborough Sarah saw a woman with an expression of fatuity on her face such that she looked even "happier than her Majesty the day of her coronation." She could not bear powdered hair, "like the Queen's when she came first into England, clotted all over with powder, when I fancy the best thing I had was the colour of my hair."

Sarah had a natural wit that enabled her to make fun of the royal family. Here is an excellent example of her racy descriptive powers. "Two or three days ago Her Sacred Majesty was in great danger of being ravished. She was walking from Kensington to London early in the morning and, having a vast desire to appear more able in everything than other people, she walked so fast as to get before my Lord Chamberlain and the two princesses, quite out of sight. Whether this proceeded from their compliments to let her see how much stronger she was than they, I cannot say. But my Lord Grantham meeting a country clown asked him if he had met any person and how far they were off? To which he answered he had met a jolly crummy woman with whom he had been fighting some time to kiss her. (I am surprised at the man's fancy!) And my Lord Grantham was so frightened that he screamed out and said it was the Queen. Upon which the country fellow was out of his wits, fell upon his knees, cried and earnestly begged of my Lord Grantham to speak for him, for he was sure he should be hanged for what he had done. But did not explain further what it was. And her Majesty does not own more than that he struggled with her, but that she got the better of him . . . Upon the whole I should be very glad that somebody would make a ballad of it. For when I was at Scarborough, I learned to sing and I fancy I could perform such a one very well without any graces."[5] This was when she was getting on for seventy-three.

There were always barbed shafts at the end of her pen for Caroline; politics came in to make their relations rancorous. "A long time since I have had the honour to pay my duty at Court, but I was told that very lately a very great lady took occasion publicly in the Drawing Room to talk of the poor dear Duke of Marlborough in the most foolish and indecent manner that ever anybody did. But I think what that person says can do nobody any hurt, not even herself, because she never passed one day without affronting somebody or other, and sometimes when 'tis intended for compliments."[6] Sublimely unconscious, of course, that exactly the same might be said of herself. Then there were squabbles about this and that: over Sarah's Rangership of Windsor Park, and over the Queen's desire to make a road through a portion of Sarah's property at Wimbledon.

This being the situation, it was to be expected that Sarah would take a hand in the scandalous squabbles in the royal family between Caroline and her miserable first-born, Frederick, Prince of Wales; and that Sarah, actuated as usual by emotion and resentment, should have taken the Prince's side and brought defeat upon herself. He was a cad and a cur—all that his mother said publicly about him. But, in order to score off Caroline, Sarah was prepared to sacrifice the happiness of her adored, enchanting granddaughter, Di Spencer, and marry her to the creature. The Duchess offered to settle £100,000 on her granddaughter, if the Prince would marry her secretly.[7] What an ambition!—like Bess of Hardwick marrying her daughter into the succession to the throne. It was resentment even more than ambition that inspired the intrigue—what a score that her descendants should occupy the throne of Great Britain! The Prince of Wales was willing. Sir Robert Walpole got to hear of it and, of course, Sarah was checkmated.

One motive in Sarah's putting up the statue to Queen Anne at Blenheim, with its grateful inscription, was to reflect upon her successors:

as the years receded, old resentments were succeeded by new. "This character of the Queen is so much the reverse of Queen Caroline that I think it will not be liked at Court. Nobody can read it without reflecting upon the difference of the proceedings in Queen Anne's reign and the present."[8] Caroline had almost as acute a financial sense as Sarah, who was convinced that the reason why the bill for the reduction of interest on mortgages was deferred was to enable the royal family to get their money out of stocks before they fell—"the Queen herself has at least a million of money in that fund."[9] Caroline died that year, 1737: "as it is no treason, I freely own that I am glad she is dead . . . His Majesty thinks that he has lost the greatest politician that ever was born, and one that did him the greatest service that was possible. Though everybody else that knows the truth must acknowledge that it was quite the contrary."[10] Everybody else did not: George II was quite right about his wife's abilities; they were of outstanding service both to government and the dynasty. On Sarah's part there was no understanding of the self-sacrifice, the restraint and self-control, the life of incessant attendance upon, and drudgery for, the King that Caroline lived—something like Lady Masham before her—which was the price she paid for power. Sarah wanted the power without paying the price: she did not get it.

In the way stood the bulky, but agile, body of the extremely competent Sir Robert. The provoking man had no sense of the obligations he owed to the Marlborough family: had no one any gratitude in politics, or in anything else? Besides, had she not done him a service by lending his government a large sum of money, for which he had given her very inadequate returns—"he never saw fit to take any notice of me till he wanted the same kindness to be repeated."[11] Even in small matters he was disobliging: he withheld her permit for passing through St. James's Park, going to or from Marlborough House, a liberty which had not been withdrawn by Queen Anne in her worst days: "I thought I might have hoped from the services that I always endeavoured to do Sir Robert, when I had power, that he would not have allowed the Duke of Buckingham's widow a greater favour than the Duke of Marlborough's." She proceeded to say exactly what she thought of Sir Robert in all companies. As time went on and there seemed no prospect of ever shifting him from power—he had the constant backing of Queen Caroline—Sarah pursued him with rancor, taking a hand in all the cabals against him, joining with her old enemies, the Tories (in particular with Bolingbroke), against him, leaving large sums of money in her will to his foremost opponents.

Not all her money could ever shift him. It is amusing to watch how almost invariably Sarah got herself checkmated.

On this subject there is a revealing exchange of letters between Sarah and Marlborough's former chaplain, the admirable Dr. Hare, who should have become Archbishop of Canterbury. "The more I esteem and admire what is excellent in your grace," he wrote, "the more concerned am I to see any blemishes in so great a character. Ill-grounded suspicions, violent passions and a boundless liberty of expressing resentments of persons without distinction from the Prince downwards, and that in the most public manner, and before servants, are certainly blemishes, and not only so, but attended with great inconveniences; they lessen exceedingly the influence and interest persons of your grace's fortune and endowments would otherwise have, and unavoidably create enemies. It is, I think, confessed to be one of the most prudent rules of life, for persons in all stations not to give needless and unnecessary offense, since no person is so great as not to want on many occasions for themselves, or relations, or friends, the favour and good will of others; and least of all is it desirable to incur the settled displeasure or ill wish of a Prince; since he can seldom want long an opportunity of making it felt in some degree or other."[12]

That may be said to be the heart of the matter; it does not detract from the excellence of the advice that Dr. Hare looked to Walpole for preferment.

It is to Sarah's credit that she took in good part this reproof—"for which I give you a great many thanks. I have read Montaigne, and I remember he says something to this purpose, that one can't give a greater proof of friendship than in venturing to disoblige a friend, in order to serve them . . ." From there she went on to pages of justification of herself against Sir Robert and repeating all her grievances. "I must own that I cannot come up to your discretion as to keeping my thoughts to myself, when I know I am in the right, and when I never had any obligation, which is my case, from *the highest downwards,* as you express it . . . I hope I shall always take care (as I have hitherto done) not to be the aggressor . . . but I don't see why I should deny myself the pleasure of speaking my mind upon any occasion . . . and I am very little concerned for what you seem to think is the sense of many concerning my behaviour, because I am sure they don't know me, and by what I have seen in most of my acquaintance, I have hardly ever found that they could take the advice in their own case that some will give . . . I think I am at liberty to say whatever is true of them, and I wish nobody went further . . . you know my way is to tumble out the truth just as it comes in my head."[13]

Exactly. The judicious ecclesiastic did not waste any more time giving advice in that quarter.

Sarah went on with her feud against Walpole to the end of her days. In 1733 Walpole brought forward his Excise Bill, which was the best scheme of the kind ever presented to the country: it would have economized immensely in the collection of the revenue, stopped smuggling and evasion of excise, increased the yield for less trouble and enabled the land tax to be lowered, if not abolished. Had it come into effect, it would have anticipated the reforms of the nineteenth century and perhaps constituted Walpole's greatest claim to fame. But the measure offered an easy target for popular misrepresentation, and a nationwide agitation was set on foot by the Opposition, in which dissident Whigs joined with Tories—the whole thing engineered by Bolingbroke, whom Walpole had allowed to return from exile, and propagated in *The Craftsman*. The highest hopes of Walpole's fall, at last, were cherished —to Sarah's joy. The great measure had to be withdrawn, and Walpole's power was seriously shaken. He dismissed Chesterfield, who had opposed the scheme from within the government, from office. Henceforth Chesterfield was a favorite with Sarah.

A general election was to follow. The Duchess issued her commands to the Dean and Chapter of Worcester, through one of the prebendaries who had been army chaplain and secretary to General Charles Churchill. "Having a very great estate in my own power I have writ to all my tenants and people that I have influence over, to desire that they would not engage to promise anybody their votes till 'tis seen what members will offer. And then I shall desire of them to give all my interest to such as have the best characters and the best estates, without distinction of that odious thing, Party—which I have seen kept up for so many years on each side, by turns, only for the advantage of the leaders, without any regard for the good of the nation." There was, as usual, something in what Sarah said; but, for present purposes, Party meant Sir Robert Walpole. The Duchess's tenants and followers were "never to be for any man that has an employment, since experience shows us how few there are that have virtue enough to vote on the side of reason and justice when they must lose by it a profitable place or the hopes of a title and other trifles not necessary to mention." Voting for "reason and justice" meant voting against Sir Robert; "virtue" consisted in doing what the Duchess wanted. It was true that Walpole held on to power by bribery and corruption: so would anyone else have done who took his place. Does anyone suppose that Bolingbroke would not?

To come to the point of the letter: "Sir Thomas Lyttleton has always voted as he is directed [i.e., by Walpole]; and 'twas for that reason, I imagine, he has an employment he can know nothing of. He is my cousin, but he ought not to take what I say ill, because I do solemnly protest if I had a son that would, from weakness or any by-end, be influenced to act anything against the true national interest—if I had a thousand votes I would give them all against him."[14] No doubt: herself being the arbiter of the true national interest.

Sarah meant what she said: she was determined to have her way, and to use all the pull she had to that end. Sir Thomas Lyttleton had to withdraw and Worcestershire fell to the Tories. She forced her grandson, the new Duke of Marlborough, son of the grand Whig, Sunderland, to go into opposition to the Court and join up with the powerful coalition forming against Walpole, extending from Chesterfield to Carteret and Bolingbroke. She would have cut the young Duke out of her will if he had gone against her: she always used this threat to hold her grandchildren to the line. One of the grounds for the disputes with her family was her unrelenting determination to keep them all solid against Walpole. Walpole won the election and was in for the next seven years: Sarah had to recognize that he would be in power virtually for the rest of his life. Bolingbroke, too, recognized the collapse of his hopes and retired to France. The Duchess failed even to keep her family united against Walpole: in 1738 the young Duke went back to the side of the Court.

Sarah's great defect in politics was the feminine one of looking at matters in excessively personal terms. No one ever impugned her business capacity: in this field her masculine propensities came into play.

In the year after the Duke's death, she bought the Wimbledon estate of Sir Theodore Jansen, who had been ruined in the South Sea crash. Thereafter, hardly a year passed but what she bought an estate or two, until at her death she left some thirty in all. What she dreaded most was a war with France, which Sir Robert would conduct very ill and we should be defeated. "I can't live long enough to want necessaries, having bought land enough to produce beef and mutton at very dear rates, which make my produce very little in comparison of money at interest; but 'twill support one, unless an entire conquest come."[15] Such a line of thought has not been entirely absent from people's minds in recent years. Sarah was in the habit of acting upon her convictions— she was both a woman of her word and a woman of action—and the very year she wrote this, the first year of the war, 1739, she was "in the city to bid for Lord Yarmouth's estate, which I believe I shall have, and I do think it necessary to do it, because land will be the last thing that will be taken from us, and I expect a little sooner or later a sponge, which will put an end to all stocks and money lent to the government."[16] Her forebodings were not fulfilled; nevertheless, at a time when money was depreciating, it was good business to buy land. In that twelvemonth she bought half a dozen different estates in as many counties.[17]

Some of her business correspondence from the years 1737 to 1740 has fetched up on the other side of the Atlantic, from which we can follow what a shrewd eye hers was in such matters, attentive to every detail.[18] And very impressive it is to note the indomitable spirit of an old woman now crippled with gout, incapable of walking and often of wielding a pen, yet holding her head high and never giving in. At this moment she is out to buy the estate of a Mrs. Armiger: "I think it is an advantage to buy an estate that one has had so long the possession of, because one knows very well what one has made of it . . . But as for the advowson, I do not believe it can be worth anything like 300 guineas a year. But whatever it may be worth, I would not give a shilling for it. So that whoever likes to buy it, I shan't oppose them." Sarah was not interested in advowsons, i.e., presentations to livings, any more than she was in their incumbents: mere encumbrances to her positive, anticlerical mind, where there was no room for mystery any more than for cant—other than political cant.

On a July evening in 1737 she is writing urgently to her agent, Mr. Waller, to bid for an estate in person for her, "because it is what I am infinitely concerned to succeed in." This estate, Hill Deverell in Wiltshire, was being sold in Chancery to pay debts; Sarah was buying not for herself, but for the Marlborough trust estate, according to the Duke's will. She goes into all the complicated conditions with the utmost clarity. She got it, but wondered whether it was necessary to name all three trustees in the documents. Surely herself and Lord Godolphin—who was almost as much under her thumb as his father had been—were enough, without Lord Sundon? Lady Sundon, as plain Mrs. Clayton, had been a dear friend: Sarah had recommended her to Caroline as woman of the bedchamber, with the inevitable consequence. Lady Sundon read divinity, of a rather heterodox kind, with her mistress: to this we owe a mordant description from Sarah's pen of a portrait of this highbrow couple in their "supposed library," shorn up by serried ranks of philosophers.[19]

The purchase of Hill Deverell was not so easily completed: the owner was in prison for debt; there were legal difficulties. "A law-suit is a thing I dread extremely; but nothing is so bad as one with the Crown ... I am satisfied that I have had very bad imposing people to deal with in this purchase. But, if I could be made safe in it, I should like rather to buy it than not." The state of the law of real property in the eighteenth century, like that relating to marriage, made estate purchases a very tricky thing. The way Sarah carries them through, off her own bat, is very impressive: the rewards of confidence in oneself. With such a vast estate, she could hardly expect to be free of legal difficulties; at one time or another she seems to have been involved in at least a score of Chancery suits.

Nor could she get quit of the legal consequences of the old rows about Blenheim: they continued, millstones round her pertinacious neck. Thirty-five years after, the executors of her old enemy, Travers, were demanding money for his work at Blenheim. "The certain truth is that Mr. Travers had a sign manual from Queen Anne to receive the money from the Treasury, and was accountable for the right distribution of it to the Duke of Marlborough ... It was reasonable, to be sure, to pay his Clerk something for the trouble he had, but not £2,100 for so small a service as receiving £220,000 in six years."

No doubt, if Sarah had been in charge, the costs of building Blenheim would have been considerably reduced; but equally, if she had had her way, it would not have been built at all.

For all her experience at Blenheim, or perhaps because of it, she was building again: in this, too, another Bess of Hardwick. She was clearly bitten with the pleasures of building, or, perhaps more exactly, of furnishing. She was very hard to please. She pulled down the half-finished house she had purchased with the site at Wimbledon, and asked Lord Burlington, whose later buildings she did not approve—in particular, the lovely Assembly Rooms at York—to plan another. This too did not please her: not simple enough; so she demolished it and made him try again. This passed muster, and it gave her much pleasure in the 1730's to furnish it and fill it with things.

Now she was buying a marble chimney piece from Southampton House for her dining room. It was a fine one, but "there is a good deal of carving upon it, which is not at all to my taste . . . I am determined to have no one thing carved in the finishing of my house at Wimbledon, my taste having always been to have things plain and clean from a piece of wainscot to a lady's face."[20] She had bespoken a set of blue and gold leather hangings, which was as fresh now as when put up, for one of the rooms at Wimbledon. By 1734 all the pictures were finished, except those of young Marlborough, her dear Di and her husband the Duke of Bedford.

In the summer of 1735, "I have now full employment in furnishing Wimbledon, and it is a great pleasure and amusement to be dressing up and making a place pretty that I designed for my dear Cordelia . . . The furniture I think extremely handsome and will be almost all new."[21] All pleasure in finishing Wimbledon vanished with Di's death, for whom it was intended. This building too had given much trouble, and Sarah concluded that it was best to do "without the help of an architect, for I know of none that are not mad or ridiculous, and I really believe that anybody that has sense with the best workmen of all sorts could make a better house without an architect."

Her favorite house remained Marlborough House;* and there, within, under the accretions of Victorian and Edwardian royalty, we see —Sarah. The great saloon, going up to the full height of the original two stories, with its splendid doorcases, is not much changed. During the years of exile, Laguerre was at work painting the Battle of Blenheim upon the walls: there is the Duke holding his baton, seated on his white horse, his generals following behind. On the main staircase is the battle of Ramillies; on the east staircase, Oudenarde or Malplaquet.

---

* For many years in our time the residence of Queen Mary, after the death of King George V.

As she grew older, she turned more to the pleasures of literature, both of reading and of writing. Montaigne was a favorite—though he does not seem to have done her much good: she read to confirm her prejudices. The appearance of *Gulliver's Travels* gave her extreme pleasure: she was ready to forgive her old enemy for the delight he had given her. Pope and Gay wrote off to Swift: "the Duchess Dowager of Marlborough is in raptures at it; she says she can dream of nothing else since she read it; she declares that she has now found out that her whole life has been lost in caressing the worst part of mankind, and treating the best as her foes; and that if she knew Gulliver, though he had been the worst enemy she ever had, she should give up her present acquaintance for his friendship."[22]

She was capable of greater magnanimity than ever Swift was: we find her writing in 1736: "Dean Swift gives the most exact account of kings, ministers, bishops and the courts of justice that is possible to be writ. He has certainly a vast deal of wit; and since he could contribute so much to the pulling down the most honest and best-intentioned ministry that ever I knew, with the help only of Abigail and one or two more, and has certainly stopped the finishing stroke to ruin the Irish in the project of the halfpence, in spite of all the ministry could do, I could not help wishing that we had had his assistance in the Opposition; for I could easily forgive him all the slaps he has given me and the Duke of Marlborough, and have thanked him heartily whenever he would please to do good."[23] She had never seen Swift in her life, but she was "prodigiously fond" of *Gulliver* and was rereading it in 1736. "I most heartily wish that in this park I had some of the breed of those charming creatures Swift speaks of and calls the Houyhnhnms, which I understand to be horses, so extremely polite, and which had all manner of good conversation, good principles, and that never told a lie, and charmed him so that he could not endure his own country when he returned. He says there is a sort of creature there called Yahoos, and of the same species with us, only a good deal uglier; but they are kept tied up and, by that glorious creature the horses, are not permitted to do any mischief. I really have not been pleased so much a long time as with what he writes."

In the autumn of 1727 Voltaire paid a visit to Blenheim. The Duchess had already written one "vindication" of her conduct in relation to Queen Anne, which Walpole had advised her to suppress—no doubt because its tone was too bitter. From time to time she would turn over her papers: "I am at present altering my account of Queen Anne's character. I have begun to love her again since the present lot have become our governors." She had the idea of asking the brilliant young Frenchman to put her materials together for her.[24] But the *rusé* Voltaire realised how many enemies it would make for him in England to have a hand in that pie; he already had enough in France: he declined the commission. It was a pity, for thereby we missed what might have been a masterpiece. The Duchess was much vexed: "I thought the man had sense, but I find him at bottom either a fool or a philosopher." She had met more than her match in Voltaire: it was he who profited by the encounter. He was writing his *History of Charles XII*: Sarah gave him a vivid account of Marlborough's mission to Charles and his impressions of the warrior-king. Of this he made good use. He seems also to have got an anecdote about Sarah's deliberately upsetting a glass of water over Abigail's court dress, upon which Scribe based a celebrated play, *Le Verre d'Eau*.

Sarah was certainly going to go down in literature. On Bolingbroke's return from exile, these two old enemies joined together on the basis of opposition to Sir Robert. The Duchess turned to Marlborough's former disciple, who had had such an admiration for him, for an inscription for her Victory Column.[25] Bolingbroke obliged with ringing words: "The battle was bloody: the event decisive. The woods were pierced: the fortifications trampled down. The enemy fled." The Duchess was touched to the heart. "When I first read it, I thought it the finest thing that was possible for any man to write and as often as I have read it I still wet the paper." She was not without literary feeling: here, too, her taste was for the plain and unadorned, the simplicity that commands.

Her relations with literary men were hardly fortunate, especially when it came to a type like Pope. She wanted to be friends with him; he boasted of it, "the Duchess of Marlborough makes great court to me; but I am too old for her mind and body."[26] Though she was eighty and he fifty, there was some truth in this. We watch this brilliant monkey flattering the old lady, angling for a legacy. "I owe you more than I dare say you remember. First, I owe you my house and gardens at Twickenham, for you would have purchased them for me when you thought me fond of them. Secondly, I owe you a coach and horses, notwithstanding I fought you down to an arm-chair, and the other day I but named a house in town, and I saw with what attention you listened to it, and what you meant by that attention." When the old lady was ill, he wrote to ask after her health: "I sincerely wish it better than my own and you younger than I, that the tables may be turned and I leave you a legacy at my death."[27]

He left her a legacy all right: the scarifying portrait of Atossa in the book of his *Moral Essays* devoted to the "Characters of Women." He read this shocking piece to Sarah, under the pretense that it was a portrait of the Duchess of Buckingham. It is fairly clear that it was a composite portrait with traits from them both, but with Sarah's predominating.

> But what are these to great Atossa's mind?
> Scarce once herself, by turns all womankind!

(The mind goes back to the Restoration Court of Sarah's childhood and Dryden's description of Buckingham.)

> Who with herself, or others, from her birth
> Finds all her life one warfare upon earth;
> Shines in exposing knaves and painting fools,
> Yet is whate'er she hates and ridicules;
> No thought advances, but her eddy brain
> Whisks it about, and down it goes again.
> Full sixty years the world has been her trade,
> The wisest fool much time has ever made:
> From loveless youth to unrespected age,
> No passion gratified, except her rage . . .

Far more unforgivable was the character of Marlborough that Pope omitted from the *Essay on Man*. It is now thought that it was for this deletion that Sarah gave Pope £1,000, rather than for the suppression of "Atossa." She cared more for what the world thought of the Duke than of herself. The malicious poet considered the piece one of the best he had written:

> What wonder triumphs never turned his brain
> Filled with mean fear to lose, mean joy to gain.
> Here see him modest, free from pride or show,
> Some vices were too high, but none too low.
> Go then, indulge thy age in wealth and ease,
> Stretched on the spoils of plundered palaces.
> Alas, what wealth, which no one act of fame
> E'er taught to shine, or sanctified from shame;

Alas, what ease those furies of thy life,
Ambition, Avarice and th' imperious wife . . .
Hear him in accents of a pining ghost
Sigh, with his captive, for his offspring lost.
Behold him loaded with unreverend years
Bathed in unmeaning, unrepentant tears;
Dead, by regardless veterans borne on high,
Dry pomps and obsequies without a sigh.
Who now his fame or fortune shall prolong,
In vain his consort bribes for venal song:
No son nor grandson shall the line sustain,
The husband toils, th' adulterous sweats in vain . . .

How shameless, how cruel, to jab at the open wounds in Marlborough's life! We have seen how this humane man grieved for the loss of his son, at the unhappiness caused by Sarah within his family. We see something of what the Marlboroughs had to endure from jealousy and detraction all their lives; we see indeed what the poisonous malice of the intellectual is capable of, the insensitiveness to the lying cruelty inflicted —all inspired by envy of the pre-eminent, masquerading as virtue.[28]

In her last years Sarah was much concerned with how posterity would view not so much herself as her actions; she wished to put her case and an official biography of the Duke to be written. It is curious, though perhaps understandable, how much difficulty each of these gave. For years she had been fiddling at her memoirs, and at last she got a reputable man: Nathaniel Hooke—friend of Pope and a good Roman historian—to put them into final shape for her. This must be the circumstance that accounts for the story that the old Duchess, though ill in bed, dictated with perfect clarity for six hours at a stretch. No one who reads the book can mistake that the language is Sarah's own, though Hooke may have toned it down; not even Sarah's resentments, however, were as bitter as they had been. The book, *An Account of the Conduct of the Dowager Duchess of Marlborough, From her first coming to Court to the year 1710*, was published in 1742 and made a sensation.

In the *Gentleman's Magazine* Dr. Johnson wrote a review which is as remarkable for its general reflections on writing history as it is for the exposure of his own prejudices.[29] He could not prevail on himself to do justice to the Marlboroughs: he did not like them—too Whiggish in their principles—and he thought their acquisitiveness vulgar. It would be too easy to allow that it was; for, on such a scale, it transcended mere vulgarity (besides, John and Sarah, of themselves, liked plainness and simplicity) and became baroque magnificence. Consider what the nation gained by it in gaining Blenheim! Dr. Johnson thought Addison's dedication of his charming opera, *Rosamond,* to Sarah "an instance of servile absurdity"—"a woman without skill or pretensions to skill in poetry or literature."[30] But what could be more absurd than to suppose that the dedicatee of a book should necessarily be so skilled? Addison, who always did what was appropriate, was a better judge of propriety. Dr. Johnson's attitude only shows that the reactionary Tory was more independent-minded, and far less deferential, than Whig intellectuals.

Sarah's book, like everything about her, at once became a subject of controversy. On the whole, she got off lightly: the extraordinary old lady had survived so long that after a lifetime of unpopularity and envy, the British public—with its usual mixture of sentimentality and gallantry —had practically taken her to its bosom. Fearlessness—not caring what anybody thought—and eccentricity had their usual reward. At George II's coronation, the old Duchess, gouty and weary with standing, had called for a drum in Palace Yard and sat down on it comfortably in all her finery, blazing with jewels, to the enjoyment and cheers of the populace. Now one of the critics began his pamphlet: "the spirit, humour, language of this extraordinary piece all proclaim it genuine; and if, from the likeness of a child, there be any guessing at the true parent, the mother of this pretty babe might have been easily known, even if she had attempted to keep herself concealed. All that vivacity, freedom and contempt of dignities, which have distinguished the lady from all other ladies, shine with such lustre in the book, as to set it beyond comparison with any other of the kind, except it be the Lord Clarendon's History."[31] That must have pleased Sarah: a warm welcome for an ill-educated girl to the ranks of authors; she had arrived there by sheer force of personality. Whatever Dr. Johnson might say about her, she was as remarkable a personality in her way as he was in his.

The unkindest, and the most effective, criticism came from the American writer James Ralph of Philadelphia—former associate of Benjamin Franklin, now working as an impecunious journalist in London. He devoted a whole book, *The Other Side of the Question,* to traversing Sarah's book point by point.[32] He had no independent source of information, so he had to proceed by a rigid analysis of what Sarah said. We may judge his tone from his opening phrases: "as your grace still seems to retain that fire which rendered you so conspicuous in power, and so impatient on being *turned out* . . . be pleased to consider that authorship as well as love sets all mankind on a level . . . your grace's notable performance, in which Mrs. Freeman is everywhere the heroine and poor Mrs. Morley no better than a foil to set her off to the more advantage . . . but the world will by no means be persuaded to endure that you should set up your own statue in the place of hers who *raised you out* of the dust." Rather thin-blooded: it is evident that Ralph did not like Sarah, did not respond to an outsize personality. Perhaps there is an unconscious difference of choice here: the English like outsize targets to shy at. It is rather fun to see the egalitarian American reduced to defending monarchs like William and Mary and Anne against the irreverent remarks of a lady bred up at Court: no idea, evidently, how independent-minded courtiers can be. The Duchess, at the height of her troubles, had declared with some improbability—like Oliver Cromwell at a similar juncture— that she would emigrate to America. The Continent, at that time, would hardly have been big enough to hold her.

Attacked by this splenetic journalist, Sarah had the fortune to be defended by the generous, full-blooded Fielding: he could appreciate a great woman when he saw one—he "never contemplated the character of that Glorious Woman but with admiration." Fielding was a gentleman and a chivalrous fellow: he rushed out his *Full Vindication of the Duchess Dowager of Marlborough* before *Joseph Andrews* was clear of the printer's.[33] It may be concluded that Sarah had the better in this warfare.

There was still the Duke's official biography to provide for, and here Sarah was defeated by the laziness of prospective authors. No one wanted to embark on a work of such serious research. Years before, it had been hoped that Steele would undertake it: papers had been unloaded upon him to flip through. The task was more than this jolly, lazy man could contemplate; and he can never have contemplated it seriously: it was beyond his powers. A complete outsider, the excellent Lediard, produced an admirable biography of the Duke, in three volumes, in 1736. He had been secretary to our envoy at Hamburg, and accompanied Marlborough on his mission to Charles XII in 1707. His book is a work of conscientious scholarship, based on public papers and on some personal knowledge. I do not know why Sarah took no notice of Lediard: it may be because his book ended up by quoting poetry—

that she could not tolerate. She entered into negotiations with two not very reputable writers, Richard Glover and David Mallet—both of them very inferior poets—to write the biography. In her will she left them £500 each and access to all the papers, but "no part of the said History may be in verse."[34]

Politics, to the last, entered into the choice. Glover had been in opposition to Walpole. The Duchess believed him "to be a very honest man and wishes, as I do, all the good that can happen to preserve the liberties and laws of England." He was at any rate honest enough to refuse the commission. Mallet was not: he accepted, went about for years professing to be "eternally fatigued with preparing and arranging materials," and never wrote a line. We have come across such people. In the event, but only after her death, the Duchess was defrauded. She hoped that the Earl of Chesterfield might oversee the History: to whom she left £20,000 and her best diamond ring, "out of the great regard for his merit and the infinite obligations I have received from him." The most famous legatee was William Pitt, to whom she left £10,000 "upon account of his merit in the noble defence he has made for the support of the laws of England to prevent the ruin of his country." In him she was justified: the true successor of Marlborough.

There remains the family: where Sarah's touch was as fallible as in the field of politics. She was on bad terms with her eldest daughter, Henrietta, who on her father's death became Duchess of Marlborough in her own right. She had a good deal of her mother's temperament, with the amorous disposition of the Villierses. She was as opinionated and self-willed as Sarah, but more warmhearted; her combination of haughty grandeur with being no better than she should be was a difficult one to carry off: she managed it with more dignity than most.

Her childhood letters reveal her as an engaging creature, affectionate, impulsive: more than a little vain and anxious for a crumb of approval from her magnificent, awe-inspiring mother.[35] "I am in pain for fear my Dear mama should be angry," she writes, "yet this is ill writ, and spelt. But if you will bileeve me, I am in such hast I hardly know what to do, and therefore hope that you will forgive all faults."

She was married at eighteen to Godolphin's only son by Margaret Blagge, aged twenty: intelligent parents, intelligent stock in every direction; nothing could be more appropriate. They soon produced a son, called after the King, William: in the family, Willigo. Godolphin reports from Holywell, "all here are very well at present and Willigo begins to make a noise, which he is pleased with himself because he takes it for speaking, but it's a language not much understood in the world hitherto; his sister is a great beauty." The marriage may be regarded as successful, as marriages go. But the younger Godolphin was as easygoing as his father and as little ambitious. Hervey tells us that he had plenty of natural ability and that he was a man of sense; but his real passion was for horses and he preferred the company of stableboys. We can hardly blame Henrietta for finding that disappointing and her husband rather tame.

With her spirit and ambition she was more taken with the wits and preferred the company of poets, particularly polite ones who knew how to commend their parts to ladies. When her brother Blandford died, leaving her the heir, the agreeable Mr. Congreve sent her sympathetic verses, "The Tears of Amaryllis for Amyntas." Verses were better than horses. The year of Ramillies, Congreve strengthened his claim by a Pindaric ode in honor of the Lord Treasurer; when he and Vanbrugh opened their new playhouse, Henrietta was referred to, as she longed to be, as "the learn'd Minerva." It was natural enough: there was ground where her mother could not meet her. Soon Mr. Congreve, who was a delightful companion, was a welcome visitor at Godolphin House, playing at cards and other things. Congreve, Gay, the detested Vanbrugh—this was not a combination that pleased Sarah. She called and found her daughter "at ombre with Mr. Congreve and a woman that I did not know. I thought he looked out of countenance, but showed more willingness to talk to me than you did; I soon put you at ease by going away."[36]

We see the kind of woman Henrietta was at this time from her portrait at Lancaster House. In coloring fair, like her mother, fine eyes and, like all the women of the family, an elegant figure. There she sits forcefully, in plain scarlet dress with a blue gown draped loosely round her; a gold scarf trailing from her hair, her literary pretensions explicit in the book drooping from her hand.

Sarah disapproved of her daughter keeping company with "low poets." "She has starts of giving a hundred guineas to a very low poet that will tell her that she is what she knows she is not, which I think so great a weakness that I had rather give money not to have such verses made public."[37] This was years later, when the breach between mother and daughter was irretrievable. It refers to the publication of Gay's *Polly*, the sequel to *The Beggar's Opera*: *Polly* had been suppressed by Walpole on account of her identification with his mistress, Maria Skerett.[38] One would think that this might have recommended the piece to Sarah. A subscription was raised by Gay's grand friends: he had spent five or six months with Henrietta and Congreve at Bath, and now she subscribed a hundred guineas for a copy. Congreve had since died: hence the reference:

> First in thy list does great Almeria stand,
> And deal her favours with a lavish hand,
> Her buried bard's resemblance does she see,
> And thinks Alphonso still survives in thee.

Henrietta's liaison with Congreve was the great affair of her life, recognized by everybody. But it was never recognized by Sarah. It led to vehement reproaches, appeals to the Duke, quarrels, reconciliations, scenes, letters—many of which Sarah afterward burnt in resentment: the regular gamut of her attempts to destroy the Queen's passion for Abigail, and equally fruitless. It would seem that Sarah, by temperament cold, did not understand other people's warmer passions: her direct assaults and violent interferences only wedded them closer. And so it was with Henrietta, who owed the happiness of her life to Congreve.

Their visit to Bath proved fruitful: the waters were apt to have "a wonderful influence on barren ladies, who often prove with child, even in their husbands' absence."[39] Godolphin, who had not been much in the habit of cohabiting with his wife, wrote complaisantly to his daughter, "you will, I dare say, my dear child, be glad to hear that your Mama is very well, after having been brought to bed, about two hours ago, of a little girl." Lady Mary Wortley Montagu—who was jealous over the possession of Congreve—was less kind: "she is as much embarrassed with the loss of her big belly," she wrote, "as ever a dairy-maid was with the getting one."

Not long after, Congreve died and was buried in Westminster Abbey. Henrietta did not hesitate to erect a monument to him with an inscription in her own name: "to whose most valuable memory this monument is set up by Henrietta, Duchess of Marlborough, as a mark how deeply she remembers the happiness and honour she enjoyed in the sincere friendship of so worthy and honest a man, whose virtue, candour and wit gained him the love and esteem of the present age, and whose writings will be the admiration of the future." Henrietta Churchill was not lacking in the courage of her family. Her mother commented, "I know not what pleasure she might have had in his company, but I am sure it was no honour." When it was found that Congreve had left almost all his fortune to his Duchess, people felt sure that it was a *dot* for his child.

Perhaps now we know, partly, why Sarah hated poets so much: one of them had taken her daughter from her. No one considers the sacrifice Congreve made to this liaison. It has always been thought a mystery why the most brilliant dramatist of the age deserted the stage at the height of his powers. Here is, perhaps, the explanation.

Henrietta's son, the second Blandford, was the next heir to Marlborough's dukedom. In him the easygoing strain of the Godolphins slackened the fiber still further and, like a lot of rich young men of the eighteenth century, he took to drink early. As a result of Sarah's influence on the Duke in making his will, the young heir had been made independent of his mother, Henrietta; and this made for bad blood between mother and son. Sarah's relations with her grandchildren followed the psychological patterns usual with such types: the boys could do what they liked and get away with it. On a visit to Holland, the young heir did the only sensible thing he ever managed: he fell in love with a rich burgomaster's daughter and married her before the family could stop him. She had a dowry of £30,000, but that was inconsiderable for the heir to the Marlboroughs.

There was uproar in the family. All the Godolphins were alarmed and on the alert. Queen Caroline was the first to tell the young man's sister "in the Drawing Room in private and in a most kind manner that she was sorry to tell her such disagreable news."[40] The one person who took it well was Sarah—perhaps this was enough to put it right: she proceeded to do her best for the young couple. No doubt she felt responsible for him, and this was a way of getting her own back on Henrietta. Then it was found that the young Dutch lady was "charming and agreeable; I envy her nothing but her good understanding and her sweet even temper; they stand her I believe in great stead. He is very kind to her in his way and she carries it mighty prettily to him."[41] Unfortunately the young man was a confirmed drunkard by this time. His grandmother put up with his eccentricities with surprising forbearance and good humor.

One day in August 1731 he went to Oxford to attend a meeting of a club, where a drinking bout at Balliol brought on a high fever, of which he died.[42] Sarah was with him at the end: "I would have given half my estate to have saved him," she said; "I hope the Devil is picking that man's bones who taught him to drink."

Among the things this young man had omitted to do was to give his wife a baby. Thus died the hopes of the Godolphins, who would otherwise have succeeded to the dukedom. And so they pass out of our story.

Henrietta grieved inconsolably, not for her feeble son, but for Congreve. It was said that she had a figure made of him which was set by her at table and at night in her bedchamber. Perhaps this was mere scandal; she had her oddities, like her mother. In 1733 she fell ill and shortly died. Too late, her mother confided to Di Spencer: "you have judged very right in thinking what has happened I should feel much more than I imagined formerly I could ever do. By which I am convinced that there is such a thing as natural affection, though I have heard many people laugh at that notion. I have made several attempts to be reconciled to that unfortunate woman and upon the report of her being in great danger, I did it in a very moving manner before I came to Woburn. But nothing I said or did had the least good effect. However, it is a satisfaction to me that I did all that was in my power. But what do I dream of satisfaction, when there are not two things upon earth at so impossible a distance as satisfaction and me?"[43]

These two events entirely altered the scene: the Godolphins went out, the Spencers came in.

With Sarah's either-or mentality, two of her Spencer grandchildren, Diana and Jack, the younger ones, were her favorites; the other two, Anne and Charles, she did not care for. Indeed, Anne, Lady Bateman, was her aversion: she answered her grandmother back, gave as good as she got, and led the cabals in the family and in society against the notorious old lady. Sarah, after some particular provocation, blackened her portrait at Blenheim and wrote underneath, "She is more black within." The Lady Bateman was as much of a tartar as her grandmother and exerted a great influence over her elder brother Charles, Earl of Sunderland, who now succeeded as third Duke. Sarah was convinced that his sister had arranged his marriage to—of all people—the daughter of one of the twelve peers created unforgivably in 1712. Marlborough's widow could not swallow this. "I do believe that my Lord Sunderland, who is certainly a very weak man, will always be governed by his sister."[44]

On the other hand, Jack Spencer was the apple of her eye. "I think your brother John has good nature, sense, frankness in his temper (which I love), and in short a great many desirable things in him; but still he wants a great deal to get through this world in the manner that I wish he should do."[45] No doubt. He, unlike his brother, had made a marriage of which she could approve: a delightful girl, whose golden locks, as Sarah's had once done, "do certainly become her. And as your brother is of that opinion I believe she will despise the fashion; for she is extremely in love, though he is always dressed like a keeper or farmer. They both appear equally happy, and I hope it will ever continue so."

Diana had been brought up by her grandmother, and had her mother's art of managing the old lady. Sarah loved her passionately, and —as her way had always been—jealously: she could not bear to think that any other woman was closer to her. It evidently fell to Diana to do what she could to bring the family together and restore her elder brother to his grandmother's affections. In this she succeeded. The young Duke paid Sarah a visit which charmed her. (The Spencers had charm.) Soon Sarah is "labouring like a pack-horse every day to save him from the cheats."[46] Unfortunately, Charles was both extravagant and negligent: he simply could not keep up with her energy or answer her multifarious business letters. "I cannot help saying to you that it is very unpleasant to go through so much drudgery for one that will not trouble himself to write ten lines in answer to things that only concern himself." The Duke did not displace plain Jack Spencer as his grandmother's favorite, nor— unfortunately for the Churchills—as the chief beneficiary of her will. The joke is that Jack was hardly less extravagant than his brother.

It was their sister Diana, however, who had Sarah's heart. "Your desiring me to take care of myself for your sake is very kind, and I return it by assuring you that I desire to live only for you."[47] When the girl married John Russell, Sarah gave her a dowry of £30,000 and designed to leave her £100,000. Her husband succeeded his brother as Duke of Bedford. "This letter is writ by my new secretary, the Duke of Bedford, which you will read with more ease than my ridiculous hand. He has turned Di out of her place of my secretary, which you know is a common thing in this age for ministers to trip up one another's heels. He is the best servant and minister that ever I had, and he is so far from being lazy that he copies out all my papers that I have. He is certainly a perfect miracle of his age. I think Providence designs to make me amends for some of my past sufferings by the goodness and kindness of this young man."[48]

Sarah took to calling Diana "Cordelia." "That is the name I intend to call you for the future, which is the name of King Lear's good child, and therefore a proper title for you, who have been always good to me . . . You are charming in all your thoughts and actions."[49] The name was ominous of tragedy. Already Di's health was not as Sarah could wish it. She hoped that the girl would go into the air on every fine day; it was impossible it could do any hurt. To aid her take the air, Sarah sent her Marlborough's famous tent. "I wish it may be of any use and please you, but I think the chief value of it is, to think that it was your dear grandfather's tent, when he did such wonderful things to secure the nation from being enslaved by the French king, besides the great provisions he made for his whole family, all which I think should make his memory dear to every one of them." Sarah did not realize that no further provision would be necessary for her Cordelia: she was dying.

Di's death left the old woman's life empty of love, the only salve for the ills of this world. The soulless round continued—indomitable activity, politics, business, society, people, dragging oneself round to the last. But at heart there was emptiness. "It is impossible that one of my age and infirmities can live long; and one great happiness there is in death, that one shall never hear any more of anything they do in this world."[50] Religion, the consolation of them that have not love, meant nothing to her. What her real belief had been is revealed in her saying, "I have always thought that the greatest happiness of life was to love and value somebody extremely that returned it and to see them often."

But love survives the venom of the snake.

She died in her eighty-fifth year, at Marlborough House, her favorite residence, on October 19, 1744. She had been born, an age before, only a few days after the happy Restoration of King Charles II.

Her will was as full and crowded as her life had been, and vastly more generous.[51] It was governed by the decision that since Charles Spencer, the elder brother, had succeeded to the dukedom, the younger should have Althorp and the succession to the Spencer estates. John Spencer, ancestor of the Earls Spencer, became her chief legatee: that is how most of her personal belongings come to be at Althorp. The bulk of her lands and estates went to him and his heirs, on condition that he should not "accept or take from any King or Queen of these Realms any pension or any office or employment, civil or military." That must have made the young Duke regret that he had returned to the government fold and accepted office before her death. Marlborough House went to John Spencer for life, afterward to go with the dukedom. All the furniture that she had bought there was for John; that bought by her husband went to Charles. The furniture at Blenheim went to Charles, provided he left the goods and furniture of Althorp to John, who was also to have the house in Grosvenor Street. His son and heir was to have £2,000 a year on coming of age. A sense of duty to Marlborough's dynastic feelings made her direct £3,000 a year for the sons of Blenheim. Their successors had reason to wish that more of her substance had been devoted to the upkeep of that house.

For a tremendously generous list of legacies to other people followed. Over a score of people were given annuities. Her man of business and trustee, James Stephens, was left £15,000 and £300 a year. (Multiply by ten.) Her companion, Grace Midgley, a girl whom she picked up at Woodstock and made her Abigail, got £15,000, £300 a year, a miniature of Marlborough, a locket portrait of him and one of Sarah by Kneller, and the Duke's striking watch. Grace's daughter was left £3,000. The Earl of Clancarty, Sarah's neighbor at Marlborough House: £1,000 down and £1,000 a year. All her gold and silver plate, her seals and trinkets and small pieces of japan, were for John Spencer; her best diamonds for his wife. Her diamond solitaire, gold snuffbox with portraits of Marlborough, a string of pearls with other pictures of him, were left to her daughter Mary, Duchess of Montagu; to the Duchess of Devonshire "my box of travelling plate," to the Dowager Countess of Burlington £1,000 and her bag of gold medals, to the Duke of Leeds £3,000, his niece £1,000; to the Duchess of Manchester, a granddaughter, the house in Dover Street. To the Godolphins nothing: they had failed in the race. Her wish was to be buried "near the body of my dear husband" at Blenheim.

They had been long apart. At length there together they lie.

Epilogue

AND SO the Churchills won, by the deeds of their ancestor, their place at the summit of English society, that small and select, but very human, Olympus. We have followed their tracks across landscape and history from their beginnings in the West Country—that sharper, more intimate countryside—to the wider and more commanding prospects of Oxfordshire, the magnificence of Blenheim, upon which their story has pivoted ever since.

Sarah was succeeded at Blenheim by her grandson, Charles Spencer, who counts—after his aunt, Henrietta—as the third Duke. His son George, the fourth Duke, reigned there for over half a century, dying in 1817: which brings us well into the nineteenth century, up to the threshold of the Victorian Age. His son, the fifth Duke, just before succeeding resumed the name of Churchill; so that all the later members of the family are Spencer Churchills.

It has been given to few families to achieve two distinct summits in the course of their history—especially two such fateful peaks as John, Duke of Marlborough, and our own fortunate Sir Winston Churchill.

In between has come a good deal of variegated country, with its diversified character and appeal, affording some contrasts as well as suggestive similarities, often rewarding and almost always interesting.

Sarah remarked, with some disapprobation, on the contrast between Charles Spencer and his grandfather, the great Duke. This was not wholly to the young man's disadvantage. Where John Churchill had been ambivalent and secretive, Charles Spencer was candid and sincere; where the grandfather had been acquisitive and mean, the grandson was generous to a fault. Where John had a cool heart and head, for every-one except Sarah and his children, Charles was warmhearted and of an open nature, a loyal and constant friend. And though, as against the first Duke's life of industry and toil, Charles was idle and enjoyed life rather than work—which seems to be thought a virtue rather than otherwise—he was a man of spirit, anxious to maintain the great name of Marlborough by service in the field; upon which, indeed, he died.

His son and successor, with his handsome good looks, carried on his father's charm and constancy of nature. In other respects a contrast: for instead of a life of action, he led a withdrawn, retired life, given up to the pleasures of connoisseurship, collecting gems, enamels, pictures; carrying through the re-designing of Blenheim Park on the grand scale (to him we owe the present landscape of lake and sward and plantations); in the end, withdrawing altogether into the pleasures of silence and astronomy.

Later generations produced those who added to the inheritance as well as those who subtracted from it; some did both. And so we come to Disraeli's Viceroy of Ireland, father of Lord Randolph Churchill, who achieved a sudden eminence of his own, before bequeathing a more substantial and more famous son.

In all this the family offers us a rich and many-sided expression of the nation's life, in some ways more opulent and exotic since such an eminence gave it the opportunities and the means to express itself as it liked. In such cases eccentricity is apt to wage fruitful war with good sense—as with Sarah herself. Yet we see the wilder flights of imagination and fantasy tugged back and kept in bounds by the pull of the soil; in two supreme instances we watch these bounding impulses of genius harnessed to the soil of the nation itself. This family gives us a mirror in which to study a fair representation of the country's history.

Sir Lewis Namier has a passage in his book, *England in the Age of the American Revolution*, all the more illuminating as a reflection coming from outside: "English history . . . is made by families rather than by individuals; for a nation with a tradition of self-government must have thousands of dynasties, partaking of the peculiarities which in other countries are peculiar to the royal family alone. The English political family is a compound of 'blood,' name and estate, this last, as the dominions of monarchs, being the most important of the three. . . . The name is a weighty symbol, but liable to variations; descent traced in the male line only, is like a river without its tributaries; the estate, with all that it implies, is, in the long run, the most potent factor in securing continuity through identification, the 'taking up' of the inheritance. . . . Primogeniture and entails psychically preserve the family in that they tend to fix its position through the successive generations, and thereby favour conscious identification."

Here is the importance of Blenheim in fixing the inheritance of the Churchills, its potency witnessed after a couple of generations—the two Spencer Dukes—in the return to the old name. (Here too, perhaps I may add, is the justification for such a family history as this.)

In the generations since Sarah it has seen changes characteristic of the nation's evolution, of the development of our society. Whig under George II, under George III maintaining a dignified independence inclining to the liberal sympathies of Charles James Fox; brought back to Conservatism by the pull of the land and disagreement with the Repeal of the Corn Laws: such is the picture until the emergence of Lord Randolph with his campaign for Tory democracy, carried forward by his son, the young Winston Churchill, into the new liberalism which, in the years 1906 to 1914, laid the foundations of the welfare state and social democracy. It is tempting to see something of the Foxite tradition of his ancestry in these early activities of Winston Churchill, since such chimes and echoes reverberate long in historic families. But he was to embody something more important—the safety of the state, the very existence of the nation in the years 1940 to 1945; and something even more significant for the future.

The Churchills today are not an English family only; they are a family in which English and American contributions share equally, are fused into one. It is not always realized how many American marriages have brought new infusions of vitality and vivacity into the stock: in addition to the famous match of Lord Randolph Churchill and Jennie Jerome—from both sides of which their famous offspring derives obvious traits—and the celebrated alliance of his cousin, the ninth Duke, with Consuelo Vanderbilt, there have been three more Anglo-American marriages in different generations, as, we may be sure, there will be more to come.

For the significance of the astonishing career of the greatest of all the Churchills is not, happily, confined to the English scene of action: it extends to that of all the English-speaking peoples, whose history he is writing, whose place in the world he is illuminating and defining, of whose rich unity in diversity he is the very human embodiment.

Notes

KEY TO ABBREVIATIONS

Cal. Com. Comp.—*Calendar of the Committee for Compounding*
Cal. S. P. Dom.—*Calendar of State Papers, Domestic*
Cal. S. P. For.—*Calendar of State Papers, Foreign*
Cal. S. P. Ireland—*Calendar of State Papers, Ireland*
D.N.B.—*Dictionary of National Biography*
E.H.R.—*English Historical Review*
H. M. C.—*Historical Manuscripts Commission publications (Ormonde, etc.)*

The following refer to manuscript sources in the Public Record Office:
C.—Court of Chancery
L.C.—Lord Chamberlain's Office
S.P.—State Papers
P.C.C.—refers to the wills of the Prerogative Court of Canterbury now kept
at Somerset House in London

CHAPTER I
Dorset Beginnings

1. H.M.C., *Marquis of Bath MSS.*, II, 173-75.
2. Quoted in Sir Winston Churchill, *Marlborough, His Life and Times*** (London, Harrap, 1933-38, 4 vols.), I, 32.
3. C. W. Dale, *The History of Glanville's Wootton*, 1-2.
4. Quoted in Churchill, *op. cit.*, 30.
5. C 8/86/101.
6. SP 23/186/410.
7. A. R. Bayley, *The Civil War in Dorset, 1642-1660*, 36.
8. *Ibid.*, 66.
9. SP 23/186/414.
10. *Ibid.*, 413.
11. *Ibid.*, 416.
12. Bayley, *op. cit.*, 405.
13. *Cal. Committee for Advance of Money*, 804.
14. C. H. Mayo (ed.), *The Minute Books of the Dorset Standing Committee, 1646-50*, 437.
15. C 6/148/27. This document is much mutilated.

CHAPTER II
Cavalier Colonel

1. J. Foster, *Alumni Oxonienses, 1500-1714*, I, 276.
2. I am indebted to Mr. W. C. Costin, Senior Tutor of St. John's, for the information concerning Winston Churchill's residence there.
3. *Admission Register of Lincoln's Inn*, I, 229.
4. *Records of Lincoln's Inn*, II, 458-63.
5. *The Oxinden Letters, 1607-1642*, ed. D. Gardiner, xxxiv.
6. Field Marshal Lord Wolseley tells us that these citations appear in the grant of augmentation of arms to Winston Churchill at Blenheim Palace, but that other names of actions in which he took part are now illegible. See Wolseley, *Life of John Churchill, Duke of Marlborough*, I, 20.
7. Clarendon, *Hist. of the Rebellion*, ed. Macray, III, 90-91.
8. Churchill, *Marlborough*, I, 20.
9. The story is told by John Prince, who was a neighbor of the Drakes of Ashe in the next generation and to whom Lady Drake's son, John, stood as god-

* Published in the United States in 4 vols. by Charles Scribner's Sons, New York, 1933-38.

father. See J. Prince, *The Worthies of Devon* (1810 ed.), 329.

10. *Cal. Com. for Advance of Money,* 1092-93.

11. Churchill, *op. cit.,* I, 21.

12. Cf. my essay on "Hillesden in Buckinghamshire," *The English Past,* and for Milton, *ibid.,* 95 ff.

13. SP 23/162/697.

14. Quoted in Churchill, *op. cit.,* I, 17-18.

15. SP 23/162/700.

16. *Ibid.,* 468.

17. SP 23/106/311.

18. SP 23/199/723.

19. A. R. Bayley, *The Great Civil War in Dorset,* esp. 129 ff., 194, 221, 234.

20. From Winston Churchill's grant of augmentation of arms; cf. Wolseley, *op. cit.,* I, 20.

21. Churchill, *op. cit.,* I, 26.

22. Wolseley, *op. cit.,* I, 23-24.

23. *Cal. Com. for Compounding,* I, 865, 1053.

24. *Cal. Com. for Advance of Money,* 1092.

25. Dymock, for example, nosed out five cases and brought them before the Committee as a means of obtaining his arrears of pay.

26. Churchill, *op. cit.,* I, 27-28.

27. *Records of Lincoln's Inn. Black Books,* II, 395.

28. Wood, *Athenae Oxonienses,* IV, 235.

29. *Letters of Humphrey Prideaux to John Ellis,* ed. E. M. Thompson, Camden Society, 27.

30. The point Churchill discusses is the legal one whether James I's commission to Ralegh on the Guiana voyage, giving him power of life and death under his command, did not imply his own pardon for former treason, "it being incongruous that he should have the disposing of the lives of others, who was not clearly master of his own." *Divi Britannici,* 333-34.

31. *Ibid.,* 1.

32. *Ibid.,* 9.

33. *Ibid.,* 11.

34. *Ibid.,* 15.

35. *Ibid.,* 311.

36. *Ibid.,* 318.

37. *Ibid.,* 323.

38. *Ibid.,* 355.

39. *Ibid.,* 357.

CHAPTER III

The Restoration in England and Ireland

1. The best account of these months, the events and moods of the time, is in the early pages of Pepys' Diary.

2. *The Diary of Samuel Pepys,* ed. H. B. Wheatley (1949), I, 145 ff.

3. Eva Scott, *The Travels of the King,* 477.

4. *The Diary and Correspondence of John Evelyn,* ed. W. Bray (1850 ed.), I, 337.

5. *Clarendon's History of the Rebellion,* ed. W. D. Macray, VI, 234.

6. G. M. Trevelyan, *History of England,* 451.

7. *Return of Members of Parliament,* I, 552.

8. *Journal of the House of Commons,* VIII, 247, 249, 263, 271.

9. *Ibid.,* 279, 281, 307, 308.

10. *Ibid.,* 318, 321.

11. *Memoirs of the Court of Charles II by the Comte de Grammont,* (Bohn ed.), 143.

12. Quoted in V. Barbour, *Henry Bennet, Earl of Arlington,* 48, 58.

13. *Ibid.,* 47, 48.

14. Clarendon, *Life and Continuation* (1827 ed.), II, 204.

15. W. A. Shaw, *Knights of England,* 227.

16. *Cal. S. P. Dom.* 1661-62, 176.

17. *Journal of the House of Commons,* VIII, 346, 354.

18. *Ibid.,* 412, and *passim.*

19. Clarendon, *op. cit.,* II, 204 ff.

20. J. C. Beckett, *A Short History of Ireland,* 87.

21. Cf. the King's reasonable expression of opinion on this, R. Bagwell, *Ireland under the Stuarts,* III, 15.

22. Quoted, *ibid.,* 22-23.

23. *Ibid.,* 30.

24. *Clarendon's Life and Continuation* (1827 ed.), II, 51.

25. Wolseley, *op. cit.,* I, 24.

26. *Cal. S. P. Ireland,* 1660-62, xl. In this volume, in which Churchill is traduced in the Preface, his name is

totally omitted from the Index, though there are many references to him in the documents.

27. T. Carte, *Life of Ormonde*, II, 273-74.
28. *Cal. S. P. Ireland*, 1663-65, 2-3.
29. *Ibid.*, 30.
30. *Cal. of Carte MSS.*, 143.
31. *Ibid.*, 47.
32. *Cal. S.P. Ireland*, 1663-65, 40-41.
33. *Ibid.*, 231.
34. *Cal. S.P. Ireland*, 1663-65, 88-89.
35. *Ibid.*, 185-86.
36. *Ibid.*, 281.
37. W. A. Shaw, *Knights of England*, 239.
38. See Barbour, *Arlington*, 78 ff.
39. *Report on the Carte MSS.* (Bodleian), 226.
40. *Ibid.*, 229.
41. Clarendon, *Life* (1657 ed.), II, 451.

CHAPTER IV
Sir Winston Churchill:
Whitehall and Dublin

1. G. N. Clark, *The Later Stuarts*, 1660-1714, 54.
2. Cf. Wilbur C. Abbott, "The Long Parliament of Charles II," *E.H.R.*, 1906, 34-35.
3. Wolseley, I, 22.
4. M. S. Giuseppi, *Guide to the MSS ... Public Record Office*, II, 135.
5. Cf. C. W. Firebrace, *Honest Harry, Sir Harry Firebrace*, 1619-91, 225 ff.
6. For an example of its business, see a letter of Boreman and Churchill to Ormonde, December 30, 1675. In July, 1660, Robert Twiford had been admitted by warrant, not sworn, into the place and service of oils and pickles for His Majesty's use. But His Majesty's Grocer, a place of ancient establishment, had always served His Majesty's household with oil, before the Restoration and since, and was a sworn officer. The other provides oils and pickles at the entertainments of ambassadors and the feasts of St. George, which he ought still to enjoy. *H.M.C., Ormonde MSS.*, IV, 643. One sees the possibilities.
7. Cf. M. S. Briggs, *Wren the Incomparable*, 171-72.

8. Cf. *A Collection of Ordinances and Regulations for the Government of the Royal Household* (Soc. Antiquaries), 352 ff.
9. Quoted in Bagwell, III, 45.
10. *A Collection of Ordinances*, 358.
11. T. Birch, *History of the Royal Society of London*, I, 26.
12. *Ibid.*, 447.
13. *Ibid.*, 111.
14. *Ibid.*, I, 508, 510.
15. *Ibid.*, II, 1.
16. Pepys, *Diary*, ed. H. B. Wheatley, IV, 289.
17. Birch, IV, 421.
18. For the Poor Law Amendment Act of 1662, see C. Grant Robertson, *Select Statutes, Cases and Documents*, 53-60.
19. Bodleian Library, "Liber Admissorum," October 4, 1665.
20. *Journal of the House of Commons*, VIII, 614, 615, 617, 618.
21. Wilbur C. Abbott, *loc. cit.*, 38.
22. Bagwell, *op. cit.*, III, 69.
23. Quoted, *ibid.*, 72.
24. T. Carte, *Life of Ormonde*, II, 320-21.
25. Cf. Bagwell, III, 43 ff.
26. Carte, *Ormonde*, II, 302.
27. *Ibid.*, 316.
28. *Cal. S. P. Ireland*, 1663-65, 622.
29. *Cal. S. P. Ireland*, 1666-69, 96.
30. *Cal. S. P. Ireland*, 1663-65, 699.
31. *Cal. S. P. Ireland*, 1666-69, 7.
32. *Ibid.*, 99.
33. Bagwell, III, 29.
34. *Cal. S. P. Ireland*, 1666-69, 127.
35. *Ibid.*, 168.
36. *Ibid.*, 369.
37. Cf. Clark, *op. cit.*, 65-66.
38. *Cal. S. P. Ireland*, 1666-69, 472.
39. Cf. Cooke to Ormonde, June 6, 1668. *Report on the Carte MSS.*, 179.
40. Cooke to Ormonde, June 9, 1668. Carte MSS., Vol. 215.
41. Carte MSS., Vol. 36, June 23, 1668.
42. Stowe MSS (British Museum), 745/-10.
43. Cooke to Ormonde, Carte MSS., June 13, 1668.

44. Cf. Carte MSS., Vol. 48; and Carte, *Ormonde*, II, 346-47.
45. Carte MSS., Vol. 51, June 30, 1668.
46. *Cal. S. P. Ireland*, 1666-69, 651.
47. *Cal. S. P. Dom.*, 1668-69, 163.
48. Stowe MSS. 745, f. 32.
49. Quoted in Bagwell, III, 88.

CHAPTER V
House of Commons: Court Member

1. "Character of King Charles II," in Halifax, *The Complete Works*, ed. Walter Raleigh, 204-5.
2. Wilbur C. Abbott, "The Long Parliament of Charles II," E.H.R., 1906, 283.
3. *Journal of the House of Commons*, IX, 100, 101, 104.
4. Anchitell Grey, *Debates of the House of Commons*, I, 174-75.
5. *Ibid.*, 186.
6. *Journal of the House of Commons*, IX, 125, 133, 139.
7. Grey, I, 219.
8. *Ibid.*, 233.
9. Quoted, *ibid.*, 246.
10. *Ibid.*, 250.
11. *Ibid.*, 257, 263.
12. Halifax, *loc. cit.*, 190.
13. *Poems and Letters of Andrew Marvell*, ed. H. M. Margoliouth, II, 101, 102, 105.
14. Grey, I, 297.
15. Marvell, *loc. cit.*, II, 109.
16. Grey, I, 337.
17. David Ogg, *England in the Reign of Charles II*, I, 351.
18. *Ibid.*, 368.
19. *Journal of the House of Commons*, IX, 249.
20. *Ibid.*, 300.
21. Grey, II, 247.
22. *Ibid.*, 373.
23. *Ibid.*, 334.
24. *Ibid.*, 418.
25. *Ibid.*, 377-80.
26. Marvell, 161.
27. *Ibid.*, 156.
28. *Ibid.*, 140.
29. Ogg., *op. cit.*, II, 450.
30. *Ibid.*, 458.

CHAPTER VI
Parliament and Popish Plot

1. *Journal of the House of Commons*, IX, 357, 360.
2. *Ibid.*, 376-77.
3. *Ibid.*, 390.
4. *Journal of the House of Commons*, IX, 370.
5. Grey, III, 455.
6. *Ibid.*, 457.
7. Ogg, I, 382.
8. *Ibid.*, II, 539.
9. *Ibid.*, 542.
10. Grey, IV, 23.
11. *Ibid.*, 196.
12. Cf. Ogg, II, 549-52.
13. Grey, VI, 2.
14. *Journal of the House of Commons*, IX, 457, 490, 495.
15. *Ibid.*, 456.
16. Grey, VI, 240-41.
17. *Ibid.*, 242-44.
18. *Ibid.*, 253.
19. *Ibid.*, 291.
20. *Journal of the House of Commons*, IX, 558.
21. A. Clark (ed.), *Life and Times of Anthony Wood*, II, 428.
22. A. Wood, *Athenae Oxonienses*, IV, 235.
23. Ogg, II, 614-15.
24. *Ibid.*, 622.
25. *Return of Members of Parliament*, I, 553.
26. Cf. *Cal. S. P. Dom.*, 1672, 236; *Cal. S. P. Dom.*, 1673-75, 427, etc.
27. C. W. Firebrace, *Honest Harry, Sir Henry Firebrace, 1619-91*, 227.
28. July 12, 1686. James II to Ormonde. To admit the bearer, Sir Winston Churchill, into the place of Second Clerk of the Green Cloth, vacated by the death of Sir William Boreman. *H.M.C. Fifth Report*, 345.
29. *Journal of the House of Commons*, IX, 723, 726, 730, 741, 744, 745.
30. Cf. F. C. Turner, *James II*, 272, 290.
31. *Ibid.*, 292.
32. Grey, VIII, 359.
33. *Ibid.*, 354.
34. *Ibid.*, 359.

35. *Ibid.*, 364.

36. C 6/460/220.

37. J. Hutchins, *Dorsetshire*, II, 257.

38. C 9/405/67.

39. *H.M.C., Ormonde MSS.*, IV, 90.

40. SP 29/441. No. 78.

41. SP 29/311. No. 206.

42. *Capel Letters* (1770), 19.

43. *H.M.C., Bath MSS.*, II, 173-75.

44. J. Foster, *Alumni Oxonienses, 1500-1714*, I, 276. Sir Winston's next youngest son Jasper, who had been born in 1659 or 1660, was also at Queen's College: he matriculated from there the year before Theobald, March 10, 1676, aged seventeen. He died young.

45. A. Clark (ed.), *Life and Times of Anthony Wood*, III, 50, 116.

46. Foster, *Alumni Oxonienses, loc. cit.*

47. P.C.C., Exton, 91.

48. P.C.C., Lort, 66.

49. A. Wood, *Athenae Oxonienses*, IV, 235. This is corroborated by the Register of St. Martin's-in-the-Fields.

50. J. Hutchins, *Dorsetshire*, II, 478.

CHAPTER VII
Arabella

1. *Memoirs of the Court of Charles II*, by Count Grammont (Bohn ed.), 107, 173.

2. *Ibid.*, 116.

3. Henry Savile to the Earl of Rochester, *H.M.C., Bath MSS.*, II, 160.

4. F. C. Turner, *James II*, 61.

5. Grammont, 173.

6. *Ibid.*, 170-71.

7. *Ibid.*, 162 ff.

8. We owe to her the scheme of having "the handsomest persons at Court" painted: the Windsor beauties. *Ibid.*, 191.

9. *Ibid.*, 274.

10. *Ibid.*, 280.

11. *Ibid.*, 137.

12. *Ibid.*, 282.

13. Churchill, *Marlborough*, I, 32-33.

14. Pepys, *Diary*, ed. H. B. Wheatley, VIII, 186.

15. Arabella paid £3.6.0 poor rate to the parish. In the Victorian Age the house was occupied by the blameless Bishops of Winchester. A. I. Dasent, *History of St. James' Square*, 18, 21, 244.

16. Godolphin to William III, July 1, 1692: a great part of the late King's estate in Ireland was settled as security for the payment of £1,000 to Mrs. Godfrey and £2,000 a year for Lady Belasyse. He advised the King to make a grant under the great seal of Ireland of the reversion of those lands for the above payments. *Cal. S. P. Dom.*, 1691-92, 346.

17. *The Life of James FitzJames, Duke of Berwick* (1738), 1.

18. *Cal. Treasury Books*, 1672-75, 641.

19. *Cal. Treasury Books*, 1676-79, 401.

20. *Ibid.*, 763, 774.

21. Turner, *op. cit.*, 109 ff.

22. *Essex Papers*, ed. O. Airy, I, 159, December 30, 1673. "The Duchess of Modena is gone away this morning . . . and the Duke hath already made his visits to Mrs. Churchill."

23. Turner, *op. cit.*, 113.

24. Cf. *Diary and Correspondence of John Evelyn*, ed. W. Bray, IV, 248, January 19, 1696. "Passed the Privy Seal, amongst others, Mrs. Sedley (concubine to ——) Countess of Dorchester, which the Queen took very grievously, so as for two dinners, standing near her, I observed she hardly eat one morsel, nor spake one word to the King, or to any about her, though at other times she used to be extremely pleasant, full of discourse and good humour. The Roman Catholics were also very angry; because they had so long valued the sanctity of their religion and proselytes."

25. Turner, 301.

26. Evelyn, *loc. cit.*, 248-49.

27. *Cal. S. P. Dom.*, 1679-80, 339.

28. *H.M.C., Seventh Report*, 536.

29. H. Ellis, *Original Letters*, Ser. I, Vol. III, 328-32.

30. *Journal du Marquis de Dangeau* (ed. 1855), V, 134.

31. *Ibid.*, 172.

32. *Ibid.*, 303.

33. Churchill, *Marlborough*, I, 97-98.

34. W. D. Christie (ed.), *Letters to Sir Joseph Williamson*, I, 64.
35. Churchill, *op. cit.*, I, 185.
36. Swift, *Journal to Stella*, ed. H. Williams, I, 363-64.
37. *Ibid.*, II, 377.
38. P.C.C., Fagg, 47.
39. P.C.C., Marlboro, 42.
40. P.C.C., Auber, 144.
41. H.M.C., *Downshire MSS.*, 204.
42. Major General Churchill was allowed 20,000 guilders by William III for Berwick's ransom—£1,205.15.3. That year Charles was able to lend the government £1,000. *Cal. Treasury Books*, 1693-96, 681.
43. *Journal*, V, 303.
44. *Letters of Horace Walpole*, ed. Toynbee, IV, 283.
45. *Letters*, V. 155.
46. *Ibid.*, VI, 87.
47. *Ibid.*, XIII, 259.

CHAPTER VIII
John and Sarah

1. *Cal. S. P. Dom.*, 1667, 462.
2. Wolseley, *op. cit.*, I, 66.
3. *Cal. S. P. Ireland*, 1669-70, 91.
4. Cf. *D.N.B.*, *sub*. Villiers, Barbara.
5. *Memoirs of the Court of Charles II*, by Count Grammont (Bohn ed.), 118-19.
6. Churchill, *Marlborough*, I, 59.
7. *Cal. S. P. Dom.*, 1671, 71.
8. H.M.C., *Portland MSS.*, III, 320.
9. *Hatton Correspondence* (Camden Society), I, 66.
10. *Ibid.*, 233.
11. Quoted in Churchill, *op. cit.*, I, 99.
12. Quoted, *ibid.*, I, 111.
13. *Cal. S. P. Dom.*, 1674-75, 367.
14. Churchill, I, 84-85.
15. *An Account of the Conduct of the Dowager Duchess of Marlborough* (1742 ed.), 9-10.
16. These are given in full in Churchill, I, 119-40, from which I quote.
17. *Savile Correspondence* (Camden Society), 49.
18. Quoted in Churchill, I, App. II.
19. Quoted, *ibid.*, I, 143.

CHAPTER IX
Court Life and Home Life

1. Wolseley, I, 226.
2. *Ibid.*, 202.
3. For our proposals, see *Cal. S. P. Dom.*, 1678, 147. For Churchill's movements, see *ibid.*, 90, 95, 101, 134. In September he was sent over to act as brigadier, commanding the first brigade, Sir John Fenwick the second. *Ibid.*, 389-90.
4. Cf. W. G. Hiscock, *John Evelyn and Margaret Godolphin*.
5. Wolseley, I, 213.
6. *Correspondence of Clarendon and Rochester* (1828 ed.), I, 45.
7. *Cal. Treasury Books*, 1679-80, 226. He was paid £300 out of the Privy Purse for his expenses.
8. Churchill, I, 162.
9. *Memoirs of Sir John Reresby*, ed. A. Browning, 191-92.
10. Churchill, I, 164.
11. *Savile Correspondence* (Camden Society), 30.
12. *Ibid.*, 124, 128-29.
13. Churchill, I, 165-66.
14. *Correspondence of Clarendon and Rochester*, I, 51.
15. Churchill, I, 167.
16. *Ibid.*, 171-72.
17. *Ibid.*, 173.
18. *Ibid.*, 176-77.
19. J. S. Clarke, *Life of James II*, I, 659.
20. H.M.C., *Seventh Report*, 363.
21. See his Introduction to Stuart Reid, *John and Sarah, Duke and Duchess of Marlborough*, xviii.
22. *Cal. S. P. Dom.*, 1683, 311.
23. H.M.C., *Seventh Report*, 365.
24. W. Coxe, *Memoirs of John Duke of Marlborough*, I, 21.
25. *An Account of the Conduct of the Dowager Duchess of Marlborough* (1742 ed.), 13-14.
26. Quoted in Churchill, I, 190.
27. Coxe, *op. cit.*, I, 22.
28. Cf. *Cal. S. P. Dom.*, 1683-84, 83, 400.
29. Churchill, I, 184.
30. *Cal. Treasury Books*, 1685-89, 892.
31. Coxe, I, 19.

CHAPTER X
The Revolution

1. L. von Ranke, *History of England*, IV, 214.
2. J. S. Clarke, *Life of James II*, II, 17.
3. Quoted in Churchill, I, 210.
4. H.M.C., *Third Report*, 98.
5. *Ibid.*, 97.
6. *Correspondence of Clarendon and Rochester*, I, 141.
7. Quoted in Churchill, I, 225.
8. The phrase is that of the sedate D.N.B., *s.v.* "Sedley, Catherine."
9. Coxe, I, 26.
10. *Ibid.*, 27-28.
11. G. Burnet, *Supplement to the History of My Own Time*, 293.
12. *Cal. Treasury Books*, 1685-89, 222.
13. *Ibid.*, 89.
14. *Ibid.*, No. 2182.
15. Burnet, III, 269.
16. Coxe, I, 26-27.
17. Quoted in Churchill, I, 239.
18. *Ibid.*, I, 248.
19. *Ibid.*, I, 253.
20. *Ibid.*, I, 271-72.
21. H.M.C., *Ninth Report*, 460.
22. Churchill, I, 291.
23. Coxe, I, 30-31.
24. J. S. Clarke, *James II*, II, 225.
25. *Correspondence of Clarendon and Rochester*, II, 207.
26. I.e., Mrs. Berkeley.
27. *An Account of the Conduct of the Dowager Duchess of Marlborough* (1742 ed.), 16-18.
28. H. Ellis, *Original Letters*, 2nd Series, IV. 166-7.
29. Ellis, *loc. cit.*, IV, 177-78.
30. *Correspondence of Clarendon and Rochester*, II, 211.
31. L. C. 3/30.
32. Ellis, IV, 173.
33. Ellis, IV, 178, 180.

3. Ailesbury, *Memoirs*, 244.
4. *Cal. Treasury Books*, 1689-92, 361.
5. Cf. *ibid.*, 1077: to clearing Marlborough's pay as Lieutenant General to Jan. 1, 1691, £1,460.
6. Ailesbury, *loc. cit.*
7. Quoted in Churchill, I, 319.
8. Wolseley, II, 216.
9. Cf. *Cal. Treasury Books*, 1689-92, 1998.
10. Churchill, I, 331; cf. Clarke, *James II*, II, 419.
11. Quoted in Churchill, I, 334.
12. Quoted in Coxe, I, 44.
13. Ailesbury, *Memoirs*, 310.
14. *An Account of the Conduct of the Dowager Duchess of Marlborough* (1742 ed.), 24-25.
15. *Ibid.*, 32.
16. *Ibid.*, 29 ff.
17. *Ibid.*, 36-37.
18. *Ibid.*, 38 ff.
19. Evelyn, II, 318.
20. Churchill, I, 388.
21. *Account of the Conduct. . . ,* 44-45.
22. *Ibid.*, 56.
23. Quoted in Coxe, I, 51.
24. *Account of the Conduct. . . ,* 65 ff.
25. *Ibid.*, . . . , 84-85.
26. *Ibid.*, 106.
27. *Ibid.*, 110-11.
28. *Ibid.*, 118.
29. Quoted in Coxe, I, 68.
30. *Cal. S. P. Dom.*, 1687, 307.
31. *Account of the Conduct. . . ,* 179-81.
32. Coxe, I, 69.
33. *Account of the Conduct. . . ,* 285 ff.
34. Churchill, I, 509.
35. *Cal. S. P. Dom.*, 1700-2, 381.
36. *Cal. Treasury Books*, 1700-1, 86, 300, 302.
37. *Cal. S. P. Dom.*, 1700-2, 348.
38. *Hatton Correspondence* (Camden Society), II, 249.

CHAPTER XI
William III and Marlborough

1. John Evelyn, *Diary*, ed. W. Bray (1850 ed.), II, 286, 290.
2. Quoted in Churchill, I, 343.

CHAPTER XII
The Duke

1. Quoted in Maurice Ashley, *Marlborough*, 41.
2. Churchill, II, 452.

3. Quoted in C. T. Atkinson, *Marlborough and the Rise of the British Army* (New York, G. P. Putnam's Sons, 1921), 199.
4. Ailesbury, *Memoirs*, 12.
5. *Ibid.*, 283.
6. *Ibid.*, 593 ff.
7. Churchill, II, 8-9, 13.
8. Quoted in Coxe, I, 202.
9. *An Account of the Conduct of the Dowager Duchess of Marlborough* 1742 ed.), 297.
10. C. T. Atkinson, *Marlborough*, 165.
11. Quoted, *ibid.*, 166.
12. *Ibid.*, 168.
13. *Ibid.*, 169.
14. Quoted in Churchill, II, 145.
15. Quoted, *ibid.*, 161.
16. Quoted in Coxe, I, 150-51.
17. Ailesbury, *Memoirs*, 558.
18. Quoted in Coxe, I, 189.
19. Quoted, Churchill, II, 247, 248.
20. *Ibid.*, 245.
21. Quoted in Coxe, I, 219.
22. Quoted, *ibid.*, I, 226.
23. Quoted in Churchill, II, 317.
24. Quoted, *ibid.*, 307, 308, 318, 340.
25. *Ibid.*, 314.
26. C. T. Atkinson, 195.
27. Quoted in Churchill, II, 370, 395.
28. H.M.C., *Downshire MSS.*, 831.
29. Churchill, II, 390.
30. Quoted, *ibid.*, 403.
31. *Ibid.*, 449.
32. Reproduced in facsimile in Coxe, I, 306.
33. Churchill, II, 459.
34. Quoted in C. T. Atkinson, 235, 238.
35. *Ibid.*, 241.
36. Coxe, I, 329-30.
37. H.M.C., *Portland MSS.*, II, 63.
38. Cf. P. Smithers, *The Life of Joseph Addison*, 91-97.

4. *Ibid.*, 569.
5. *Ibid.*, 570.
6. *Ibid.*, 565-66.
7. H.M.C., *Downshire MSS.*, 841.
8. Churchill, II, 591.
9. Churchill, III, 116.
10. C. T. Atkinson, 294.
11. Quoted in Coxe, II, 37.
12. *Ibid.*, 32-33.
13. Quoted in Churchill, III, 141-42.
14. Quoted in Coxe, II, 37-38.
15. *Ibid.*, 55.
16. *Ibid.*, 57.
17. Churchill, III, 171.
18. Quoted in Coxe, II, 271.
19. Churchill, III, 419.
20. *Ibid.*, 424.
21. Quoted in C. T. Atkinson, 342.
22. Quoted in Coxe, II, 480.
23. *An Account of the Conduct of the Dowager Duchess of Marlborough* (1742 ed.), 216.
24. Quoted in Churchill, III, 485.
25. *Ibid.*, 483.
26. *Ibid.*, 504.
27. C. T. Atkinson, 365.
28. Quoted, *ibid.*, 367.
29. Quoted in C. T. Atkinson, 371.
30. Cf. my essay, "Mr. Churchill and English History," in *The English Spirit*, 10-11.
31. Quoted in Coxe, III, 104-5.
32. *Ibid.*, 287-88.
33. Quoted in Churchill, IV, 249.
34. *Ibid.*, 245.
35. Quoted, *Ibid.*, 255.
36. Quoted in C. T. Atkinson, 425.
37. Quoted in Atkinson, 448.
38. R. Parker, *Memoirs* (1746 ed), 160-61.
39. Churchill, IV, 457.
40. *Parliamentary History*, ed. Cobbett, VI, 1037-38.
41. Coxe, III, 480-81.

CHAPTER XIII
Summit and Fall

1. Quoted in Coxe, I, 400.
2. Churchill, II, 547.
3. *Ibid.*, 564.

CHAPTER XIV
Sarah and the Queen

1. *Cal. Treasury Books*, 1703, 101, 414.
2. Quoted in Coxe, I, 103.
3. *See An Account of the Conduct of the*

Dowager Duchess of Marlborough (1742 ed.), 177 ff.

4. *Letters of Sarah, Duchess of Marlborough . . . at Madresfield Court* (1875), xii.

5. H.M.C., *Eighth Report*, 52.

6. Quoted in Stuart J. Reid, *John and Sarah, Duke and Duchess of Marlborough*, 146.

7. *Ibid.*, 54.

8. *Account of the Conduct . . .* , 125 ff.

9. *The Letters of Queen Anne* (ed. B. C. Brown), 98-99.

10. H.M.C., *Eighth Report*, 51.

11. Quoted in Coxe, I, 162, 164.

12. Quoted, *ibid.*, 168, 169.

13. Quoted in Churchill, II, 237.

14. *Letters*, 126-28.

15. *Ibid.*, 144.

16. *Ibid.*, 177.

17. *Ibid.*, 172.

18. *Ibid.*, 196-97.

19. *Ibid.*, 200-201.

20. Quoted in Churchill, III, 233-34.

21. *Letters*, 203.

22. *Ibid.*, 213.

23. *Account of the Conduct...* , 183 ff.

24. H.M.C., *Portland MSS.*, IV, 454.

25. *Letters*, 227.

26. H.M.C., *Eighth Report*, 52.

27. Coxe, II, 508.

28. *Letters*, 189.

29. *Letters*, 244.

30. *Account of the Conduct . . .* , 219 ff.

31. Quoted in Stuart J. Reid, *John and Sarah, Duke and Duchess of Marlborough*, 280.

32. Coxe, II, 604, ff.

33. *Ibid.*, III, 129-30.

34. *Private Correspondence of Sarah, Duchess of Marlborough*, I, 235.

35. Sir John Vanbrugh in H.M.C., *Report VIII*, 100.

36. *Private Correspondence*, I, 268.

37. *Account of the Conduct . . .* , 224-25 ff.

38. H.M.C., *Report VIII*, 43.

39. *Letters*, 301.

40. *Ibid.*, 302.

41. Quoted in Reid, 322.

42. *Account of the Conduct . . .* , 238 ff.

43. Quoted in Reid, 327.

44. Coxe, III, 352 ff.

45. H.M.C., *Report VIII*, App. III.

CHAPTER XV
Exile and Return

1. *An Account of the Conduct of the Dowager Duchess of Marlborough* (1742 ed.), 218.

2. Quoted in L. G. Wickham Legg, *Matthew Prior*, 130.

3. Swift, *Prose Works*, ed. Temple Scott, V, 76.

4. *Ibid.*, 99.

5. *Ibid.*, 101.

6. Swift, *Prose Works*, IX, 97.

7. *The Poems of Jonathan Swift*, ed. Harold Williams, I, 157.

8. The ninth Duke of Marlborough, in Stuart J. Reid, *op. cit.*, xx.

9. Quoted in Coxe, III, 457-58.

10. Swift, *Journal to Stella*, ed. Harold Williams, 145.

11. *Ibid.*, 452.

12. *Ibid.*, 159.

13. *Ibid.*, 452, 460.

14. *Ibid.*, 451.

15. *Ibid.*, 481.

16. *Ibid.*, 631.

17. *Memoirs of Sarah, Duchess of Marlborough*, ed. W. King, 247.

18. H.M.C., *Portland MSS.*, V, 686.

19. *Parliamentary History*, ed. Cobbett, VI, 1132.

20. Quoted in Churchill, IV, 564.

21. *Memoirs*, 235-36.

22. Swift, *Journal to Stella*, 568.

23. *Ibid.*, 597.

24. *Letters of Sarah Duchess of Marlborough . . . from Madresfield Court*, 26.

25. *Ibid.*, 28.

26. *Ibid.*, 32.

27. *Ibid.*, 36.

28. *Ibid.*, 41.

29. *Ibid.*, 64.

30. *Ibid.*, 76.

31. *Ibid.*, 72.

32. *Ibid.*, 74.

33. *Ibid.*, 94.

34. *Ibid.*, 58.

35. *Ibid.*, 89.

36. *Ibid.*, 99.

37. *The Letters of Queen Anne*, ed. B. C. Brown, 393.

38. *Ibid.*, 401.

39. *Ibid.*, 403.

40. *Journal to Stella*, 557.

41. *Letters*, 397.

42. *Account of the Conduct . . .*, 263.

43. Swift, *Prose Works*, V, 454.

44. *Ibid.*, 451.

45. Quoted in Churchill, IV, 607.

46. Cf. *The Correspondence of Jonathan Swift*, ed. F. Elrington Ball, II, 199.

47. L. G. Wickham Legg, *Matthew Prior*, 133.

48. *Correspondence of Swift*, II, 200-201.

49. *Ibid.*, 206.

50. *Ibid.*, 222.

51. *The Wentworth Papers*, *1705-1739*, ed. J. J. Cartwright, 408.

52. *Ibid.*, 416.

53. *Correspondence of Swift*, II, 232.

54. Quoted in Churchill, IV, 623.

CHAPTER XVI
Blenheim Palace

1. Churchill, IV, 319.

2. Introduction to Stuart J. Reid, *John and Sarah, Duke and Duchess of Marlborough*, xxvi-xxvii.

3. *Ibid.*, xlii.

4. Quoted in David Green, *Blenheim Palace*, 50.

5. Coxe, I, 403.

6. Quoted in Green, *op. cit.*, 67.

7. Cf. *ibid.*, 70-71.

8. Ailesbury, *Memoirs*, II, 586.

9. Coxe, II, 40.

10. *Private Correspondence*, I, 35.

11. *Ibid.*, 41.

12. *Ibid.*, 240.

13. *Ibid.*, 263.

14. Vanbrugh, *Works*, IV, 214.

15. Vanbrugh, IV, 23.

16. Quoted in Green, 94-95.

17. Vanbrugh, IV, 29-30.

18. Quoted in Green, 106.

19. *Private Correspondence*, I, 178.

20. Quoted in Green, 105-6.

21. *Private Correspondence*, I, 189.

22. Vanbrugh, IV, 33.

23. Vanbrugh, IV, 36.

24. *Ibid.*, 38.

25. *Private Correspondence*, I, 30.

26. *Ibid.*, 58.

27. Coxe, II, 426.

28. H.M.C., *Portland MSS*, VII, 14.

29. Coxe, III, 309.

30. Vanbrugh, IV, 231.

31. Quoted in Green, 120.

32. Quoted in Stuart J. Reid, *op. cit.*, 357.

33. Vanbrugh, IV, 54.

34. *Ibid.*, 66.

35. *Ibid.*, 85.

36. *Ibid.*, 123. The printed text of the letters says "hand'd"; I suggest hang'd is a more likely reading.

37. *Ibid.*, 130.

38. Quoted in Green, 156.

39. Vanbrugh, IV, 170.

40. *Letters . . . from Madresfield Court*, 121-22.

41. *Ibid.*, 145.

42. Quoted in Coxe, III, 646.

43. Quoted in Green, 158.

44. Quoted in *ibid.*, 160.

45. *Letters . . . from Madresfield Court*, 166.

46. Vanbrugh, IV, 69-70.

CHAPTER XVII
The Three Brothers

1. Cf. J. H. Owen, *War at Sea under Queen Anne*, *1702-8*, 3-4.

2. *Ibid.*, 6-7.

3. *Cal. S.P. Dom.*, 1675-76, 486; *Cal. S.P. Dom.*, 1677-78, 578.

4. Cf. *D.N.B.*; Owen, *op. cit.*, 4; *Cal. S.P. Dom.*, 1682, 160.

5. *Return of Members of Parliament*, *passim*.

6. H.M.C., *Hastings MSS.*, II, 193.

7. Owen, 4; H.M.C., *Lothian MSS.*, 137; *House of Lords MSS.*, App. Report XIV, Pt. VI, 228.

8. Narcissus Luttrell, *Brief Relation*, II, 340, 343.

9. *Cal. S.P. Dom.*, 1699-1700, 273, 316.

10. *Cal. S.P. Dom.*, 1702-3, 277.

11. *Cal. Treasury Books*, 1704-5, 354.

12. H. B. Wheatley and P. Cunningham, *London Past and Present*, II, 296.

13. Owen, 30.

14. Luttrell, V, 272.

15. Cf. Sir Julian Corbett, *England and the Mediterranean*, 1603-1713, ch. XXVIII.

16. In June Admiral Churchill was busy discussing with Methuen, the ambassador there, the resources of Lisbon and the preparations necessary for a base. Owen, 46.

17. Luttrell, V, 295, 297.

18. Quoted in Corbett, II, 498.

19. Corbett, II, 567-68.

20. Churchill, II, 101.

21. Coxe, II, 275-76. From a previous letter to Godolphin, *ibid.*, 274, it seems that Churchill had some thoughts of resigning.

22. Churchill, III, 334.

23. Coxe, II, 256.

24. Luttrell, V, 234-35.

25. Coxe, II, 504.

26. *Private Correspondence*, II, 288.

27. Coxe, II, 600.

28. J. L. Chester, *Registers of Westminster Abbey*, 268, 328.

29. *Cal. S.P. Dom.*, 1673-75, 236.

30. *Cal. S.P. Dom.*, 1680-81, 131. This entry relates to Charles, not, as the Index states, to John.

31. *Cal. Treasury Books*, 1693-96, 681, 907.

32. *Return of Members of Parliament*, *passim*.

33. F. Taylor, *The Wars of Marlborough*, 1702-9, I, 155.

34. *Ibid.*, 157.

35. Cf. *Letters and Dispatches of Marlborough*, ed. Sir George Murray, I, 253, 281.

36. *Ibid.*, 293.

37. *Ibid.*, 299-300.

38. *Ibid.*, 301.

39. *Ibid.*, 320, 321.

40. *Ibid.*, 389-91.

41. *H.M.C., Portland MSS.*, IV, 255.

42. Luttrell, V, 284.

43. *Ibid.*, 685.

44. P.C.C., Fagg, 3.

45. P. Smithers, *Life of Joseph Addison*, 255.

46. W. Egerton, *Memoirs . . . of Mrs. Oldfield*, 121.

47. *Wentworth Papers*, ed. J. J. Cartwright, 422-23.

48. *The Works of Sir Charles Hanbury Williams* (1822 ed.), I, 74-81.

49. *Letters of Horace Walpole*, ed. Paget Toynbee, I, 42.

50. *Ibid.*, 192.

51. *Collins' Peerage*, V, 674; *Complete Peerage* (G.E.C.), X, 89.

52. Coxe, III, 595-96.

53. Basil Williams, *Stanhope*, 210.

54. *Diary of Mary, Countess Cowper*, ed. Spencer Cowper, 118-20.

55. Coxe, III, 616-17.

56. *Ibid.*, 618-19.

57. *Letters . . . from Madresfield Court*, 126.

58. *Ibid.*, 127-28.

59. *Correspondence of Sir Richard Steele*, ed. Ray Blanchard, 367, 466.

60. *Letters . . . from Madresfield Court*, 135.

61. *Ibid.*, 131

62. Quoted in Churchill, IV, 645-47.

63. *Ibid.*, 648-49.

64. Chester, *op. cit.*, 306.

65. P.C.C., Marlborough, 42.

66. Coxe, III, 654.

67. *Poems*, I, 295-97.

68. *Chesterfield's Letters*, ed. Bonamy Dobrée, 1261, 1893, 1968.

CHAPTER XVIII
Sarah in Old Age

1. *Diary of Mary, Countess Cowper*, ed. Spencer Cowper, 196-97.

2. *H.M.C., Bath MSS.*, II, 180.

3. Coxe, III, 629.

4. *Letters of a Grandmother*, 1732-5, ed. G. Scott Thomson, (1943) 58, 147, 156.

5. *Ibid.*, 74.

6. Lady Charnwood (ed.), *Call Back Yesterday*, 47.

7. R. L. Arkell, *Caroline of Ansbach,* 266.

8. *Memoirs,* ed. W. King, 276.

9. *Ibid.,* 297.

10. *Ibid.,* 279.

11. *Private Correspondence,* II, 462, 465.

12. *Ibid.,* 455, 457.

13. *Ibid.,* 468-72.

14. Maud Wyndham, *Chronicles of the Eighteenth Century,* I, 33 ff.

15. *Memoirs,* ed. W. King, 289.

16. *Ibid.,* 300-301.

17. Cf. table in O. Colville, *Duchess Sarah,* App. IX.

18. Huntington Library, MSS. H.M. 16600-16635.

19. Cf. *Letters of a Grandmother,* 155-56.

20. *Letters of a Grandmother,* 70, 142.

21. *Ibid.,* 52, 151.

22. *Correspondence of Swift,* III, 359.

23. *Memoirs,* ed. W. King, 313-15.

24. Cf. J. C. Collins, *Bolingbroke and Voltaire in England,* 247-48.

25. D. Green, *Blenheim Palace,* 174.

26. *Correspondence of Swift,* VI, 129.

27. S. J. Reid, *John and Sarah,* 452-53.

28. With characteristic lack of self-reflection, Pope described Marlborough as "a man who had everything from without to make him happy and yet was very miserable, from the want of virtue in his own heart." Cf. *The Minor*

29. It is reprinted in his *Works* (1825 ed.), VI, 4-9.

30. *Lives of the English Poets,* ed. G. B. Hill, II, 89; *Boswell's Life of Johnson,* ed. G. B. Hill, V, 376.

31. *A Review of a Late Treatise . . . ,* 1742, 2.

32. Published by T. Cooper, 1742.

33. G. M. Gooden, *Henry Fielding,* 137.

34. P.C.C., Anstis, 259.

35. Sir Tresham Lever, *Godolphin,* 111-13.

36. Quoted, *ibid.,* 149.

37. *Letters . . . from Madresfield Court,* 143.

38. Cf. *Correspondence of Swift,* IV, 70.

39. Quoted in Lever, *op. cit.,* 257.

40. National Library of Wales, Brogyntyn MSS., 169.

41. *Ibid.,* 601.

42. *Ibid.,* 441.

43. *Letters of a Grandmother,* 96.

44. *Ibid.,* 44, 51.

45. *Ibid.,* 110, 135.

46. *Ibid.,* 137.

47. *Ibid.,* 56.

48. *Letters . . . from Madresfield Court,* 152-53.

49. *Letters of a Grandmother,* 150, 163, 166-67.

50. *Memoirs,* ed. W. King, 302-3.

51. P.C.C., Anstis, 259.

Poems of Pope, ed. Norman Ault, 358-59.

Index

Addison, Joseph, 211-13, 263, 272, 319, 345
Admiralty, Board of, 305, 309-14
Ailesbury, Thomas Bruce, 2nd Earl of, 90, 172, 173, 195, 202, 290-91
Almanza, battle of, 104, 312
Althorp House, 354
America, 29, 86-87, 140, 346
Andover, 165, 316
Anne, Queen, accession of, 197-98, 281, 309; character of, 141-43, 272; death, 279-80; and Marlborough, 198-99, 201-2, 204, 208, 209-10, 221, 225-27, 233-35, 249, 257, 261-62, 265, 268, 271-73; as Princess, 94, 122, 154, 156-57; as Queen, 96, 110, 143; and Revolution of 1688, 157-58, 162, 164, 165-69; and Sarah, Duchess of Marlborough, 122, 136, 141-46, 156, 176-85, 198, 199, 201-2 241-62, 333, 334, 342, 345; and the Tories, 247-48, 276-78, 279-80; and the Whigs, 219, 223, 243-45, 247-48
Arbuthnot, Dr., 252, 280
Argyle, Archibald Campbell, 9th Earl, 89, 139-40
Arleux, 236-37
Arlington, Henry Bennet, Earl of, 35, 36-37, 38-39, 45, 47, 56-57, 62, 74, 75; and Ireland, 41-44
Army, the, 31, 35, 162-63, 167-68, 172
Arran, Earl of, 92, 100, 119
Ashe House, 20-22, 24, 25-26, 112, 119, 271
Austrian Empire, 204, 206, 210; Emperor Leopold I, 210, 236, 238, 328
Auverquerque, Dutch general, 217, 226

Axminster, 21
Aylmer, Matthew, Admiral, 308, 314

Bank of England, 156, 172, 233
Barillon, Paul, French ambassador, 83, 137, 149, 159-60, 168
Bath, 17, 151, 184, 224-25, 349
Bavaria, 205, 206
Bedford, John Russell, 4th Duke of, 340, 352
Belasyse, John, Lord, 89, 154; Lady, 106
Bentinck, William, 1st Earl of Portland, 172
Berlin, 210
Berwick, James, Duke of, 103-4, 105, 108, 109, 111, 113, 158, 162, 174, 186, 222, 228, 312, 316; and Marlborough, 200, 229, 279
Blake, Robert, 22, 150
Blandford, William Godolphin, Marquis of, 134, 350
Blenheim, battle of, 96, 192, 195, 206-9, 244, 307, 318, 339; Palace, 146, 193, 211, 212, 272, 282-307, 324-25, 328, 333, 339, 341, 345, 354, 355, 357
Bolingbroke, Henry St. John, 1st Viscount, 218, 223, 268, 270, 276-77, 279, 322, 334, 337, 342
Boscawen, Edward, 38
Bouchain, 237, 271
Boyne, battle of the, 174
Brabant, Lines of, 202, 214, 318
Bridgewater, 151, 152,
Bridport, 150
Bristol, 11, 19, 23, 150, 151
Brodrick, Sir Allen, 41, 43, 53, 54, 57, 62

Brussels, 96, 135-36, 196, 219, 297, 318

Buckingham, George Villiers, 1st Duke of, 9, 20, 114

Buckingham, 2nd Duke, 49, 50, 61, 62-63, 74-75, 116

Burgundy, Duke of, heir to French throne, 224-26

Burnet, Gilbert, historian and bishop, 155, 161

Byde, Sir Thomas, 76

Cabal ministry, the, 70-71, 74

Cadogan, William, 1st Earl, 225, 273, 322, 325

Cambridge, King's College, 94

Carlisle, Charles Howard, 3rd Earl of, 304

Caroline, Queen, as Princess of Wales, 321, 331-32; as Queen, 332-34, 339, 350

Castle Howard, 288, 304

Castlemaine, Barbara Villiers, Lady, 44, 48, 49, 72, 84, 101, 106, 115-19, 123, 124, 162; her daughter Barbara, 118-19

Castle Rising, 321

Catherine of Braganza, Queen, 49, 50, 77, 114, 168

Charles I, King, 8-9, 11, 13, 23, 27, 29, 30, 42, 76, 159

Charles II, King, 2, 3, 13, 27, 28, 31-34, 36, 37, 41, 50, 62-63, 69, 79-88, 92-93, 95, 100, 109, 110, 114, 136, 138, 140-42, 171; Court of, 65, 67, 97-101, 115-19, 122-25, 171; and Ireland, 40, 41-43; Marvell on, 73; and Parliament, 38-39, 45, 53, 70-76; 77; and women, 98, 105, 116-19, 126

Charles II, King of Spain, 190

Charles III, Habsburg candidate for Spanish crown, 218, 220, 230, 231; afterward Emperor Charles VI, 238

Chesterfield, Lady, 99

Chesterfield, Philip Stanhope, 4th Earl of, 329, 337, 347

Churchill, in Devon, 6; manor of, in Somerset, 94, 122

Churchill, Fort, on Hudson's Bay, 173

Churchill, Arabella, 23, 61, 93, 97, 101-13, 136, 146, 309, 315, 328; her children by James, Duke of York, 103-4, 106, 108-9, 111-12

Churchill, Awnsham and William, booksellers and publishers, 315

Churchill, Charles, General, 24, 95-96, 103, 111, 144, 165, 174-75, 197, 201; career, 316-19, 334-35; Charles, General, the 2nd, 319-21; Charles, the 3rd, 321-22

Churchill, George, Admiral, 24, 56, 95, 103, 112, 165, 199; career, 305-15

Churchill, George, the 2nd, 315

Churchill, Henrietta, see Marlborough

Churchill, John, father of Sir Winston, 6-8, 11-14, 20-21, 24, 91, 94-95; Mary, 2nd wife, 13, 23, 91

Churchill, Sir John, Master of the Rolls, 6-7, 78, 94, 122

Churchill, John, son of Sir Winston, see Marlborough

Churchill, Lady Mary, wife of Charles 3rd, 321-22

Churchill, Lord Randolph, 356, 357; and Jennie Jerome, his wife, 357

Churchill, Theobald, son of Sir Winston, 24, 41, 94

Churchill, Sir Winston, Cavalier Colonel, 7, 8, 13-14, 15, 16, 129; on his ancestry, 5-6, 94-95; and the Civil War, 11-13, 16, 20, 23; death and will of, 95-96; Divi Britannici, 27-30, 93; and Dutch deputies, 93-94; and Board of Green Cloth, 46-47, 67, 77, 87, 129; and Ireland, 41-44, 53-54, 54-62, 115-16; marriage of, and births of children, 20-21, 23-24; in Parliament, 34-39, 45-46, 51-54, 64-90, 148-49, 150; petition of, to Charles II, 92-93; wife of, 20, 21, 60, 94-95, 107, 110, 126, 132

Churchill, Sir Winston (b. 1874), 2, 3, 6, 27, 51, 79, 83, 121, 142, 170, 178, 179, 183, 189, 192, 357

Church of England, 83, 148-49, 153, 154-55, 159, 243-44, 269

Cibber, Colley, 166

Civil War, the, 1, 8-13, 17-20, 21, 22-23, 25

Clanmalier, the O'Dempsey, Lord, 41-43, 44, 47

Clarendon, Edward Hyde, 1st Earl of, 1, 9, 17, 18, 33, 35-36, 38-39, 58, 61, 62, 64, 99-100; fall of, 44; and Ireland, 41, 42, 52-53; and Parliament, 45-46

Clarendon, Henry Hyde, 2nd Earl of, 105, 162, 163, 165, 172

Clarendon Code, the, 33, 46, 52

Clifford, Thomas, 1st Baron, 37-39, 71

Cockpit, at Whitehall, the, 48, 157, 160, 165, 168, 172, 177, 180, 182, 219, 241, 243
Coleman, Father Edward, 86
College of Arms, 5, 92
Committee for Compounding, 12, 24
Commons, House of, 31, 33-39, 45-46, 51-53, 64-90, 105, 168, 171, 176, 189-90, 203, 239, 272
Compton, Henry, bishop of London, 154-55, 157, 160, 165, 167
Congreve, William, dramatist, 147, 348-50, 351
Conventicle Act, 46, 52, 68-69, 71
Cooke, Colonel, 41, 43, 54, 57, 59, 61-62
Corfe Castle, 11
Cork, 174, 316
Cornbury, Edward Hyde, Lord, 162
Cornwall, 11, 23; the Cornish Foot, 11, 17-18
Coventry, Henry, Secretary of State, 38, 41, 42
Coventry, Sir John, 71
Crewe, Nathaniel, sycophantic bishop of Oxford, 106
Cromwell, Henry, 42
Cromwell, Oliver, 1, 2-3, 26, 31, 52, 53, 58, 140, 158, 194, 346

Danby, Thomas Osborne, Earl of, 74, 83, 86, 160, 161-62, 165
Danube, River, 195, 206-8, 316-18
Dartmouth, George Legge, Baron, 135, 139, 157, 165, 168, 175
Davis, Moll, dancer, mistress of Charles II, 105, 116
Dean, Forest of, 80
Declaration of Indulgence (1672), 72, 74, 159; (1688), 159
Defoe, Daniel, 197, 233, 263
Delamere, Henry Booth, 2nd Lord, 153, 165
Denmark, 144; King Christian of, 96, 144, 307; Prince George of, husband of Queen Anne, 96, 144-45, 162, 165, 177, 199, 204, 209, 226, 256-57, 305, 306, 313, 314-15, 316
Dering, Sir Edward, 41, 54, 58-59, 61-62
Devon, 5-6, 20, 26
Digby, Sir Kenelm, 49
Dissenters, the, 46, 64, 68, 72, 84, 159
Dorchester, 6, 7, 8, 11, 13, 96, 315
Dorset, 5-8, 10, 11-14, 23, 88, 150, 315

Dover, 32, 69, 106, 158, 281; Secret Treaty of, 44, 58, 70, 73
Drake, Sir Francis, 20, 29
Drake family, of Ashe, 20; Sir Bernard, 20; Eleanor, Lady, 20-23, 24-26, 60, 88, 150; Sir John, 20-21; John, 21, 22, 24, 37
Dryden, John, 116, 283, 302-3
Dublin, 41, 42, 50, 54, 62, 114
Dunch, Elizabeth, 113
Dutch, the, 81, 193, 195, 220-22; war, the (1665-7) 53, 57, (1672-4), 72-73, 93, 120-21
Dykvelt, Everard van, Dutch emissary, 157

Ecclesiastical Commission (James II's), 153, 161
Edinburgh, 137-38
Elizabeth I, Queen, 9-10, 29-30, 183, 186, 230, 232; as Princess, 286
Enzheim, battle of, 120-21
Essex, Arthur Capel, Earl of, 93
Essex, Robert Devereux, 3rd Earl of, 22
Eton College, 94
Eugene of Savoy, Prince, 190, 206-7, 225-26, 227, 229, 232, 236, 237, 270
Euston, 44-45
Evelyn, John, 32, 134, 171, 363
Exclusion Bill, 69, 84-85, 140

Falmouth, Charles Berkeley, Earl of, 99-100, 111
Fenwick, Sir John, 119, 186, 364
Feversham, Louis Duras, Earl of, 105, 151-52, 158, 162, 168, 176
Fielding, Henry, 346
Fitzharding, Lady (Mrs. Berkeley), 166, 255
Flanders, 173-74, 174-175, 178
Florence, 297
Fox, Charles James, 357
France, 73-74, 79, 230-31, 234-36, 237-38
Frankfort, 205, 274-75, 317
Franklin, Benjamin, 345
Frederick, Prince of Wales, 333-34

Galmoye, Lord, 109-10
Gay, John, 341, 349
George I, King, Elector of Hanover, 143-44, 203, 224, 247, 263, 279, 281, 300, 319, 328, 332
George II, King, 320, 334, 345, 357
George III, King, 103, 357
Germany, 170, 204-9, 222, 317-18

Gibbons, Grinling, 291
Gibraltar, 310
Ginkel, Godert, 1st Earl of Athlone, 175, 193, 196
Gloucester, William, Duke of, Queen Anne's son, 144, 176, 184-85, 186, 187, 242
Glover, Richard, 347
Godfrey, Colonel Charles, 110-11, 113, 120
Godfrey, Francis, 95, 315
Godfrey, Sir Edmund Berry, 86
Godolphin family, the, 133
Godolphin, Margaret, 133-34
Godolphin, Sidney, Cavalier poet, 11, 133
Godolphin, Sidney, 1st Earl, 105, 133-35, 141, 145, 175, 177, 184, 185, 186, 263, 265, 277, 278, 279, 298, 347; character of, 134, 272; and Marlborough, 134-35, 199, 203, 210, 213-214, 217-19, 223, 246, 249-50, 266, 294, 312; and Queen Anne, 145, 198, 219, 226-27, 233-34, 247-48; and Sarah, Duchess of Marlborough, 134, 242, 265, 274
Godolphin, Francis, 2nd Earl of, 296, 339, 348, 349
Godolphin, William, see Blandford
Gould, Mary, of Dorchester, heiress, 96, 319
Grafton, Henry Fitzroy, 1st Duke of, 44, 162-63
Grand Alliance, the, 73, 82-83, 159, 164, 190-91
Grantham, Thomas Robinson, 1st Lord, 332-33
Green Cloth, Board of, 47-48, 67, 77, 87, 110, 129
Grenadier Guards, 114, 121, 237
Grenville, Sir Bevil, 11, 18, 31, 165
Grenville, John, 1st Earl of Bath, 31, 165
Gwyn, Nell, 88-89, 105

Habeas Corpus Act, 66, 89, 149, 182
Hague, the, 137, 157, 191
Halifax, George Savile, Marquis of, 65, 69, 78, 105, 149, 159, 182, 362
Hall, Jacob, ropedancer, 118
Hamilton, Anthony, 97, 98, 101
Hanover, 210, 235, 238, 278
Harley, Robert, 1st Earl of Oxford, 36, 204, 223, 233, 235, 239, 244, 250, 252, 254, 259, 263, 267, 268, 270, 276-77, 280-81, 299, 322-23
Hawksmoor, Nicholas, 291, 303

Heinsius, Anton, Grand Pensionary of Holland, 199, 201, 202, 204, 221
Herbert, Captain, 119
Hill, Abigail, see Masham, Lady
Hill, John, Major General, 241, 270
Hogue, La, battle of, 183
Holland, 46, 58, 66, 73, 93-94, 133, 134-35, 149-50, 191, 196, 199
Holywell, near St. Albans, 122, 146, 173, 245, 272, 319
Hooke, Nathaniel, 344
Hooke, Dr. Robert, 49-50, 197
Hopton, Ralph, Lord, 17-18
Hudson's Bay Company, 173
Hull, 69, 70, 158
Hussey, Sir Thomas, 90

Innocent XI, Pope, 153, 159
Ireland, 154, 173-74, 177; Irish Cattle Bill, 52-54; Restoration Settlement in, 39-44; Act of Settlement for, 40-41, 42, 43, 174; Act of Explanation of, 43, 44, 45, 54-55
Italy, 193, 216, 222

James I, King, 20
James II, as Duke of York, 32, 53, 59-60, 64, 77, 81, 84-85, 86, 88, 132-33; as King, 89-90, 148-68; and Arabella Churchill, 60-61, 102-8, 109, 112, 113; at Brussels, 136; and Ireland, 58-60, 98, 173; Sarah, Duchess of Marlborough on, 140, 347; in Scotland, 136-40; and women, 98-108, 126, 154
Jeffreys, George, Judge, 152, 160, 161
Jennings family, the, 94, 122
Jennings, Mr., 273, 302
Jennings, Frances, Duchess of Tyrconnel, 102, 122
Jennings, Sarah, see Marlborough
Jermyn, Henry, Earl of St. Albans, 105
Jermyn, Henry, Baron Dover, 117, 118, 154
Jewel House, the, 117, 191
Johnson, Dr. Samuel, 322, 344-45

Kensington Palace, 180, 185, 257, 259, 292, 321, 332
Keppel, Joost van, 1st Earl of Albemarle, 171
Killigrew, Thomas, 100
Killigrew, Sir William, 85
King's Evil, the, 29, 155
Kinsale, 174-75, 316

Laguerre, Louis, 291
Landen, battle of, 111, 316
Lansdown, 11, 17, 19, 31
Lediard, Thomas, 346
Legge, *see* Dartmouth
Lely, Sir Peter, 97, 101, 112
Lille, reduction of, 228
Lincoln's Inn, 15
London, 22, 23, 32, 68, 71, 159, 210, 211, 238, 281; Fire of, 51; Plague of 1665, 52
Louis XIV, 3, 98, 120; and England, 65, 70, 72, 81, 106, 136, 143, 180, 190, 228; and Europe, 66, 70, 73, 77, 79, 81-83, 135, 149, 159, 170, 174, 186, 284, 297; and Revolution of 1688, 159, 160-61; and War of Spanish Succession, 190-91, 209, 213, 228, 230, 234, 240, 268, 271, 312
Louvain, 214
Luxembourg, 88
Lyme Regis, 11, 19, 21-22, 88, 150
Lyttleton, Sir Thomas, 337

Maastricht, 110, 120, 202, 273
Macaulay, Thomas B., 27, 155
Madrid, 36, 238
Maintenon, Mme. de, 98
Malplaquet, battle of, 233, 259
Manley, Mrs., a low writer, 258
Marines, Royal, 307
Marlborough, James Ley, 3rd Earl, 172; Countess of, 22
Marlborough, John Churchill, 1st Duke of, 2, 3, 5, 26, 41, 72, 95, 103, 110, 111, 144, 145, 146-47, 342, 353, 354, 355; character of, 25-26, 174, 347; service of, in Africa and Mediterranean, 114-16; and his brothers, 310-14, 316-18; and Lady Castlemaine, 118-19; and Dutch Deputies, 199-200, 201, 213, 214-15; in exile, 272-73, 279; and return from, 280-81; and James II, 132-33, 135-42, 149, 155-58; and courtship of Sarah Jennings, 121-31; and Netherlands, offer of Governor Generalship, 220-22; and Revolution of 1688, 158-69; and sea power, 115, 305, 309-10; and Sedgemoor campaign, 150-53; and war of Spanish Succession, 192-240; in the Tower, 180-83, 308; Pope on, 343
Marlborough, Sarah, Duchess of, 112, 132, 134, 137, 139, 195, 263-64, 267, 312, 356, 357; on the Duke's

ancestry, 5; and Princess Anne, 122, 136, 141-45, 165-67, 172, 177, 181-85, 187-89, 245; and Queen Anne, 198, 199, 201, 203, 226-27, 241-62; and Blenheim Palace, 282, 283, 285, 289-93, 296-303; and Queen Caroline, 331-34, 339; and Marlborough House, 294-95; 334, 340, 354; in old age, 330-54; and Pope, 342-44; on Swift, 269, 341; *Account of the Conduct of,* 344-47
Marlborough, children of 1st Duke and Duchess; Anne, Countess of Sunderland, 188, 241, 251, 269, 323, 328; Elizabeth, Countess of Bridgwater, 246, 275; Henrietta, Lady Godolphin, afterward 2nd Duchess of Marlborough, 110, 134, 147, 172, 187, 241, 268, 296, 325-28, 347-51; John, Marquis of Blandford, 187, 202; Mary, Duchess of Montagu, 246, 321, 326, 354
Marlborough, Charles Spencer, 3rd Duke, 351-53, 355
Marlborough, Charles Richard John, 9th Duke, 331, 357; and Consuelo Vanderbilt, 357
Marlborough, 5th Duke, 355
Marlborough, George Spencer, 4th Duke, 355
Marsin, Marshal, 206-9
Marvell, Andrew, 69, 70, 73, 77
Mary I, 148
Mary II, as Princess, 81, 135, 143; as Queen, 108, 177, 179-84
Mary of Modena, Queen, 104, 106, 108, 112, 122, 134, 154, 157, 166
Mary, Queen of Scots, 29
Masham, Abigail Hill, Lady, 233, 239, 242, 243, 251-59, 262, 263, 270, 278, 279-80, 334, 341, 342, 349
Masham, Samuel, Lord, 239, 252, 263
Massachusetts, 11
Maurice, Prince, 22, 23
Maynwaring, Arthur, 258, 319
Mediterranean, the, 114-15, 308, 310-11
Meggs, Nicholas, and his widow, 6
Meuse, River, 200, 214
Midgley, Grace, 354
Milton, 21
Mindelheim, 210
Minterne, 6, 7, 24, 33, 46, 62, 90, 95-96, 132, 174, 319
Mohács, battle of, 109

Monk, George, 1st Duke of Albemarle, 31, 32, 57, 164, 175
Monmouth, James, Duke of, 71, 87, 89, 120, 136; Rebellion of, 149-52
Montague, Admiral, see Sandwich
Morland, Sir Samuel, 75
Moselle, River, 204, 205, 214
Musbury, 21, 26

Namier, Lewis, 356
Nantes, Revocation of Edict of, 73, 226
Napoleon I, 170, 193, 210, 213, 236
Navestock, 109, 112
Navy, the Royal, 32, 35, 72, 158, 168, 305-6, 308, 311-13; naval building program (1675), 79; retrenchment in, 88
Ne Plus Ultra Lines, 235, 236, 237
Netherlands, the, 81; the Spanish, 190, 196, 199, 214-18, 220-21, 223, 231, 270, 273
Nijmegen, Peace of, 83
Nonsuch Palace, 117
Northampton, James, 3rd Earl of, 166, 167
Nottingham, 166, 318

Oates, Titus, 85-86
Occasional Conformity Bill, 203
Oldfield, Anne, actress, mistress of General Charles Churchill, 319
Orkney, George Hamilton, Earl of, 209, 216, 217, 318
Ormonde, James Butler, 1st Duke of, 40, 41-42, 47, 53, 54, 57, 61-63; James, 2nd Duke, 111, 270-71, 316
Orrery, Roger Boyle, 1st Earl of, 54, 55, 68
Ossory, Thomas Butler, 61, 100, 156
Oudenarde, battle of, 223-24, 255
Oxford, 15, 17, 19, 27, 51-53, 94, 153, 167, 313, 351; Balliol College, 351; Bodleian Library, 51; Christ Church, 36, 153, 167; Magdalen College, 153; 161; Queen's College, 94; St. John's College, 15, 51

Paris, 97, 119, 214, 227, 229, 235, 238, 268
Parliament, the Long, 17, 31, 81; the Cavalier, 34-39, 45, 52-53, 57, 64-87, 149; of 1679-81, 87; of James II, 148; of Anne, 197, 200, 203-4, 271-72, 279
Passive Obedience, 155
Paulett, Earl, 270

Paulett, John, Lord, 21, 271
Penn, William, 159, 206
Pepys, Samuel, 32, 50, 52, 63
Petre, Father Edward, 109, 153
Petty, Sir William, 43, 50
Philip II of Spain, and Antonio Perez, 143, 259
Philip V, 218, 230
Pitt, William, 347
Plymouth, 165, 308
Pollard, Sir Hugh, 39
Poole, 11, 13
Pope, Alexander, 283-84, 341, 342-44
Popery, legislation against, 71, 77, 79, 83-85; Popish Plot, 71, 85-88, 136
Portman, Sir William, 50
Portsmouth, 83, 158, 308, 316; Louise de Quérouaille, Duchess of, 72, 81, 88
Pretender, James Edward, the, 159-60, 224, 276, 313, 322, 332
Prior, Matthew, 218, 263-65, 269
Pym, John, 9, 17, 23

Quebec expedition, 270

Ralegh, Sir Walter, 28
Ralph, James, of Philadelphia, 345
Ramillies, battle of, 192, 194, 216
Restoration, the, 5, 6, 31-35, 46, 97
Revolution of 1688, the, 73, 83, 148-69
Reynell, Sir Thomas, 22
Rheims, Archbishop of, 107
Rhine, river, 200, 209, 213, 222
Robartes, Lady, 98
Rochester, John Wilmot, Earl of, 118
Rochester, Laurence Hyde, Earl of, 136
Rooke, Admiral Sir George, 309
Roos, Lord, divorce case of, 69
Rosewell, Sir Henry, 24
Roundway Down, battle of, 18, 19
Royal Society, 28, 50
Rupert, Prince, 2, 19
Russell, Admiral Edward, Earl of Orford, 160, 306, 308
Ruvigny, Henri, Marquis de, 1st Earl of Galway, 83, 157
Rysbrack, John Michael, 291, 303
Ryswick, Peace of, 170, 186

St. Albans, 205, 242, 246, 308, 324
St. Germain, 109, 112, 186, 190, 278
St. James's Palace, 86, 117, 168, 185, 257, 262, 280, 309
St. James's Park, 113, 334
St. James's Square, 105, 126, 154

St. Paul's, 32, 197, 255, 283, 291
St. Winifred's Well, 99, 155
Salisbury, 162, 163, 164, 165, 172, 179
Sandwich, Admiral Edward Montague, 1st Earl of, 32, 56, 307
Savile, Harry, 126, 137-38
Scarborough, 332
Schellenberg, storming of, 206, 210
Schomberg, Frederick, Duke of, 172
Scotland, 13; James II in, 138-39; Sir Winston Churchill on the Scots, 30
Sedgemoor, 151-52, 316
Sedley, Catherine, mistress of James II, 103, 107-8, 126, 154
Sedley, Sir Charles, 107, 126, 130
Seven Bishops, trial of, 159-60
Shaftesbury, Anthony Ashley Cooper, 1st Earl, 9, 50, 52, 53, 81, 84
Sherborne, 6, 7, 11; Castle, 11
Sidney, Algernon, 149
Sidney, Henry, Earl of Romney, 160, 175, 198
Skerrett, Maria, mistress of Sir Robert Walpole, 321, 349
Slangenberg, Dutch general, 215, 318
Sole Bay, battle of, 72-73, 120, 172
Somerset, 10, 17, 18, 150-53
Somerset, Charles Seymour, 6th Duke of, 150, 180; Duchess of, 255, 262
Sophia, Electress of Hanover, 143, 210, 321, 332
South Sea Bubble, 325
Spain, 190, 230-31, 238, 308; war of Spanish Succession, 199-271
Spencer, Anne, Lady Bateman, 351
Spencer, Charles, 3rd Duke of Marlborough, see Marlborough
Spencer, Diana, Duchess of Bedford, 303, 323, 333, 340-41, 351-53
Spencer, John, 351, 354
Steele, Sir Richard, 276, 324, 346
Steinkirk, battle of, 185
Sunderland, Robert Spencer, 2nd Earl of, 141, 153, 160-61, 185, 188
Sunderland, Charles, 3rd Earl, 188, 233, 248, 313, 331
Sundon, Lady, formerly Mrs. Claydon, 339
Swift, Jonathan, 110, 233, 263, 265-69, 270, 273, 277, 280, 328, 341
Syon House, 180, 184

Tallard, Marshal, 186, 206-9, 318
Tangier, 114-15, 315
Taylor, Jeremy, *The Whole Duty of Man*, 258

Temple, Sir Richard, 90
Test Act, 71, 74, 87, 89, 149
Texel, battle of the, 73
Thornhill, Captain, 59, 61, 62
Thornhill, Sir James, 291
Tichborne, Sir Henry, 108
Torbay, 161
Tories, Irish (i.e., robbers), 56
Tory party, the, 35, 88, 141, 155, 168, 176, 179, 203-4, 223, 238, 243-45, 248, 276-79, 312-13, 322
Toulon, 310, 311, 313
Tower of London, 160, 181-83, 316
Travers, Mr., Treasury agent for Blenheim Palace, 293, 339
Trelawny, Brigadier, 165, 315
Trelawny, Sir Jonathan, 84
Tunbridge Wells, 147
Turenne, Henri de, Marshal, 121, 130, 214
Tyrconnel, Richard Talbot, Duke of, 100, 122, 153, 174; Duchess of, see Jennings

United States, 85
Utrecht, Peace of, 263, 266, 271, 276, 277

Vanbrugh, Sir John, 197, 283, 285-86, 287-302, 304, 348
Vendôme, Marshal, 224-28
Versailles, 120, 136, 149, 157, 193, 229, 282, 284-85
Vienna, 204
Villars, Claude de, Marshal, 120, 232, 234, 235-37, 271
Villeroi, Marshal, 215-16
Villiers family, the, 20, 114
Virginia, 49
Voltaire, 212, 341-42

Waldeck, Prince of, 173, 174, 175, 316
Waldegrave family, 103, 108, 111, 113
Waldegrave, Henrietta, Lady, 103, 108-9, 111
Waldegrave, Sir Henry, 108, 109
Waller, Edmund, 9, 29, 76, 82
Waller, Sir William, Parliamentarian general, 11, 17-18
Walpole, Horace, 12-13, 321-22
Walpole, Sir Robert, 269, 272, 302, 313-14, 321, 322, 331, 333-37, 341, 347, 349
Waterloo, an unfought battle at, 215
Wellington, Arthur Wellesley, 1st Duke of, 192-93, 195, 196, 210

Westminster, 17, 68, 89, 165; Abbey, 315, 319, 349
Weymouth, 12, 34, 87, 316
Whig party, the, 34, 69, 80, 82, 88, 89, 140, 203, 219, 223, 230-31, 243-45, 247-49, 312
White, Rev. John, of Dorchester, 11
Whitehall, 27, 43-44, 47-49, 51, 77, 86, 106, 117, 149, 161, 165, 166, 168
William III, 66, 73, 81, 109, 135, 143, 198, 296, 297, 309; in Ireland, 174; and Marlborough, 155, 157, 171-75, 176-91, 221, 309; and Monmouth, 150; and the Revolution of 1688, 158, 160-69, 308
Wimbledon House, 337, 340
Winchester, 155; College, 7, 95

Windsor Castle, 75, 108, 136, 167, 321; Lodge, 241, 324, 327; Park, 309, 333
Winston family, the, 8
Winston, Sarah, mother of Sir Winston Churchill, 8
Wise, Henry, gardener, 290, 292, 295
Wood, Anthony, 27
Woodstock, 211, 286, 291-93, 295, 298, 301, 303-4
Wootton Glanville, 7-8, 13, 14, 24, 90, 95
Wren, Sir Christopher, 49, 68, 89, 285, 290, 291, 294

York, 102, 137
York, Anne Hyde, Duchess of, 60, 98-101, 104, 122
York, James, Duke of, *see* James II